# JAMES CHALMERS

## HIS AUTOBIOGRAPHY AND LETTERS

Ever yours
Tamate

# JAMES CHALMERS

## HIS AUTOBIOGRAPHY AND LETTERS

BY

### RICHARD LOVETT, M.A.

AUTHOR OF 'JAMES GILMOUR OF MONGOLIA,' ETC.

*WITH TWO PHOTOGRAVURE PORTRAITS, MAPS, AND SEVEN
OTHER ENGRAVINGS FROM PHOTOGRAPHS*

NEW YORK
LAYMEN'S MISSIONARY MOVEMENT

# PREFACE

JAMES CHALMERS was a man of God's own making. He early recognized the Divine influence within and around him, and like St. Paul himself he did not 'refuse to be persuaded by the heavenly vision.' He owed little to education or to the influences that mould the majority of men. He owed all that he was to his sense of the boundless love of Jesus Christ; he gave his whole being in loyal and enthusiastic surrender to the Saviour who had redeemed him; he caught a large measure of the Master's own Spirit; and he counted it his highest joy to be spent in the effort to win for Christ the drunkards of Rarotonga and the cannibals of New Guinea.

Chalmers was absolutely unconventional. He paid little heed to the common standards of life, and made no effort to direct his course along the ordinary grooves of thought and of action. He was restless, impulsive, to some extent the creature of mood. At times he appeared to be easily elated, easily depressed. But at the base of his personality there was a strong will, an indomitable purpose, a plan in life that refused to be modified by opposition or suffering or external difficulties of any kind.

The author has chosen the plan followed in this book deliberately, and from the conviction that it will best accomplish the ideal at which he has aimed. That is to present to the reader the real James Chalmers, with no attempt to round off angles, to reduce seeming incompatibilities, or to paint a fancy picture. As in the case of *James Gilmour of Mongolia*, wherever possible Chalmers speaks for himself. This method has its difficulties; but it delivers the author from the temptation to work up glowing pictures. The superficial reader may think it an easy method, yet as a matter of fact the balancing and comparing different accounts of the same series of events, and the fitting them into a compact and clear whole, mainly in the words of Chalmers himself, has often taken much more labour, time, and thought than would have been needful to rewrite the whole story.

Chalmers has left an autobiography, but one all too brief. This was found under the circumstances described on page 15, and constitutes the backbone of the life. There is also in existence a large quantity of letters and reports, both official and private, and of these very free use has been made. Those who are acquainted with Chalmers' letters and reports know that he was no master of style or of exact expression. Like his great fellow-countryman Carlyle, Chalmers was fond of elliptical expression, and it is often much easier to see exactly what he means, than it is to trace clearly the grammatical relation of his phrases and sentences. Here and there the author has ventured by occasional changes in the order of words to render the meaning easier of comprehension.

Considerable space is devoted to the ten years which Chalmers spent on Rarotonga. Many people who have a fair knowledge of his New Guinea work hardly know that he ever lived in the Hervey Group. Those ten years, moreover, were the severe apprenticeship which fitted Chalmers for his later achievements as a master craftsman in dealing with savage humanity. Those ten strenuous years were the training period which enabled him later on to gain his foothold at fierce Suau, to open up the whole south-eastern coast of New Guinea, to say of the wild cannibals of Namau that he loved them.

Parts of the fifth chapter traverse ground covered by *Work and Adventure in New Guinea*. But as Chalmers gave much space to these events in his autobiography, and thereby indicated the importance he attached to them, the author did not feel at liberty to delete them. Moreover, though dealing with the same events, the descriptions are by no means identical with those in the book.

Chalmers was a many-sided man, and his vigorous personality attracted to him men of widely different types. He fascinated the common sailors on a British man-of-war; he could hold the gun-room table spellbound by the hour; he drew out the sympathetic side of men of science; he could thrill huge assemblies; and he was never happier than in the company of little children. But his life-work was that of a missionary of Jesus Christ to the heathen, and it is mainly from that point of view that he must be studied if he is to be understood.

It is impossible to acknowledge here the kind help of all the many friends who have gladly co-operated in this labour of love. But I am indebted in the first instance to Mr. Harrison-Chalmers for placing at my disposal the entire manuscript material in his possession as stepson and representative of Mr. Chalmers. My thanks are also due to the Directors of the London Missionary Society for allowing me the fullest access to all their official correspondence. I am also indebted in an especial degree to the Rev. Gilbert Meikle, Mr. Chalmers' pastor when a lad at Inveraray; to the Rev. R. Wardlaw Thompson; to Sir J. Erskine, of the Royal Navy, under whom the Protectorate over New Guinea was proclaimed in 1884; to the Rev. Joseph King, the London

Missionary Society's representative in Melbourne; and to Dr. Lawes, Tamate's life-long friend and colleague.

I owe also an especial debt to Mrs. Arthur Edwards (Miss Kate Blomfield), who has greatly enhanced the value of this book by allowing me to consult a large number of letters, written to her by Tamate, between 1886 and 1901; also to Mrs. Robert Dawson, Miss Emily Blomfield, Miss Searle of Kew, Melbourne, the Rev. J. J. K. Hutchin, and a host of other friends who have all most willingly co-operated in the work by allowing me to consult letters in their possession.

I owe a word of thankful acknowledgement to Mr. Graham Balfour, for sanctioning the publication of the three letters from Robert Louis Stevenson to Tamate, written in 1890, letters as characteristic as any that ever proceeded from that skilled pen.

The book is sent forth in the hope that it may recall much that was gracious and inspiring to many who have clasped Tamate's strong hand, looked into his flashing eyes, and heard the trumpet-tones of his voice from the pulpit and the platform. It is hoped also that, in the words of Admiral Bridge, 'it does justice to the character of this great Englishman,' using the term in its widest sense.

But Chalmers above all was a great servant of Jesus Christ, and, to use his own phrase, 'a whole-souled missionary.' May the Head of the Church deign to use this story of a noble life to inspire others to go forth and carry on that great work which fell from the veteran's hands when the awful but glorious crown of martyrdom descended upon him and his young colleague at Dopima!

# CONTENTS

# LIST OF ILLUSTRATIONS

## PHOTOGRAVURES

## ENGRAVINGS

## MAPS

# CHAPTER I

## EARLY YEARS

JAMES CHALMERS sprang from the Highland pea-
santry, and to his ancestry and environment were due
many of those qualities which made him in later years
a prince among men.  He grew into youth and manhood under the shadow of the ancient castle of Inveraray,
and amid the influences and associations of the Argyll
clan.  He ever considered himself, and that with pride,
a clansman of the great duke.

All who in later life came to know him well, and
could induce him to talk of those early years, found that
the child was father to the man.  To the invigorating
air of his native hills, and to the free, open, if hard
life of his boyhood, James Chalmers owed the strong
physique, the dauntless courage, the almost exhaustless
energy of his later years.  Strange as the statement may
seem to those who came to know him only after 1886,
in early manhood he was slim, and not entirely free
from symptoms of physical weakness.

James Chalmers' parents were simple, God-fearing
folk.  His father was exceedingly quiet and reserved
in manner, but very thoughtful.  His mother was active
and energetic, and transmitted to the son much of her
own strong individuality.  To the careful, if somewhat
rough, upbringing of his parents Chalmers owed a debt
which he ever thankfully acknowledged.  In youth he
came under the pastoral care of the Rev. Gilbert Meikle,

minister of the United Presbyterian Church at Inveraray. The following pages abound in testimonies to the abiding and life-long blessing which this relationship brought him.

Argyllshire in 1841, and for those in the humble rank of life into which James Chalmers was born, was a somewhat hard and severe training-ground. But from conditions not dissimilar in essentials sprang Morrison of China, Moffat of South Africa, and Gilmour of Mongolia. It was amid these primitive surroundings that Chalmers developed a sound mind in a healthy body ; it was there, before going forth into the great world, that he came to know and love and reverence Jesus Christ, the Saviour of the world. It was there that quenchless love for the savage heathen came into his heart; and the energizing resolution that, God helping him, his life should be spent in bringing to their darkness the light of life. The breezes from hill and sea, the simple yet strenuous life, the atmosphere of adventure in which as a schoolboy he lived and breathed, gave him as an abiding equipment his love of fresh air and the ocean, his quickness of eye and instant appreciation of the right act for an emergency, his readiness and ability to cope with all manner of men and of things. In this school he acquired that strength and fearlessness and skill which in after days enabled him to steer his whaleboat through wild seas and the wilder Pacific surges which thunder over the coral reef. The tact and quickness and courage with which he held his own in early schoolboy rivalries enabled him in later years to keep his head, though surrounded by fierce and excited cannibals, when his own life and the lives of all who were with him depended upon his power to control the restless passions of fierce savages, and to turn their thoughts from murder to those of peace.

Only a short time before his death Chalmers wrote a brief autobiography. The manuscript bears the heading, 'Notes for Lizzie,' and was doubtless completed in this form at the request of his second wife. It was originally composed of five quires of quarto letter-paper, but one of these quires disappeared, in some way unknown, in New Guinea. After his murder this autobiography was found among Chalmers' papers at Daru, and sent home after the visit of the Government steamer to the scene of the tragedy. In this document he has sketched his own early years.

'I was born in Ardrishaig, Argyllshire, on August 4, 1841. My father was an Aberdonian, a stonemason, who came in the thirties to Inveraray to assist in the building of the quay, and who never again returned to his home near Peterhead. My mother was a Highlander, born at Luss, on Loch Lomond. I never met any of my father's people; but in after life I came to know several of my mother's. The first three years of my life were spent in Ardrishaig, which was then only a small fishing village on Loch Fyne, about twenty-three miles below Inveraray. From Ardrishaig we removed to Lochgilphead, and remained there for a year or two. Then, after a short interval spent at a place near to Tarbert, we again returned to Ardrishaig.

'My first school was on the south side of the canal, and I can well remember my mother leading me to the master, and giving him strict injunctions not to spare the rod. I do not remember his ever thrashing me; but I shall never forget a punishment which I consider much more severe than the taws. From my infancy I was very fond of sweets, and a lad several years my senior had some, and said he would share them with me if I would first chew what he gave me. I gladly offered to do so, and he gave me a piece of tobacco, which I chewed with avidity, because of the prospect of sweets. Little did I imagine the effect it would have upon me; and when my class was called I staggered and fell as I was going to the master. I was picked up, and for punishment placed in the master's box desk, with a tall chimney-pot hat placed on my head, which rested on my shoulders. I can remember being very ill, and at length sent home, and to bed.

'Great was the sorrow when the schoolmaster left to go to Australia. He had been in the habit of occasionally holding a service on the Sunday, the only service ever held in the place, except when a minister came round to baptize children, and this was very seldom. The nearest place of worship in those days was in Lochgilphead.

'My next school was on the north side, a new building, and the master was liked by us because of the sweets we got from him; but I fear his liking for whisky was very great, and we had many holidays and half-holidays.

'My father was very seldom at home, and I can remember that I earned my first money on one occasion when he had walked from Inveraray, and was spending the Sunday with us. He promised to give me a sixpence if I could repeat the twenty-third Psalm before night. I did it without a mistake, and I got the prize; but this large sum of money was too much for me to deal with, and so I handed it to my mother, and I got one penny of it as my share.

'I can remember that the people of Ardrishaig were very superstitious; but at that time I thought there was nothing wrong in this. Whooping-cough was thought to be bad, and when a child was ill with it a donkey

THE MOTHER OF JAMES CHALMERS.

was procured, and women stood on each side of the creature and passed the sick child under it and over it as a means to a cure. To hear a dog crying was a sure sign of a death. I can remember that once when we were playing and heard a big dog cry we stopped our noise, and wondered who was dead. We were on the left bank of the canal, and shortly afterwards there approached us a horse dragging a boat, and in the boat there was a coffin. This made a wonderful impression on me, so much so that even now I cannot bear to hear a dog crying.

'I paid a short visit to my father in Inveraray in 1846 or 1847, and what I best remember was being taken on Sundays in the evening to the United Presbyterian Church. My father was much interested in the young preacher who had come as minister there not long before. I can remember that many could not get inside the church because of the crush. The preacher was the man who in after years became my beloved pastor, the Rev. Gilbert Meikle. After a few months I returned to my mother.

'I suppose it was from living near to the sea that when quite young I became passionately fond of it, and I was happy if only I could get into a boat or on to a log or plank of wood. I have had many narrow escapes, many thrashings from my mother and friends in consequence, but the supposed salutary effects of these were not lasting. Three times I was carried home for drowned, but my father was wont to say in after years he feared my fate was to be something else. I was very restless, and dearly loved adventure, and a dangerous position was exhilarating.

'I was a great favourite with many of the fishermen, and was often allowed to spend some time on board of their boats. It was when in the school on the north side that four of us thought we could build a boat for ourselves, and even attempted it. But we soon gave up the effort, and took to caulking and tarring a herring-box, which we finished quickly. As I was captain, I must have the first sail. We got a long line, and I, sitting in the herring-box, was dragged along the beach until the line broke, and I was carried out to sea. There was a difficulty in saving me because of the strong current.

'In 1848 or 1849 we all went to Glenaray, near to Inveraray, to live; and in after years I came to look upon that as the place to which I belonged, rather than Ardrishaig. In 1850 I spent a day in the latter place, but have never visited it since. I can remember it was a fearful place for whiskey, and I often wonder if it has changed since for the better. The continual dramming of the fishermen, from the coming in with the fish until all had been passed over to the buyer and the curer, was bad for all. There were frequent fights, frequent arrests, and frequent trips to Inveraray.

'Our first home in Glenaray was at High Ballantyre, and here I spent several happy years. I had two sisters, and together we used to go to the Glenaray school. The master then was Mr. John McArthur, and he continued master until 1894, when he died, a very old man. We had over three miles to go to school, and often were the only travellers on the road. In the winter months we were joined by a large contingent from Sallachary, made up of Morrisons, Bells, and MacVicars. Of these I only know of one (1900) alive, my dear old friend Dugald Morrison, now of Inveraray.

'In these years a great number of scholars came from the town, a distance of four miles, and others from points along the road between the town and school-

house. There were the Mintos and Blairs, who considered themselves of the town party, and in fights
joined that party. I joined the Glen party, and many
were the fights we had, which generally began with
throwing turf and ended with stone throwing. On
fighting-days we considered it safer, when the fight
was over, to take the high road by way of Kilmun,
where we left two of our number, McNeil and Turner,
and then on to Sallachary and home. If there was no
fighting we came on to the Three Bridges, and then
up that way. The single fights were many.

'The schoolmaster had often to punish his pupils for
black eyes and other signs of battle. He seemed to
know everything that took place, and so also did the
good parish minister, Dr. Smith. The doctor generally
visited the school after some serious broil, and spoke
kindly to us, and urged on us that we should love one
another. His own son, Jack, was a sprightly youth,
and was in every bit of fun going. He was frequently
unfortunate in getting wounded in the fights and in
burning himself with gunpowder. On two occasions he
nearly lost his life from the latter, and on each occasion
we had a visit from the doctor.

'We were taught in school up to elementary Latin, and
in mathematics Euclid. Several times our school stood
highest in the competitive examinations. Mr. McArthur
turned out clever boys, and these are now scattered all
over the earth, many of them having done well. He
was proud of us, and we were certainly proud of him,
and loved him. Yet for one thrashing he gave me,
quite unjustly, I felt sore at heart for years; and remembered it all through my life. I was accused wrongfully,
and he, thinking I was guilty, and I stoutly denying it,
in wrath broke several canes over me. More than thirty

years after, on my first return home, I visited the Glen
with my dear old pastor, and met the old schoolmaster.
He referred to that thrashing, and told me how sorry
he was afterwards, when he found out that I had had
nothing whatever to do with the affair.    The voice
quivered as he said, " Do you remember it, James? "
and I don't think my answer was more steady, as I
replied, " Yes, I remember it well, but now it is all
right," and we turned the conversation to other and
more pleasant memories.    To my old schoolmaster
I am greatly indebted, and so are we as a family.
His kindness is a memory that lives.

' When I was about ten years old I saved one of the
Mintos from drowning.    There had been very heavy
rain during the morning and until near school closing
time, when the sun came out, and we had a fine afternoon to get to our homes.    There was a very big spate
on, and the Aray was rushing, tumbling, and roaring.
The affluents were all full, and rushing on to swell the
Aray's volume of water.    Some of us were a short distance ahead, and a few were coming up behind.    When
at the Three Bridges, which were wooden then, the old
stone ones having been carried away the year before,
there was a cry from a short distance up the river that
Johnnie was being carried away.    A rush, and in the
course of it off went my jacket, and I could see the boy
come rolling down.    I got quickly to the down side of
the bridge, and holding on to the timbers beneath the
bridge and stretching well out, I, as he was passing under,
seized his dress, dragged him near, and held him tightly
with my left hand.    I then slipped down a little, and
allowed us both to be carried a little distance on, when
I seized a branch, and getting near the bank was helped
up with the saved boy.    Why I went to the down side

and acted as I did, I cannot say; but it was the only way in which he could have been saved. He was carried home, and for some days did not come to school. I had the thanks of his parents, and, what pleased me still more, the admiration and cheers of the master and scholars. A few years ago I had a letter from Mr. Wm. Minto, the eldest son, in which he refers to his brother John, who was saved by me on that autumn afternoon at the Three Bridges.

'I remember, some years after this event, standing one afternoon at the further end of the quay, there being only one or two others beside on the quay. Suddenly there was a loud scream, and on looking round I saw a woman in great agony, shouting out that a child was drowning. I was a good swimmer now, so running along a short way, and taking off my coat as I ran, I sprang in, swam off, and seized hold of the dress of a child who was floating away with the current, and was apparently dead. I got the child ashore, who was then taken charge of by friends, and brought round to life.

'My father was a thorough old moderate churchman, a steady auld kirk. Blow-high, blow-low, rain or snow, sunshine or storm, all were alike, to church he would go, and I had to accompany him. My mother and sisters went with us on fine days. My father had a great respect also for Mr. Meikle, the United Presbyterian minister, whose Sunday school I had been induced to attend by some of the boys who came to Glenaray school. My father put no obstacles in the way, and so when I was about eleven years of age I joined the United Presbyterian Sunday school. Mr. Meikle himself was the superintendent of the school. My first teacher was Mr. John Campbell, merchant, a very earnest Christian man. He died soon after I joined the school; and if

I remember rightly, I was advanced to the class that met in the small vestry, and was conducted first by Mr. Hally, and afterwards by Mr. Meikle. His interest in every scholar was great, and absentees were always sought for. We had left High Ballantyre, and had gone to an old house on the hill near to the schoolhouse. One Sabbath I was absent, and during the following week Mr. Meikle came to seek me out, and meeting my father near to the fourth mile from town, he said he had come out to inquire why I had not been at Sunday school, and he hoped I was not ill. On my father coming home, I was told this, and urged never to be absent again; and so save the good man from that long walk.

'When I was thirteen years of age I removed from the Glen school, and attended the Grammar school, the master being Mr. Smith, who is still there, and much respected by all.

'My father was anxious I should become a civil engineer, but was too poor to help me. A way opening, I was taken on, as a boy, to carry the chain when he was surveying, by a Mr. Darroch, whom I have since met in New Zealand. For a short time I rather liked this, as it took me away from school, of which I thought I had had enough. But this did not last very long, and so I had to return to school. Once my father was in the Blackmount, and I persuaded my mother to allow me to go out bark-beating; but on my father's return I was glad to be ordered to leave off, and to get back to school. At another time I was allowed to leave school, and to go herding for a fortnight; but, liking amusing books, and so neglecting my duties, I was kindly told I had better go back to school.

'When between fourteen and fifteen I entered the office of Maclullich and Macniven, lawyers, Inveraray,

Mr. Maclullich was also Procurator Fiscal.  I remained there three years, and then removed to the office of Wilson and Douglas in the same town.  It was a time of sowing wild oats, and I was generally blamed for everything out of the ordinary way that took place, whether I had taken part in it or not.  Off and on I still attended the Sunday school; but I could not bear to meet Mr. Meikle, though I loved him.  If I saw him coming along the road, I got out of his way as quickly as possible.  He lived in the Newton, and as I had frequently to go there, to Sheriff Maclaurin's, with and for papers, I often saw Mr. Meikle walking along; and then I was over the wall by a gas lamp about half way between the smiddy and the Newton.  I was nimble, and as he was short-sighted I used to get right away. Going to the Sheriff's was always spoken about as going to Avingandum.

'It was at the beginning of these somewhat reckless years that I came to the great decision of my life.  I remember it well.  Our Sunday school class had been held in the vestry as usual.  The lesson was finished, and we had marched back into the chapel to sing, answer questions, and to listen to a short address. I was sitting at the head of the seat, and can even now see Mr. Meikle taking from his breast-pocket a copy of the *United Presbyterian Record*, and hear him say that he was going to read an interesting letter to us from a missionary in Fiji.  The letter was read.  It spoke of cannibalism, and of the power of the Gospel, and at the close of the reading, looking over his spectacles, and with wet eyes, he said, " I wonder if there is a boy here this afternoon who will yet become a missionary, and by-and-by bring the Gospel to cannibals ? "  And the response of my heart was, " Yes, God helping me, and I will."  So

impressed was I that I spoke to no one, but went right
away towards home.   The impression became greater
the further I went, until I got to the bridge over the
Aray above the mill and near to the Black Bull.   There
I went over the wall attached to the bridge, and kneeling
down prayed God to accept of me, and to make me a
missionary to the heathen.

'For some time I was greatly impressed; but the impression passed away, and at last I forgot all about it.'

In a letter to Mr. Meikle dated April 29, 1863, written
from Cheshunt College, Chalmers refers to this episode:

'Often do I think of days gone and spent in the chapel,
especially in the Sunday school, where I should like to
be remembered to scholars and teachers.   Nothing can
afford me more pleasure than to feel I am still one with
them; and even in the future, when, it may be, in some
foreign clime I shall have to teach little black children
the way to Jesus, I shall still feel happy in the thought
of our Sabbath school at home, where I can safely say,
many years ago, when you were reading or telling us of
the Fiji Islands and of their dreadful state, I felt so great
a fire in my soul that I then prayed God, young as
I was, to make me a missionary and send me to tell
them of Jesus; but alas, I went astray, yet that prayer
I believe will be answered, if not to the Fiji, to some
other place.'

Chalmers was twenty-one years old when he wrote
these words, and about fifteen when the missionary fire
first burned in his heart.   The 'going astray' meant that
for a season he fell into bad company, and suffered
a temporary loss of his first love for and zeal in the
service of Christ.

We turn again to the narrative in the autobiography:
'Of course at home and in school we had the Shorter

Catechism *ad nauseam*, and when on a Sunday evening we were not at chapel we read a chapter of the Bible, and then were catechized upon it. In looking back to that time over all these years I wonder what effect that catechism has had on my life. I fear in many cases it has soured the unwilling pupils against religious things. It may have been a help to me. I do not think that the so-called religious teaching in day schools has the beneficial effect that many think; and in my opinion religious teaching is very much better omitted in our public schools, and left entirely to the Sunday school and the home. I delighted in reading the Old Testament and the Revelation to St. John; but was often perplexed as to many Old Testament statements. The God of the Highlands at that time was a terror, and we heard more of Him as such, than as the God of love. Mr. Meikle was not considered quite orthodox, as he preached and taught a God of love. I have heard preaching, as a boy and a youth, at which I have shuddered, as the bottomless pit of fire and brimstone has been shown. I have heard preachers say that the saved parents would say Amen and shout Hallelujah as they saw their children who were unbelievers cast forth on the day of judgement to everlasting punishment in the lake of fire. My flesh has creeped, until I was able to get rid of the fearful nightmare.

' The effect of teaching like this was to lead me to give up altogether for a time religious things, and even to create in my mind a great antipathy to them, since I felt sure that I was not one of the elect. Still, two men held a wonderfully fascinating power over me and others, and we believed that they were true Christians. These were Mr. Meikle, and Mr. Duncan Munroe, a merchant in the town, and one of the United Presbyterian elders. Many quiet and kindly words did Mr. Munroe speak to me, and, strangely enough, I never felt inclined to spurn him. Nearly forty years have gone since that time, and still I see the quiet, godly man. In the winter, with his plaid wrapped around him and his genial smile as he came near to you when out walking, he would ask in kind words how you were getting on. How ashamed one felt when in as kindly a manner he referred to some incident, and said he hoped it would not happen again, and that Jesus loved us, and wanted us much to love Him! But then he and Mr. Meikle were Arminians, and very unorthodox.

'Time passed, and I thought I was too big for Sunday school, and so I left. How strange it was that soon after I returned to the Sunday school, not as a scholar, but as a teacher!

'In November, 1859, two evangelists from the North of Ireland arrived in Inveraray, at the urgent request of Mr. Meikle, to hold a series of meetings. Several of us young fellows decided to do all we could to interfere with the meetings, and so to prevent what were called conversions. One of the first meetings was held at the Maltland, in the joiner's loft; and at about seven o'clock in the evening of the day on which it was to be held I had no intention of going. But I called at the shop of Mr. Archibald MacNicoll, as I often did, he being a friend of mine, and he asked me why I was not going to the meetings, and said that I ought to go that night. I raised many objections, but he was so resolved on my going that he gave me a small Bible for use at the service, and got me to consent to go. It was raining hard, but I started, and on arriving at the bottom of the stairs to the joiner's loft found that the meeting had begun, and that they were singing " All people that on earth do dwell" to Old Hundred. I thought I never heard such singing before, so solemn, yet so joyful. I ascended the steps and entered. There was a large congregation, and all were intensely in earnest. The younger of the evangelists was the first to speak, and chose as his text Rev. xxii. 17, and seemed to speak directly to me. I felt deeply impressed, but at the close of the meeting hurried away back to town, returned the Bible to Mr. MacNicoll, but was too upset to speak much to him.

'The following Sunday night, in the Free Church, I was pierced through and through with conviction of sin, and felt lost beyond all hope of salvation. On the Monday Mr. Meikle came to my help, and led me kindly to promises and to light, and as he quoted " The blood of Jesus Christ His Son cleanseth us from all sin " I felt that this salvation was possible for me, and some gladness came to my heart. After a time light increased, and I felt that God was speaking to me in His Word, and I believed unto salvation.

'Soon after my conversion, I began addressing meetings in public, and established several cottage meetings in the town. I also went to places in the country and addressed the people, as far away as Lochawe and Furnace.

'After my conversion I soon remembered my vow in the Sunday school, years before, to bring the knowledge of Christ to the heathen, and never again was it forgotten.

'My parents were too poor to give me a university course, and I often wondered how it could be managed. I had joined the United Presbyterian Church, and become a teacher in the Sunday school. Mr. Meikle assisted me in many ways to increase my stores of know-ledge, and especially with Latin and Euclid. He also told me that many students supported themselves whilst at college by doing work as missionaries in connexion with the Glasgow City Mission and churches. During the summer of 1860 or 1861, a gentleman who took great interest in religious work visited Inveraray, and was much pleased with the various meetings, and took part in them. He was Mr. William Turner, of Glasgow, brother of the well-known South Sea Missionary. He often talked to me about his brother, and about mission work, and increased my desire to become a missionary.

'In 1861 I joined the Glasgow City Mission, and a few days after my arrival in the city I called on Mr. Turner, who introduced me to his brother, who was then in Scotland, carrying through the press an edition of the Samoan Scriptures. My district was in the High Street, my hall near to a mission church connected with Greyfriars. I was a member of that church, and worked in connexion with it. Dr. Calderwood was then minister. All our evening meetings were well attended, and my Sabbath morning Bible class was regularly attended by over one hundred and twenty young men and women.'

It is not possible to add anything to the graphic picture Chalmers has sketched of his boyhood and youth. Nor can any details be given, unfortunately, of his Glasgow experiences. He toiled in that great city only eight months; but though the period of service was brief the discipline was invaluable to him in after life. In the slums of Glasgow he had to deal with men and women hardly less degraded and even more difficult to influence for good than the heathen of New Guinea.

# CHAPTER II

## COLLEGE LIFE

CHALMERS, in his autobiography, has given a very rapid outline of his college training and experiences.

'In the course of my Glasgow life I began preparing for the university, with the intention of entering the ministry of the United Presbyterian Church, but after several conversations with Dr. Turner, I applied to the London Missionary Society, was accepted by them, and sent to Cheshunt College. I was sorry to leave Glasgow, as I had been greatly blessed in the work.

'My anxiety to get to the mission field helped me to apply to the Directors of the London Missionary Society. I have often grieved over the unmanning of myself by becoming a student on charity. But I thank God for Cheshunt, and more especially for Dr. Reynolds. That first interview with the Principal is to-day a blessed memory. We met in the parlour belonging to the matron, Miss Aldridge. He asked many questions about Greek, Latin, mathematics, and being satisfied, then said, his whole face speaking, " But, brother, the most important thing of all is your state in relation to our Lord Jesus Christ." Every student of our " St. Anselm's " time looks back with holy, blessed memories to Cheshunt.

'After leaving Cheshunt I spent a year at Highgate with Dr. and Mrs. Wardlaw, in the home for students soon going to the field. It also was a pleasant time.

I might have to go to Africa, and so for some time gave myself to the study of Dutch, also attended lectures given by a Dr. Betts near to Highgate, and also attended the Homoeopathic Hospital recommended by Dr. Epps. It was whilst at Highgate that I paid a visit to Cheshunt to assist in the Missionary Anniversary services at the village stations, especially at Hertford Heath. The weather was delightful and warm for the season, and several proposed a row on the Lea. I accompanied, and had a good pull. In the afternoon all stripped to bathe, I remaining in charge of the boats. I was resting leisurely when I saw one sink and rise and scream and sink again. A fellow student near by swam out and tried to seize him, but he got hold of the rescuer, and together both were sinking in the mud and locked fast to one another. I sprang into the river, clothes and all, and diving, seized hold of one by the hair, and then the other students, who had formed a line from the bank to the centre of the river, drew us all three safely on shore. We hurried back to college, and I, getting into a suit belonging to a fellow student named Pringle, hurried away to Hertford Heath. We thought to keep the knowledge of what had happened from the Principal, but twenty-three years after he related the whole affair to me, adding, " You thought to keep it quiet."'

Dr. Turner, referred to above, a Scotchman himself, an Ayrshire man, was then at the height of his fame. He had been at work in Samoa since 1841, and had passed the Nineteen Years in Polynesia which are described in his book with that title. He had helped to found and to bring to a high pitch of efficiency the Seminary at Malua, which is to-day one of the best training-schools for native evangelists in the Pacific. His chief task in Britain, at the time when Chalmers

met him, was to carry through the press an edition in
Samoan of the complete Bible, and also four volumes of
Scripture exposition in the same language, for the use
of his Samoan students. Dr. Turner had had some
terrible and thrilling experiences on the island of Tanna
seventeen years before Dr. Paton landed on it. He was
well acquainted with the type of savages among whom
Chalmers was eager to labour. A man of Dr. Turner's
force and experience was certain to exert a powerful
influence over the earnest and enthusiastic city missionary. Dr. Turner continued his work in Samoa
until 1882; and he died in London in 1891. He had
lived to see the youth whom he directed to the London
Missionary Society, and to Cheshunt College, become
one of the foremost figures in modern missionary
enterprise.

The reference which Chalmers makes in his autobiography to the conditions under which he entered
Cheshunt College is both strong and characteristic.
He states: 'I have often grieved over the unmanning of
myself by becoming a student on charity.' This refers
to the fact that he was unable to pay his way through
college, and that he entered Cheshunt as a student
whose expenses were paid by the London Missionary
Society. At this time, for the great majority of the
candidates which it accepted, the Society paid to the
college authorities a sum of thirty pounds a year.
This sum was only the lesser half of what the education
cost, since every student who passes through the college
costs the authorities at least eighty pounds a year,
exclusive of rent for college buildings. Hence in Chalmers' case, and in the case of all students who were
similarly situated, the authorities of Cheshunt College
conferred a bursary worth at least fifty pounds a year.

The London Missionary Society also allowed each student ten pounds a year for personal expenses. Many of the students in Cheshunt College at this time were so placed that their friends could supplement this somewhat scanty provision. This was not the case with Chalmers, and he seems to have felt humiliated by his inability to make both ends meet. On January 22, 1863, he wrote to Mr. Meikle:—

' I lately had an interview with an under Secretary in connexion with the Society, and he said the Directors did not at all understand student life, or they would never offer their students only ten pounds a year to defray all their expenses, as it would take that nearly to pay for washing, fire and light. I asked him if nothing could be done to have it increased, but he feared not. I told him that if they would give twenty pounds for the first year, or even fifteen pounds, ten pounds or less would do for the second and following years, as I then came on to the Box[1], which after the first year pays of itself the student's college expenses; but he still seemed to think they would not change. I am the first student from the Society in this college on that sum. I have no doubt but I will get this session battled through in some way, and it may for after life prove one of the best lessons I had while at college. It teaches how to economize, but in rather a difficult way.

' I do not intend to be at many meetings for the next five months, but just to get on with my studies. I am beginning to make use of the Greek for my Testament, and I rather like it, although I cannot say I like the languages as well as theology and mathematics. But,

[1] The fees received by the students for preaching were put into a common fund called the Box, and divided among the men at the close of the term, in proportion to the number of services taken by each.

by the blessing of God, I am determined to master all the languages I have to undertake.'

In another letter to his old pastor, dated April 29, 1863, Chalmers wrote :—

'Nothing, it seems, can be done to increase my allowance, from what Mr. Prout says. I spoke to him of our two months' vacation, and told him if they did not increase it I would have to remain in the south. I shall strongly object to remain in the south, and shall endeavour to get home by some means. It tries faith to see so many difficulties, and I believe they cannot be worse than they really now are ; but yet, and although darkness hovers around the future months, I feel the missionary zeal stronger—the desire to glorify our dear Lord, and to be the means of saving though it be but one, now surmounts every difficulty, and casts down every barrier. If I thought next year was going to be as this—but it will be better seeing I will come in for a share of supplies—I would make application to be appointed to some part of the field, and yet I feel thoroughly unqualified for so great a work. Might I ask to be remembered in the Wednesday evening meeting, that my love may be stronger, and that I may be qualified for this great and glorious work ?

'I need not revert to that which I doubt not you will have already learned. I mean my engagement. The reason of my becoming engaged so soon was because her parents and the whole family are leaving shortly for New Zealand, where she has a brother who is getting on well. This one thing I can say, she is a thorough missionary.

'I am reading Livingstone's travels in Central Africa during my spare time, and feel very much interested in that portion of the field. Mission work

C

would be difficult for the first two or three years, but oh, the pleasure of taking the Gospel to the Africans! '

In after life Chalmers had the feeling that it would have been better, and more in accordance with his self-respect, had he waited until, by his own labour, he had earned enough to pay his way through college. But this, in his case, would have postponed for years entrance upon the missionary work so dear to his heart. And it is practically certain, as he surmises in the letter just quoted, that the severe economy which he was compelled to exercise during his student days, was a fine and helpful discipline for his after life.

The system now in force with the London Missionary Society is radically different from that which obtained in Chalmers' time. The Society does not accept a candidate until his college course is completed, and it now recognizes no financial responsibility whatever for him during his education. But Cheshunt College, now as then, never receives from any student more than forty pounds a year, and in the vast majority of cases the annual payment stands at a much lower figure.

Many of those who were students at Cheshunt College from 1862 to 1865, during the time Chalmers was a student, are still alive, and retain pleasant and vivid recollections of him as he was at that time.

The Rev. G. Lyon Turner, M.A., writes:—' From the autumn of 1862 to the summer of 1864, I knew him in the intimacy of college life at Cheshunt. He was tall, but thin, not at all portly, as he became in later years. His complexion was then rather pale and freckled. His hair was black, his eyes hazel, with an endless sparkle in them. He was active and muscular, lithe, but strong. He had the frame of an athlete, and was a powerful skater, and a vigorous football player. By all his natural qualities of body, mind and spirit he was a born pioneer and leader of men.

'He was possessed of boundless energy, and was always ready for noise, pranks, and practical jokes. In 1887, he wrote to me, "Do you ever feel old? I don't." The only way in which peace could be preserved in the college corridors was to make him and another, now a man known and honoured in all our churches, "policemen," to keep the peace. Chalmers was a vigorous, magnetic speaker, who laid hold of his audience and moved them mightily, and touched them by his loving earnestness. He had great will-power. On one occasion a series of lectures was given in the village hall on electro-biology. The lecturer, whose name was Von Humm, professed by mesmerism to make people do things impossible to them in the normal way. Two lads who were evidently in collusion with him were brought by him upon the platform in a pretended mesmeric condition. He passed his hands over their arms and these at once became rigid. He made them drink different nauseous mixtures and then declare these to be what they had previously stated was their favourite drink. Chalmers came to the conclusion that the man was an impostor, and with the help of a confederate determined to test this. On the second evening they attended the lecture, and when the lecturer's confederates appeared Chalmers took his place on the platform. The fellow student who was gladly assisting him passed his hands over Chalmers' arm and it at once became rigid as a bar of iron. They had also prepared a liquid consisting of a mixture of tincture of assafoetida and cayenne pepper. Chalmers challenged the lecturer's lads to drink this.

They did so, and pronounced it to be coffee. Chalmers perforce as challenger had to do the same, and he also drank off a glass and stated that it was coffee. This he did by the exercise of his will power, but with the wryest of wry smiles.

'He was very warm in his attachments, and he had a big, loving heart. To the last the vigour of his hand-clasp was a testimony to his muscular power. One of my tenderest memories is one of my earliest, and it is one which illustrates the earnest simplicity of his Christian life. One afternoon during my first three months at the College he found me in my study, and we passed a quiet half hour together in prayer. This was quite natural to him, for he was a real man of God, and a tender-hearted Christian disciple. I felt then, and have often thought of it since, that fervent power with God which was the secret of his power with men.'

Another fellow student, the Rev. William Harris, who after many years of service in the Presbyterian Church of England is now (1902) living in retirement, and who, prior to entering Cheshunt had fought with Hedley Vicars in the trenches before Sebastopol, writes :—

'I remember him the day we entered college, and his face is still with me. Round, slightly freckled, smooth and winsome. He was known to me as a fellow of boundless geniality, good temper, and to any brother in "the blues" his face was a means of grace and if you were a wet blanket and stayed in his company long enough you would become dry. He was very modest and unpretentious, full of goodness and harmless fun. What he did, he did with both hands earnestly. He was a lovable character, but no one supposed that there was such latent spiritual force in him—a force ever increasing as he moved on in life—revealing him to be of the order which is not after a dying commandment, but after the power of an endless life.  I count it one of the joys, the great joys of my life to have known James Chalmers.'

Another fellow student, the Rev. James Thomas, of the British and Foreign Bible Society, describes an incident of Cheshunt life already referred to in the autobiography, but in a manner which strikingly illustrates Chalmers' skill and courage in a moment of great and unexpected danger.

'One hot day, near the end of April, eight of the students, including Chalmers, agreed to go for an afternoon's boating on the River Lea.  Having pulled for an hour, as the day was so hot they agreed to have a swim; but Chalmers, not being very well, resolved to remain on the river's bank.  Of the seven who entered the water six were good swimmers—the one unable to swim did not venture far from the river's brink.  Having been ten or fifteen minutes in the water the six swimmers landed, and were drying themselves, one of them being a little distance from the rest.  The one man unable to swim remained in the water for a little time longer.  Suddenly there was a splash and a scream; but one man (the writer), who was apart from the others, clearly saw that the man in the water was beyond his depth, and ran the few yards to the margin of the river and jumped in.  The others thought that the man who screamed was only larking.  Instantly the drowning man clutched hold of his deliverer in such a way as made it impossible for him to swim; and, although he pleaded with him to relax his hold, saying that he could easily save him if he did so, the frightened man clung all the closer; and both men were in the greatest danger of being drowned. Their struggles forced them towards the middle of the river, when Chalmers perceived the greatness of the peril, and called upon the other six men, who were still undressed, to plunge into the river, and to swim out one a little beyond the other, so as to be able to make a chain of hands, when he, having only thrown off his coat and waistcoat, jumped into the water, and swam towards the drowning pair. Having taken a secure hold of one of them as they were sinking together for the last time, with the other hand he seized one hand of the outermost set of the swimmers, and called upon them to haul him and the endangered men ashore. By this means both of their lives were saved. Chalmers' skill, as well as courage, was revealed by the instantaneous formation of the plan that saved his colleagues from what otherwise would have been certain death.'

The Rev. W. Garrett Horder, who entered Cheshunt College the same year as Chalmers, writes :—

' The portrait which faces page 48 represents James Chalmers as he was just before leaving Cheshunt College. Those who knew Chalmers only when he had become famous—broad-shouldered and deep-chested, his face widened beyond the dimensions of that of Charles Dickens, to whom he had grown very like, but rendered larger-looking by thick moustaches and ample flowing beard—will be astonished that he was ever so slightly built and with a face so small. The camera, however, is a surer witness than any that memory can summon. And in this case it gives, as it does not always, an absolutely accurate impression of the original. Such was the man as he set his face resolutely toward mission work in far-off lands—lithe, sinewy, with not an ounce of superfluous flesh ; with a face alert and determined, eyes

that looked you through and through, as do those of
the great preacher of Manchester, Alexander Maclaren.
Indeed, the eyes gave the distinctive character to the
face.

'Chalmers entered Cheshunt with a culture of the
slenderest, and a very small acquaintance with literature,
native or foreign, modern or ancient. But he had the
advantage that every Scotchman I have ever known
enjoys, that of never revealing by his speech the slender-
ness of his early education. In the case of Englishmen
want of early culture is often revealed by some vulgarity
of speech, especially in the use, or rather the abuse, of
the letter H, a failing which in many cases no after
training can eradicate. The Scotchman may have his
own way of rendering the English tongue, and to
Southerners he may be difficult to understand, but no
one catches in his speech the note of vulgarity.

'The training at Cheshunt did little to alter his manner
of speech. He would have been a strange Scotchman
if it had. Nor did it do much to make him, in any
department, a scholar; that he never became. He put
in his appearance regularly at the classes assigned to
him, and did his best to prepare for the periodical
examinations; but if his fame had rested on his acquirements, it would be very near a minus quantity. Men-
tally he left the college pretty much as he had entered it.
Over Chalmers, as over every other student who could
appreciate it, the spell of the lovely character and spirit
of the beloved Principal, Dr. Henry Robert Reynolds,
was strong, and exerted a refining and uplifting influence. Beyond this the Principal's teaching gave the
young Scotchman a wider outlook, and probably softened
a good deal the hard outlines of the Scotch theology in
which he had been brought up, throwing into greater

prominence the thought of the Divine Fatherhood. But from the class-rooms at Cheshunt he drew a general emotional influence rather than a compact and ordered knowledge of theology. Surely a greater result! "If every one that loveth is born of God, and knoweth God," the education of the heart is more than that of the head.

'During his stay at Cheshunt he continued the mission work begun at Glasgow. But there were no scenes in Cheshunt such as had met his eyes in the slums of Glasgow. I remember his telling me, in later years, that, apart from its cannibalism, even New Guinea presented no sights more terrible for degradation and impurity than Glasgow. Among the sparser and less virile dwellers in the village hard by the college he now laboured. He visited the poorest and most neglected in their homes, preached in the open air, and carried on a vigorous campaign against drink.

'The College at Cheshunt is the centre of a great number of village stations, to which the College chapel stands as a sort of tiny cathedral, and the Principal of the College as the Bishop. Each of these village churches was placed under the direction of a Dean, who was responsible for the pastoral work, and went as often as possible to conduct the services on Sunday. I suppose it was because of his muscular build that Chalmers was appointed Dean to the farthest off of these, at Hertford Heath, some eight miles from the College, and to which no railway offered any alleviation of the toil of walking. This station had a special interest, as it was under the fostering care of Professor Johnson, the well-known Sanskrit scholar of Haileybury College, then the great training-school for the Indian Civil Service. Between Professor Johnson and Chalmers a warm friendship sprung up, and the young Scotch student was an ever welcome guest at his house. Whenever it was possible, and he had sermons to deliver—a question of much moment to most students—Chalmers was always ready to cover the sixteen miles involved in the journey to Hertford Heath and back. There he worked his way to a warm place in the affections of the little company who met for worship. To this day one of the proudest memories of the congregation, for which a new and beautiful little sanctuary has been erected, is that the Apostle of New Guinea was one of their earliest Deans. In work of this kind Chalmers found the best spiritual preparation for the after and noble work of his life.

' No account of Chalmers at Cheshunt, however, would be complete without reference to his fellow students, and indeed to some of the frolics in which from time to time they were associated. Among the men of his time Chalmers was a universal favourite. His manliness, his sincerity, his simplicity, endeared him to us all. There was in him that touch of nature that made him kin. To use John Henry Newman's favourite motto, it was a relationship of " Heart to heart." Men might think little of his intellectual equipment, but every noble soul recognized the greatness of his heart.

' Chalmers was usually the ringleader in the practical joking of his time. Some will perhaps think that in a college of theology such things should be unknown. May I tell them for their comfort that most of the men who have been conspicuous for devoted work in after years had, at some time or other, some part in such practical joking? A too demure childhood is not a good augury for the after life. And a too serious behaviour at college is not always the precursor of the most devoted work in the service of Jesus Christ. A little harmless effervescence shows that there is abundance of life. And the life in Chalmers was so abounding that it demanded expression. Long-sustained thought or study was an impossibility to him, and so in the interval between an early tea and supper, occupied by most men in preparation for class or the composition of sermons, he often grew restless, and would wander about the corridors bent on some harmless mischief, to the disturbance of the more studiously inclined.

'I remember how one evening when an extra bad fit of restlessness was on him his much disturbed neighbours resolved on condign punishment. He was closely fastened in his room—the key-hole filled with cayenne pepper, to which a match was applied, so that for him to breathe was impossible, and he had to throw wide his window and put out his head to get air; but as soon as his head was out a volley of water was fired upon it from a sentinel stationed on the roof above. Such punishment, however, neither aroused revenge nor cured his restlessness.

' All this reminds me of a story told by Dr. John Ker: " On one occasion, William Guthrie, author of the *Christian's Great Interest*, had been entertaining a company with mirth-provoking anecdotes, and being called on afterwards to pray, he poured out his heart with such deep-felt fervour to God that all were melted. When they rose from their knees, Durham of Glasgow, a ' grave solid man,' took him by the hand and said, ' Willie, you are a happy man; if I had laughed as much as you did a while ago, I could not have prayed for four-and-twenty hours.' " Chalmers was like Willie Guthrie—he could play a prank, and right upon it pray. Surely not only the happiest, but the truest way for a Christian! Christianity does not mean the exclusion of fun from the life, but its sanctification.

'The New River runs through the beautiful grounds at Cheshunt. My most vivid memories of Chalmers are of him on that river—steering a raft or being upset and floundering in the water. Against both the rules of the College, and of the New River Company, who owned the river, Chalmers persisted in launching a raft and disporting himself thereon—working it with all the skill of a Canadian lumber-man. He ran along it almost as a squirrel would, but every now and then he would lose his balance and disappear in the water. I have often thought that the best preparation he had for many an adventurous voyage in New Guinea waters was on that raft.

'But whether at play or work, in class-room or field, in mirth or in prayer, his heart was always beating for the things of God and His kingdom. The great enthusiasm for humanity kindled by Jesus Christ burned within that heart, and made his life a living sacrifice. He fulfilled to the full the great thought of Joubert—"Let us be men with men, but always children before God; for in His eyes we are but children." "He carried the child's heart with him through life," as Baldwin Brown in his ordination charge advised me to do. And so he became "The Great Heart of New Guinea," as Robert Louis Stevenson called him. One of the most cherished memories of my life is that for two brief years I held fellowship with him, and so I can claim a friend among the noble army of martyrs.'

James Chalmers and Ralph Wardlaw Thompson were fellow students at Cheshunt. They were far asunder in many respects; they were alike in their love of healthy, harmless fun. The future Apostle of New

Guinea and the future Foreign Secretary of the London Missionary Society were confederates in many a raid upon the peace of their more studious brethren. And the survivor concludes, as only he can, these reminiscences of college days.

'My acquaintance with James Chalmers commenced when he entered Cheshunt College, at the beginning of the session in September, 1862. He did not enter for the full course, and as I had been a session at college before he arrived, our knowledge of each other was entirely outside the class-room. My recollections of his Cheshunt career do not point to any conspicuous mental power, nor to any reputation gained as a student; yet I imagine few men have left a more vivid or a more pleasant impression on their fellow students than he did. As I recall the memories of those happy days of student life, through the light of later years, I see how the qualities which won our respect and affection then, were the qualities which were most conspicuous and influential in his later career.

'The big, powerful Scotchman, with his exuberance of animal spirits and enthusiasm, was not long in discovering that his fellow students, though in training for the ministry, were not under strict monastic discipline. The monotony of student life was relieved from time to time by an outburst of the spirit of mischief and practical joking. This undoubtedly served as a most useful safety-valve, was almost invariably thoroughly good-natured and innocent; but while the fit was on study was impossible, and any unfortunate who could not enter into the spirit of the fun promptly became the butt of the good-humoured mischief of his neighbours. Chalmers entered into this side of college life with great zest, and was soon known as one of the most prominent of a little band of mischievous spirits, *quorum pars magna fui*, who were ringleaders in those outbreaks. Many a laugh have some of us had when we have met in the soberer days of ministerial life, and talked over those merry times when we were students, and in all such reminiscences the name and figure of Chalmers had a prominent place.

'Who, for instance, that was at Cheshunt at the time can forget the awful apparition of the great brown bear? Chalmers had made the acquaintance of Mr. Tugwell, curate at Goff's Oak. Mr. Tugwell had been for a time a missionary among the North American Indians, and had brought home with him some interesting curios. Among others, there was an enormous bear's skin, with the head and paws complete, prepared by the Indians to be worn in some of their dances. Chalmers promptly borrowed this skin, and brought it down by night to the College. He confided his secret to only one or two confederates, and at the close of a very quiet evening, when prayers were over, and the men were all in the dining-hall at supper, the door was suddenly flung open and the bear appeared, standing on its hind-legs, and roaring ominously. It shambled quickly into the room among the startled students, made for one of the quietest, subjected him to a terrible hug, and then pursued others. At this juncture a confederate turned out the gas, and the scene of excitement in the dark may be better imagined than described. When the light was turned on again it was discovered that it was Chalmers who was masquerading in this fashion. For a week after that bear was the central figure in numberless jokes. I shall never forget the abject terror on the face of an old Irishman who used to come into the College as a vender of fruit and other luxuries, when the bear suddenly met him at the end of the corridor, and seized him and his basket in its ample embrace.

'This same exuberance of animal spirits and love of adventure were carried through his missionary life. Those who went out with him to the South Seas can tell of the impression he produced upon the sailors. While detained on Niue by the wreck of the second John Williams, he narrowly escaped drowning in his effort to emulate the natives in the exciting, but to a novice very perilous amusement of surf swimming with the aid of a small plank. When I met the members of the New Guinea District Committee at Vatorata in 1897, it was remarked that Tamate could not be well, for he was so quiet! Usually at the annual gatherings of the committee he was a moving spirit in fun and mischief, and when the serious labours and deliberations of the day were over, he would devise some practical joke, at the expense of the more sober members of the committee.

'While the spirit of fun was so strongly marked, I should be very sorry to give the impression that it was the most prominent feature in the college life of my dear friend, James Chalmers. Quite as pronounced, and all the more influential because of its association with such lively qualities, was his deep religiousness. His faith was very simple, very decided, and had all the fervour of the Highlander. The earnest outpouring of his soul in the broad Doric of his West Highland speech, made a deep impression upon us all at the first of our students' weekly prayer meetings in which he took part, and his work at the village stations, especially at Hertford Heath, left an impression so deep that his memory still remains among those who are left of the village congregations at the time of his student life.

I remember going over to Hertford Heath for the Sunday just after he had paid his first visit to that station. I found the little congregation in quite a furore of excitement, in consequence of the powerful appeals he had made to them in the missionary interest. His personal life of simple earnest devotion was the source of all his enthusiasm in speaking for Christ, while his dashing fearlessness of spirit gave a certain tone to his utterances which made them very impressive.

'After Chalmers left college he was for twelve months under my uncle, Dr. John Wardlaw's care, with other missionary students, at Farquhar House, Highgate. I had the opportunity of seeing him frequently there. It was my privilege, shortly after settlement in Glasgow, to take part in his marriage to his noble-minded first wife, Miss Hercus, of Greenock. Then he went abroad, and for several years we had very little communication with each other. He gave me a very warm welcome when I entered upon my present duties as Foreign Secretary; and since then I have by correspondence and by personal contact, got to know a good deal more of my old fellow student.

'He had his faults, as we all have, he was too impulsive; he was sometimes inclined to be very strongly prejudiced, and to take up very unreasonable positions; nor was it easy to get him to alter his views when once formed. But these failings were but spots on the sun; the great qualities which impressed his fellow students remained with him, and were his power throughout his missionary life, an intense humanity, absolute fearlessness, a beautiful simplicity of nature, and absence of selfishness, and a whole-hearted devotion to the work of the Lord Jesus Christ, to which he had given his life, and for which he was prepared to do anything that might be required in the interests of the great cause.

'Some of his fellow students were greatly amused when they heard of him at Rarotonga as presiding over a Training Institution for the preparation of native evangelists. We could scarcely imagine our old associate tethered to the desk, or methodically teaching and lecturing; yet when I saw the same Chalmers at Saguane, walking up and down the sanded floor of his little rush school-chapel, and for the love of Christ teaching some three-and-twenty wild young New Guineans arithmetic, geography, and the English language, I fully understood and appreciated the way in which he would undertake the duties of a tutor of theological students. The great missionary explorer, with his boundless energy, seemed grotesquely out of place in giving an elementary lesson to the young New Guineans by means of the Gouin system of language-teaching, but he did not feel it to be so ; it was work which had to be done, there was no one else to do it, he therefore quite naturally and simply took it up, prepared to hand it over to any one who could do it better, or to stick to it as long as it was necessary for him to do so. I laughed heartily with him, and I fear chaffed him unmercifully, but none the less, I got a new view of his simple and noble character, and admired and honoured him more than ever for his devotion to duty.'

Chalmers spent two years only at Cheshunt. He entered the College in September, 1862, and he left it at the end of his second session, in June, 1864. During his first year, the President, the Rev. Henry Robert Reynolds, B.A., who had, as recently as 1860, relinquished the pastorate of East Parade Congregational Church, Leeds, suffered a severe breakdown in health.

JAMES CHALMERS AND HIS FIRST WIFE IN 1865.

This necessitated changes in the teaching staff, and to some extent disorganized the educational arrangements of the College. It is already obvious to the reader that hard study and theological reading were not Chalmers' strong points. The bent of his mind, the condition of the College, and last but not least, the state of his finances, all tended in the direction of making his college course as brief as possible.

In 1861 the London Missionary Society had founded a college at Highgate, intended for the completion of the training of their students. The theory was that the student should spend a year there, and devote himself to attending lectures on comparative religion and upon missionary work and history, and to the beginning, as far as possible, of a study of the language of the people among whom he was likely to labour, and further to gain such elementary medical and mechanical knowledge as might prove of special service to him when abroad. To this college, in 1864, Chalmers was transferred.

Cheshunt College has always been limited in the number of its students. In Chalmers' first year it contained twenty-seven students; in his second, twenty-six. It has never had more than forty-two or forty-three. It is residential, and in consequence the influence of personality, the action and reaction of man upon man, is one of the most potent and abiding forces in the training. Dr. Reynolds had many and great gifts, but perhaps the greatest of them all was his constant perception of the heavenly vision, and his power of making it visible to those who came under the magnetic influence and abiding sway of his own deep spirituality. Cheshunt has never lacked scholars, and among Chalmers' fellow students were two who graduated brilliantly at the University of London, one taking the Master of Arts degree in both classics and philosophy, and the other taking the gold medal, the same year, in philosophy, at the same degree. There was the outside stimulus of the University of London for the stronger students; there was the natural, human rivalry of the class-room; there was the abiding and powerful attraction towards theology, exegesis, and philosophy, necessarily strongly felt by men looking forward to a life spent in the ministry of the Gospel. And over all and above all were the charm and almost resistless attractive power of Henry Robert Reynolds—the St. Anselm, as Chalmers calls him, of Cheshunt—the man of quite unforgetable sweetness, and uplifting and spiritual insight.

Dr. Reynolds and James Chalmers were as far asunder as the Poles in many respects; yet they learned in the close relationship of life at Cheshunt to respect and to love one another. A bond was established that only strengthened until the elder man passed within the veil. A letter of Chalmers to Dr. Reynolds, dated December 11, 1895, lies before us as we write. He says:—

'Your giving me *The Lamps of the Temple* was an inspiration. I have been listening to you again and again, and drinking in new life from the Water of Life flowing through you. I have read them all, and to-day begin them again. At times of devotion may they be to me as the very Lamp of God. These *Lamps* will bring back to every Cheshunt fellow the past, and flash anew through his soul thoughts and inspirations that in the past were his through you. God spare you to us yet a while! To know you are with us is a comfort. I carry with me, and it will remain with me, your sacred benediction.'

Dr. Reynolds, writing long years later of these college days, said: 'Chalmers gave me the idea of lofty consecration to the Divine work of saving those for whom Christ died. His faith was simple, unswerving, and enthusiastic, and while he could throw a giant's strength into all kinds of work, he was gentle as a child and submissive as a soldier. He used to pray for help as if he were at his mother's knee, and to preach as though he were sure of the message he had then to deliver.'

Thus though the scholastic opportunities of Cheshunt did little for Chalmers, its spiritual life tended to deepen even his devotion and enthusiasm and intense longing for the salvation of men. The testimonies from his fellow students, quoted above, show that Chalmers was a force in the spiritual life of the College. And his vigorous physical life, his high spirit, his love of fun, his freedom from all conventions, combined to render his brief stay at Cheshunt a memorable experience for all who shared it with him. William Harris was not the only man who counted it one of the great joys of his student life to have known James Chalmers.

# CHAPTER III

## 'IN PERILS OF WATERS'

THE last year in the home training of a missionary student is usually a season of uncertainty, unrest, and mental excitement. The future field of service has to be determined by the Directors of his Society. The question of engagement and marriage is often very prominent, and sometimes very disturbing. If the definite field of service is known, there are tentative efforts to acquire the elements of the language, and to store up information about the country and the people where the life-work is to be carried on. In addition all the harassing and yet important questions of outfit have to be dealt with, frequently in the face of very scanty means for their consideration.

Chalmers was no exception to this rule. He had had many searchings of heart and many trying experiences, but in the course of the year 1865 his future course began to shape itself both certainly and attractively. He writes in his autobiography :—

'After leaving Highgate I went for some months to Plumstead, near to Woolwich, where with my lifelong friend, Saville, we studied Rarotongan with the Rev. George Gill of Rectory Place, who had laboured for many years as a missionary in Rarotonga. We lived in the very happy home of the Rev. Hugh Hercus, my future wife's uncle. On October 17, 1865, I was married to Miss Jane Hercus, daughter of Peter Hercus, Esq.,

Greenock, and afterwards of New Zealand. She was
a worthy Congregationalist, and a member of the
Greenock Church. Her grandfather Hercus was the
first minister of the church, and her grandfather
Robertson was a well-known Congregationalist minister
in the north and west of Scotland in the early years
of the century. She was a whole-hearted missionary.'

Miss Hercus was a lady of quite exceptional gifts and
graces. She was the eldest of four children, and was
left motherless at the early age of five years. By nature
bright and happy, the responsibility which fell upon her
as the eldest child rendered her staid and thoughtful
and eminently practical. Her mother's father, the Rev.
George Robertson, died in 1854, when Miss Hercus was
about fourteen, and the widow removed to Kirkwall in
the Orkneys, whither her granddaughter went to take
care of her. There Miss Hercus remained for five years,
giving herself absolutely to the engrossing duties of her
charge. And she did this at the age when such restraint
is most irksome, and yet in such a way as to appear
unconscious that it involved any sacrifice. She was
trained from early childhood in Christian life and
thought, though she did not become a Church member
until 1858. In that year also her grandmother died,
and she returned to Greenock. In 1861 her parents
removed to Glasgow, and here she met her future
husband. She spent some time in Leeds as a schoolmistress. Here she lodged with a family named Large,
and became very intimate with the daughter Lizzie, who
afterwards became the second Mrs. Chalmers. Before her
marriage, in 1867, she also spent some time at Inveraray.

Possibly in no department of Christian work is the
choice of a life-partner more important than in the
mission field. The two have to live together under

circumstances which test to the uttermost every weakness of body, of temper, of spirit, of faith. On the other hand, in hardly any other walk of life can a woman by her health, her tact, her sympathetic support, and her wise and zealous co-operation, be such a true helpmeet to her husband.

The annals of the London Missionary Society are rich in records of the noble and successful and devoted lives of the wives of missionaries. And yet in the vast majority of cases these lives do not make much stir, they seldom receive, except from the few who really know the facts, their due meed of appreciation and gratitude, and although they are often 'succourers of many,' their deeds are not well in the public eye.

On the other hand, the same records show not a few cases of lives crippled or even ruined by unsuitable and incompetent wives. Most frequently the failure is on the side of health. So often does this occur that not a few missionary administrators now think that the medical standard should be inflexible, and that if the slightest sign of weakness is present the bar to foreign service should be absolute. This has always been a matter of great concern and of great difficulty to missionary boards. Perhaps the chief change of recent years is a different inclination of the balance. Whereas if there was a slight doubt, it was usually given in favour of allowing the woman to go abroad, now it is frequently given against that course. And in our judgement this is wise, and had it been acted upon more rigidly in the past, much sorrow and failure and unnecessary expense would have been avoided.

But great as are the hindrances to mission work caused by ill-health, these are as nothing to those sometimes caused by defective moral and spiritual quality.

The woman who goes to the mission field with a man, and is yet not in fullest accord with him as to the great work and purposes of his life, inflicts a grave injury upon both him and the cause dear to his heart. Every mission can show such cases. They naturally do not figure in reports, but now and then the fruitlessness of a promising career is due to the fact that his life is linked to one who cannot govern her tongue, or who will not throw herself into her husband's work, or who cannot live at peace with others. And the worst of such cases is that they often seem beyond the reach of cure, and inflict a daily crucifixion upon those who have to endure what is incapable of improvement.

But in the case of Chalmers there was almost absolute freedom from every risk of this kind. Her early training had been an admirable discipline for the work and experience which came upon her as the wife of such a husband. It is possible that there was in Miss Hercus a strain of physical weakness. But this did not prevent her from giving years of happy and fruitful labour to the great cause upon which her heart was fixed. In Chalmers' words, written long years after she had passed away, 'She was a whole-hearted missionary.'

Chalmers in a letter from Highgate, dated March 17, 1865, deals with his views and hopes at this time :—

'I have delayed writing till the time would be fixed when we should sail, and now that it is about settled, I shall write. It has been decided that I shall go to Mangaia, in the Hervey Group of Islands, as a beginning. I shall have the charge of a church with over 500 members and a school of about 700 children. The island has a population of 3,000. I do not expect to remain long in it, as I hope to have more direct missionary work. There are still very many islands in

the South Seas where Christ is unknown, and to some
of these I live in the hope of yet carrying the knowledge of Him.  To-night I feel the desire stronger to
preach Christ among the heathen than I did three years
ago.  My desire grows, and as I become better acquainted
with redeeming love, I long to go.  God has helped and is
still blessing my labours, and I feel assured that He whose
the work is will ever continue to bless them—when put
forth in His name—for His glory and the good of man.

  ' You recollect our last missionary ship was lost, and
they have now begun building a new one in Aberdeen,
which cannot be ready before the end of the year; so
that we shall be in this country till then.  To send us
out before then would entail an expense of £500, and
the ship would sail without missionaries, to which of
course the churches would object.

  ' Nothing has as yet been decided as to what I am to
do after June.  I have no wish to return here, and
I have spoken to Mr. Wardlaw, our president, about
remaining north, and continuing my studies privately.
As it is, here I have very little to do with the College,
and what I do, I do privately.  I attend the hospital for
medicine, but that I could get in Glasgow, besides help
from a medical friend I became acquainted with in the
City Mission.  My other studies I could pursue alone.
I should like your opinion on this.  I feel I must
study botany, for the use of my medicines.  I am getting
on pretty well with the language, and hope to be able to
preach in it soon after getting to the island.'

  The next letter is of interest not only because it gives
a few details of his life at this time, but also because
it was written to the Miss Large referred to above.
There had been some understanding that as soon
as the young couple were established in Rarotonga

Miss Large should come out to help them in their work. The letter is dated Plumstead, July 25, 1865.

'What do you think now of our long absence—longer than either Jeanie or I contracted for? Dear lassie, I wish I could see her! She is in Inveraray now, and expects soon to go to Ould Ireland. As yet we cannot fix the consummation of all things. I wish we could, and soon too. I expect to go north in October, and hope to be married immediately afterwards. The new ship is expected in the Thames in September, and will be sure to sail this year. How long we are kept waiting ere we get into full harness! May God in His infinite love help us to make up for this in the future somewhat! I trust and pray ours may be a happy and useful future—that we may be the means of saving multitudes of souls, of cheering many on their way heavenwards.

'I am now lodging with Jeanie's uncle, and am very much at home. I spent a few holidays lately at South-end, but have now got back to work. I wish Jeanie and you were near here, we could have such fine times of it just now. Jeanie speaks of our spending a few days after our marriage, and just on our way south to sail, with you in Leeds.

'Good-bye now. May God bless you and be with you ever. On Christ lean for all support. He alone can strengthen you. Be strong in faith in Him, for He alone can save and bless and make truly happy. Let Him have *all* our hearts.'

Chalmers' ordination[1] took place two days after his

---

[1] This service took place on October 19 in Finchley (East End) Chapel. The Rev. William Gill described the field of labour; the Rev. John Corbin, of Hornsey, asked the questions and offered the ordination prayer; and the Rev. J. S. Wardlaw, M.A., delivered the charge. The Rev. Thomas Hill and the Rev. S. W. McAll, minister of the chapel, also took part.

marriage, and after it the young couple were eager to get to their appointed work. In the normal order of things they ought to have been settled in their new home within a year after leaving England. But for them it was ordained otherwise. It was not until May 20, 1867, that they set foot upon Rarotonga, and their experiences in the interval form a striking chapter in the annals of missionary adventure.

In those days there was no regular communication with any of the South Pacific Islands. Even to-day there is a regular mail connexion with only one or two groups. Hence for the work of visiting its widely scattered stations in Polynesia the Society has to employ their own vessel. The first great extension of London Missionary Society work in Polynesia was due to the energy and enthusiasm of John Williams. His visit to England in 1834 aroused great interest in the Society's work, and led to the purchase of a vessel of 400 tons called the Camden, whose duty it was to visit the missionary stations regularly, conveying missionaries and their wives, native agents and teachers, and all necessary stores. During the Camden's first voyage, in 1839, John Williams was murdered by the natives on the island of Erromanga. The Camden returned to England in 1843, and was then sold. As a memorial of the martyr the children of England raised over £6,000 to build a new missionary ship, to be called the John Williams, and from 1844 until 1864 the vessel did noble service. In the latter year, on December 10, she became a total wreck on the reef of Pukapuka or Danger Island. The children of a later generation enabled the Society to build a second John Williams, and in this entirely new vessel Chalmers and his wife sailed for Australia on January 4, 1866.

'The first John Williams,' writes Chalmers in his autobiography, 'was wrecked on Danger Island, and to replace her a very fine clipper ship was built in Aberdeen, and also named the John Williams. In her, on January 4, 1866, we left Gravesend. The vessel was commanded by Captain Williams, and his mate was Mr. Turpie, afterwards so well known as captain of the third John Williams.

'We had a rough time in the Channel, and at one time it was thought we should certainly be wrecked, and every soul lost. We met, and survived the gale of wind in which the London was lost. We suffered a good deal of damage, and put into Weymouth for repairs, where we remained for over a fortnight. The missionaries and their wives landed, accepting the kind and pressing invitation of the many friends ashore; but my wife and I preferred staying on board. Mrs. Williams, the captain's wife, was also on board. Throughout January the weather continued bad. Towards the end of the month we weighed anchor, and stood away to sunnier climes.

'We had a long stiff beat in getting to the South, but how we did enjoy the warm weather when we got into it! Our party consisted of Mr. and Mrs. Michie, Mr. and Mrs. Watson, and Mr. and Mrs. Davies, bound for Samoa; Mr. and Mrs. Saville, bound for Huahine; and Mr. and Mrs. Chalmers, bound for Rarotonga. I am now (1900) alone in the field.'

A letter dated, Ship John Williams, near Australia, April 25, 1866, gives some pleasant glimpses of life on the missionary ship after their stormy start was over:—

'We are now within 900 miles of Adelaide, and hope to get there in a few days. It has been a truly happy, pleasant, and blessed time to us all. We have felt none of the monotony of sea life, so much spoken about, but on the contrary have enjoyed change and variety in the heavens, sea, and atmosphere.

'The Bible class and prayer meetings with the men have been blessed. Prayers offered on our behalf have truly been answered, and God has blessed souls. The careless have been led to inquire for salvation, and the praying on board have been aroused to greater earnestness. Our Sabbath services and prayer meetings in the saloon have been to thirsty ones wellsprings of salvation. I have enjoyed and benefited much by the voyage thus far, and sincerely trust it will prove all through a grand spiritual preparation for the great work. Souls and God's glory are all that we desire.

'In health God has largely blessed us. We have been in excellent health all the way. After leaving Weymouth we had a slight touch of sea-sickness, by which I think we benefited much. I hope we won't be getting like the sailors, land-sick after being on shore a little. Mrs. Chalmers has proved the best sailor of the ladies in the saloon, in fact, beating some of the gentlemen.'

'On May 20,' continues the autobiography, 'we arrived in Adelaide, and received a right hearty welcome from Mr. Sunderland and the Christian people of that beautiful city. My wife's father came from New Zealand, and met us there. We visited Melbourne, Geelong, Ballarat, Hobart, and Sydney, where we spent some weeks. The interest taken in us, and the kindness shown in each city and town we visited was great. We left Australia feeling we had many friends whom we should long remember, and although many have passed on, there are still a few friends of those days remaining who remember with pleasure that happy time. Eh, it was a happy time!

'In August we left Sydney, and stood away for the New Hebrides. We had Dr. and Mrs. Geddes and Mr. and Mrs. Nelson on board as passengers from Sydney, and they were to be landed on Aneiteum. The afternoon we entered the harbour of Anelicahaut Aneiteum was clear, and there was a good south-east breeze blowing. We were all charmed with the new scenery, and were standing aft, entranced with watching the many beautiful colours of the reef near by, when suddenly several were thrown down upon their backs. The vessel had gone upon an unobserved reef with every stitch of canvas set, and there she hung for some days. Her forefoot was smashed, and a great piece of her false keel carried away. She was making much water, and the pumps had to be kept going. She was got off at last, and the forepart patched so as to enable her to get to Sydney for repairs. The Presbyterian New Hebrides Synod, who were then in session, decided that their vessel the Dayspring should accompany the John Williams. Mr. Robertson, now of Erromanga, with twenty-two natives, came on board to keep the pumps going. We had a long passage, nearly three weeks, and day and night the pumps had to be kept going. If I remember right, she was making from eighteen to twenty-two inches of water an hour.

'The Sydney friends were astonished to see us back so soon, and sorry indeed were they when they heard the reason. We lost everything by salt water. My wife and I were the only missionaries who accompanied the vessel, the others, with the greater part of the cargo, remained on Aneiteum. Again we experienced the exceeding great kindness of Sydney friends. We stayed with a widow lady and her four children, and all through life it has been a pleasant, loving memory.

After six weeks we were once again outside of Sydney Heads, and standing away from Aneiteum, and in one week we anchored in the Anelicahaut harbour.

'All were well. Passengers and goods were taken on board, and in a few days we sailed away to the Loyalty Islands. We were intensely interested in the mission work we saw on Aneiteum, and our whole self became enthused with it in the Loyalty Group. We all thanked God for calling us to so grand a work. The missionaries and natives gave us a kind reception at each island.

'From the Loyalty Islands we worked across the Pacific, south of Fiji, to Niue or Savage Island, an outlier of the Pacific. We landed at Niue, and had a kindly welcome from George Lawes, and his wife and people.

'We spent a day or two at Niue, and then the goods having been landed we were to sail for Samoa on January 9, 1867. Captain Williams suggested that some of us should go on board the night before, so as to leave less boating for the following day.'

What happened that night is more vividly described in a letter to Dr. Tidman, which Chalmers wrote on Savage Island nearly a month later, February 4, 1867 :—

'On the 8th ultimo, about 11.30 p.m., our much loved and thought of John Williams became a total wreck on the reef which surrounds this island. For some days the wind had been blowing very strong from the WNW., so causing a heavy swell to drive in towards the shore, and preventing the landing of the remainder of Mr. Lawes' goods, part of which had been landed on the 3rd, the wind then blowing off the land. On the afternoon of the 3rd all the passengers, with the exception of Mr. and Mrs. Davies—Mrs. Davies being unwell—came ashore to see Mr. Lawes. During the night the wind changed, and so prevented all communication with the ship, until the Tuesday. After getting the boats discharged, and reladen with yams, taro, bananas, cocoanuts—presents from the natives— Mrs. Williams, Mrs. Chalmers and I accompanied the captain to the ship, leaving Mr. and Mrs. Saville, Mr. and Mrs. Watson, with our carpenter, ashore. The latter was to buy from the natives the following morning pigs, &c., for ship use. We were glad to get back, for we loved to be on board ship, looking upon it as our home.

'About seven o'clock it fell calm, but as we were out a long way from land, no uneasiness was felt. About half-past seven, just as we were going to evening worship, the ship was noticed to drift astern. This was rather strange, as the current set the other way, but the swell was very heavy. Before worship was over orders were given for all hands on deck, and to lower away the whaleboat, which was soon done. She was sent ahead, well manned, having the ship in tow; still the ship went astern. The pinnace was next sent ahead, but both boats having no effect upon her, a third, the gig, was sent to assist. But with three boats well manned—manned by men who felt truly interested in our noble ship—she continued to go astern faster than ever.

'All now felt very anxious. We, the passengers, went below, and committed the ship and all on board into His hands who in the calm as well as in the storm could save His own ship. Nothing was left undone that was possible for men to do. Soundings were taken, but no bottom found. Rockets were fired, and blue lights burned, to warn those ashore of our danger, but we could not hope for any assistance from the land. Nearer and nearer the ship approached the dreaded reef, and by ten o'clock the reef seemed close under the stern. The white surf, through the dense darkness, could be distinctly seen, and it became evident that the sooner means were taken to save life the better. We had on board about seventy souls, including men, women and children. Shortly after ten o'clock the gig came alongside, and the ladies were handed down into it. Next the whaleboat and pinnace came, and were soon filled. About half-past eleven Mr. Turpie got into the pinnace, the rope was cut away, and the three boats lay off, to watch what might become of the ship. She very soon struck with a fearful crash, and as the rain now came down in torrents we made for the Mission station, a few miles off.

'By three a.m. on Wednesday morning we got off the reef under Mr. Lawes' house. A canoe came off, into which we got two and three at a time, and were paddled into the break of the surf, when, between the waves, natives seized us, and carried us with all speed to the shore. Inside the reef torches were kept burning by the natives, and without this it would have been impossible to land until daylight. By half-past four all were landed and comfortably housed with Mr. Lawes, whose kindness, with that of Mrs. Lawes, cannot be overlauded.

'Morning light revealed the ship in the midst of the surf—lifted up on the reef, and lashed mercilessly by the waves. Attempts have been made to save part of the cargo, but very little has been saved. Captain and Mrs. Williams seem heartbroken; but for Mrs. Williams and me I fear the captain would not have left the ship that night. He was proud of his ship, and justly so too. In their hearts the interests of the Society and missionaries found a large place. They have lost a great deal at this time. Many of their most valuable things have been either lost or destroyed, yet that does not seem to affect them at all. Should Captain and Mrs. Williams not return to these Islands again, they will be much missed, for they were true friends of all the missionaries. Too much cannot be said in the way of praise, for all who know them, I believe, love them.

' Do not for a moment suppose that we feel discouraged; we have no intention of turning back, and leaving our mission work. God forbid! If possible, we shall go on now. God is our strength. All our trust is in the Lord.'

It was while thus detained against his will on remote and solitary Niue that Chalmers nearly lost his life in the fascinating and exciting, but except to a native, excessively dangerous pleasure of surf swimming. We continue the story again from the autobiography :—

' During our stay on the island, I nearly lost my life. I was greatly interested in the surf swimming, and often watched the lads at it. One day the sea was particularly big, and I determined whilst bathing to try and run in on a sea with a plank. I got too far out, and was sucked back to the big boulders, and the seas washing me about, I got much bruised and cut. I can remember feeling that all was lost, when a great sea caught me, and threw me on to a boulder, and I felt now or never, and with a terrible effort I clung to it, and then rising, gave one spring, and landed where help could come to me. I was picked up, and carried to the house. I was in bed for several days. I never again tried surf swimming.'

The autobiography continues the story of this adventurous voyage :—

'Again everything was lost. When I left the John Williams for the boats, I had on a shirt and a pair of trousers and a pair of socks, no boots, and my watch, which had been the gift of the poor of the High Street, Glasgow. Some things were saved, but all much spoiled. The kindness we received from Mr. and Mrs. Lawes exceeded all praise. We had to remain six weeks on the island, and were at the mission house all the time. When a schooner belonging to the Samoan Trading Company called, the mate, Mr. Turpie, some of the crew, Mr. and Mrs. Davies, Mrs. Chalmers and I took passage in her to Samoa. We were eleven days getting to Apia, and ran out of water, and were put on very short rations in food. The captain was truly kind, and did all he possibly could to make us comfortable. My wife had been very ill on Niue, but picked up considerably on this voyage. We were kindly received by all in Samoa. The consul did all he possibly could for the shipwrecked crew, and we were entertained by the missionary, Mr. Murray. The missionaries lost much by the wreck; some of them were very short of clothing, and all were short of food.

'Soon after we arrived at Samoa, Captain Williams and his wife, and remainder of shipwrecked missionaries and sailors (only the second mate and a few sailors remained behind), were brought to Samoa in the Rona, a brig of one hundred and fifty tons, owned and commanded by the notorious Bully Hayes. On the arrival of the captain the wreck was sold, and Hayes bought it with all belonging to the ship that had been saved.

'Hayes was then chartered to return to Niue, and bring to Apia the remainder of the crew and all the saved spoiled cargo. On his return the things were equally divided between the missionaries in Samoa,

Society Islands and Cook Islands, and lots were drawn. The cloth was spoiled. I had a chest of tea in my lot, and believed it was good; but on opening it on Rarotonga we found it had been wetted, and was quite rotten.

'After spending six weeks on Samoa, Hayes was chartered to take us to Rarotonga, and Mr. and Mrs. Saville to Huahine. Before leaving Apia the foreign residents presented me with a testimonial in money, "feeling grateful," as they expressed it, " to you for the great interest you have taken in our spiritual welfare." The crew having saved the forecastle Bible presented it to me "as a token of our esteem for the religious instruction we have received from you while on board the said vessel." These marks of love and kindness I prized then, and still prize much. The Bible is to be sent to 14, Blomfield Street.

'Hayes seemed to take to me during the frequent meetings we had on shore, and before going on board for good I met him one afternoon, and said to him, " Captain Hayes, I hope you will have no objection to our having morning and evening service on board, and twice on Sabbaths. All will be short, and only those who like to come need attend."

'"Certainly not; my ship is a missionary ship now, and I hope you will feel it so. All on board will attend these services."

'" Only if they are inclined," I replied.

'We were well treated on board, Hayes was a perfect host, and a thorough gentleman. His wife and children were on board; and although we had fearful weather nearly all the time, yet I must say we enjoyed ourselves. Instead of going to Rarotonga first, we had gone so far south that we could easily fetch Tahiti, and so we

stood for it, causing us to be much longer on board,
Hayes several times lost his temper, and did very
queer things, acting under the influence of passion
more like a madman than a sane man. Much of his
past life he related to us at table; especially such
things as he had done to cheat governments; but as
much has appeared in print concerning him I forbear
retailing these stories.

'Leaving our friends, the Savilles, at Huahine, we
came to Mangaia, where we were very kindly received
by Mr. and Mrs. Wyatt Gill and their people. We
arrived on a Sunday in very dirty weather. I landed
just after sunset.

'On Monday morning I returned to the ship for
Mrs. Chalmers, and about midday we went ashore
with the captain, hoping to return in the evening.
The wind was easterly and very strong. The boat
remained outside the reef, going to and from the ship
with goods and provisions. About dark, a wet and
disagreeable night, the boat was ready to leave for
the last time. Both of us, with the captain, were
anxious to get off, and were quite ready to go, when
the natives refused to put us over the reef, as it was
very rough. The captain offered them five dollars
to get on board, but they would not be moved, the
pilot saying, "It is easy for me to take them to the
boat, but I feel certain that boat will never reach
the ship." Little did we suppose that by their refusal
to comply with our request our lives were preserved.

'The boat left for the ship, which lay off and on,
at no great distance from the reef. All night we felt
anxious about the ship, for the night was dark and
stormy. The next morning no ship was to be seen,
and it was not until Thursday she hove in sight.

The captain went on board immediately. Soon a
flag went up, but alas! it was only half-mast, then
another. It too was half-mast—What can be wrong?
Mr. Gill and I got a canoe and went off, but before
getting to the ship saw what was wrong. No whaleboat was seen on the starboard davits, and getting
on board we found she had never reached the ship.
There were two men in the boat, one a native of the
Sandwich Islands, who was second mate, and the other
a native of Ireland, named Hughes, who was working
his passage from Huahine.

'The supposition is she swamped, or was run down
by the ship. They were last heard cooeying close
to the ship, but could not be seen. We had had
many merciful deliverances since we set sail from
Gravesend on January 4, 1866, and again our prayer
was that life thus preserved might entirely be devoted
to the service of God.

'While we were waiting the return of the vessel
Mr. Gill had decided to accompany us. The plan was
that we should visit Aitutaki, pick up Mr. Royle, the
missionary on that island, and proceed thence to Rarotonga, where a meeting of Committee might be held.
On arrival at Aitutaki, a boat came off into which we
got, and on reaching the shore Gill stepped out, and
the boat was seized by an excited crowd, and with
much shouting we were carried right in through a
cocoanut grove to the foot of the hill on which the
mission house stood. There Mr. Royle met us, and
gave us both a hearty welcome. The shouting informed him that something very unusual was taking
place, and he had come down to see what it was.
A day or two after we left for Rarotonga laden with
presents from the Aitutakians, and with a bull and

a cow from Mr. and Mrs. Royle. What a splendid missionary couple they were, and what excellent work they did! We did not see eye to eye on some points, but I have always had a great admiration for their earnest service. He was a zealous man, and given to prayer.

'When near to Rarotonga I had a very kind letter from Hayes, thanking me for the services I had held on board the ship, and for my kindly demeanour towards him, saying, "If only you were near me, I should certainly become a new man, and lead a different life." Yet a few days after arriving at Rarotonga, the vessel being anchored in Avarua, he nearly killed his supercargo with a bag of dollars which I had given him as the last payment of the charter for the voyage now successfully completed.

'On May 20, 1867, we anchored in the harbour of Avarua. I was the first to land, and on being carried ashore from the boat by a native, he asked, "What fellow name belong you?" so that he might call it out to the shore. I answered, "Chalmers," and he roared out, "Tamate;" hence the name.'

# CHAPTER IV

## LIFE ON RAROTONGA

IN the manner described in the closing paragraph of the last chapter, Chalmers set foot on the island, and began the work to which he had looked forward with eager longing for years. Very few, even in those days of rough experience in travelling by sea, traversed in search of the desired haven such stormy seas, or entered port after such varied and dangerous experiences. Looking back through the years, we may discern in and through it all a discipline that bore good and speedy fruit. The open-air childhood and youth at Inveraray had fitted Chalmers to rejoice in 'moving accidents by flood and field' that would have discouraged a less robust nature. The combination of events, fortunate and disastrous, good and evil, that placed seemingly endless difficulties in the path to Rarotonga did but strengthen his faith, cause his enthusiasm to burn with a steadier flame, and render him daily more and more determined, were life spared to him, to reach his new home and to enter upon his lifework.

Moreover it is not unlikely that the long and exciting strain of the seven months' voyage rendered it easier for him, after a while, to settle down to those ten years of quiet, active, fruitful labour, within the limits of one Pacific island. Had it not been for the severities of the road that led him to the island, he might have been much more impatient than he was for

new scenes and more arduous duties. Even Chalmers might well rest and be thankful after a voyage
which nearly ended in total wreck almost at its beginning; which suffered partial wreck as soon as the ship
entered the Pacific; and reached the climax of total
wreck at Savage Island. To have faced death not once
or twice, but many times; to have left England in the
John Williams, the vessel built in faith and love and
prayer, and to have reached Rarotonga in a pirate
vessel commanded by one of the most notorious of
Polynesian desperadoes, to have been plucked from the
very jaws of death in the surf of Niue, partly by his
own courage and endurance, and partly by the skill and
wonderful power in the water on the part of the Savage
Island natives—these and many similar experiences
probably led even Chalmers to be willing for a time
to live the life of an ordinary mortal, and to occupy
himself in the quiet drudgery of uneventful missionary life.

And what of his new home? Rarotonga is one of the
most beautiful of the multitudinous isles of loveliness
which dot the surface of the vast Pacific Ocean. The
Rev. William Gill, who laboured there as a missionary
from 1839 to 1852, has left on record a description of
the island itself, and of the character and qualities of the
people in their heathen life that enables the reader to
picture the new surroundings in which Chalmers and
his wife now found themselves.

'Rarotonga is situated about six hundred miles
south-west of Tahiti, in 21° 20" south latitude and 160°
west longitude, and is the largest island of the Hervey
group. It is encircled by an outer reef thirty-five miles
in circumference; and its mountains rise three thousand
feet above the level of the sea. The barrier reef is a

protective wall of immense, deep, compact, block coral, from a quarter of a mile to half a mile broad. And this at low tide is almost bare, but at high tide is submerged to the depth of from four to six feet. The openings in the reef towards the sea vary from ten to twenty feet in width, and allow canoes and boats to pass in and out ; one of these, on the north side of the island, is large enough to admit a vessel of forty tons burden, but affords no protection; and on the south-east side there is another, which forms a miniature harbour, deep and safe, and is beautifully adorned by four ever-green lovely islets; but being exposed to windward is not available for ships. With these ex-ceptions there is no anchorage round the island. It is a reef-bound coast, shelving slightly seaward, then sinking perpendicularly thousands of feet towards the foundation of the sea.

'Against this vast barrier of coral reef the mighty waves of the Pacific, of deepest blue, rise in majestic grandeur to a height of more than twenty feet, then, curling over, break in innumerable myriads of silvery white spray, and dash in subdued, yet graceful, beauty on the shore.

'A long white sandy beach, varying from ten to a hundred feet wide, forms a natural margin to a com-paratively level tract of land, round the whole of the island. The soil is richly and constantly covered with fruitful groves of chestnut, cocoanut, breadfruit, and banana trees.

'Beyond this, inland, there is for the most part a long, low slip of marshy ground, cultivated as taro swamps, at whose base rise hills innumerable; then deep, wild, rugged, fertile valleys intervene between another range of higher hills; then other valleys; and thence, hill on hill, and mountain on mountain, piled on each other in rich variety of size, and form, and verdure. The lofty summits of the highest mountains can be seen by the voyager when sixty miles distant at sea.

'In each settlement the *ariki* or chief was supreme in power, and despotic in rule. Next in rank to him were the *mataiapo*, a class of independent landholders, either related to the *ariki* or having gained their position by deeds of valour. Under these were the *rangatira*, a kind of dependent tenantry, having certain privileges which distinguished them from the mass of common people, who under the above three ranks were in the condition of serfs. Caste did not exist as a system, yet each grade had its distinct position in the heathen society of Rarotonga.

'A family, as the term signifies to an English ear, was not known among this people. The chiefs, *mataiapos*, and *rangatiras*, were wont to have from three to ten wives each, according to rank, or property, or renown. Their habitations were long, narrow, low, reed huts, the ground being covered with dry grass, and the whole of the furniture consisting only of sleeping-mat, native bark-cloth, cloth-making block and mallet, stools and bowls. Licentiousness, deceit, and theft prevailed to a fearful extent; and so general and constant were the enmity and jealousy of one tribe towards another, that the majority of the people were confined to the range or district where they were born, only hearing vague reports, but knowing little definitely, respecting the tribes beyond them.

'War, either offensive or defensive, was their continual employment and delight. A state of peace was rarely ever known to continue long between the tribes. Frequent quarrels arose, sometimes by the people of one tribe trespassing the boundary line of their neighbour's land; at others, by the absconding of wives from their husbands; sometimes they were occasioned by acts of plunder on the cocoanut and breadfruit and taro plantations; and at others by revenge of former wrongs. These quarrels invariably led to fighting in which the warriors of each tribe engaged with the utmost desperateness and cruelty.

'The first victims secured in war were presented to the gods, and the head of each was taken in savage triumph, while yet reeking in its blood, to the chief of the tribe, and the bodies of such were eaten in their cannibal feasts. Cannibalism prevailed, but not to so fearful an extent as among the tribes of Western Polynesia; and infanticide was committed on a large scale, but was chiefly confined to female children, when there were already two or three in a family. The inhabitants of this lovely garden-island of the sea were sunk in an abject state of naked, barbarous, savage heathenism. Gross darkness covered the people, and their dwelling-place was full of cruelty and abomination.'

The story of the rediscovery of Rarotonga by John Williams in 1823, and of the successive steps by which Christianity was introduced, and the victory won over the vice and cruelty and cannibalism of the old heathen life is one of the most romantic in the fascinating annals of Polynesian missionary enterprise.

The early missionaries, Charles Pitman and Aaron Buzacott, who built wisely and well upon the foundation laid by the heroic Papeiha and the great John Williams, transformed a wild, fierce, and warlike race of savages into a semi-civilized, law-abiding people. Long before the eye of Chalmers gazed upon the many lovely mountains, valleys, lagoons, and reefs of

Rarotonga, the old heathenism had disappeared. Many of the islanders had been truly converted, and many had entered into the full joy and liberty of salvation. But large numbers were Christians only in name, and of those who professed to have realized the uplifting power of the Gospel many were still babes in Christ.

It was to a lovely home, and to quiet but necessary and not at all easy work that Mr. and Mrs. Chalmers came when they landed on Rarotonga on May 20, 1867. And here we pick up once more the thread of the autobiography.

'The reception we had from Makea Abela, and Tinomana and Pa, and Kainuku, and Mr. and Mrs. Krause, pastors, deacons, and churches surpassed all our expectations. Thirty-two years have gone since then, but the memory of it seems as fresh as ever. Mr. Krause had been ill for some time, and was glad of our arrival, so that he might leave.

'We had been appointed to Ngatangiia, and Pa and the people on the other side of the island had been informed of that by their beloved Pitimani. But since they had been informed of this it had become evident that it was not wise for us to go there. There was likely to be trouble, and one morning a great crowd came marching up to the mission house, shouting and dancing as they neared the steps, and demanding their missionary. Mr. Krause became terribly excited, and to us the state of affairs began to seem really serious. I suggested that we should accompany the natives on their return, and remain a few days with them. But we were convinced that we should have to make Avarua our headquarters, because the Institution was there, and it was the residence of the Makea, the leading chief, and the largest population was there. Poles were lashed along chairs, and we were actually run away with. Outside of Avarua I was allowed to dismount, and to walk the rest of the way. We stayed with the native teacher or pastor, Maretu, a prince of men, and one of the finest men I have ever known, white or coloured. We learned in time to love him dearly, and he to love us. We stayed a few days, and then we returned to Avarua. Six weeks after Mr. and Mrs. Krause and family left us for Germany.

'For years I had longed to get amongst real heathen and savages, and I was disappointed when we landed on Rarotonga and found them so much civilized and Christianized. I wrote to the Directors at Blomfield Street, stating my disappointment, and begged them to appoint us to Espiritu Santo in the New Hebrides. At the District Committee meeting held very shortly after we landed, the first I ever attended, I stated my feelings to the brethren, and suggested that Mr. Green, formerly of Tahiti, and at that time on Tahaa, should be appointed to Rarotonga. A minute to that effect was actually passed, but nothing came of it, and we lived on Rarotonga for ten years. Those years were full of happiness, of life, and of work.

'We got the place set in order, the houses which had been sadly injured by hurricanes repaired, and regular classes arranged with the students. I also paid constant visits to the different stations, and held frequent meetings with the native pastors. All this took some time, but we succeeded at last in getting the work well in hand.

'A few years later students were sent to the New Hebrides in the Dayspring, and five fine young men and their wives were sent out to begin work on the mainland of New Guinea. In Samoa they were joined by Piri and his wife, making up the total to six couples. Mr. Wyatt Gill was then going home on furlough, and these native missionaries were placed in his charge by the Committee. Their names were :—Ruatoka, Anederea, Adamu, Henere, Rau and Piri. Of them only the noble Ruatoka remains, and may his grand life be spared long!

'At Somerset, Gill was joined by Mr. A. W. Murray, and together they placed the above in Redscar Bay at Manumanu. Years after, when I called at Manumanu, the old chief Naime came to me, pretending to be very cold, and sitting down, I asked him if he were ill, and he answered, "Yes, very. Tamate, listen! What have I done, that I am thus left out in the cold whilst others are happy ? Why have I no teacher ? Was not I the first to receive teachers, and did I not treat them kindly ? When many wished to murder them, did I not prevent it ? And now you leave me alone. Tamate, you must give me a teacher."

'We had a grand year of refreshing before that first contingent left. Many were the meetings for prayer, and the church, I believe, had never had such a time of refreshing since Buzacott's time. Many were led to Christ and joined the church. What a day the Sunday before their leaving was! The excitement was intense, old men with tears streaming down their faces begged to be also sent, alleging that their knowledge of savage life and heathen customs well fitted them for the work. Never before or since have I experienced such emotions, and I felt that I must go too.

'Our Institution increased in numbers, and we had nearly forty students with their wives, and we had also a high school for boys, numbering fifty at one time.

Every day had its well-filled work, and I preached every Sunday. One Sunday in the month I went right round the island, and preached at three stations. My wife was also full of work, and we saw little of one another during the day. It was during these busy years that I prepared commentaries on all the Prophets, and all the Epistles, and wrote many things for the use of the students.

'In that paradise of the Pacific there was one fearful curse, strong drink, and that we tried to combat. I turned policeman, and used to find out where the meetings for drink were held. My experience is that native chiefs and policemen are not fit in themselves to carry out laws. They put on a spurt for a fortnight, and then things drift back, and are left to become worse than before. During Makea Abela's time we succeeded in putting it down to a considerable extent; but he was a great hindrance, being himself much addicted to drink, both foreign and native.

'Thinking that if they were allowed to drink their orange beer openly at their meals, a stop would be put to the large gatherings where all got drunk, and the orgies can only be described as beastly, I proposed this to Makea. But he decidedly opposed it, saying it would never do, as there would be no rejoicing then at all. He would not give his consent to the plan. Many of the *mataiapo* were on our side; but without Makea and the other chiefs they were useless.

'I remember once getting some of the inferior chiefs together and going on deputation to Makea and Mana-rangi, who was chief justice, and had lapsed from church membership, and from his social position through drink. They both received us well, and listened to all we had to say. One of the *mataiapos*

spoke very seriously to Abela, and Manarangi pulled
him up by asking, in a bit of song, "Whence is Makea?"
and the old *mataiapo* replied in song, " From heaven he
came," and then Manarangi wound up with, " Who then
can speak ? " and we returned, forced thus to remember
that Makea was beyond and above all law and all
human beings. In the light of an incident like this, one
could understand how and why in heathen times any
one who crossed even his shadow was instantly clubbed
to death. Abela died very suddenly, and was mourned
greatly; for although he was a great drinker, he was
exceedingly kind to all, and especially to his missionary.
The Earl of Pembroke and Dr. Kingsley described him
as a perfect gentleman.

' After Makea's death Takau, wife of Ngamaru Atiu,
was sent for, and they both were elected to the position
of head chief. She is an excellent woman, and has
done much good; but has not succeeded in putting
down the drink. All natives can be bought by the
white man, and so they wink at grog being landed.
A silk dress given as a present, a few bottles of grog, or
beer, or wine as medicine, given in the right quarter,
well known to all traders, and the island may be
swamped with drink. If the chiefs wished to stop the
curse, they could have done so long ago, for the law
passed in conjunction with the British Resident was that
no native could get drink unless he had a permit signed
by Makea or one of the chiefs. But this law led to the
selling of permits, and thus the drink traffic became
legalized, and the state of the island worse than ever.
Neither Makea nor the chiefs were earnest in the effort
to get rid of drink, and their frequent protestations were
made at the request of the white missionary, and only
to please him.

'We spent a very pleasant time on Mangaia in 1871 with the Wyatt Gills, and came to love them dearly. We visited many of the caves in the company of Mr. Gill, who was a thorough missionary, and an enthusiast in all things native, anthropology and ethnology included[1]. How dearly he loved the natives, and both he and Mrs. Gill gave themselves entirely to the natives for Christ's sake! For a young missionary there could have been no better friend; he was lenient to faults, and praised what was done well. His mode of dealing with the many faults into which a young missionary is certain to fall was one of kindness and love; and his suggestions were so put that no one could have any difficulty in adopting them.'

This somewhat meagre outline of the autobiography can here be supplemented from the letters and reports of the period. One of the first communications sent home by Chalmers was a brief note to Dr. Mullens, then the Foreign Secretary of the Society, giving a few of his early impressions of the island and its people.

'On our arrival we found Mr. and Mrs. Krause in a very bad state of health, and although they had been so for more than two years, I was pleased to find the stations in such good condition. The native agents seem to do their work well, and although there is much to deplore, yet there is much, very much, to rejoice in. The seed sown by the faithful servants of God in the past still bears fruit, and doubtless will continue to do so. The names of Pitman and Buzacott are dear to the natives; they are the Rarotongan standards, next to the Bible. The people attend church well, and the morning prayer meetings throughout the week are

[1] See Dr. Wyatt Gill's book, *From Darkness to Light in Polynesia.*

F

well attended. The people are kind to the missionary, and ever ready to do what they can to help him. The schools are well attended, and great pains seem to be taken to instruct the children.'

Before he left Rarotonga, the retiring missionary, Mr. Krause, came under the spell of Chalmers' personality, and on June 11, 1867, wrote to the Directors : ' And now allow me to congratulate the Board on the choice of my successor. He is all I have prayed for, and for so many years—a man without guile, a Nathanael—without fear, and filled with tender love for the people. I trust he is the right man in the right place.' This testimony was true at the time, and was amply verified in the succeeding ten years.

Chalmers soon began to take the measure of his first field of missionary enterprise—the population, their habits, attainments, difficulties, necessities. By November 16, 1867, he had written home to state that as he found the entire population of the island amounted only to 1856 souls, he should no longer ask for a European colleague, but only for all needful assistance from native helpers. He soon began to introduce reforms into the management of the Institution. He took the education of the young in hand, and began a system of competitive examination among the school children of the different villages. He proclaimed war to the knife against the drink traffic and drinking customs of every kind. He was instant in season and out of season in preaching the Gospel, and in work of every kind that tended to uplift and benefit the souls under his charge.

The position of a capable missionary on one of these remote, self-contained Pacific islands forty years ago was very peculiar. He was a kind of head chief, and although always careful not to interfere in matters merely political, in many respects the missionary wielded an influence far greater than that even of the chief himself. Only in very rare instances indeed was there ever open and aggressive opposition to his wishes. But heathen custom was often too strong for the rudimentary Christianity which the natives had accepted so far as they understood it; and both the wishes and exhortations of the missionary were evaded and neglected. So Chalmers found, and although his new broom swept vigorously, and he was most ably seconded in all his efforts by his energetic wife, yet he could not sweep away effectively many of the abuses that vexed his soul.

From one of the first long letters which he sent home after he had fairly settled down to work we take a few extracts.

' That curse of all curses has come to this island— strong drink. There is a law against its being brought ashore, but unprincipled foreigners manage to smuggle it, and sell it to the natives. The effects are fearful and heartrending. I believe were thinking men at home to see the effects of drink amongst these natives, they would never taste another drop, but would rise up to a man and cry shame upon those men who not only break the laws of a weak people, but also give them, in exchange for their labour, money, or coffee, a poison which is destroying them fast. The churches have suffered fearfully from it. Our young men have given themselves up to intoxication, and one after another falls a victim. All the people are scrofulous, so that firewater takes effect sooner upon them.

'As missionary I am consulted on every important point, and my decision generally is taken as settling any question. Take as an illustration this : Before Mr. Krause left we had been talking on the *kava* (strong drink) question, and thought that it might be best perhaps to abolish the restrictive law, and allow drink to be landed under a heavy tax, and the holding of a licence for its sale. I was not quite clear on the point. However, Mr. Krause laid it before the king and his *mataiapos*, and urged the acceptance of it. This action I thought premature, but said nothing. Two or three were anxious to have it settled at once; but I advised delay, and also suggested the calling of a meeting of all the chiefs and judges of the island before doing anything. However, it was taken as settled that the old law was abolished, and all that was required was to call a meeting of the head chiefs and get a new law passed.

'This was on a Monday. On the Friday following Mr. Krause left Rarotonga, so that I stepped into the entire charge of the Mission. The meeting of chiefs was held on the Tuesday following Mr. Krause's departure. I was in trouble—great trouble. I prayed to God, and I felt it was my duty to oppose this abolition or repeal of the old law. On the morning of the meeting a few of the old men who hold a strong position in the land, and who know what Rarotonga was in its heathen state, came to me, and asked what I meant to do. They advised me to oppose the abolition. This strengthened me. We prayed to God, and asked His direction.

'I went to the meeting. There sat all the chiefs and great men with a number of foreigners. I felt that a trial of strength was at hand. All were assembled in the full expectation of the promulgation of a new law, and the foreigners were all ready to take out licences. The parliament was opened by prayer. The chief judge of the Avarua district laid the matter before the neighbouring chiefs, and only asked them for their assent.

He sat down, and as he was addicted to drink himself he was pleased with the thought that he could now drink as much as he chose. At that time I myself did not know he was given to the evil habit. Next, one of the chiefs—a known and confirmed drunkard—was asked to speak. He declined, saying, "What does my missionary say?" I tried to avoid speaking at this stage, and wished that some other chiefs should speak first; but they all pressed me to give my views. At length I said that I had earnestly prayed to God that the law might not be changed so long as I was in Rarotonga. I added a few words to this, but my speech was short.

'It was sufficient; nothing more was said by the chiefs, but the chief judge of Avarua was enraged. The missionary holds great power in cases of this kind. May he hold it for Christ! I need not say that my countrymen love me none the more for the action I felt bound to take.

'After this decision I felt we must not stand still, but at once put the law in force. Yet I had not then a right understanding of the working of this engine of Satan— I mean the strong drink. I spoke alike to the chiefs and to the people; still drunkenness did not cease from the land, but the foreigners were becoming a little more afraid. Bit by bit I began to get information. I was told that the foreigners, assisted by natives, brought it ashore during the night, and gave it out to natives to sell for them. My native teachers and students also were all on the look-out. Something had to be done.

'But I could do little or nothing, until one Saturday I was out riding, and looking about. My horse stopped at the house of the chief judge. He had been ailing for some time, so I went to see him. It struck me as strange that the doors were all shut, and that there was a commotion within. At length I gained admittance, and found the chief judge's wife, with dishevelled hair, in the centre of the room, crying. The son of the chief judge was the worse for drink, and I charged him with it, and instantly asked for his father. But the father had fled.

'I left the house, and made for the king's; but on my arrival I found that he was not at home. I rode up to our own house, and heard loud crying, as of one in deep distress. It came from a house near by. I left my horse, and went over to the place. There I found a husband drunk, and beating his wife. After some persuasion, I got him to accompany me. Mrs. Chalmers gave him tea with a good quantity of carbonate of soda in it, and this brought him to his senses. He told me that the king, the chief judge and others could all be found drinking.

'I made for the king's house. He had come home, and was afraid of meeting the missionary. I took him with me, and he slept that night in our house. Now what could be done to put an end to this? A week before I had refused to permit two casks of wine to be landed on the island. I spoke to the deacons and others, and we decided to hold meetings in all the villages, or rather in three of the principal villages. The drunken party were all at church on the Sabbath. Although they had been drunk the night before, they did not absent themselves from the House of Prayer. This made it more difficult to find out the real doers of evil.

'On the Monday our king, the chief judge, his son, and the other man were all tried, fined, and admonished faithfully by the judges. The chief judge was disrated,

his power being taken from him. On the Wednesday
we had our first meeting, and several spoke. The king
promised to do better, and asked the people to pray for
him. The law was upheld, and prayers were presented
earnestly to God. On Thursday, at another village, we
had a meeting, and there was much shedding of tears,
and all the people said Amen when they were called
upon to uphold the laws. It was a glorious season.
On Friday we went to another village and held another
meeting, which was truly solemn. At each of these
gatherings the chiefs promised to uphold the law, and
the people pledged themselves to assist them. The
ringleaders and the men who sold the spirit have
confessed their faults, and to all human appearance feel
truly humbled before God. They have declared openly
their desire to leave off strong drink. They were
urgent in their desire to live with me, and at the people's
and their own earnest request I have received them into
the Institution. God alone knows what the future is,
but we leave them in His hands. Nor is this all; two
foreigners on the island who have been grog-sellers
have solemnly promised not to sell any more.'

Writing to his old pastor, Mr. Meikle, at this time,
Chalmers said:—

'The people are well advanced in knowledge and in
civilization after forty years of teaching. Sins such as
theft and adultery they do not consider very bad. The
former is not an evil to which they are much addicted
now; but the latter, I am sorry to say, prevails to a great
extent.

'There is work in abundance for two on this island,
but when I consider the state of other parts of the world
I dare not ask for a colleague. We have no time to
rust here. We are both in excellent health and spirits.

Christ's glory and man's eternal good are all we seek. Oh that we saw all on this island Christ's; and until we do we dare not rest, but by prayer and supplication and labours oft we must wrestle and struggle and patiently wait and look for the promised blessing. I trust that already the clouds are breaking, and there are the droppings of an abundant shower to follow. Will Inveraray give another for foreign work? Christ calls; souls are perishing; the grain is white, white unto harvest, but where are the labourers? It would cheer my heart to hear that one or more of my old companions had so given himself to Christ that he heard the call, "Come over and help us," and responded, "Here am I, send me." '

Mrs. Chalmers, writing home a few months later, gauges the situation accurately, with her clear woman's insight:—

'Lately there has been less strong drink amongst us, but it will take some time to know whether the apparent reformation is real. Many are anxious to abide by the laws, and do what is right, and of late some vigorous efforts have been made by the judges to enforce the laws. The secret is that the king sets no good example, and does not keep up his position or dignity. He is not at all respected, and if he does not take care, soon no one will give any heed to what he says.

'It will take us a long time to thoroughly understand the native character. Their standard of morality is low, and the sins of theft, lying, and adultery are very common. They know that such actions are wrong, and when any one has been proved to have been guilty of such offences they are put out of church membership, and are fined by the judges; but there it stops. After the fine is paid they are received as formerly. Real shame for such sin they do not feel, nor can it easily be impressed upon them that such deeds are truly great sins in God's sight.

'It will take a long time, probably several generations, before the natives see and feel as they ought on these points. But when we remember that fifty years ago the inhabitants of the island were wild savages, it is a marvel to see them as they now are. The change is great, and remembering what they then were, and seeing what they now are, we are constrained to cry out, " What great things hath God wrought ! " in our midst.

'The natives have to be treated and led in all things more like children at home than men. They soon get weary and discouraged in any work, but a few words of praise or encouragement put fresh spirit within them.'

Early in his life in Rarotonga Chalmers, like all men of bold, decisive action, found himself exposed to criticism. And although the chiefs and natives never offered active opposition to his wishes and doings, his efforts were constantly foiled in many quarters by passive resistance. Rumours of his views and deeds, usually through imperfectly informed channels, reached his missionary brethren in other islands, and even came to the ears of the Directors at home. In reply to a letter from them asking what changes he had been introducing into the mission, he gave, in June, 1869, an apologia for his methods of a very characteristic order. He writes :—

'I have returned to the old ways of Pitman and Buzacott in several respects, I grant, believing them to be best and right. True, I have entirely done away with the purchase of food for the students, and have every cause for thankfulness I did so at the outset. The students now have more and better food, and have more time to plant, weed, and prepare for classes than they ever had in former days. It may be well for me to explain.

'Since the establishment of the Institution in Mr. Buzacott's time the students had never more than two days in the week to themselves—Saturday and Sabbath. From Monday to Friday they were employed. At eight a.m. they came to class, and at nine retired for work, manual labour, and continued at said manual labour till three p.m. when they bathed, and prepared for the four o'clock class. If they were not employed in the workshop, or on the premises, they were in the woods searching for wood. They were fed in those days at the Society's expense. Now they plant their own food, and the following is the routine.

'On Monday at eight a.m., after dispensing medicine, I meet the students for two hours, when we go over part of one of Dr. Bogue's lectures on theology, printed by Mr. Buzacott. From nine to ten we go over a Psalm together, and at ten they are free for the day. On Tuesday we meet at the same hour and go over the Scripture lesson for the day. At present we are going through the Book of Daniel. From nine to ten geography and arithmetic. On Wednesday we have no classes, this being the day I have appointed to meet with inquirers and those seeking admission to the church. On Thursday from eight to nine Romans, and from nine to ten grammar. Friday eight to nine church history, and nine to ten sermon class. Mrs. Chalmers has also two hours on like days with the women for Bible instruction, arithmetic, and sewing. For each of the classes, Psalms, Daniel, Romans, and church history, I write out the lessons, and allow them to take copies for their own use. They keep the premises in order, and get through that part of their work in a very short time. At present they are cleaning the coffee subscribed this year to the Society. I allow them a little food every day whilst at it, seeing it is a long, heavy task.

'The students are making progress in their studies, and I believe those at present in the Institution know more than any former students, this being due to their having more time for preparation. They are required to prepare for all the classes. They are good earnest men and women, not, I hope, mere moral characters, but men and women who know what faith in Christ, the Crucified One, means. They are men and women who have tasted of the Water of Life, and who having experienced the joy of believing, and the salvation of their souls, are anxious that others, especially those shrouded in heathen darkness, should become partakers of like blessings. They are anxious to carry the Light of Truth to dark lands, and although we may tremble to think that real and new advance on the kingdom of darkness is always attended with suffering, they, knowing it also, are anxious to go. The Father will baptize them for the hour of suffering.

'Allow me here to say *we* also would willingly go, and to that holy sacred work of lifting up Christ before a heathen people consecrate ourselves and our all. Another, who has long laboured, and by experience been truly fitted for work like my present duties on Rarotonga, might do better than we can; and we who are yet young, and in good health, enjoying tropical life thoroughly, might, with a few of these students, go down to the west, and in the Northern New Hebrides establish a mission, and lift up Christ, the dispeller of all darkness. Send Brother Gill or Green here, and we two will go west to the heathen.

'Another change I have made is in the church. For many years, since the first missionaries left, as stated by the deacons—the ordinance of the Lord's Supper has been sadly abused by the church members. They literally drank of the wine or the mixture—cocoanut milk and wine. At all the stations I preached on the subject, and exhorted them to better behaviour; but still the abuse continued. So eventually I did away entirely with foreign wine, and confined ourselves entirely to the cocoanut milk. Since then the ordinance has been observed decently and in order.

'We have no great numbers coming to seek admission to the church. Still a few are attending the classes. Our greatest enemy at present is strong drink—foreign and native. Auckland traders supply us with the former, and the oranges the latter. Sometimes a church member is enticed away through drink, and falls. Occasionally one or two are led to see the evils of it. They leave it off, and seek to live better for the future. Much prayer is being presented to the throne of God's grace for the revival of religion among us. All our services are well attended, and we hope that soon we will hear the sound of rain, blessed with God's great blessing, the Holy Spirit.

'Since our arrival I have visited all the stations, alternately preaching at each once a month. During the week—on Wednesday especially—I sometimes ride out to one or other of the settlements, see the teachers and deacons, converse with them, and if there are any matters requiring attention, attend to them. Once every three months I meet my teachers, when we discuss the state of the churches, and pray together for God's blessing on the work. These meetings are fountains of blessing to the whole island. At all the stations great attention is being paid to the training of the young, and at present all are preparing for our next August competitive examination.

'I am well pleased with the teachers, more especially with two of them: Maretu, Mr. Pitman's old helper, and Teava, Mr. Buzacott's co-pastor. With pleasure I can listen to their preaching. The latter and Mr. Krause disagreed, and could not draw together; but I am happy to say I find him a good, intelligent, earnest teacher—one of the best. The sick and the dying are visited by him. He does not, as many teachers do, throw off the fallen, but he constantly visits them, and by reading, exhortation, and prayer strives to win them back again to God. He alone of all of us commands the entire and solemn attention of the people on the Sabbaths when he preaches.'

In August, 1869, Chalmers received the sad news of the very sudden death of his father, an event which had happened long months before the tidings could reach that out of the way corner of the Pacific. It was his father's business to keep some of the roads near Inveraray in repair. He had gone out one morning as usual to attend to his duties, and was found by the workmen, a little later, lying dead by the roadside. It was an additional sorrow to him that this loss came just at the time when he was hoping and planning to make the closing years of his parents' lives free from pecuniary cares. His letters at this time are full of gracious plans for lightening the sorrow and needs of the mother, towards whom he always so lovingly expressed the deep respect and tender affection he cherished.

A year or two later there came from Inveraray news of a very different kind. 'We are delighted,' he writes, 'with the prospect of Lord Lorne marrying a princess. Britain's sons will marry Britain's daughters! If Britain is ever a Republic Argyll will be President! So we think in this far away island of the sea.'

Chalmers' freedom from conventionalism, and readiness to take advantage of passing events for the furtherance of his great work, is well illustrated in his Report for 1870.

'We are near the close of a year which has brought to us many blessings as a church and people. We began the year with the week of prayer; old and young, chiefs and people, all came, and every morning for one week, one hour each morning. All engaged in asking blessings; only the sick remained at home. It is true that many attended from a superstitious feeling that if they were not present something might happen to them. Since then I believe we have been moving steadily forward. Many have come asking what they must do to be saved, and have been told of salvation by faith in Christ. They have returned, having, I trust, been led to Christ, and have sought admission to the church. A number of men and women who for years have been out of the church, being expelled because of sin, have come desiring to return, having by their profession repented of their sins and believed in Christ as their Saviour. The young people formed themselves into classes for prayer, and the reading of the Word of God, a deacon or returned teacher being placed over them. On my return to the island from visiting the out-stations I found large inquirers' classes of men and women, old and young, the majority of them old church members. The teachers and deacons at each of the settlements were teaching them of Christ.

'About two years ago there was started by the beer drinkers at this settlement a volunteer corps. They were drilled by a man who had been in Tahiti for some time. They had been practising drill some time before I knew anything of it. They were recognized by the chiefs, and the majority were men who for many years had never attended any service of any kind. I knew them only by seeing them in their sacred grove at night, around orange beer barrels and a great fire, naked and fierce. Sabbath and week-day were both alike to them. They were unknown to the missionaries. Well, these men met for drill, and I felt that here was a new thing growing up amongst us, which, if seized and guided, might be turned to good account. If it were left alone, or if any attempt were made to put an end to it, evil would result. I had no power to stop it, even had I desired to do so, which certainly I did not.

'Weeks passed, and at length I saw these men and said to them, "You meet for drill, why do you not come to church on the Sabbath instead of living even worse lives than your fathers when in heathenism? If you remain volunteers you must come to church." I told them I did not wish them to give up drilling. And I did so because I felt that I had a better chance of speaking to them when they were sober and at drill. The following Sabbath a few came to the service, but not all. I addressed them as young men belonging to a volunteer corps of their own formation, and I pressed them to make Christ their portion, their captain, and to believe on Him as their Saviour.

'The idea took; they were now volunteers, and of some account, and soon all began to attend church regularly. I then asked them to meet separately at other times for instruction and prayer, and this they did. Drinking diminished, and the drilling became very popular. I formed them into classes for reading, writing, and arithmetic. On Sabbaths they met by themselves under the superintendence of a teacher, after the conclusion of the forenoon service, and went over the sermon which had just been preached, sang a hymn, and engaged in prayer. I held a Bible class with them every Sabbath evening, and on Thursday morning taught them English. They all began planting their lands and doing everything possible to get new clothes to attend drill, meetings, and church. They became interested in the services, and I kept on encouraging volunteering, as I felt good was being done. The beer drinking diminished, and we had full instead of empty seats in the gallery.

'When it was necessary to repair the church these young men cut all the coral required for the platform and the staircase. They became thoroughly concerned about all that belonged to the church, and very many of them are now, I trust, very much interested in the Great Head of the Church. God has answered prayer, and the majority, if they have not found Christ precious, feel their need, I trust, and will be found of Him. But for the volunteering, begun, as described, by themselves, they might still be living unknown in the bush in wickedness. I could not frown upon them. I thought it a good opportunity to be of help to them.

'For some time we have felt it desirable to interest the natives in what was taking place outside of our island. There are also many things we wish to speak to them about which can hardly find a place in the pulpit, so we have begun a monthly newspaper of four pages. It contains short articles on the subjects that happen to be uppermost at the time, shipping news, news from other islands, pieces culled from newspapers and books, letters from natives, articles on history and also small pieces on Scripture. The natives are much interested in it, and look out for the first of the month when it is issued. Our printing-press is bad and our materials few. The children say they will buy a new press, but it remains to be seen if they can secure enough.

'Every Tuesday evening is set apart by the students here for prayer for those who have gone forth to link Rarotonga anew to the work of God among the heathen. We are all in good health and have plenty to do. I am engaged from four a.m. to nine p.m. I rest by going round the island occasionally. I occasionally ride out on an afternoon and meet the teachers at their homes with a few deacons or church members, or have those seeking admission to the church to come and meet me. When not very well, I set off to the mountains, getting where natives have never been, and feel all right the following day.

'Now and again I visit the evening prayer meetings, or it may be a meeting in the bush where some have met to drink beer or orange rum. I am not very welcome at the latter, yet they know me, say nothing, and when told, empty out their rum upon the grass. After they have done this I speak to them of Christ.'

These unconventional actions of Chalmers came to the ears of his nearest neighbour, the venerable Henry Royle of Aitutaki, who had spent over forty years on that island with only one brief furlough, and who was a splendid missionary of the early type. In a long letter, Mr. Royle expostulated with his 'young friend' for hankering after work among the heathen, and

G

quoted the following passage from a letter which Chalmers had written to him.

'We left our home for the heathen—to teach unenlightened people the way of salvation through Christ—and there still are our hearts. The few years spent here will be useful in the future. My dear brother, keep us not—urge us on. We desire—desire earnestly, to spend and be spent among the heathen. Christ urges us on.'

Royle stated that this expression of earnest desire produced in him 'a gush of pity,' and he tries to convince Chalmers that his restlessness was dishonourable to the Board of Directors, and otherwise to be deprecated. At the 'novel method of administering religious ordinances through the medium of military evolutions,' he is almost aghast. He thinks that those who neglect 'the cultivation of home virtues, and the peaceful pursuits of industry to learn the barbarous art of carnage and slaughter ought not to be admitted into instruction classes.'

Chalmers returned the letter to Royle endorsed with the assertion that it was unlike his old friend, that it was 'full of misstatement,' and added, 'We are both very well, very happy, and very busy.'

Royle dispatched another letter to Chalmers, and finally sent the whole correspondence home to Dr. Mullens, who seems to have approved of some of the actions which Royle condemned. Both were Christian men, both were noble missionary workers, both had the welfare of the nations and the extension of Christ's kingdom at heart. The cloud soon passed and the old friendly relations re-established themselves. In the heart of the younger man the desire to be off to the tribes still in the darkness of the shadow of death grew ever stronger. With the retirement of Henry Royle in 1876 there passed from the Polynesian Mission the last of the old type of missionary, the men who laid so broadly and so well the foundations of the Christian Church in Polynesia.

From the early days of his settlement on Rarotonga Chalmers made no secret of his desire to be chosen as a missionary to the fierce and barbarous heathen, of whom there were still so many who had never yet had an opportunity of hearing the Gospel, and to whom not even a native evangelist or teacher had been sent. Like Livingstone he felt that the islands and tribes which had been long evangelized might now safely be left to native pastors and teachers, with only slight European supervision. For this work, and for the duty of training native teachers, he felt that there were many better qualified than himself, who would feel these quieter and safer duties less irksome than he did. He had the instinct of the pioneer; he was dominated by that energy of a noble restlessness which was ever urging him onwards towards 'the regions beyond.' John Williams, in an earlier generation, had had to overcome the opposition of colleagues and the objections of home authorities; and Chalmers now had to convince similar gainsayers, although he was not without encouragement both at home and in the field. But God had a noble work in store for His whole-hearted and devoted servant, and step by step the way was made plain for the young missionary that led from the quiet round of daily tasks in Rarotonga to those thrilling years in New Guinea, so full of adventure, of peril, of hairbreadth escapes, of successful presentation of the glad tidings to multitudes who had never before heard the name of Jesus, or realized the meaning of such graces as love and peace and pardon and light.

As early as January, 1872, Wyatt Gill of Mangaia wrote home to Dr. Mullens :—

'I would again earnestly beg of you on no account to remove the Rev. J. Chalmers from Rarotonga. He has acquired the language and wields great influence over the natives. He occupies a most important position as head of the Institution for training the native ministry, besides superintending the printing-press. To insist upon his removal at the present juncture involves the destruction of the Hervey Group Mission.'

The occasion of this letter was the determination of the Directors of the London Missionary Society to begin a mission in the then almost absolutely unknown island-continent of New Guinea. This was an undertaking entirely after Chalmers' own heart. He earnestly besought the home authorities to allow him to go, and already the keen insight of Dr. Mullens had enabled him to mark the young Rarotongan missionary as a man likely to render effective service. In the decrees of Divine Providence it was already settled that he was to go in due time to what was then considered the darkest, most degraded, and most savage tribes and land in unevangelized Polynesia ; but five long years of missionary toil yet lay between his heart's desire and its gratification. These years he filled with honest work, not with idle or fruitless complainings. Not allowed to go himself, he did all in his power to select and equip, from the men under his care in the Institution, capable native teachers for this dangerous service.

On January 24, 1872, he wrote to Dr. Mullens :—

'The students are all looking forward with great earnestness to their being required for New Guinea. I do hope the Directors see their way clear to begin the mission, and so allow us to go forth. If you cannot begin it in force, let us try it by skirmishing. We will go with two or three students and take possession. The churches on Rarotonga have had special meetings for prayer, that God might open the door, so that His Word should be known on New Guinea. At every Sabbath service and at every meeting during the week Papua is mentioned in prayer. We cannot rest until it is thoroughly commenced. Let nothing hinder us to take possession in the name of Christ. . . . Funds will be forthcoming at once if the work is begun.'

That year the great work was begun, and from Rarotonga six teachers and their wives were carried by the John Williams, under the care of the Rev. A. W. Murray and Wyatt Gill, to New Guinea, and landed there on the mainland in the Red Scar Bay district at Manumanu. The dedication and the sending away of these pioneer evangelists, as Chalmers notes in his autobiography, stirred the whole Christian population of Rarotonga to the depths.

But Chalmers could not yet be spared, and work went on as usual under his care. His popularity with the natives increased daily, and his power over them deepened week by week. 'Even the drunkards on Rarotonga,' he wrote at this time, ' rather like the missionary, and are ever ready to help him in work. I have frequently been in the midst of the large drinking meetings, when they existed, and found the natives in all stages of drunkenness, and fighting, yet I always felt quite safe, and never met with the least insult or abuse from any Rarotongan. I made it a rule that, as I am neither policeman nor judge, those I find drinking are not to be fined ; the chiefs agree with me in this.'

This action and statement were alike characteristic ; and so is another from his correspondence at this date.

He had for years been anxious to visit Mr. and Mrs. Gill on the island of Mangaia, and towards the close of 1871 he and Mrs. Chalmers were able to spend several happy weeks with these lifelong friends. In the account which he sent home of this visit he sketches the following picture, the accuracy of which all who knew him will at once recognize:—

'All work and no play is just as irksome for missionaries—I mean those of the Rarotongan stamp—as for boys. I have been on every mountain-top in Rarotonga, and there are few valleys I have not explored. I find a mountain trip excellent medicine, and so, when out of sorts, and not quite up to the mark for Jeremiah or Ezekiel, the Acts of the Apostles or Ephesians, the history of the Jews from Malachi to Christ, or my condensed History, ancient and modern, I throw down the pen and away I go. And it is the same here in Mangaia. It is impossible to be with Mr. Gill and not have plenty of work, and it is just as impossible to be with him and not have some play.'

The traders and others who visited Rarotonga at this time frequently denounced the mission and all its works. Statements and descriptions already quoted give the true inwardness of such criticism. And often they were in no sense criticisms of men or of methods, but false statements deliberately made and with very evil intent. But occasionally men of another stamp gave their views of the work done in these islands. In 1872 a Christian merchant touched at Rarotonga, and was so pleased with much that he saw there that he wrote an account home to the Directors. This is what he found:—

'On Sunday I attended Divine service, morning and

afternoon, in the large stone church at Avarua; also two
class-meetings held in two of the deacons' houses after
the morning service, for the purpose of discussing the
sermon. In the afternoon I addressed a large and
excellently-conducted Sunday-school—Mr. Chalmers
interpreting; and in the evening I attended two of
the prayer-meetings, similar to those held on the week-
nights. I had also the privilege of addressing them,
and was afterwards loaded with presents of mats, bags,
coffee, fruit, &c. At the morning service in the church
Mr. Chalmers, in his exposition of 1 Chronicles xvii,
urged the people to repair the walls of the church
and churchyard, which considerably needed it. When
I called at the island the next time, about two months
later, I found that the call had been promptly responded
to, and all the work done. The text was from John
xii. 32, and the sermon was a powerful appeal to young
men to recruit the ranks of the native teachers, several
of whom had left the previous week, in the Presbyterian
mission schooner Dayspring, for Western Polynesia.'

This merchant engaged at Rarotonga a crew of
natives for a voyage that extended over some months.
'We sailed from Rarotonga,' he wrote, 'on the Tuesday
evening following the service described above, and
during the whole voyage of twenty-two days, services
were held uninterruptedly at six o'clock in the morning
and evening, and in addition to these, two full services
every Sunday. A native teacher, Meariki, accompanied
the party, and, as customary, was chosen by the men
themselves, his election being confirmed by Mr.
Chalmers. He usually officiated, but six or seven of
the men were able to lead in prayer, and three or
four to preach also. I question if I should have found
this state of things among a party of young English

labourers, selected without any inquiry on this subject. I never shall forget the quiet enjoyment of those evening services on the beautiful South Pacific—all my men gathered around me on the vessel's poop, singing hymns, which, although I could not understand, were yet set to old tunes, which I had known from my childhood, and sung apparently with the heart and understanding also: and the prayer, although in another language to my own, was yet, I knew, ascending with mine into the ear of Him in whose sight we were all equally His children. The first Sunday at sea a young Rarotongan sailor, named Lameke, who had been engaged by the captain, stood up, at Meariki's request, to give out the hymns and engage in prayer, and I could not but think that there were not so many English sailors who would have had the moral courage to do this in the presence of " all hands." The conclusion to which I came was, that the men would have as soon thought of going without their food as without their services.'

In this connexion also we may quote Charles Darwin's striking testimony, in his *Voyage of the Beagle*, to the reality of the religious life of these Polynesian natives:—

'Before we laid ourselves down to sleep, the elder Tahitian fell on his knees, and with closed eyes repeated a long prayer in his native tongue. He prayed as a Christian should do, with fitting reverence and without the fear of ridicule or any ostentation of piety. At our meals, neither of the men would taste food without saying beforehand a short grace. Those travellers who think that a Tahitian prays only when the eyes of the missionary are fixed on him, should have slept with us that night on the mountain side.'

At the close of the year 1872 Chalmers drew up, in

his own peculiar style and manner, a report of the state of the mission at that time :—

'The Sabbath services are well attended by all. The Rarotongans are truly a church-going people. Our services are short, not exceeding an hour and ten minutes. I dislike long services anywhere, and in this climate I find, should they exceed the time above stated, the interest flags, and we all get drowsy.

'The mission here is quite changed from what it was formerly. In many respects I think the change is for the better. There is less of the menial crouching and more independence of spirit and action. There is a something which makes the natives more manly, and leads them to think for themselves, and to act according to their own judgement. They now wear plenty of clothing, and foreign habits are taking the place of the native customs. A man must now work or go unclothed, or nearly so, and this is considered altogether shameful in the present state of things.

'Strong drink still does much harm, yet it is not nearly so much used as formerly. The traders do not sell it in such large quantities, and some of the chiefs seem anxious to put down the use of it altogether. The large meetings for drinking are now unknown. Two or three drinkers now meet at a time, but generally in hidden places. Women do not now join such assemblies. Formerly a large number of women met with the men in places cleared in the bush for these meetings, and the scene then enacted had better be left in the dark. In former days a drinking meeting on the Sabbath would frequently number as many as four hundred. These large meetings are now entirely a thing of the past. All the young men, those who drink as well as others, are now regular in their attendance at church, and the Bible classes. In the days of the large drinking meetings the young men were seldom or never seen in the settlements, and never at church.

'Three years ago we adopted a plan of visitation, by which Mrs. Chalmers and I visited every house in each of the settlements. The native pastor of the settlement with his wife accompanied us. We have a double object in these visits. 1. To encourage the natives to keep their houses clean and in good order. 2. To meet the people in their homes, and so have an opportunity of speaking personally to all. We read the Word of Life, and engage in prayer in each house before leaving. We take the people's own Bibles, and thus we see if all are supplied with the Word of God. We were in only one house on the island which had no Bible to offer us, while several had one for each member of the family. We have reason to believe these annual visits have been blessed. The stone and lime houses look cleaner and better, and the reed houses are renewed. The traders tell us they have had large orders for timber, doors and windows, nails and paint from the natives ever since these visits began. If they spend their money on their homes and dress they will have less to spend on strong drink. The various members of the households, and even the wildest young men, assemble in their houses, and there wait patiently until we come. We are cordially received by all. To us it is a great pleasure to feel that there is no home on the island where we have not preached Christ, and that there is no one who has not heard of salvation through Him, that prayer has been offered to the Hearer and Answerer thereof in every inhabited house.'

Two years later Chalmers carries war into the

country of those who criticized adversely the methods of the mission while their own conduct was open to very serious reproach.

'Many people seem to think there can be no harm in orange beer, and that the natives might be allowed to drink it. I read lately in a newspaper that the attempt to put it down was only a puritanical whim of the missionary's. If these flying visitors had seen one half of what I have seen of the evils arising from so-called harmless orange beer, they would soon bless the missionary and sober chiefs for trying to stop its use, unless they be visitors who delight in hellish scenes and think wife-beating a pleasant pastime. I have seen the natives in the bush in large and small companies in all stages of intoxication. I have seen them in the thirsty stage, the talkative stage, the singing stage, the loud talking, quarrelling stage, the native fighting stage, and the dead drunk stage. I have seen them fighting among themselves, I have seen them after returning to their homes beating, kicking, and cutting their wives, and pitching their children out of doors. I have known them to set their houses on fire, or to tear up every stitch of clothing belonging to their wives and children. I have heard cursing and swearing in English (a native when drunk talks and swears in English more than in native) in a manner that would make the hardened English swearer blush. God forbid that such days should ever again be known on Rarotonga! I have attended many young men whose strength had gone from the free use of "harmless orange beer," and have buried not a few whose death was caused by this drink. Visitors who stay only a few days ashore should be careful about reporting intelligence received from beach-combers. These men are the lowest of the low, loving evil and hating the missionary because he tries to teach the natives truth, sobriety, and righteousness.

'We have foreign drink here too; gin and rum of the worst possible quality are brought here by men who would sell their own souls to make a few dollars, and who from early morning until late at night are more or less under the influence of these drinks. The British Government has put down kidnapping in the South Pacific, but this was harmless as compared with this traffic in spirits. However, we have much less of this evil than formerly. These miserable traders are from Tahiti. Of late years traders of a very different stamp from Auckland have taken up the trade of the island. These bring Manchester and Sheffield goods, excellent in quality and abundant in quantity, as well as provisions and whatever other things may be desired by the natives. These find it to be to their interest to oppose the liquor traffic. As these new traders succeed, the Tahitian traders are retiring from the field, and we hope soon to be entirely rid of them. We thank God for the success of the past, and work on hopefully, expecting yet greater success for the future. As men we missionaries must stand up for the good of the native race, and laugh at the attacks of the so-called friends.

'Somehow or other there are very few young Englishmen whose moral character is strong enough in this sunny clime to withstand the immoral influences of these so-called weak natives. The immoralities of weakness seem stronger than the morality of strength. Is it that the morality of England is merely superficial, so that when away from all restraint, and the glass house has been left behind, the repressed inclinations spring forth?

Such men lack the higher Gospel morality springing from within out to the life, and so are soon caught by this poor weak race. These are the men who are ever talking, and some even daring, to write of the immoralities of the native race, and that the missionaries do not know the character of the natives as they do, and so forth. I sometimes think they talk and write of the degraded immoral race as a salve to their own consciences, to show that others are as bad as they are themselves. I dare to say that I know of Englishmen far more degraded than the most degraded of natives. There are Englishmen, Europeans and Americans, on these islands who make the most degraded natives blush for very shame.

'Well, we blush for our countrymen, and try to do what we can to make them different. We know the Gospel of Christ, when applied by the Spirit of God to the heart, can change the most depraved; so we wait anxiously for the Almighty Power. A change for the better has come over our foreign population here, and I am safe in saying that we now have a more respectable class of foreigners than any other island in the South Pacific where foreigners reside ashore can show.'

Chalmers by this time (1874) had formed the opinion, from which he never afterwards swerved, that in the older Polynesian mission fields the natives should be encouraged to rely more upon their own efforts, and to take a more active part in the conduct of church life and affairs.

'I think it is time these churches were left to their own resources, under the superintendence of one foreign missionary, who could take charge of the Institution. So long as the native churches have foreign pastors so long will they remain weak and dependent. Why

should not one white missionary do in the Hervey
group ? [1]  By living at Rarotonga he could always hear
of what is passing at the other islands, and in a case
of urgency could soon get a chance in one of the trading
vessels to visit any one of the islands.  We have been
nearly eight years on Rarotonga.  During that time
I have visited all the islands of this mission at various
times, and am compelled to admit that the out-stations
under the charge of the native pastors contrast very
favourably with the stations under the care of European
missionaries.  Surely the Society should stretch forth
into new and larger fields, not with one or two new
missionaries, but with larger numbers.  The age of
rush and advance requires advance in missionary effort.
The many islands yet in heathen darkness which have
not heard of our glorious Redeemer should soon hear
of Him.  Why not try to reduce the staff of missionaries
on old fields, leave the churches there to bud forth, and
to think and act for themselves, and the Society take
up new fields of labour ?  I fail to see why some new
field should not be taken up every year, neither can
I see why these churches in the Hervey group require
foreign pastors.  Well-trained native pastors under the
supervision of one foreign missionary ought to do the
work.  Such men will keep the natives together better
than any foreigner can.  Again I assert that there is
no mission in the South Pacific under the control of
a white missionary which surpasses the stations that
are under native pastors superintended by a European
missionary.'

In confirmation of these somewhat strong general
statements we may adduce some examples of these

[1] At this time the Society was maintaining three European
missionaries in the group.

native pastors and teachers, and some illustrations of the work which they accomplished. Chalmers delighted to number among his dearest friends many of these humble fellow workers. They were generally of limited intellectual capacity, although some of them displayed considerable mental power. They were necessarily men and women of small experience and contracted horizon. They were only one or at the most but two generations removed from cannibalism, many loathsome heathen customs, and from the wildest licentiousness. But the Gospel had enlightened them; the love of God made known to them in Jesus Christ had sanctified and purified their hearts. They were in the main men and women of only one book, but that book was the Word of God whose entrance giveth light to the simple. And they not only themselves rejoiced in this new life and light, made known to them in and through Jesus Christ, but they also gladly met exile, sickness, privation, even death itself in their determination to carry the glad tidings which had so richly blessed their own hearts to those dark places of Polynesia which were still the habitations of cruelty. There is no nobler chapter in the church history of the nineteenth century than that which depicts the devotion and self-sacrifice of the Christian natives of Polynesia. Here is one of many testimonies afforded by the correspondence of Chalmers to the type of Christian life, exhibited in the lives or developed by the labours of the Rarotongan native teachers and pastors:—

'We have had a good deal of sickness during the last few months, and a number of deaths. One young girl about fourteen was very ill when the epidemic came to the island. She was soon seized with it, and became very ill indeed. She lingered on for some time, and it was hoped would have got over it, but this was not to be. She was a quiet girl, very obedient to her parents, and never absent from school or church. When she knew she was dying she told her friends that they were not to be sorry for her, or anxious about her, as she knew Jesus was with her, and she was only going to be with Him. I believe during all her sickness she was never heard to complain. She looked happy. I saw her the day before her death, just two or three days after my return from the Northern Islands. She was then very weak, and not able to speak much. I read to her a few verses from the Bible, and when speaking to her of the love of Jesus she smiled and looked as if entirely happy in that love. She seemed much pleased with the few verses read from the Second Corinthians, the fifth chapter. We engaged in prayer with her, and then bade her good-bye.

'The following day at sunset her soul bade farewell to its earthly tabernacle, and entered into the presence of her Lord and Master. I met one of the deacons two days after her death, who told me that he had frequently visited her, and the last time he was there he asked her, "My child, do you hold firmly on to Christ?" She answered, "He holds me, I cling to Him." "Are you afraid?" "No; the rope is strong, I shall see Him, I love Him." The old deacon wept while he told me of that visit. So Vainemuri is now with Jesus.

'Titi is an old man in the village, very ill. He says he is going home, and will soon be there. Mrs. Chalmers and I called on him lately. He said, "I am glad to see you, as I wanted you to know that it is all right with me. Jesus has a good hold of me, and I have a good hold of Jesus. My missionary, I am going soon, but do not feel troubled because of me. The ship is anchored on Christ, and it cannot be broken on the reef. You know Christ is everything to me." To us it is cheering to meet these who were born in heathenism, who have received the truth of Christ, and are now, when nearing the grave, joyful in the anticipation of meeting Christ. Glorious love thus to bless man!

'Our old pastor, Maretu, has lost his wife, after a union of at least fifty-two years. For fifty years she was connected with the mission, and for forty years was a church member. For thirty-nine years she was a good earnest worker for Christ on Mangaia, Manihiki, and Rarotonga. No one could ever accuse her of wrong. All loved her and spoke of her as an example to be followed in things good and holy. During her illness she remained happy in Christ, and her last words were, "I should like to have seen my friends at Aro-rangi; but it doesn't matter, I am now going home." She lived for Christ, and she died victorious through Him.

'Maretu would not allow any of the native wailing over her body. He made the friends, who according to custom sat round the body from the afternoon of her death till the time for burial the next day, pray and sing hymns. He spent the greater part of the night in a room alone in prayer. He would not allow black to be worn as mourning for her, remarking, "My one half has gone to heaven to be with Jesus, where I will soon follow her. Dress in white." We sent a present of dark cloth to him on Thursday (the day of the funeral), but as he appeared at the Friday morning prayer-meeting dressed in white we sent him another of white. On Sabbath we, in company with all on the island, men, women, and children, dressed in white, as a mark of respect for and sympathy with the good old man.

H

'I question if there be another couple in the South Pacific to approach in holy living what Maretu and his wife were. Maretu is now old, but his heart is ever fresh. Now that his wife has gone on he looks more wistfully beyond, and hopes soon to meet Jesus, his wife, Barakoti (Buzacott), and the many Rarotongans who have gone on beyond the river; and he adds, with a smile, "My beloved Pitimani (Pitman) will soon join us all there."'

In the spring of 1876 a native pastor named Teava died. In his work among the heathen Teava had proved himself apt to teach, and as the result of his labours whole tribes abandoned idolatry and expressed their readiness to place themselves under Christian instruction. He was the first Christian evangelist sent to Samoa, and on Manono and in the Samoan Islands he spent more than twenty years. 'With his life in his hand,' writes Mr. Buzacott, 'he travelled in an open canoe from island to island striving to remove the prejudices of the people, and to prepare the natives to receive European missionaries.' He subsequently returned to his native island of Rarotonga, where he spent the evening of his days.

Of this man Chalmers bears this testimony:—

'During the last nine years I have seen much of Teava, and learned to admire the man. He lived much in prayer, and in the study of God's Word. At prayer-meetings he was always first there, coming at least half an hour before any one else, so that he might have time to pray and receive a blessing for himself and others before the service began. He was never absent from the deacons' Saturday afternoon prayer-meeting. He was always ready to speak to the church, ever pointing the members to Christ, and warning them against the many evils to which they are exposed. From his long, true, and earnest life he was able to speak to them as only very few could. He spoke very plainly, not at all mincing matters when occasion required. He had great regard for the *Pilgrim's Progress*, and his delight was to have me sit with him and go over a part of Christian's journey to Mount Zion, the heavenly Jerusalem.

'From his position in the island he was able to speak faithfully to the chiefs. He rejoiced greatly in the good the present Makea has been the means of doing. For five weeks before his death he was unable to attend the services in church, but he welcomed any who could spend a short time with him in prayer in his own house. He told me some days before he died that he was just waiting on; he knew the Master had sent for him. He said he was done with all below, and looked only for Christ's presence. Not in what he had done did he trust, but in the Cross of Christ alone. On March 16 he asked for a little food. It was given him, but he could not eat it; he got up and walked a very short distance in the house, when he said, "I think the messenger has come to fetch me; I shall die." His wife and another woman laid him down on his mat, when he quietly passed away.

'What a change! In his youth he was a heathen, had fought with, and had captured men and cooked and helped to eat them. In his manhood he was converted to Christ, became a true soldier of the Cross, and led many to the Saviour. In his death he trusted alone to Christ, conquered death in Christ, and went up to hear Him say, "Well done, good and faithful servant, enter thou into the joy of thy Lord."'

We take up once again the autobiography for the closing years of Chalmers' life on Rarotonga:—

'Before 1877 three bands of teachers were sent to New

Guinea, who were cared for by our old friend W. G. Lawes of Niue. All suffered terribly from fever, many died, a few returned home, and only a very few were left at work in the great island. Dr. Mullens was then Foreign Secretary in London, and I had several notes from him, saying that we were to hold ourselves in readiness to go to New Guinea.

'At length it was arranged that Wyatt Gill should take charge of Rarotonga, and so relieve us to visit New Guinea on our way home to Britain. The Directors had expressed a wish to see us before settling down to our new work. The Rarotongans did not appreciate our leaving Avarua, and hoping to detain us they repaired the church, expending in money between £600 and £700, besides labour and food. At the end of 1876 the church was finished, and ready to be opened on January 1, 1877. I called a special meeting of deacons to make the needful arrangements. There was still a sum of £25 owing, for wood which had been obtained from one of the merchants. But I felt sure the collections on the opening day would cover that debt, and that there would be a good balance in hand. The deacons met, and I told them what I thought should be done. They listened without remark until I had finished, when the good old deacon doorkeeper asked, "How are you going to get in?" "Why, by the door, of course." "No, you will not. I have the keys, and will not open a door until every cent is paid. Of course you may try the windows." I was somewhat taken aback, but replied, "It is very little, and the early morning collection on the opening day will clear it off." "No, no door will be opened unless the debt is paid." Feeling that the deacon's view was sound, I acquiesced, and we closed our meeting with prayer. About an hour after there was a great commotion in the village, drums beating and people shouting, and on inquiry I found they had already begun to collect the money to pay off the debt. That afternoon all was paid, and in addition there was a good substantial balance in hand. The opening day was a great success, and there were good collections, sufficient to pay their pastor's salary, and to leave a balance with which to carry on the work.

'It was a long pull to get the natives to become willing to pay their own pastors. The native pastors themselves opposed the plan most, since they did not like becoming dependent upon the church. Some of our missionary brethren also thought that by this action we should lose our hold upon the churches and the people. But the churches on this point agreed with me, and a few years before I left the island this reform was carried out and has since worked well. Of course subscriptions to the London Missionary Society declined, but that was to be expected, and had been used as an argument against the change. The native pastors henceforward did all a pastor's work; they married, baptized, received candidates, and excommunicated lapsed members, subject to the vote of the church; and at our quarterly meeting a full report of the actions of the pastors was made to me. I visited each station once a month, and preached, and frequently rode round the island, visiting each pastor, and learning what was going on.

'When we left home in 1866, I fully intended never to return, but when in 1876 the Directors invited me to come home, calling at New Guinea on my way, I decided to go, and so see my dear old mother, who was hoping also to see me once again. But it was otherwise ordered by Divine Providence. In December, 1876, we received news of her death, and our going home in consequence became very uncertain.

'In 1876 Mr. Royle retired to Sydney. For nearly forty years he and his good wife had laboured on Aitutaki, and only once during all that time had he been away from the island. I fancy the missionaries of the past thought more of their work than the missionaries of the present day. The latter seem to come out for ten years, even if they can stand the work so long, and the years and the months are counted, and often the furlough time is longed for. In 1863, Mr. Royle was induced to leave Aitutaki and pay Sydney a visit. On the way the John Williams was wrecked on Danger Island (Pukapuka), and Mr. Royle always afterwards spoke of this as a punishment that befell him for daring to leave his work! When the vessel was nearly on the reef, and all had taken to the boats, Mr. Royle was seen seated calmly on a chair on the poop. The mate, Mr. Turpie, who was just getting over the side of the vessel, being the last to leave, noticing him, said, " Mr. Royle, why are not you in one of the boats ? " " I must wait orders." " Well, be quick and get out of her." I know of only one other missionary who stayed so long at work without change, and he laboured for forty years without a break. That was the late Rabbi Pratt of Samoa. He knew the native language much better than any native, and was more conversant with the past of the Samoans than any single Samoan.

'In April, 1877, Mr. and Mrs. Wyatt Gill arrived to take charge of Rarotonga, and on May 21 we left it. The parting with our beloved Rarotongans was a very great trial, but we were nerved with the thought that we were going to work side by side with their children, the teachers sent out by us in past years. The people too felt that though far apart we should still be one in spirit and in heart.'

Here, as throughout the autobiography, we wish the writer had gone more into detail. As he has not done so, we must have recourse to other sources of information. Very soon after the Directors had definitely decided to take up the New Guinea Mission, Chalmers began to hope that his future field of labour would be that island, and no enterprise could have been more after his own heart than to go thither as a messenger of the Gospel. Everything that rendered New Guinea repulsive to an ordinary mortal heightened its attractive power over him. On November 22, 1875, he wrote :—

'In each of the settlements there is visibly a greater interest in things belonging to the eternal good of man. We have just appointed six men with their wives to be ready for Papua by next visit of ship. They go willingly, yea more, they greatly desire it. Quite a number of those who have gone are dead, yet the desire decreases not in these who are now with us. How I should rejoice to accompany them, and stand in the centre of Papua, and tell of infinite love! The nearer I get to Christ and His cross, the more do I long for direct contact with the heathen. The one wish is to be entirely spent for Christ, working, consumed in His love.'

In May, 1876, he continues :—

'We shall be ready to move on to Papua next year. I feel happy in the prospect of being engaged in teaching the heathen of Christ, and I believe Mrs. Chalmers will be so also. We have sent eight students

and their wives to Papua this year. God grant that
their lives may be spared to do good in Christ's name!
We are both happy in the prospect of being engaged
in the work of Christ among the heathen.'

At the same time Chalmers wrote to the Directors,
in reply to their request that he should visit England,
expressing his reluctance to return home 'so soon.'
He had been in the mission field nearly ten years, but
to his zeal and enthusiasm, while he continued well and
strong, there seemed no reason why a long furlough
home should be taken. And as events turned out he did
not see the shores of England for another eleven years.
His remarks with regard to Mr. Royle and Mr. Pratt
are not without point, in reference to the missionary life
and practice of to-day. The conditions of travelling
and of life generally now are widely different from those
which obtained in the earlier half of the nineteenth
century. In those days the bulk of missionaries iden-
tified themselves much more closely with the place and
people of their work than many of them do to-day.
A man like Benjamin Rice could spend over fifty years
of service in India, and yet revisit England only once.
And while there are splendid exceptions, like Dr. Griffith
John, of Hankow, whose last visit home was in 1881, the
custom now is shorter spells of service, and much more
frequent visits home. This is recognized and allowed
for in the regulations of the different societies. It is,
perhaps, inevitable; but there is room for grave doubt
whether it does not too often affect the work adversely.
No one can have much experience of committee work in
connexion with our great societies without feeling that
the furlough system tends at times to develop human
weaknesses. The facilities for return home are so
great that the temptations to leave work on account

of ill-health and other causes are greatly increased; and there is far more ground in some quarters than is desirable for the fear which Chalmers expresses—that the missionaries of the past gave themselves more wholly to their work than some missionaries of to-day.

Towards the close of 1876 it was decided by the Directors that Chalmers should remove to New Guinea. On May 10, 1877, a committee meeting of the European missionaries of the Hervey Islands was held at Avarua. There were present W. Wyatt Gill, G. A. Harris, and James Chalmers. At this meeting the following minute was passed, which closed Chalmers' official connexion with the mission :—

'We most deeply regret the departure of our dear friends and fellow labourers the Rev. J. and Mrs. Chalmers from this mission, in which they have laboured with such remarkable diligence and success for a period of ten years. We take this comfort, that in New Guinea they will doubtless be able to succour the Rarotongan teachers in their sorrow and suffering, and will, we trust, be enabled to open up a successful mission in the neighbourhood of China Straits. We shall follow them with our prayers and sympathies, and hope that their lives may long be preserved.'

Mr. and Mrs. Chalmers sailed from Rarotonga to New Zealand on May 21, 1877. The parting was keenly felt by both missionaries and natives. During the ten years many abiding ties of friendship and affection had been formed. But these years of vigorous and faithful service had been a fitting apprenticeship for the harder tasks now to be taken in hand.

# CHAPTER V

## AMONG THE CANNIBALS AT SUAU

NEW GUINEA, at the time when Mr. and Mrs. Chalmers took up mission work there, was an unknown land, full of terrors, savagery, and human degradation. The Rev. W. G. Lawes, who had passed between three and four years of hard and discouraging labour in the district of Port Moresby, gave in 1878 the following description of the land which Chalmers was to know and to love so well :—

'New Guinea is the largest island in the world. It has been known by name for about three centuries, but so little has really been known about it, except the extreme north-west end, that it has been practically an unknown country, and writers have found in it a field for the exercise of a most exuberant tropical imagination. A sort of glamour has rested over this island with the golden name. It was supposed to be a country flowing with milk and honey. Spice groves were said to lade the air with their sweet perfume; gold and precious stones abundant, while valuable woods were so plentiful that although it was extremely probable any visitor to its shores might be clubbed, his friends would have the satisfaction of knowing that the deed was done with the best ebony.

'Notwithstanding this character for commercial wealth, although separated from Australia only by Torres Straits—and our friends in Australia are by no means wanting in the spirit of adventure—yet the uncertain navigation and the ferocious character of its inhabitants were such that, until it was opened up by our mission only five years ago, the south-east part of New Guinea was almost an unknown and unexplored country. In an island 1,400 miles long, with an area about three times that of Great Britain, there is great diversity of climate, of product, and of race, and it is always important when a statement in reference to New Guinea is made, to know to which part of this great island the statement refers.

'Every village lives in suspicion of its neighbours, and at enmity with them, so that they are practically as isolated and separated as if they were living on some lone island in mid-ocean. The natives of the south-eastern coast are a light-coloured race, belonging to the Malayo-Polynesian family, of which the Maories of New Zealand, the Tahitians, and Samoans are the best-known representatives. Physically they are a fine race; but, whatever good looks they possess, they certainly owe neither to the tailor nor the dressmaker. There is the usual profusion of barbaric ornaments in the shape of nose-sticks, earrings, necklaces, feathers, tattooing, and paint. Whether they are more successful than others in their attempt to improve on Nature is, after all, a matter of opinion and a question of taste.

'They live in lake dwellings, such as those of which relics are to be found in different parts of Europe. Some of the villages are always surrounded by water, so that the mission steamer can anchor in the main street with safety at any time. The stone age still prevails. No implement, utensil, or weapon is to be found made of iron or any metal; but after visiting the canoe-making yards at Hood Bay, and seeing the carving from Orangerie Bay, the observer will have a much greater respect for the stone age than ever before. The fine houses testify to the excellence of their tools, as well as to the industry, perseverance, and skill of their builders. Their houses, however, are utterly devoid of furniture. They can dispense easily with chairs, and every man sleeps on a plank bed without a pillow.

' So primitive are they in their habits that neither the use of money is known, nor its want felt. They are supremely indifferent to the state of the money market. There is a wonderful absence of that abject squalor and wretchedness only too familiar to dwellers in the large towns and cities of civilized life. A man without a penny to his name, a coat to his back, or a bed to lie on enjoys life fairly well in New Guinea. He has no morning newspaper to disturb his peace of mind. He has no pile of letters to answer, no telegraph boy to alarm him. But there are some dark features which detract from the inviting character of this picture. There are some uncomfortable habits and vices. Cannibalism in all its hideousness flourishes on many parts of the coast. At Port Moresby cannibalism is not practised, but the sanctity of human life is unknown, and every man is a thief and a liar. The thing of which the men are the most proud is the tattooing marks, which mean that the man who is tattooed has shed human blood. He has no right to this distinction until he has murdered some one. They "glory in their shame."

' Woman is not so degraded and down-trodden as in many parts of the heathen world. They are certainly the burden-carriers of the community; but that does not imply the degradation which it would do with us, and they resent any interference on the part of the men with the fetching of water and the carrying of wood, as an infringement of their women's rights. Domestic affection exists to a degree which surprised us. Parents caring for the children, long after they have grown up to maturity, with great affection and tenderness, and, what was more remarkable, the children caring for the parents and watching over them when they had become infirm or sick. We were glad to miss the vice of drunkenness, for no man, as far as we know the country, drinks anything stronger than water. There is a wonderful absence, too, of open immorality. The natives are industrious. They culti-vate the soil with great care, and I have seen there what I have never seen before out of civilized life, flowers cultivated in their gardens, and this alone speaks hopefully for their future development.

'Religiously all is a blank; their only religious idea seems to consist in a slavish fear of evil spirits and a belief in the deathlessness of the soul. The spiritual darkness may be felt, but it can scarcely be described. It is most intense at the grave. The hope which Christianity gives of re-union after the grave catches their attention in a way which nothing else seemed to command.'

These graphic sentences of Mr. Lawes permit the reader to form definite ideas about the new home to which Mr. and Mrs. Chalmers went in the year 1878.

We take up once again, at this point, the thread of the autobiography, and see through Chalmers' own vivid sketches their progress from the settled and peaceful Rarotonga to the wild and turbulent district of Suau.

'On leaving Rarotonga we visited New Zealand and Sydney. It took us three weeks to get to Auckland and thence to Dunedin. With my wife's friends we stayed six weeks, also doing deputation work. This led to the beginning of an auxiliary of the London Missionary Society in Dunedin. Of that visit I take the following account from *The Story of the Otago Church and Settlement* by the Rev. C. Stuart Ross :—

'"In July, 1877, the Rev. James Chalmers arrived in Dunedin from Rarotonga, where he had been labouring for some ten years. He was on his way to join the New Guinea Mission. His addresses in some of the churches were listened to with intense delight, and in the following month a great public meeting was held in the Temperance Hall, to bid him and his wife God speed in their heroic and arduous enterprise. The building was crowded in every part, and those who were privileged to be present then will never forget the grand enthusiasm of the great audience. Deep interest was excited in the mission to which Mr. Chalmers had devoted himself, and substantial promises of help to him in his work came from every side. With many a prayer and commendation to the grace of God the noble missionaries went forth to their field of labour ; and all too soon the tidings came back that one of them was smitten down by the deadly fever which is bred under sweltering heat in jungle and morass. Mrs. Chalmers had remained at her husband's side—a noble helpmeet to him in the labours to which he had put his hand—until failing health compelled her to seek change in some more healthful and bracing clime."

'"One permanent fruit of Mr. Chalmers' visit to Dunedin was the formation of an Auxiliary to the London Missionary Society, which stimulated practical interest in the Society's work, and gave cordial welcome to any of its agents who happened to come this way." '

'Many dear friends urged my wife to stay in Dunedin

until I could get somewhat settled, but she would not be moved, saying to each and all, " No, my place is by my husband's side." We reached Sydney in the beginning of September, and after a few days stay proceeded to Somerset, where we were to meet a mission vessel for the voyage to New Guinea.

'We arrived at Somerset on September 30, 1877, and were met there by Mr. (now Dr.) Macfarlane in the Bertha, a schooner which had been chartered in Sydney for the mission, the steamer Ellengowan having broken down and being under repair. The Bertha was certainly not a clipper, and it took us a whole week to get to Murray Island, the chief station of the Western Branch of the New Guinea Mission, and Mr. Macfarlane's home.

'We spent a Sunday at Darnley Island, and we were delighted with what we there saw of the beginnings of mission work.

'On the Monday we attended the first Christian burial on the island, and I suppose the very first in the whole mission.

'On Wednesday, October 10, we sailed for Murray Island, but the weather being boisterous, and the channel not well defined, we took three days to get there. The people were emerging from savagery and heathenism; services were well attended and many attended school.

'From Murray Island we crossed to Port Moresby. When in Caution Bay we stuck on a reef for some time, and so were too late to get to Boera for the Sabbath. In the evening we reached that village, and Mr. (now Dr.) Lawes came on from Port Moresby, and gave us a right hearty welcome to New Guinea. He had suffered much from fever, and was waiting for a chance to go home. The following day the Bertha beat up to Port Moresby. I made the journey from Boera in the boat with Piri and his wife and some teachers who were to be taken east. It was my first experience of boating, and it tired me much, as I had been long exposed· to the sun, and very wet with salt water. I have had many worse trips since, but none which I remember so well.

'The first night at Port Moresby we slept on board the Bertha, but the following day we landed to stay with Mr. Lawes. He had been very ill with fever, and was anxiously waiting for us to arrive, so that he might get away. Mrs. Lawes had gone away very ill the year before, and had decided never to return. We made a short inland trip, but not for any great distance. On the return journey I got thoroughly knocked up.

'Some folk had incited the native teachers to insist on getting much higher salaries, and there was something among them resembling a strike. But this difficulty soon passed, and we became better friends than ever. We were delighted to meet Ruatoka and his wife, and Piri and his wife. These were two of the finest teachers sent to New Guinea. Piri I had never met before, but he was a noted Rarotongan character. He was a very powerful man, stronger far than any New Guinean I have met. He was born at Avarua about the year 1835, twelve years after the landing of Papeiha, who was the first teacher to bring the Gospel to the islands. Piri attended the village school, and was taught to read and write there. As he grew up towards manhood, he cast off all restraint, and gave way to all the evil passions of the youthful native. Orange beer drinking was introduced about this time from Tahiti, and spread all round the island.

'Piri was one of the ringleaders in making the orange beer and drinking it, and was often fined. In 1857 the law was executed with a little more stringency, and several times Piri came under its ban. For this he blamed the white missionary, and determined to kill him with his own hands.

'Once when drunk Piri took a spade and made for the mission house. He was seen, and a party armed with sticks and having a rope set off in pursuit of him. As he was getting on to the verandah of the mission house they seized him, and with great difficulty bound him, and led him back to the coast. He was kept in charge for some days, and when really sober saw the terribleness of the crime he had been saved from committing, and vowed that, with God's help, he would never again taste drink. He began attending the services, and became truly converted.

'Piri became a man so filled with the Holy Spirit as to earnestly seek the salvation of souls, and felt compelled to go to the heathen. He joined the Institution, and after a four years' course was sent to Samoa to take charge there of a colony of Cook Islanders. He hoped in this way to get nearer than he could at home to the fulfilment of his great desire. He did good work whilst in Samoa. His wife died there. Some time after, Maki, the widow of a teacher who died in the New Hebrides, landed at Apia on her way to her home on Mangaia. Piri asked her in marriage, and she consenting, they were married.

'This wife was a very fine woman. Piri was her second husband. In the New Hebrides fever attacked the missionary party, and all except two women, Piri's wife one of them, died. These women were at first afraid they would be taken by the chiefs and kept as their wives; but one old chief took them, and treated them as his daughters. For long they waited, and every morning they used to ascend a small hill at the back of the house, and scan the horizon for a sail. Even when sick with fever they used to crawl up. It was a long weary waiting, and then one died, leaving Maki alone. All hope of ever getting away was given up, but after nearly two years, when Maki one morning ascended to the look-out she saw a speck in the far-away distance. As the speck increased, and the ship came near, the poor woman was overjoyed, and wept profusely. The old chief was sorry to lose his daughter, but when the vessel, which turned out to be the John Williams, was off the island, and the boat came ashore, he accompanied her to the boat weeping bitterly. The John Williams had been to England in the interval, hence the delay.

'In 1872 Messrs. Murray and Wyatt Gill had been appointed to take the first batch of teachers to New Guinea, and see them landed safely somewhere on that savage island. In July, 1872, they left Rarotonga in the John Williams, calling at Samoa on their way to New Guinea. There Piri and his wife pressed Mr. Gill so hard that they might be taken to New Guinea that he consented, and so they made the sixth couple in the company of native teachers.

'Piri was a very fine specimen of humanity. He was about six feet two inches in height, and large in proportion. When they arrived in Redscar Bay Mr. Murray and Mr. Gill decided to land them all at Manumanu. Piri landed in a flaming red shirt, which to the present day (1898) is remembered by the older natives. The natives respected him much and feared him. He was not easily moved to anger, but when he was once aroused it was advisable to keep out of his way.

'I remember on one occasion arriving at Boera in the night, and going up to Piri's house to have a sleep. Everything was left in the boat, so as to be ready to

start when the tide suited, we then having no fear of
thieves. After breakfast, the boat being afloat, I went
on board with the crew, and we found that not a row-
lock was left. Piri was on the beach with his wife,
and I landed and told them what had happened. His
wife got very wroth, but no one seemed to mind her as
she went through the village demanding the return of
the rowlocks. We then sent for the chief and headmen,
and met them in Piri's house. Piri quietly told them
that the rowlocks must be returned to the boat. The
chief and headmen had a run through the village, but
it was of no use. Piri, now thoroughly roused, stalked
to the end of the village and demanded the rowlocks,
and said that no one should leave the village until they
were returned, and that every house should be searched.
He looked as if he meant what he said, and then in a
very strange way we received back the rowlocks from
a woman who said she had found them in the street.
I never again missed anything when at Boera.

From Manumanu Piri and his wife were removed with
the others because of serious illness, fever being very bad
there. One man had died and three of the women.
Finally all were removed to Somerset, to be near
Mr. Murray. In November, 1873, being much better,
the teachers were returned to New Guinea and placed
at Port Moresby. Piri and his wife went to Boera.
For sixteen years they did good service, and their
work was blessed.

' Piri accompanied me in many of my trips, especially
to the west in the Gulf. Several Gulf natives who had
stayed at Boera, and received many kindnesses from
Piri and his wife, gave us a good welcome to their
villages, and made our stay with the people much more
satisfactory than it might otherwise have been. He is

said to have introduced the large potato, and for years along both the east and west coast it was called by his name. In 1878 he and his wife spent a few months with us at Suau, and I saw much of Piri then. He was a good man, and a man of prayer, and when addressing new teachers he always told them to live much in prayer, and to remember that Jesus our Master was never far away, but ever near. In 1887 he and his wife accompanied us to Motumotu. While there he was attacked with dysentery. He got better, and as soon as he was able to travel he left us, we hoping to meet him again at Boera, but his work was done. They got safely to Boera, where he had a relapse, and they were taking him to Port Moresby to Mr. Lawes when he died on the way, in January, 1888. In May of the same year his wife followed him. She was to have gone home to Mangaia, but I was glad she was called to higher service where her husband was. They both rest side by side at Boera, near to the house on the hill by the village. Piri was supported by our friends in Anderson's Bay, near Dunedin, New Zealand.

'What can I say of Ruatoka, who now (1898) for twenty-six years has toiled on, enduring many hardships, in sickness often, knowing what hunger means, his life often threatened, and yet who has outlived all his compeers, including his wife? As a young man, we were greatly attached to him and his wife. He was born at Tamarua, Mangaia, in the year 1846. His parents dedicated him when young to the work of God. When a lad he attended Mr. Wyatt Gill's school, and made fair progress. He joined the church, and afterwards came to live with the missionary in order to prepare for entrance into the Rarotonga Institution. He married Tungane, the daughter of a very excellent

Christian couple. Her father had for many years been the missionary's right-hand man. He and his wife came to the Institution. As a young man he was very tall and very thin, and I feared not very strong. He was all that could be desired, and I never once heard anything against him or his wife. We became very much attached to them.

'The year before sending the first contingent of teachers to New Guinea, and before any had been selected for the work, Ruatoka broke down in health, and I feared would never been able to go out. Recovering a little, I appointed him one of the pioneer band, contrary to the strongly expressed views of many in Rarotonga, who thought I was throwing away a valuable life. Both Ruatoka and his wife were in ecstasies at the thought of going, yet they were afraid with a great fear that I might be influenced to change the appointment, and detain them. Going about to the villages agreed with him, and he certainly grew stronger. Those opposed to his going even in the last week thought it was a sin to send him only to die shortly after landing on New Guinea. But I felt convinced I was right in sending them, and now (Nov. 1898) he is the only one remaining out of that band and of several subsequent bands that were sent.

'In the first years Ruatoka and his wife had very hard times, knowing much sickness, often suffering from hunger, and their lives frequently threatened. They have often had to keep watch all night, lest they should be attacked unawares; for the natives everywhere prefer that style of fighting. All subsequent bands of teachers were landed at Port Moresby, and then placed at their stations by the white missionary. Ruatoka and his wife were as father and mother to these newcomers. When the sick teachers were brought to Port Moresby they nursed them day and night. Many died, and Ruatoka and his wife made their coffins, superintended the digging of their graves, and gave them Christian burial.

'In 1878 a large party of gold prospectors came to New Guinea, making Port Moresby their headquarters. Very many of them became sick, and many died, and to them all Rua and his wife were ever kind. Ruatoka did much for them. Once he heard the prospectors were about to be attacked by inland tribes, and he determined if possible to stop it. Getting together a few Port Moresby, Motuan, and Koitapuan natives, he marched inland, visited the prospectors, and told them what he had heard. They feared that something was about to happen from the stealthy ways the natives were seen to move about. At times some had approached near to the camp at night, and one prospector had been badly used by some natives.

'Rua had heard the tribe were to meet at Moumiri, and so he determined to go right in amongst them. The prospectors chose a party from amongst themselves, all armed, to accompany Rua, and if necessary fight for him; but Rua decidedly objected, and went with his natives right into Moumiri, where there was a great gathering of armed men from all the region round. At first the natives threatened him, but he took no further notice than to say, "Why do you want to kill me? what have I done?" He then reasoned with them, preached to them, prayed for them, and the end was that they all dispersed to their homes. The prospectors on his return thanked him, as they were very anxious to be on friendly terms with all the natives, and succeeded in being that right through.

'On two occasions Ruatoka carried prospectors a long distance on his back to his own house, and so saved their lives. One was Neville, a gentleman by birth, and an army man, who begged of the prospectors in Sydney to be allowed to accompany them for the sake of adventure. He was on his way in from the Larogi to Port Moresby, and was taken very ill, and lay down to die. Natives found him, but as it was getting near night, and he looked like dying, they were afraid to touch him. They, on arriving at Port Moresby told Rua, and he begged them to return with him, and help him. But no New Guinea native could do such a thing, as the spirit might ever afterwards haunt them.

'Ruatoka got a long piece of cloth, a small lantern, and bottle of water, and started in the dark. About five miles out he was searching in the long grass when he heard low moaning, and going whence the sound came he found poor Neville nearly dead, quite unconscious. He gave him a little water, then fastening the cloth round him he bent down, and taking the two ends in his hands, and using all his strength, he got the sick man on his back, and began his return journey. He had to cross a range of hills over 300 feet high, and as day was breaking he arrived at his house, and laid the sick man on their one bed, to be cared for by his wife, whilst he lay down dead beat. Neville was nursed back to life, and was able to return inland, where some time after he died from another attack of fever.

'Rua is a true Sabbatarian, and it often vexed his soul to see the abuse of that sacred day. No Sabbath passed that Rua did not make some reference to it to the few natives who attended the services. It was hoped gold would be found in large quantities, and a German thought the best paying concern would be a store. So he built one a little way from the back of the mission ground. When the store was finished he wanted a cook-house, and that he got a Scotchman who was in from the river to put up. The roof was put on, and on the Sabbath, when Rua was holding his forenoon service, there was the loud noise of hammering iron. For a short time he stood it, but at last, telling his audience to go home, he went to his own house to get an English Bible, in which he found the chapter and verses containing the Fourth Commandment. He then marched to where the cook-house was being put up. The German and a friend were sitting on the doorstep of the store, and saw the teacher coming, and wondered what was the matter, as he looked very solemn. The Scotchman was on the top of the cook-house. Rua came just beneath him, and knowing only a little Pidgen English, he said, pointing to the man on the house, " Say, come down." The white man was somewhat astonished to have such a peremptory order from a coloured man, and did not answer. " Say, you know savee, I speak come down." The white man found his tongue, and in very strong language sent the " nigger " to a very hot place. I believe the wrath of the white exploded in fearful cursing. Again Rua said, " What do you talk ? You white fellow send missionary along my country, and my country he get good, and he like Sabati much. Before my countrymen he eat you, but no now. I come along New Guinea, I speak man Sabati he tapu, no work, no fish, no hunt, no build house on Sabati ; and New Guinea man, he say, Ruatoka, you make lie, white man, he work Sabati. What for you make him ? Come down." Once again very forceful adjectives, and the teacher's wrath rises. The tall, powerful man at last makes as though he would ascend the ladder, when the German, knowing well what would take place, shouts out, "Rua, my friend, stop!" and to the white man, "You fool, come down at once, can't you see it is our friend the teacher, and we are wrong?" Rua was roused, so when the white man came down, he handed him the Bible, and ordered him to read the verses he pointed out, and at once. The white man did it, and then the teacher said, "God, He speak, you no work now. Put down hammer belong you." There was a quiet Sabbath for the remainder of the day.

'I have taken many trips with Rua along the coast and inland, and have ever found him an excellent travelling companion. It was when away on one of these, looking out for an inland position as a head station, that his wife was left in entire charge, and she conducted schools and services just as when Rua was at home. One Sabbath morning she was speaking about God's love in giving Jesus, and that day the services were well attended. In the afternoon she spoke of the need for the Holy Spirit to work in all their hearts, and said that when He did they would be changed and love Jesus. Nearly midnight, long after she and her girls had gone to bed, there was a knock at the door, and she called out, "Who is there?" she was answered "I." "Who are you?" again "I." No native likes giving his name. The girls were awakened, and one of them recognized the voice as that of Aruadaera, and said so. Then she called out, "Is it you, Aruadaera?" and he answered, "It is." "What do you want?" "Open the door and let me in, and I will tell you." He was evidently in great distress, but she replied, "It is now very late, and we are all in bed, so come in the morning." "No, now; I cannot wait until the morning." She had to strike a match, and light the lamp, and let him in. "Now, what is it?" "I do not know what it is, but I am afraid, and I think it must be the Spirit you spoke of working in my heart. I am afraid to lie down, lest I should die, for I know I am bad." So then and there she told him of Jesus, and prayed for him, and advised him to go home, and come back in the morning; but he insisted on hearing more, and being prayed for again. He left, but before daylight was back again, and sitting outside the door waiting for it to be opened. He accepted pardon through Christ, and became quite a changed man. He was the first baptized native in New Guinea. For many years he has been a deacon in the Port Moresby church, and an earnest Christian man. He was well advanced in years when he was converted, but he has learnt to read and write. Three of his daughters became wives of teachers, and have done very excellent work. He has been a great help to Ruatoka in many ways.

'In December, 1885, Ruatoka lost his wife, after a very short illness. She had shared the sufferings of the first hard years of the mission, and had been the first to teach girls to read, sew and iron. Some time after Ruatoka married the widow of a teacher, and she has since been a very great help to him in all his work.

'There have been many changes of white missionaries at Port Moresby, but Rua has stuck to his work. In twenty-six years he has had only one change, and that to Cooktown, where he spent a few days. He is greatly respected by all. The governor, government officials, and all the whites speak highly of him, and the natives look to him as to a father. His has been a grand career, and we pray it may continue for many years.

'But much of the work of these two noble men lay

in the future. When we first set foot in Port Moresby very little direct result of mission labour could be seen among the natives. A few children could repeat the letters of the alphabet, but no one could read. I visited the school frequently, but was disappointed in what I saw. We then went on to the east, leaving Mr. Lawes at Kerepunu, to return once again to Port Moresby, and then away on furlough to England. I did not again meet him until he and Mrs. Lawes returned to resume work in New Guinea in 1881.

'The first place we called at was Teste Island, and there Mr. Macfarlane left two teachers. I felt that this station was too far away from my teacher at Kerepunu. We had picked up a few words, and we got on very well with the people. From Teste Island we went to Hoop Iron Bay on Basilisk Island, but the people there were not inclined to be friendly. The Mayri, a small lugger, had followed us up, and Macfarlane and his teachers, some in the lugger, some in a whaleboat, I accompanying, went to Milne Bay, where the teachers were placed at Killerton. My wife remained on board the Bertha. We returned to Hoop Iron Bay, but the Bertha was not there, and on going out towards Teste Island we met her and got on board. An attempt had been made to murder the crew while ashore getting water, and a party of natives on board had turned nasty at the same time. Those ashore got to the boat, leaving casks, water-bags and buckets. As they came near the vessel all the natives sprang over the side and went ashore. The captain did right in leaving that part as soon as possible.

'I did not much like the look of any place we had seen so far. Macfarlane was anxious to get back to Murray Island, so we stood in for South Cape. When some miles off we came to a reef, and not knowing of any passage, the boat was lowered, and I accompanied the captain to explore a bit, and try and find an anchorage inside.   We found a fine bay between South Cape and Suau.   A canoe was there with one man in it fishing.   He was not able to get away from us, and we pulled towards him.   When some distance off we called out and held up a piece of red cloth and some red beads.   He looked as if in great terror, and it took us some time to get him alongside; but when he came he was comforted with small presents.   He was an evil-looking man, and wore on his arm a man's jaw-bone. We left him, and he paddled away as for dear life to the shore.   Getting on board we stood over the reef and in towards the land, and came to an anchor in the bay, under the lee of Suau Island.   It was still early in the afternoon, and we were soon surrounded by a number of canoes.   The noise was terrible.   My wife sat on deck knitting, and one old fellow, wearing a necklace of human bones, took to her and became her friend. When the sun had set they all had to leave the ship, as we allowed no canoe to remain alongside the vessel after sundown.   This native gave Mrs. Chalmers to understand by signs that he was going to sleep, and in the morning he would return with food.

' A watch was kept all night.   At three a.m. a large canoe was seen coming towards the vessel, and was warned off.   At four o'clock, some distance up the bay, a flotilla of canoes was seen, as if they were intending to cross the bay.   Then horn-blowing began and wild shouting, and we felt as if they were going to attack us; until at length it became evident that there was an opposing party coming from the mainland, and the fight, if any took place, would be amongst themselves.   At five o'clock the first flotilla bore down upon us in a body, but we warned them off until the sun appeared.

'When the sun was rising, in the first canoe alongside was my wife's friend of yesterday, bringing with him a present of taro. We gave him a return present. Several of our new friends wore human jaw-bones on their arms, and also many bones from other parts of the body. Not a few seemed evil-disposed, and as though they would soon have picked a quarrel. After breakfast we got into the boat, taking Kirikeu, the friend of Mrs. Chalmers, with us, and went in search of a suitable place for a mission station. One thing we specially wanted was a good supply of water, near to which we might build. We had a look at several places, and at last rounding the point we came to two small villages with a bit of unoccupied land between, and a point of white sand running out into the Pass, which was afterwards named Mayri Pass, and ending in black rocks. The position was good, and in the bush behind was water, and a short way along the beach a good supply of fine water, which the old man told us never dried up. We decided on the spot for the house, and as the season was nearly over, and the schooner had to return to Port Moresby and Murray Island, we had to make haste. I wanted to hire a house during the time our own was being built. There was a house belonging to the chief Manuegu, but he would only let us have one end of it.

'I got tomahawks and knives from the Bertha, and landed with a number of young men, and distributing the tomahawks and knives went into the bush, and showed them what kind of wood we wanted. Soon we returned, all carrying timber, and we measured the space for the house—thirty-six feet by eighteen feet—

and showed them where to dig holes for the posts.
Then I returned to the vessel, and began to land the
teachers' things. Securing some old sails we rigged
up tents ashore, and all the teachers landed, and slept
ashore that night. In the morning they were all right.
All our things being landed on the Saturday we left the
vessel, and took up our quarters in the chief's house.
Hanging close by us were human skulls, and all round
us the bones of pigs and cassowaries and fishes. The
division between our small apartment and the chief's
was about two feet high, and in the early morning,
about three o'clock, he and others stepped over it, and
across our mattress. The whole surroundings were
peculiar, and it was a weird sight to look out in the
moonlight between these human skulls. The chief's end
of the house contained also clubs and spears and shields.
A very fine Tamano tree grew close by, and had been
growing there for ages, and one could only wonder
what scenes had been enacted under its shade.

‘ The natives informed us they were cannibals, and that
human flesh was good. I once had a conversation with
an old cannibal, converted to Christianity when I knew
him. “ Is man good to eat ? ” “ You savee bulamakau ? ”
“ Yes.” “ Well, no good.” “ You savee pig ? ” “ Yes.”
“ Well, no good.” “ You savee sheep ? ” “ Yes.” “ Well,
no good ; man he too much good,” and he smacked
his lips.

‘ Sabbath came, and we held Rarotongan service, and
sang many hymns under the shade of the old Tamano
tree. We were all in excellent health, and just fit for
work. The Mayri was anchored opposite and close by.
A few days later the Bertha sailed. We had put some
of our things on board of the Mayri, and landed them
as we wanted them. We were anxious not to excite

the native cupidity by a display of tools, tomahawks, and cloth. One afternoon, after resting, we were turning again to work, and I went down the beach to the water's edge, and called to the captain of the Mayri to look in a certain box, and find a saw, and send it ashore. I heard a noise, and on turning round saw our house surrounded by an armed, ugly-looking mob of painted savages. I signed to the captain not to send ashore, and I rushed up and got through the cordon, and upon the platform in front of where we slept. The excitement was intense. The men were demanding tomahawks, knives, hoop-iron, beads ; and by signs gave us to understand that if they did not get them then they would murder us. I felt vexed, since we had been particularly careful to avoid trouble, and had given no occasion for offence.

'One evil-looking fellow, wearing a human jaw-bone, and carrying a heavy stone club, rushed towards me as if to strike. Through his paint I recognized the man of the canoe when we first came in the boat. Looking him steadily in the face our eyes met, and I demanded in loud, angry tones what he wanted. He said tomahawks, knives, iron, beads, and that if they were not given they were going to kill us. "You may kill us, but never a thing will you get from us." Some of the teachers suggested it would be better to let them have a few things than for us to be murdered. I replied, "Can't you see if we give to these men, other parties from all round will come and make demands, and the end will be that we shall all be murdered?" "No," I said, "let them do it now, and be done with it." I was in quite a don't care mood. Kirikeu then approached, and advised me to give a small present, as those who were troubling us were people from the other side of the island, and our friends at Suau could not do much for us against them. Again I replied, " No, my friend, never to people carrying arms do I give a present. All the time we have been here we have never carried arms, and have dwelt amongst you as friends."

'Kirikeu then began to harangue the crowd, assisted by the chief Manuegu, and all retired to the bush behind the house. A deputation waited upon me from the bush, again asking me to give something, but they received the same answer, " I never give to armed people."

'This commotion stopped our work, and that night, for the first time since we landed, we kept a watch all night. There was a good deal of unrest throughout the night, and natives were seen moving about in the bush. The next morning we resumed work just as if nothing had happened. We were getting the wall plates on when Kirikeu came, accompanied by a very decent-looking native, and saying, " This is the chief of yesterday, and he is sorry for what took place." I liked the look of the man, and tried to explain to him his error, and that now he was unarmed and clean we were glad to make friends with him, and I went over to the house, taking him with me, and there gave him a present.

'When the house was finished, and half the flooring down, we left the chief's house, and were glad to get quarters of our own. We had begun sawing wood for flooring and other necessary work. During our stay in the chief's house my wife used to sit on the platform sewing or tatting, and every day Bocasi, a very fine-looking young warrior, wearing the shells that marked him out as a fighting-man, came and sat in front of her. He helped her to learn the language, and she

taught him tatting and knitting. The shifting of the
goods from the chief's house to our new home was no
easy matter; and twice spears and clubs were handled
by the natives very suspiciously. They claimed everything we had taken into the house, but at length we
got all our property away. Many things were stolen.
The loss which troubled us most was the theft of our
camp oven. We never saw it again for two years, and
then found it had been stolen by a man who had been
most friendly towards the teachers. I afterwards sent
the chief a present, in addition to paying him for the
use of his house, and for the ground the teachers
occupied with their tents.

'We now began to feel ill and feverish, I suffering
most because of a severe attack of diarrhoea. It was
nearing the end of the year, and I, having bought
a piece of land for planting purposes, was anxious to
have it cleared and planted, so that on January 1, 1878,
I might be free to travel along the coast to Orangerie
Bay on the one side, and Leocadie on the other. We
missed Bocasi for some time, and wondered what had
become of him. We got news that some white men
had been murdered on an island, and everything they
possessed divided out among the murderers. This led
to great unsettledness amongst the natives; but we
went steadily on with our work.

'We were getting to know many of the people, and
we fancied that we had gained their confidence. Many
of the natives showed kindness in bringing us vegetables
and fish. We also received numerous invitations to
feasts, some of which were to cannibal feasts. It was at
this time that Kirikeu, as a kindly attention to Mrs.
Chalmers, brought and offered to her as a present a
portion of a man's breast already cooked! We were

still watched day and night. I was told frequently that I should be a great chief had I only more than one wife. One chief offered me his eldest daughter as a beginning.

'Just before Christmas with some natives I was in the bush at the back clearing, the teachers were at the seaside sawing, when Johnnie, one of the crew of the Mayri, who was ashore getting wood and water for our trip to the west, came to me in the bush, and said, "I think we are going to have trouble. Natives all look bad, and he been off trying make row we fellow." "Oh no, I think it is all right," I replied. But I told the men to knock off work, and come to the cook house, where I would pay them for what they had done. I was paying them, when I heard two shots fired from the Mayri. I quickly picked up my things, and made a bound for the house. The sawyers did the same. Two of the crew were with us. This left on board the Mayri the captain and cook, a Darnley Islander named Kangaroo.

'I insisted that the crew should return on board, and on looking out towards the vessel, I saw that she was in charge of natives, and the long sennit hawser kept on deck had been passed ashore to natives on the reef, and some natives were pulling up the anchor, and that in a few minutes more the vessel would be ashore. I also heard shouting from the beach where the dingey was, and one of the crew came running up to say that they would not let them get the boat away. I sprang down from the house, and vaulted over the fence, ran to the boat and sent the natives flying, and got her off. The natives on board the vessel seeing the dingey coming off, let go the anchor, and sprang overboard, and those on the reef ran along the beach to the village.

'Firing began from the vessel as soon as the crew

got on board, and the shots came to the village, and into the bush. Natives were arming, and the bush seemed all alive with them. I went on to the beach, and as far as the chief's house, where I saw two men who had been wounded, and came back to the house for bandages. A crowd was gathering round the house, all carrying arms, spears and clubs. When at the chief's house I was told that Bocasi was on board the vessel, and so getting into a small canoe I took two men with me, and they paddled off. I thought that possibly the native was being detained as a hostage for peace, but on nearing the vessel I called out, " Is there still a man on board?" and the answer was, " Yes, he board." I felt he was dead, and so I said, " Is he shot?" " Yes, he shot dead, yes, he dead."

'Getting on board, I found the deck covered with blood, and the captain leaning against the mainmast white and weak from loss of blood. He had been speared in the side, and he had a fearful cut on his foot. In the small hold was the body of Bocasi, and my canoe men decided to take it ashore; they were getting it on deck, but I felt that it would never do to allow them to land it. To take the body to land with me would mean instant death to us all at the hands of the enraged natives. To allow it to land before me would mean the death of those ashore, and also that I would not be allowed to return to the land. So I stepped quickly into the canoe, caught the man in it under his arm and made him come with me. He was a son of our old friend Kirikeu, and I asked him to let me get to the house before he said anything.

'The principal people seemed friendly, and kept assuring us that all was right, we should not be harmed. Great was the wailing when the body was landed, and arms were up and down pretty frequently. Canoes began to crowd in from the regions around.

'At dusk I sent off to the Mayri some things for the native who was going to act as captain, and for the mate, and I told them to send by the native teacher in the canoe all the barter that could be spared us, and stand in readiness for the signal to be off. A native then came in to us quietly through the bush and said, "Tamate, you must get away to-night if you can; at midnight, perhaps, you may have a chance; to-morrow morning, when the big star rises, they will murder you." "Are you sure of it?" I asked. "Yes; I have just come from their meeting at the chief's house, and that is their decision; they will do nothing till to-morrow morning." Just before that there had been a rush of the natives, as if they were going to take the mission house; but still they did not break the fence. They simply came close up, defying us and vowing vengeance. The chief himself came to the house at dusk and said, "You must give compensation." "Yes," I said, "I will give compensation; but, remember, I have had nothing to do with Bocasi's death." "You must give it now," he said. "I cannot," I replied; "if you come to-morrow when the big star rises, I will give it you." He then went sulkily away; and it was then that the native told me about the probability of our being murdered in the morning.

'I told Mrs. Chalmers what the chief had told me, and I said, "It is for you to decide. Shall we men stay and you women go, as there is not room enough for us all on the vessel? Or shall we try all of us to go? Or shall we all stay?" The answer I received was, "We have come here to preach the Gospel and do these people good; God, whom we serve, will

take care of us. We will stay. If we die, we die; if
we live, we live." The teachers' wives then came up,
and I put the same question to them; and they said
that whatever my wife did they would do; "Let us
live together or die together." We decided to stay, and
we then had evening prayer. We dared not sing the
evening hymn, because it would draw the people about
us. I read the forty - sixth Psalm and engaged in
prayer. As I was praying in the Rarotongan dialect
we heard the anchor being pulled up, and when I had
finished I could see the last of the Mayri going out of
the bay. The bridge was then broken, and we had
simply to trust Him who alone could care for us.

'The noise during the night had somewhat abated,
but in the morning we could hear the natives coming
all round from very long distances, from which the
war-horn called them. At four o'clock the chief came
to see me. During the night I had got tomahawks,
hoop-iron, red beads, and cloth together. Mrs. Chalmers
and myself made parcels of them—a large parcel for the
friends of the one who was killed, and smaller parcels
for the wounded. These were shown to the chief. "It
is not enough," he said; "cannot you give any more?"
I replied, "If you will wait till the steamer comes
I may be able to give you more; but at present I
cannot." "I must have more now." "I cannot give
you more now." The man then went away, and we
expected that the natives would attack us immediately.
Several of them came as far as the fence and demanded
more, but we took no notice, and they went away.

'During all that day (Sunday) we could not tell
when the attack would be made. Of course during the
night and day we had to keep watch and watch. On
Monday, when a funeral feast was going on, and the

man who was killed was being buried, we thought that surely the attack would be made. The old man, who seemed to be very friendly, kept close by us, and told us that we must not on any account go outside, and that he would be our friend. A Tanosine canoe came in with a number of natives, all fighting men, and demanded that they should be allowed to do as they liked. They were told that the white man and his friends would be murdered in payment for what had been done, and the natives of Suau told those from Tanosine that they would attack us at once.

' I had been on watch in the night, and at three o'clock I had just turned in. I had not been long asleep when Mrs. Chalmers called out: " Quick! they have taken the house." I sprang from my bed and rushed to one of the doors, which was simply made of a piece of cloth. I threw the cloth aside, and there was a large armed party standing in front of us, and others at the end of the house. I could see in the dimness of the morning that they were led by the old chief from the mainland. Standing before him, I said, " What do you want?" " Give us more compensation," said he, " or we will kill you and burn the house now." " Kill you may," I said, " but no more compensation do I give. Remember, if we die we shall die fighting; and there is an end of it." The old man got frightened. Then, for the first time, we took down the musket, and showed it to the old man. Some powder was put in and some small shot. The people had seen us shoot birds before. I said to the old man, " Go! tell them that we are going to fight, and there must be an end to this. The first man that crosses where that fence stood " (for it had been thrown down) " is a dead man! Go "! They retired, leaving us alone with Him who ever cares for His children.

'For about an hour and a half they had a long discussion. At last the old man came back, calling me by name. I challenged him; I would not allow him to come inside the fence, as we feared treachery. He said, "It is all right," and looking out we saw a large war canoe manned, and several hundred smaller canoes being lifted into the water. The natives in the war canoe were standing up and saying to the people on shore, "To-morrow we return, not only to kill the white man and his friends, but to kill all of you." It ended simply in this way. The chief had said, "Before this white man came here with his friends I was nobody; they have brought me tomahawks, hoop-iron, red beads, and cloth; you have no white man, and if you try to kill him, you kill him over my body." So our lives were saved. We dared not, however, go far into the bush or into the eastern side of the village.

'Amidst all the troubles Mrs. Chalmers was the only one who kept calm and well. The people became much quieter, and no new demands were made upon us. A few days later a cannibal feast of which we had heard was held, and some of our friends took part in it.

'The Ellengowan arrived on January 20. The natives were beginning to think no vessel would come; but when it arrived they were frightened, and willing to forget the Mayri affair. After her arrival we were able to go about among the people again.

'Early in 1878 I began the exploration of my district, and one of the first places I visited was the Leocadie group of islands. The people were kind, and did their best for us. We arrived on a very stormy night, and had wretched quarters, and were glad when morning came. In the morning the people looked unsettled, and as if they were likely to become hostile, and we got away as quickly as possible. At the Leocadie, not very long before our visit, the natives had murdered a whole crew of Chinamen.

'From Leocadie we went to the Brumer Islands. I was very thirsty, and at the first place we called I asked for water to drink. After a short time a cocoanut cup full of water was handed to me, and I drank it, and felt a peculiar nasty taste in my mouth. A teacher who was sitting aft asked me to pass it to him, as he too was thirsty, but I told him not to drink, as the water had a nasty bitter taste. Soon after we left I became very sick, and vomited with very severe retching. We had to put into Baibeseka and be helped up to a house. I remained there until nearly sundown. The crew were very kind and attentive. On getting home I went to bed, and was ill for a month.

'On my first visit to Tepauri we had an exciting time. The Suau people were at deadly enmity with the Tepauri people, and only a short time before our arrival there had been a big cannibal feast at Suau of captives taken from the other side. I determined to make peace between the two, and that the Tepauri natives should be allowed to visit us. I proposed visiting them, but our Suau friends opposed it. On a Sunday afternoon I said, " To-morrow I go to Te-pauri, and I want Kirikeu and Manuegu to accompany me." But no one would accompany me. In the evening I was sitting at the front door with my wife, when a number of natives came before us, some of them carrying skulls. The skulls were placed in a row, and then our old friend Kirikeu said, " Friend, are you going over there to-morrow?" and I replied, " Yes, I intend going." " Do you see these skulls? They belonged to people we killed from over there, and on these rocks " (black rocks on the water's edge in front of the house) "we cut the bodies up, cooked and ate them. They have not been paid for, and your head would be considered good payment, as you are our great friend." Looking at me he went on, "Will you go now?" "Yes, I go to-morrow morning, and God will take care of us."

'I had one teacher who was a widower, and I said to him, "Beni, you heard all the natives said yesterday. I am going to Tepauri, will you come with me?" After prayers we went to the dingey, and the excitement on the beach was great. Every effort was made to prevent our going. We got off to our small mission lugger, the Mayri, and sailed over. We anchored well off, and then Beni and I pulled in the dingey to the reef, where we got out in three feet of water. There was a noisy crowd of armed natives ashore, and I feared that they might seize the dingey, so I sent her back with the man to the vessel. We waded ashore, and the noise was great, and the spears and clubs numerous. They danced around us, shouting all the time. Then we were seized by the hand and hurried along the beach, I protesting all the way, but to no purpose. Beni was just behind me, and around us the crowd kept up a swinging dance, using their spears and clubs, pretending to throw them or to strike a blow at an enemy. One word we thought we could make out, *goira*, *goira!* This we interpreted to mean, "spear them! spear them!" On Rarotonga the word would have been *koia*, and we fancied that which we now heard might be the same word.

'We came to a dry watercourse, and up that they constrained us to go, but getting my heel against a stone I protested, and Beni did the same. But it was no use; we were just lifted over. I turned to Beni, and

said, "Try to get back, they may let you return."
"I am trying all the time, but it is no use." "Well,
what do you think of it?" "Oh, they are taking us to
the *marai* to kill us." "It looks like it." The *marai*
is the sacred place in Eastern Polynesia where the gods
are supposed to live, and where sacrifices are offered.
We had only recently left the Cook Islands, and knew
nothing of New Guinea, so it is no wonder we thought
that there might be sacred places in the thick bush.

'The bush was dense. I turned to Beni, and said,
"No use, Beni, God is with us, so let us go on quietly."
We reached the hill, and near to a large rock, with moss,
ferns, and lichens in abundance around it, there was
water dropping into a cool pool below. It was a fine
cool, refreshing place. I was made to stand on a stone
near the pool, and Beni on another, and the crowd all
round us, when the man who held my hand spoke,
and this is what we made of it. Their word for water,
we discovered later, was *goira*. "Tamate, look, there
is good water; it is yours, and all this land is yours,
and our young men will begin at once to build you a
house. Go and fetch your wife, and leave that bad
murdering lot you are now among, and come and
live with us." They had heard that when we arrived
at Suau our first inquiry had been for good water.
This was their reason for at once leading us inland.

'Our return to the beach greatly relieved our friends
on board the Mayri, for they had begun to think we
were murdered. We remained a while to accept the
hospitality of the natives, and then returned to Suau.
Our own people kept away for some time, and then
a few came saying, "They did not kill you, but did you
eat anything?" "Oh yes, plenty." "You should not
have done that, as they will have poisoned you." I

had an attack of fever the following day, and the people became very excited, lest I should die, and they were sure I had been poisoned; but no harm came of it.

'My first visit to Farm Bay was interesting. About forty years ago one of Her Majesty's ships stood in to the bay, but seeing the natives coming out in numerous canoes, and apparently hostile, rather than come into collision the captain put about, and stood away. The reports of Farm Bay from our natives and others were very bad; but I determined to get to know them. Before going on any of these expeditions we always had a meeting for prayer. I landed at Navapo in my whale-boat. As we neared the beach I stood on the bow, and sprang ashore; the boat was then backed into deep water. The beach swarmed with natives, but they gave me a wide berth as I walked up to the nearest house. I was dressed in white except my boots, which were black. The natives kept at a good distance from me, and discussed me. Some thought it better to get their spears and clubs, and many of these were in the long grass close by. My clothing bothered them, and the black feet frightened them. One came and touched and tested the shirt, and found that it was all right; it was cloth. Then the trousers were tried, and also pronounced right. The brave ones who came to try returned to the others to discuss the position; but no one had yet had the pluck to touch my feet. At last one old woman could stand the uncertainty no longer, and she came slowly up, tears rolling down her cheeks, and covering her heart with her arm, lest I should see how excited she was, she tried first the shirt, then the trousers. She then looked piteously up at me, and I nodded, as I knew well what she was going to do. She then placed her hand on my left boot and was feeling it. I picked my right foot up and drew off my boot. Poor woman! she screamed and rushed away, and with her the whole crowd, helter skelter into the bush, and I saw no more of them. In after visits to the Bay we became capital friends, and teachers were settled among them.

'The Suau natives quite appreciated our living with them, and they were right, as they thought afterwards, in not permitting us to be murdered. For if they had, they never again would have had a white man living amongst them, and then where would they have been able to get knives, hoop-iron, tomahawks, large knives, beads, and cloth? Now they were people of note, and even their enemies acknowledged this. I remember that a few months after we landed they made up a very large party from other villages, and proceeded west to visit their friends and to trade. They had now a good bit of trade in hand from house-building, and land purchase, food, water, and few curios. For the purchase of land they had received, amongst other things, large sugar-cane knives, and I certainly made a mistake in giving them these. As soon as they got them they began to brandish them, and to imitate playfully the cutting off of heads. Many canoes all strongly manned went west, and in about a fortnight returned with much conch-shell blowing, shouting, and dancing, and carrying on as if returning from a great victory. They told us that they had had a very good time, and that everywhere they had proclaimed that they had a white man living with them, and all those who heard this respected them much. They brought us presents of sago and bananas, and we were now the very best of friends.

'Some time after this I went along the coast, and in

what we called Fife Bay very nearly came to grief.
I landed in the whaleboat, the mate of the steamer
Ellengowan landing with me. The tide was far out,
and we left the boat in charge of the crew, two South
Sea Islanders, with instructions to be sure and keep her
afloat. Just when landing some natives who had come
down to the beach strongly objected to my leaving the
boat; but I insisted, and stepped into the water, followed
by the mate. We got right up the beach through the
mangrove to the house of the chief, for whom I had
asked. He was a sulky, sullen fellow, and would have
nothing to do with me. I told him who I was, and he
replied he knew all about me. He was nursing a
baby, a grandchild I supposed, and I thought of getting
at him through the bairn. So I placed a small present
on the child. These things he picked up, and threw at
me, and I could see that a row was brewing. I asked
the mate, who was a little way off, how he thought
things were, and he answered, " Bad, sir ; the bush is full
of natives, and there are arms everywhere. They have
stolen all my beads and hoop-iron. It looks like mischief." " Then let us get away quietly to the boat."
We walked away, and as we reached the mangrove we
could see natives crouching in it with spears and clubs.
As we made our way through the mangrove the natives
gathered thickly behind us, and we realized that their
plan was to do the mischief at the boat. We were about
halfway down the beach, I ahead, when the mate
shouted, " Look out, sir, there's a native just behind you
ready to strike with his club." I wheeled suddenly round,
our eyes met, I hurriedly took a piece of stock iron from
my satchel, and held it out close to his face. I know
not how it was, he stretched out one hand to get the
iron, and with my right hand I seized the club, and

wrenched it from him, and carried it as if I meant work—and I did! The natives, months afterwards, told me that at that moment I looked bad. We reached the boat, but the crew, in their excitement as they saw what was taking place, had allowed it to ground. I held the club facing the natives whilst I stood in the water, and the others got the boat off. The natives were undecided, and so we got safely away. It seems our Suau friends had been there, and had challenged them to fight, showing the big knives, and taunting them with the fact that they had no white man to give them such things. And so when they saw me their feeling was, "Now the Suau white man is in our hands. Let us kill him, and those with him."

'Our first visit to Dahuni, near Mullens' Harbour, or rather what should be called Mullens' Harbour [1], was full of much native experience. Early in the afternoon we steamed up to an anchorage, and soon after coming to anchor we had several hundreds of canoes around us. I had given orders that no natives were to be allowed on board, and that any curio-buying must be done over the side of the ship. I ordered the cook to put all his gear away, so that no one could touch anything, and asked the captain to see that sufficient steam was kept up, at all events until sunset. They were a noisy crowd, and ugly as well, and some made very significant insulting signs; but we wanted no trouble, and so pocketed the insults. I had frequently heard that this was a bad place, and so determined, if possible, to avoid all rupture.

'I had just gone down to the cabin to have a bit of food, when I heard a great commotion amongst the canoes, and the mate shouting, "Look out, all hands." I rushed

[1] Mr. Chalmers here refers to the fact that the names of many of the places he originally discovered and named have since been changed.

on deck, and saw our Chinese cook in a canoe, and very
excited. I ordered him back, and those on board helped
him back to the vessel. " Now, you fool, what did you
want to get into a canoe for ? Can't you see the spears
all ready ? " " He steal knife belong me." " I told you to
put all away, what for you no do it ? " " I keep knife
work ; he steal him." " All right, you leave him to me
now." I went aft, the canoes were closing round us,
and spears and clubs were all handy. I called out,
"Every canoe go away. No more canoes to come
alongside until knife is returned. Now go." There
was some jeering, some defiance, and a few canoes made
off at great speed towards Dufaure Island. The clearing
out was not to my liking, so I asked the captain to blow
the whistle, and then there was great excitement, and in
a few minutes not a canoe near us.

'Special watches were set that night with only trusted
men. I had my hammock slung under the main boom,
and was fast asleep, when the captain shook the hammock, and called me hurriedly. " Up, sir, quick ! they
are going to attack us ; the war horns are blowing."
I sat up in my hammock and listened, and then I said,
" Why, captain, there is no fighting, but they are
bringing in a pig from somewhere and rejoicing. Go to
sleep, and learn to distinguish the blowing of the conch-
shell." I went to sleep again, but just after daybreak
was again called, as a canoe was coming off. Those in
the canoe told us the chief was coming, and soon a
large canoe with many on board drew near. There
were many paddlers, many sitting still, and one man
standing up. As they neared I could see the one
standing was holding something in his stretched-out
arm, and he was calling out, " Tamate, Tamate, it is
peace and friendship." When the canoe came along-

side, I allowed the one who was standing up, an old man, to step on board, and then he gave me the stolen knife, a pig, and a large quantity of native vegetables. I took the chief to the cabin, and gave him a suitable present. He had been to Dufaure to get the knife, and had insisted on their giving me a suitable present; hence the pig and vegetables. I explained to the chief that it was Sabbath, and that no canoes were to come off, but that I would land later.

'After service I landed, and got a few natives together, but they were very impatient to get away. It seemed that early that morning a man had died suddenly, and they were mourning. In some parts of the village the people were far from cordial, and I thought it would be better for me to get on board. I went to where the dead man was laid out, and offered a present, but was not well received. I stood there a little while, and a young man came hurriedly, and threw himself on the corpse, crying bitterly, and saying, "O my father, my father! speak but one word to me, one word only! Why have you left me, O my father, my father?" The corpse was in a sitting posture, and was decorated with leaves and flowers, and all round were many crying and cutting themselves with shell until the blood flowed freely. A youth, whom I found out afterwards to be the chief's son, came to me and said that I ought to go on board, and that as I had nobody from the vessel with me, having landed in a canoe, he and one other would paddle me off. On the way they told me that it was not safe for me to be on shore, as the friends were saying that the blowing of the whistle the previous day had killed their friend, and they might kill me in payment.

'The following morning we went up the Poroai

Lagoon, but not very far, as it was full of sand and mud-banks. I had walked over to it before from the seaside. We anchored a very long way off, and I landed in a canoe, the mate accompanying me. We told the paddlers to keep the canoe afloat, and we went up to the houses, but our reception was not good. Spears and clubs were being taken down and placed handy, and after a little a young woman signed to me to get away. We quietly went to the canoe, wading through the water. I ordered the paddlers to take us off, but they were undecided, so we seized the paddles, and made the canoe move through the water. Meanwhile there was a rare row going on ashore, and we afterwards learned that a few opposed our being murdered. Hence the delay that took place, and now that we had escaped they quarrelled amongst themselves. The tide was well out when we got to the Ellengowan, and all round the steamer it was dry. About six o'clock, when the tide floated us, we got away.

'At Dufaure Island I had a strange adventure. On springing ashore from the boat I called out for Meaudi the chief, and a dapper little fellow approached. We looked at one another, and became friends. The boat had backed off after landing Jack, a Loyalty Islander, who had accompanied me in some of my travels. The first thing to do after meeting was to exchange names, I becoming Meaudi, and he becoming Tamate. I then tied a print handkerchief round his neck, and gave him a small present, a piece of hoop-iron and a few beads. We then marched on, having some distance to go to his village. The crowd increased, and amused themselves with relating to every newcomer, in very loud voices, the landing, the meeting, the exchange of names, and the presents.

'At one point, hearing very loud shouting as if in anger, I turned round, and saw my man Jack armed with a long spear, and showing off. I asked him what he meant, and he replied, "I think some bad men here. I get spear and I show I savee all right about throw spear, spose them want fight. I keep spear now, and look out good for you." I told Jack to keep quiet, and not to excite the people.

'On arriving at the first village, I was introduced as Meaudi, and found that I had numerous relations, grandfathers, grandmothers, fathers, mothers, uncles, aunts, brothers, sisters, cousins of every degree, and each and all expected a present. I was careful to give the old ladies a present of Turkey red calico, and to call them mother. I have always done that when landing at a new place, and if they have accepted the compliment I have then felt perfectly safe. At one place, when the men were gathering round me with their spears and clubs, the old women collected near me, and ordered the men away, and they obeyed.

'From the first village we went to others, and went through the process of friendship and presents a second time. I had to send the boat back to get my satchel replenished.

'We remained good friends all through my stay at the east end. In 1878 I received a number of teachers from Rarotonga and Raiatea, and I placed a man and his wife at Meaudi's own village. He and the people gave them a good reception. After staying some time at Suau, and visiting Teste Island and Milne Bay, I went west, calling at Isuisu, where I had placed two men and their wives and one little girl. I called at Dufaure, and found the teacher and his wife well, and getting on well with the people and language. I proceeded west to Port Moresby. On my return I called at Dufaure again, and found both sick, and heard that the Isuisu teachers and their wives were dead; that they had been poisoned, and that the girl was at Suau. I took the teacher and his wife with me. They told me that Meaudi had warned them to keep their pans and bucket in the house, cook their own food, and only employ a certain lad to fetch their water, as he was afraid that they might be poisoned. We called at Isuisu, and found the place nearly deserted. I visited the graves, and all I could get out of the natives was that the teachers died in one night, and that the Suau teacher came and buried them. I said nothing as to what I had heard. The house was much injured, and the boxes broken open and their contents taken. I proceeded to Suau, where I was told that the teachers were poisoned at the instigation of an island chief. He had come down and professed great friendship, and begged tomahawks, hoop-iron, cloth, and beads from them; but they told him they could not give them, as they were the only things they had with which to buy food, but that if he brought food they would buy it. He was very wroth, and employed a sorcerer to destroy them. The teachers, so as to have cool water, hung the bucket full of water under the house close by the door, and all they had to do when thirsty was to bend over and dip their pannikin into the bucket. During the night the sorcerer went through his magic, and finally put poison into the bucket. The teachers, their wives, and the child drank, had severe vomiting and great pains, and before morning all died except the child. News arrived at Suau during the day, and at once the teacher started in the whaleboat with a Suau crew. The bodies were in the house, the child was being cared for by an old woman.'

L 2

The narrative contained in this chapter has been given almost entirely in the words of the autobiography. But at the point in his story now reached a large portion of the manuscript is missing. There is consequently a considerable gap, extending to the period, many years later, when Chalmers had taken over the work of the Fly River Mission. But fortunately, from the year 1878 there is a considerable mass of letters, both private and official, in existence, and also a long series of reports. From these it has been possible to construct a continuous narrative of his work, and also to glean many of his thoughts upon men and affairs.

In 1878 Chalmers and Macfarlane were the only European missionaries of the Society in New Guinea, and in 1879 the latter returned to England on furlough. W. G. Lawes had sailed for England in December, 1877. The three years he had passed in and around Port Moresby had been a season of great trial to his wife, himself, and the native teachers. Depressed by fever and by the difficulties of the work, he had expressed some doubt about his returning to New Guinea, but in April, 1881, he and his family resumed work at Port Moresby. Since that date he and his wife have given long years of devoted service to the mission. He became the great literary and educational missionary, and Chalmers the great pioneer in opening up new districts.

In a letter dated January 23, 1878, Chalmers referred to his old friend and colleague, and to the depression caused by fever. 'Lawes,' he wrote, 'is a splendid fellow, and a first-class missionary, and is well liked by the people. He must have been writing to you as to me when ill with fever, and when dark dense clouds alone were seen. I remember Mrs. Geddie telling me she never allowed Dr. Geddie's letters written by him when down with fever to be sent, and that frequently, if they had not been burnt, when the doctor had read them after recovery he used to say, " But that this is my own handwriting, I would not have believed I could ever have written such things." '

It is difficult for those who have never passed through the experience to form even an approximate conception of what a reference like the above implies. Climatic influences in an island like New Guinea are a deadly foe to missionary enterprise. It is hard enough when health is good to keep bright and strong and hopeful. Nothing but a large share of the grace of God and a clear realization of His sustaining Presence can keep faith bright and active under repeated attacks of fever. This is one reason why so many native teachers have died in New Guinea. When repeated attacks of fever seized them they soon gave up even the wish to recover, and hence often died when, could they have been a little stimulated and encouraged, they would have recovered. Even Chalmers at times found it very hard to conquer the awful weakness and depression caused by this vigilant foe, ever lurking by, ready to attack him when least equal to resistance.

During 1878 Chalmers and his heroic wife were alone on the mainland of New Guinea, Macfarlane's head-quarters being on Murray Island in the Torres Straits. On January 24 Chalmers wrote, ' We are tolerably well. I have got much lighter during the last few weeks, but am so much better that I shall soon pick up again. We have begun speaking of God's love to the people in very broken language, yet I hope sufficiently well to make them think a little. The people here are dreadful cannibals. Their finest decorations are human jawbones and other bones, and sometimes the wretches appear with pieces of human flesh dangling from their arms. There is no doubt that many of them had hoped to secure our bodies for a feast. We are warned even now not to wander too far away from the house. The hopes of the mission are bright, and assuredly we shall not be forsaken.'

In New Guinea, even from the first, Chalmers had no idea of limiting his care and labour to one station or district. He was soon to verify the almost prophetic sentence written of him by Wyatt Gill in 1877, ' It may be he is the Livingstone of New Guinea.' He had secured a foothold, one entirely after his own heart, and in the very centre of savagery and cannibalism. But he had hardly obtained a shelter for his wife and himself ere he was away, exploring the coast-line, with a keen eye for suitable districts in which to station native teachers.

In March, 1878, Chalmers wrote to Dr. Mullens, ' I have made my first trip in the Ellengowan, and find her very comfortable, and a good sea boat. We left Suau on February 5 for Port Moresby, Mrs. Chalmers remaining with the teachers. There was really no accommodation on board for her, and she thought it was not well for us both to leave the teachers at Suau so soon after the disturbances, and in the unhealthy season. The natives of the place were highly pleased with her remaining, and promised to treat her kindly. They saw we had confidence in their friendship.

' We arrived at Port Moresby on February 7, and found all well. Ruatoka was pleased to see me, as they feared we had all been killed and eaten. I was pleased with the progress which had been made in the school. When we were there in October none could read, and now five stood up and read well. I had a visit from all the teachers from Kerepunu to Boera. They had all been afraid that they would never see us again. The churches at Kaile, Hula, and Kerepunu are all finished. The book translated by the Kerepunu teacher Anederea, and revised by Mr. Lawes, is being printed in Sydney. I think when a teacher does translate a book it would be well to give him credit for it. Poor fellows! They have to bear the brunt of the fight, and we, the white missionaries, follow in and get the bulk of the credit. We are the men who make peace, not so much these humble teachers, and yet they have smoothed the way and have spoken of us to the heathen. It is we who reduce the language to writing and translate books, and yet often they have taught us and helped us, and have first written the language and first been able to speak in it to the people!'

From Port Moresby Chalmers went on to Murray Island, and thence to Thursday Island and Cooktown. From Cooktown, after coaling and refitting, the Ellengowan returned to South Cape.

'Mrs. Chalmers was well, and had been treated right kindly by the savages, they bringing her food, and telling her that she must eat plenty, so that when Tamate returned she might be looking well and strong. Mrs. Chalmers says it is well she remained, as the natives saw we had confidence in them, and the day following our departure they were saying amongst themselves, "They trust us; we must treat them kindly. They cannot mean us harm, or Tamate would not have left his wife behind."'

It would be difficult in the splendid record of nineteenth-century missions to find a more courageous and self-denying action than this consent of Mrs. Chalmers to remain alone amid a horde of cannibals for the sake of

Christ's work among them, and for the benefit of her Rarotongan fellow workers. When her husband left her there was no possibility of receiving any tidings of him until he himself brought back the tale of his wanderings. She knew him well enough to realize that places of danger attracted rather than repelled him, and that the worse the reputation possessed by any tribe or place the more likely he was to visit it. They had only a few weeks before passed through experiences which might well have unnerved the strongest. Chalmers came to know afterwards, from one of the chiefs, that again and again the murder of the whole missionary party had been determined, and that those appointed to do the deed had come once and again to the low fence which surrounded the rough mission home. They had only to step over it and rush in upon and murder the unarmed man and his wife. Had they done this they would have been hailed as heroes by local Suau opinion. But the same chief told Chalmers that at the low fence they were restrained by some mysterious thing which held them back. What was it? To the devout mind there can be no doubt. It was the restraining Hand of that God and Father in whom both His servants so firmly trusted, at whose call they had come to Suau, and for whose sake they were willing to lay down their lives.

Yet when we recall that Mrs. Chalmers allowed her husband at the call of duty to go from her, leaving her at the mercy of savages who were only just beginning to know them and their ways; when we remember that her only helpers were two or three Rarotongan teachers and their wives; that all her possessions were eagerly coveted by her savage neighbours, and that the bodies of herself and the Rarotongan

teachers would have been considered choice dainties
for a great cannibal feast, we marvel at her courage, at
her faith, at the quiet heroism which led her to endure
the almost unendurable because she did not think it
right to leave the weaker teachers to bear the strain
alone, and because she thought that if she accompanied
her husband the absence of both would injure the work
so well and so hopefully begun.

But though her courage and her faith rose supreme,
the strain upon her health was great. Probably some
inherent weakness in her constitution would never have
permitted her long to endure the life in New Guinea.
And there can hardly be a doubt that the nervous excitement of the thrilling scenes through which she had
passed during the last three months, and the intense
strain which she had to bear through her weeks of
loneliness, rendered her more susceptible to fever, and
hastened the end. Neither she nor her husband yet
seemed to have realized how serious her state of health
was; and when one remembers how ill-health depresses,
and tends to weaken courage, we find only more reason
to wonder that she was able to act as she did. There
is extant a pathetic document, a journal written in her
own hand of what took place day by day, during those
lonely weeks at Suau. We give some extracts, that the
reader may picture her in this time of hard duty.

'Saturday, February 9. A fine day, but the air is
heavy, not nearly so light and dry as the last three
days. Toudi and wife brought me to-day four bread-
fruit and a few red bananas. I gave him some fishhooks
before he left; he asked for them. My leg is very
much easier to-day. To-day a strong fence is put
round a small enclosure under the tree at the back for
our pigs, and to be ready for those from Port Moresby.

All well, except Tamarua's [1] eyes are rather sore.  We have not had one shower since you left, dear, but I think we will soon have rain.  The outline of the hills along the coast has been remarkably clear to-day, and it is now very close and sultry.  I feel very feverish, and all my bones ache terribly.  I wish, my husband, that you were back again, but I am sure, dear, that we have done a good stroke, and made a good impression by my remaining here.  I think the people see and feel that you have confidence in them, or you would not have left me here alone.  At any rate all seem very much pleased at my staying, and they are not at all troublesome.

'I told Tamarua to be on the outlook for strangers, who should get flour or a present, and either tell me or give it to them.  He has done so, but as yet none of any importance have called since you left.  How I wish I knew your whereabouts this Saturday night, dear!  Are you near Murray Island, or still at Port Moresby?  May our God bless and keep you always, dearest!  I do hope you are well.

'Friday, February 15.  Manuegu brought me some bananas before I was up.  I did not see him.  He left them for me.  Pi much better to-day.  Tamarua complains.  His wife came for medicine for him.  I gave camphor.  The wind is rising.  Clear night, no rain yet since my dear husband left me.  How long ago it seems, and how very much I miss him!  I keep as busy as I can, but still the time seems long, and I feel very lonely.  Yesterday and to-day Tamarua and Ngativaro have been busy with the gates.

'Sabbath, February 17.  Ngativaro and Pi took the services.  Both seem better to-day.  Tamarua is still

[1] One of the Rarotongan teachers.

ill. Head aching and very feverish. I gave him aconite, and to-night he seems a little better. This has been an intensely hot day. A great deal of thunder, no rain since you left us. A good shower would lighten the air. It is so heavy and sultry to-night. I have felt very ill all this warm close day, and oh, how much I miss my James, and wish I knew where he spent this Sabbath day! May God bless and keep us!

'Monday, February 18. As I was getting ready for bed last night, quite a commotion got up outside. The shell was blown, old Kirikeu shouting as loud as he could, and men and women were running and screaming. The noise wakened the teachers. Ngativaro went to see the cause. It was an eclipse of the moon, and a very fine one; the natives believe that many of them are to die in consequence of it, hence the excitement. Another intensely hot day. Great deal of thunder and lightning, air very close and sultry, no rain. I should like to hear it pour down.

'Tuesday, February 26. Tamarua a little better. I dosed and fed him same as yesterday. Tamarua Vaine ill. I was obliged to keep on the bed most of the day. None of us very bright. It was very sultry all day, with constant thunder. About four in the afternoon heavy rain fell, which relieved us all. With the exception of a very little on Friday, this is the first rain we have had since you, my dear husband, left us. Three long weeks this morning, dear, since you left me. When shall I see you back? I do hope very soon.

'Thursday, March 6. What a terrible disappointment we have had to-night! About five, great excitement. A vessel (not a canoe) close up to us. It was thick, and raining fast, so that we could not see far off. Of course all thought it was the Ellengowan, there could be no two thoughts on the subject. The flag was hoisted, the gate unlocked, and I got dry clothes all ready. When all was done the vessel was close to us, and oh, how disappointed we were to see a small vessel instead of the Ellengowan! It is Mr. Goldie's. He came ashore at once and had tea.

'Thursday, March 14. This has been a dark, squally day. Very, very dreary; rain, wind, and thunder in the morning and forenoon. Not much rain in the afternoon, but heavy squalls and very cloudy. What a stormy night! I wonder where my husband is. I cannot help feeling a little anxious about him. God grant he is safe and well!'

The extract just quoted concludes the journal. Mr. Chalmers returned from Cooktown about March 15, and we can imagine what the meeting must have been after six weeks of such strain. His thoughts had often been with the lonely wife, and in the joy of reunion the darker side of the experience was soon forgotten. The effect upon the natives was excellent, as Mrs. Chalmers had foreseen. They responded to her confidence in them. They brought her constant supplies of food, always impressing upon her, however, that she must be sure to report their goodness to Tamate when he returned. They knew that local custom rendered it imperative that he should make them return presents, and this, of course, he did. There was rejoicing in many a native hut, as well as in the missionary's home, when Tamate returned.

The voyage which had separated husband and wife was one of business. Chalmers felt it needful to visit Port Moresby and the stations thereabout, to see how the native teachers were faring. Since Mr. Lawes' departure they had been without superintendence, and experience shows that the South Sea teachers, as a rule, do well only if kept in frequent touch with the European missionary. The man Pi, referred to in Mrs. Chalmers's journal, was a native teacher quite above the average, and Chalmers himself has left on record a sketch of him that enables us to understand better how he could have left his wife alone at Suau.

' Pi was the first of the Rarotongan boys brought up under my care who desired to become a teacher. He was a quiet, good boy, and although not over quick, was a good plodder, and made progress. His father, Paniani, was a queer mixture, a man full of good intentions, but weak, and ever stepping forward, only to drift back again. He gave his son gladly to the work of Christ, and he ever spoke of his son, who was for Christ's sake preparing for foreign work, as an honour to his father. After some years Pi wished to prepare for New Guinea. He married a quiet, intelligent girl, and they both lived happily with us. After four years of student life he and his wife were sent to New Guinea. No one could ever say an evil word of either of them. During all the years Pi was with us I never once heard his name connected with any evil.

' He stayed with us for some time at Suau, and then I placed him at the Leocadie. But in a short time so many teachers died that I was forced to bring Pi back to take charge of Suau, and right well he did his work. There he lost his wife, and after some time he married the widow of one of our teachers, and she dying, he was again left a widower, and for a long time simply gave himself to his work. In 1885 he married the widow of one of the teachers murdered at Kalo, but she only lived a short time, and in 1887, when on a visit to Port Moresby, Pi died. He was greatly mourned by the natives of the east end of New Guinea, for whose uplifting he had worked hard during ten years. He was quiet and lovable, and yet very firm. These were qualities not found in the New Guinea savages, yet thoroughly appreciated by them.

'In 1878, at Suau, I translated a few hymns and two chapters of Mark's Gospel. For a long while these were all the literature we had to help us in our work. Pi gained a wonderfully correct knowledge of the language, and I urged him to translate the Gospel of Mark and to get the assistance of the most suitable natives. After a long time he finished the Gospel, revised, and re-revised it, and then, accompanied by the natives who had helped him, brought the manuscript to me at Port Moresby, and we together again revised it, and then sent it to Sydney, where it was printed. The New Guinea Mission could do with many more men like Pi.'

Having established the mission at Suau on a sound footing, and the heroism of Mrs. Chalmers having greatly strengthened the hold upon native interest and sympathy, Chalmers felt that the station could now be left for a time entirely in the charge of Pi, and of the other Rarotongan teachers. He had long been eager thoroughly to explore the coast-line from Suau to Port Moresby. Hence, on May 24, this time taking Mrs. Chalmers with him, he started in the Ellengowan to see as much as possible of a large portion of the New Guinea coast, never before visited by a white man. It is sufficient for our purpose to give the brief statement in which Chalmers summed up the chief results of this, the first of his many lengthy exploring expeditions.

'I went inland from Meikle Bay to Orangerie Bay. I explored inland at the back of Kerepunu, where no man had ever been before, and I visited the districts of Animarupu and Kuaipo. I have walked all along the coast in the bay from Keppel Point to the point of Macfarlane Harbour, and found two of the most populated districts yet known in New Guinea. I have been ashore, during the voyage, at 105 villages —at most of them a white man had never before been seen—and I had communication in all with nearly 200 villages. We have discovered and named several bays, harbours, rivers, and islands. We have had communication and mixed with tribes hitherto looked upon as fierce savages. We have had, on more than one occasion, to leave suddenly in order to save our lives. I am never armed, and frequently not an arm was carried in our party. We have been truly watched over by Him, whose we are and whom we serve. Mrs. Chalmers has accompanied us throughout[1].'

Chalmers did not remain long at Suau after his return from the trip just described. To understand his position at this time the fact must be kept in mind that he expected almost every month to visit England on furlough for rest and change, after nearly twelve years' service in the tropics, and in order to confer with the Directors as to the future conduct of the mission. Had Lawes been well enough to continue at Port Moresby he would probably have returned to England in 1877 or 1878. But Lawes had gone home, Macfarlane was contemplating doing so, and Chalmers felt that until a colleague had been sent out to relieve him the risks involved in leaving so many South Sea Island teachers alone in New Guinea were too great to be faced.

[1] See *Work and Adventure in New Guinea*, chap. ii.

Even at this early stage divergent views as to the proper working of the mission had appeared. Macfarlane, not unnaturally, was wedded to his view that the mainland was for the most part too unhealthy for the permanent headquarters of the mission. He held that these should be at Murray Island, that thither promising natives should be brought from different parts of New Guinea, and that these should, when properly trained and evangelized, become the evangelists of their own dark land. He also hoped Murray Island might prove a sanatorium for both the native teachers and the European missionaries. But Macfarlane did not stay in the Gulf Mission long enough to prove whether this scheme could be successfully worked or not. And in the end the view of Chalmers and Lawes prevailed, and many centres of work, with European missionaries at their head, were gradually established on the mainland.

In May, 1878, in order to see for himself exactly how matters stood in the Gulf Mission, Chalmers visited the stations in Torres Straits, the islands Mabuiag, Dauan, and Saibai. Of the last-named he wrote, June 5, 1878, 'Everywhere you look there is nothing but low sickly-looking land to be seen. It would be a pity to forsake these people now, and we can only hope that the work carried on by Mr. Macfarlane will be so blessed, that from amongst those brought to Murray Island some will be found who will become teachers to their own people, and to the people on the mainland.

'If Mr. Macfarlane is able to carry out his present plan of an Institution, it will be a great thing, and, I believe, the life of this branch of the mission. There are many difficulties, arising from difference in language and race, which will take a long time to overcome, but overcome they will be. I hope, before visiting England, to see all the country between Saibai and Yule Island, and so be able to give my opinion as to its suitability or non-suitability for missionaries. Mrs. Chalmers has had fever very badly, and is still suffering. If she does not get better soon, I shall send her to Sydney.'

Towards the end of June, Chalmers was back at Suau. Thence he forwarded to the Directors letters from the teachers, 'that you may see,' as he characteristically remarks, 'all is well down at our end. Do not fear, we shall not let go our hold, God helping us. The devil will be sure to bother us, but his powers must yield, and conquered he will be.'

From the correspondence of this period we select one or two typical examples. The first, a letter dated August 23, 1878, illustrates the methods adopted when placing teachers at new stations, and the risks involved, due, not unfrequently, to either the ignorant or the wicked action of white men.

'We arrived at Boera on July 15. Mr. Chester, police magistrate at Somerset, accompanied us. In the evening we obtained from Piri and the natives much valuable information about the Gulf, and the character of the natives along the coast as far as the Aird River. From all we learned I believe the Gulf could be worked from Port Moresby or Kerepunu easier than from any other part. Having filled up with wood, we took Piri and his wife on with us for a change, and left for Port Moresby on July 16, where we arrived the same after-noon. Three of the diggers had died, many were ill, and at Port Moresby; others were at the camp at the Laloki, and only a few were out prospecting. The

M

diggers speak in the very highest terms of Ruatoka, one saying, "Yes, sir, we believe that man to be a thorough Christian."

'We left Port Moresby on July 23, and Mr. Chester and I landed at Hula on July 24. We walked the following morning fifteen miles to Kerepunu, passing through Kamari and Kalo and crossing the Kemp Welch River. I arranged with the chief of Kalo to have Materua placed there. On our arrival at Kerepunu we found Tamarua, the teacher we had left there, very ill, and not likely to live. On July 29, Mr. Macfarlane and I placed Materua at Kalo. His reception was good.

'Some days before we returned from the west to Kerepunu, the people of one of the villages near to Keppel Point attacked a *beche de mer* station about six miles from Kerepunu. They threw several spears, and wounded one man very seriously. On the foreigners using their rifles they rushed to their canoes, and made off. I was truly sorry for this, as I hoped, notwithstanding the attack they had determined to make on us at Aroma in May last, to have left teachers with them this year. With some difficulty I persuaded an elderly man of Kerepunu to go to Maopa and tell my friend Koapena to come and see me.

'We all feared the latter would be afraid to come in, but were agreeably surprised on our return from Kalo to find Koapena, and another chief, with several youths, awaiting us. He came to the mission house, and after some conversation we cemented our friendship in the strongest manner. I gave him a tomahawk, and he took from his leg a bunch of white shells fastened together with human hair and tied them on my arm. He pressed on me to return to Maopa, and asked for teachers who could live with them as Anederea does at Kerepunu.

'H.M.S. Sappho being in harbour, the captain invited Koapena, the other chief, Anederea and myself, on board. Through the teacher the captain examined the chiefs, and found that the beginning of the trouble with the white men arose from a misunderstanding as to the price of fish. A boat belonging to the station was on the reef fishing, and a canoe came alongside wishing to sell *beche de mer*. The foreigners wished to buy all that was offered at once, the natives wished to sell it in lots, and were asking what was considered too high a price. Words passed, the canoe was shoved off by those on the boat, a boy in the canoe threw a stone and struck the boat, the foreigners seized their rifles, fired three shots, and wounded one man in the arm. When they got ashore the natives told all that had passed to their friends, and they arranged to attack the station that afternoon. Koapena, hearing of their intentions, prevented them from carrying them out. A few days after they got into their canoes, saying they were going to trade with the foreigners, went down, and attacked them. Koapena denied, as chief, having had anything to do with the attack ; it was only the young swells, he said, and the foreigners would be quite safe to return.

'At present our eastern teachers are too far apart ; and the eastern end being as unhealthy as the western, I propose leaving South Cape and settling down somewhere in the known healthy locality of Hula, Kerepunu, or Maopa.

'By eleven p.m. we arrived at Kerepunu to find sorrow established in the mission house, Tamarua having died about four p.m. He told them not to weep, as he was going home. Christ was near, he said, and his end was peace. He hoped just to see me once more before he left, and wished for our return. On the day following we buried him on the sand-hill at the back of the village. Anederea's influence is so great with the people that there was no difficulty in securing a piece of ground for burial.

'We left Kerepunu on August 3, and anchored first at Grange Island for wood. We anchored next in Mayri Bay. The natives would not allow us to ascend the hills to their villages, but received us kindly on the beach, and helped us to collect plants. Thence we went to Dufaure Island, and on to Port Dudfield. The natives were pleased at our returning to them, and were greatly delighted with the hoop-iron we gave them. We left the following morning, and after anchoring for an hour in Meikle Bay proceeded to South Cape, anchoring there about three p.m. We found all well. The natives were glad to see us. They had heard that I had been killed at Aroma, and they said that their sorrow at these tidings was great.

'On the Monday after our arrival, just after dark, we heard a great noise, and went out to see what was up. The men had determined to send away all the women, or to kill them, as they were an abominable lot. It seems that a woman of a village close by, whose husband died a few days before, had dug up the body, and made a feast for her friends of Brumer, Tissot, and Stacey Islands. The men determined to punish this action, saying, " If we pass this over our bodies will be treated in the same way." However, the women may be trusted to take care of themselves.'

At this early stage of the mission there was no intention of limiting work to the coast-line. Chalmers had already made one or two attempts at inland journeys, and had penetrated some few miles at one or two points into the interior. And these attempts were to continue for some years, since it did not become evident, until a later date, that the difficulties in the way of inland extension were insuperable. They are due partly to the nature of the country, partly to the climate, but in far larger degree to the paucity of the resources placed at the disposal of the Society by the Christian people at home. Costly as the coast mission has been, a still greater proportionate expenditure will be involved in carrying the Gospel to the inland tribes of New Guinea, unless the happy day comes when the natives trained in the various colleges and schools become, both in character and acquirements, equal to the great task of evangelizing their countrymen.

But ever since landing at Suau Chalmers had been eager to penetrate into the great region lying behind the coast villages nearest to his home.

A report dated August 26, 1878, gives very interesting details of the journey, especially of some of the curious customs of the natives who accompanied him. The main result of the journey is summed up in the sentence, 'I should not advise that teachers be sent inland at present.' A few extracts from the journal may be of special interest to the reader.

'Mr. Chester, the representative of the Queensland Government, was anxious to join our party, and I was glad of his company. He with Ngativaro, Pi, and Reboama, made up our company. We knew nothing of either the country or the people. We have had several visits from inland tribes, but could not discover exactly where they came from. A chief named Kuaiani was to lead us across, an elderly man and a staunch friend.

'We crossed the river while the sun was shining, and went on, shouting joyfully. At a place where a woman had died long ago each man took a branch of a tree, one also was given to me, and we ran along beating our feet and legs to prevent the woman from retarding our progress. All right; we passed the place, and then we went a little more leisurely. Later it was amusing to see the old chief march spitting at the rain which had come on, and talking angrily to it and calling upon us to exert our powers too.

'By half-past six we entered the chief's house at Diodio, somewhat tired and glad to rest. The chief and people were delighted to see us. The excitement was great, and our old friend had an attentive audience to listen to all he knew of these wonderful *dimdims* (foreigners). Stretching out on the floor alongside of the fire I slept the sleep of the wearied, only awakened now and then by our old friend, who was expatiating at various times during the night on the day's proceedings, and on the mighty war canoe, Sappho, which had called at Suau; that, he said, was nothing but a great floating land with a large population.

'We were now at the base of the range, and at a part where no mountains appear on the chart. A great work had to be accomplished, and before doing it the mountain spirits must be propitiated. We were made to assemble on the small island; an old cocoanut, which must have been carried for the purpose, was broken and scraped into a large leaf, several kinds of leaves were taken and cut small and placed alongside of the scraped cocoanut, the old chief and five others sat round mixing all together and chanting in a low, monotonous tone. When they had finished they stood up and gave a loud shout. All except the women and foreigners seized some of the mixture, squeezed it over their heads, chests, and backs, and then going into the stream up to the thighs, stood, and with hands closed and uplifted to mouth, and looking up towards the mountain, repeated some words in a very low tone, after which they all shouted and plunged into the water. The old man continued some time in the water after the others, in a crouching position, and looking steadily up the mountain and repeating something as if in prayer. When he had finished, and had come out, I asked him if it was all right. " Yes, yes, good, very good; they have gone, and Buniara (chief of Vakavaka) will be prepared for us. Pigs we shall eat on the other side of that mountain; armlets we shall put on, and there shall be more taro and yams given to us than we know what to do with."

' We had to ascend again, but before doing so incantations again had to be gone through. On this occasion a seed from a tree was taken and beaten until quite soft, and was then squeezed into the eyes of the chief. His eyes were soon inflamed. All decorated themselves with their ornaments and put their hair to rights, the old chief leading, and we foreigners behind, followed by the men and women. All the way up the chief was picking leaves from various plants, and then addressing them threw them down and went on speaking in a very low tone, not deigning to smile at anything. A bird settled on a branch a little distance ahead of us. The chief at once stopped and called out to it to get away from there as it was preventing our advance.

' We climbed to a height of 900 feet, then along the face of the hill to a village 900 feet above sea level. A number of men were seated on a stone circle; we were marched round them, the chief chewing viciously at betel-nut and squirting it out to right and left as he went along. When he had gone quite round he spoke thus to the men on the circle, " Here are great foreign chiefs come to see you, and here am I, Kuaiani, with a number of my people." Room was made for us foreigners on the circle, but Kuaiani went out in front of the houses. The men of the place left us and sprang out in front of the houses, one had a spear and another a native axe; they harangued and shouted, and rushed up to our old friend, and feigned an attack upon him. At one time men, women, and children were all shouting. Kuaiani took his tomahawk and threw it down before them. Another threw down two pieces of hoop-iron, then an old woman came and wept with our chief. All now appeared friendly, and our people and the people of the village mixed freely. It seems that some time ago an unpleasantness had occurred when a party from this village were at Varauru, and they had been settling their difference in this way.

' On our return I was sorry to find Mrs. Chalmers very unwell. Unless she gets better soon we shall visit Cooktown, when she may proceed to Sydney, and remain there for a few months. Do not fear, we shall not run any useless risks if we can help it.'

Later in the year he made another inland journey in which incidents of the kind just noticed occurred.

' I returned to the chief's house, and received a present of six earthen pots of cooked taro and a fine pig. Oh, how the people did scream with delight when I showed them my arms! The possessions which gain me most admiration are my nose and boots. That nose, and, oh, those boots! They shouted from ridge to ridge, " Tamate has come," and then the natives came in crowds. I bought taro for our party, but they brought more than I had hoop-iron to spare, as we had still the return and the coast. I said I could buy no more, but if they liked to trust me, all right, and when their chief came to visit me I would pay him. "Certainly, take all, and some day our chief will visit you, when you will give him the iron." The house was crowded, but a small space was reserved for me, where I enjoyed a good night's rest. By daylight we were off, and by another route, passing through several villages where we had to halt to be admired.

'When we got to the village where our boat and canoes were anchored, we found great crowds from all round waiting our arrival. A deputation waited upon me to allow the boat to be seen, and to this I assented with pleasure. One of my boys went off and brought her in to the beach, where she was examined all over and greatly admired. The excitement, though great, was of the most genial kind. We had some feasting, and by sunset were on our way home. We had chewing of betel-nuts and squirting of the juice to the north, south, east, and west, to keep off the wind. A streak of light, from under a small cloud, from a star, caused a consultation, and this turned out to be in their judgement the spirit of some woman, and our journey by sea would be prosperous. One of the lads was very ill with a bad cold, and had a severe pain in the side, this was attributed to a woman who had speared him. I, thinking it might be some old wound, asked when and how: "Oh, it was a spirit; our eyes did not see the spearing."

'In the moonlight, in Lawes Bay and round by Free Point into Farm Bay, we saw a romantic picture. In the background was the great mass of mountains, part of the Lorne Range, close to us was the bold coast with the surf breaking white upon it, and on each side of the boat was a large war canoe manned by savages. It was not unpleasant to hear them singing

translations of the hymns, " Come to Jesus " and " I
have a Father in the promised land." They cannot
yet understand them, but I hope they will soon.   God
grant that the day is near when these poor fellows
shall love our Lord Jesus as their Saviour and Friend!

' We have been in twenty new villages and two new
large mountain districts.   We have discovered a new
bay and three islets and four rivers.   We have mixed
freely with people hitherto thought to be great savages,
and above all, we have been with them as friends, living
in their houses, sleeping surrounded by them, and eating
out of the same dish with them.

' I hope Mrs. Chalmers will be able to return in
January.   The natives prefer her being here.   I believe
it is that they think it is all peaceful when she is with
us, and they have perfect confidence in her as their
friend.'

The separation from his wife, which Chalmers had
long dreaded, came in October of this year.   He took
her to Cooktown on the way to friends at Sydney.
The hope was that change of scene, rest from work, and
the kindly attention of friends, would lead to such a
restoration of health that she might be able to accompany her husband to England.   Chalmers had now in
his turn to endure something of what she had so bravely
gone through earlier in the year—loneliness in life and
work at Suau.   Chalmers kept at this time, evidently
for his wife's benefit and interest, a somewhat full journal,
which shows that in his own way he felt no less than she
had done the burden of loneliness and separation.

' Suau, October 18.   Your birthday, my ain lassie,
and God grant you many returns!   Sincerely do I
hope you are keeping better.   We had a rough and
unpleasant passage across, the decks being too much

lumbered. However, all got across safe. We made Dufaure Island, and had to steam up from there, arriving here yesterday about one o'clock. There was true sorrow when it was seen that you were not on board. The boat is much thought of. So, love, you are steaming along to Island Point now. How suitable for us both is the Scripture passage for to-day in the Daily Book, "The Lord shall be thy confidence, and shall keep thy foot from being taken." Our trust is in Him; nearer still to our adorable Lord Jesus; to live His life and to be filled with His love, to be lost to self; His alone, safe in His arms; rest!

'October 20. We had a comical scene in church this morning. A boy came in dressed in a shirt, and looking of the greatest importance. Soon quite a congregation assembled, and when the service was about to begin, in stalks one of Ngativaro's big lads with a jacket in his hand. He spotted the youth with the shirt, and ordered him then and there to undress. The boy had to get up, and was helped by several others out of the stolen shirt, which was handed to its rightful owner, who immediately set to dressing, quite a large number helping in the operation.

'October 22. Ah, darling Jeanie, it is dull coming home, especially when down with fever, and not having you to meet me! We set off in the morning. Pi, Reboama, Manuegu, and I in boat with five lads. The two war canoes, one on each side of us. All were armed, and there were fifty-one men in all. We got on to the reef near Varauru, and poled and paddled to Delina, where we arrived about three p.m. Delina is only a food land with a few houses, which are merely for the people when planting. All of us sat still in the boat for a long time, then Porokau went ashore, squirting the saliva from the betel-nut, and mounted the platform of the chief's house where I was when we called there in April. Shortly the people got cocoanuts, and threw them on the beach near to the boat. Then Porokau came down, and he, Manuegu, and I went ashore with our presents. The cocoanuts were divided, and all went ashore, leaving only a few in charge of the boat and the canoes. We bought several hundreds of cocoanuts, some taro and yams, and were soon feasting. Night came on, and some of us took up our quarters in the chief's house, a wretchedly small concern with a great smoking fire. Eight of us were packed together in a place very little larger than our bed. It blew a terrible gale of wind, and rain poured down in torrents. Morning broke at last, and right thankful I was for it.

'We left and crossed to Bonarua, but ague threatening me we did not stay. It rained and blew, and we made for Baibeseka (Tissot). We left the canoes far behind, I shaking all the way. Manuegu got me into a nice comfortable house alongside a fire. I was soon in a high fever. It was pleasing to see the kindly interest all the people took in Tamate, keeping out of the house, and inquiring every now and again for me. Poor people, they thought it a great honour that I should run into their place when sick.

'October 25. How it did rain this afternoon! It was well we did not go to the mountain to-day. Our Tepauri friends visited us to-day again. It is now pouring, and although still very early, I think I'll away to bed. The nights are long and dull, not a creature but myself in the house. God grant us both health and strength to live together for Him.

'October 26. I have had another dreadful attack of fever and vomiting, and am now better, yet my head is light; eh! my ain Jeanie, I do miss you much, very much. It has been raining all day. With the exception of colds all the others are well. I wonder where you are. May we both be safe in His arms, whose we are and whom we serve!

'October 28. I am in hopes of getting away in the morning for Oopu. I look forward to your being better to meet me in January at Thursday Island. If you feel well, and the doctor says it is safe, come on, but if you feel weak, and the advice given is to remain, do so, darling; do not risk too much, you are too precious to me for me to drag you in uncertain health into this climate. I hope the Directors will relieve us soon so that we may get home. God, our Father, ever guide us aright and keep us for His own glory only! How I long for more entire consecration to His service, that we both may evermore dwell in our Lord Jesus, our adorable Redeemer!

'November 30. We have just had our Saturday evening prayer-meeting. I hope to-morrow to be able to sit down at our Lord's Table. There are eighteen of us altogether, and it will be well for us " to do this in remembrance of Him." Glorious Saviour! would God we were more enthusiastic in our love, simply and solely His. How very formal we get in our routine worship, and how seldom we break away from self and mere form up into the true spiritual region, to be lost in burning love for Christ! Oh to dwell at His Cross, and to abound in blessed sympathy with Him and His great work! Then would the heathen wonder and inquire. God help us by His Spirit! We want the heathen for Christ. May you, darling lassie, be richly blessed this night, and truly enjoy the loving presence of Him whom you love and delight to serve!

'December 6. One year yesterday since we arrived here. The house is up, and it is a fine, large-looking place. Where are you, pet, and what are you doing? These are questions often passing through my mind. Under the shadow of the Almighty may you ever rest. Oh, how I do hope you are well and strong, and that we may very soon meet!'

The closing days of this eventful year were passed by Chalmers at Port Moresby. Thence, on December 31, he wrote to the Directors :—

'As to going to England I cannot see my way clear. We have eighteen stations in the eastern branch of the mission, and to leave these poor fellows at present would be cruel. I am in excellent health and good working trim, and so I shall remain until relieved. You can safely send out two or three young missionaries—men altogether Christ's, who will think nothing of a few hardships, and spurn the notion that the work here involves any sacrifices; I think the word " sacrifices " ought never to be used in Christ's service. Let them be men and women without any namby-pambyism. The latter—ladies—might be kept back for a year or two, and yet a man is none the worse off with his wife alongside of him. I hope to see mine here again very soon, as I get through more work and do it more satis- factorily when she is with me.

'I still have a strong desire to cross the peninsula to Huon Gulf. I have no wish whatever to turn explorer, but I do wish to know all that is to be known about New Guinea. But only in the capacity of a missionary would I travel.'

During January, 1879, Chalmers was busily engaged in visiting the old and in stationing new teachers along the coast. It was at this time that he made his first

trip westward, and that only a short one.   But it fixed
the plan which had been slowly maturing in his mind.
'The whole trip,' he wrote on January 15, 'was a most
enjoyable one, though we had wind, sun, and rain in
abundance.   What a magnificent district for a missionary
with a good staff of teachers, from Keokaro Bay to Yule
Island, and eventually along the coast to the Aird River,
where he would be met by the western teachers and the
black race.   What a grand prospect for the future, the
whole coast divided into small districts and worked
inland by English missionaries and native teachers who
claim all for Christ.   God grant we may be spared to
see that day !   Already the teachers are gaining great
influence over the savages, and are doing much to prevent strife and bloodshed, and we have reason to believe
that some who hear us are beginning to think of the
things they hear.   We need help—missionaries willing
to live amongst the savages, men and women who will
joyfully endure the hardships of the climate for Christ's
sake.   We must show the world that the Gospel is still
the power of God unto salvation, and that there are
those who believe thoroughly in it, and are willing to
endure much for its sake.'

The journal, under the date January 26, records :—

'I had sad news concerning my wife's health.   She
was no better, and the doctor considered her in a very
critical state.'

These sorrowful tidings were brought to Chalmers by
the vessel which also carried Mr. Thomas Beswick, who
had been appointed to the New Guinea Mission, and
who, in July, 1879, made Hula his station.   ' I was truly
glad to welcome Mr. Beswick to New Guinea,' writes
Chalmers.   ' His arrival is, I trust, the beginning of
a good time for New Guinea.'

The arrival of a colleague brought the return visit to England within the range of the possible, but the dangerous state of Mrs. Chalmers' health upset the plan. Before Chalmers could complete the arrangements needful ere he could leave his work, on February 20, 1879, his wife died at Sydney. So uncertain was the postal communication of those days that Chalmers' first intimation of his great loss was a paragraph in a newspaper shown to him at Cooktown.

The Rev. S. Ella, a retired Samoan missionary, resident at Sydney, in a letter to Dr. Mullens, dated February 26, 1879, gave some particulars of her closing days:—

‘ You will be grieved to receive the sad intelligence of the death of Mrs. Chalmers, although you have probably been prepared for such news. The medical opinion of our dear sister's complaint from the first gave very little hope of her recovery, though she herself was more hopeful, and spoke longingly of her speedy return to her husband, and to the work to which she was so ardently devoted. It was painful to witness the ravages which consumption was daily making on her enfeebled frame, till she was at length reduced to the utmost limit of attenuation, and passed away from utter exhaustion.

‘ Her mind to the last was bright and vigorous. She delighted to talk on the missionary work, and especially on scenes and events in the New Guinea Mission, regarding the prospects of which she was very hopeful. Had it pleased God to spare her to return to that mission, she would have proved a most valuable labourer ; but He has, in His inscrutable will, called her away to the heavenly rest, and New Guinea and the Missionary Society have lost one of the brightest heroines the mission field has known. Our sympathies and earnest prayers are drawn forth on behalf of the bereaved husband, who is working still far away from the mourners here, and not knowing that the fond partner of his toils has left him for the eternal rest.

'Our dear friend received every kind and loving attention from the family of Mrs. Mander Jones she could have found among her nearest relatives, and this kindness was continued to the last. Mr. Edward Jones has given her mortal remains a place in his family tomb, alongside of his two infant children, in the beautiful cemetery at Rookwood. A large number of friends followed her to the grave.'

Chalmers went on with all speed to Sydney as soon as possible after the receipt of this grievous intelligence. He then paid a flying visit to Dunedin, where his wife's parents and other relatives lived.

Two brief letters were written at this dark time from Dunedin to Dr. Mullens, one dated April 9 and the other April 23. In the first he writes :—

'You are already aware of my great loss, and to enlarge upon it I cannot. I write asking you to do me a great favour by getting the consent of the Directors to my returning to and remaining in New Guinea for the present. In my dear wife's last letter to me, she says, "On no account leave the teachers," and I feel I must return to them. I had left New Guinea to meet her in Sydney and proceed to England, but the Master has done His will, and I will be happy nowhere but in the work. I should have returned to New Guinea from Thursday Island, but had no particulars from Sydney, only a newspaper report that I received from one of the shellers. The Port Moresby and Kerepunu districts are in fine working order, and I long to see the same in the east end. Leave me then to bury my sorrow in work for Christ, with whom my dear wife is.'

And in the second :—

' I am leaving to-day for South Australia on deputation, and I hope to be in time at Cooktown for the Ellengowan. I must to work. It would have a bad impression on our teachers were I to go home now. They have suffered, and some of them have lost their wives, and with them I must be. The Master is with us, and all is well. Were I to go home now, the colonial press would glory in it, and say, " See how true our remarks on these English missionaries have been. Here is one who has lost his wife, and he must needs run home and leave the poor South Sea Islanders alone, although some of them have had the same trial to endure." I feel so certain of the future success of the mission that I am eager to return and have part in it. It must be all for Christ, and Christ our all.'

From Adelaide, on May 9, he wrote to Mr. Meikle :—

' I am at present in South Australia as deputation from the London Missionary Society to the churches. I do not much like the work. I hope to leave the colonies for New Guinea in July. At times the feeling of loneliness is depressing. When I left New Guinea I had hoped we should have been with you this month, but the Master has ordered and arranged otherwise. I have meetings every day, and preach twice every Sabbath. The people are remarkably kind and sympathizing ; still, I want to be with my savage friends. May I live more for Christ, all for Christ, and Christ all !'

The death of his wife was a sore blow to the lonely missionary. Those who have read the preceding pages can measure the greatness of his loss, and the suffering which it inflicted upon his affectionate nature. But it is most characteristic that the loss which would have disturbed and seriously upset a weaker man sent

Chalmers back to his work. In many cases such a blow would have been an additional reason for a visit to England; but in his ears there ever sounded the message from his dying companion—'on no account leave the teachers.' The colonial press was usually kindly and just in its references to mission work. Yet then, as now, ignorance and prejudice, and even hatred, based upon the realization that the presence of missionaries placed some check upon avarice and lust, sometimes inspired unfriendly references to the New Guinea Mission in colonial papers. The charge referred to by Chalmers had been occasionally made, and baseless though it was, he determined that it should have no countenance from his actions. And so, sad of heart, lonely and depressed, and yet sustained by the Master's presence and an unquenchable conviction that great things were in store for New Guinea, he returned to his work. Seven long years of splendid service were to pass before he revisited Britain. Years full of rich blessing, immediate for those whom his labours directly affected, remote yet none the less fruitful for tribes who may never even hear his name.

Chalmers reached Cooktown on his return journey on June 12, and paid a short visit to South Cape. On June 28 he wrote to Mr. Meikle:—

'I have again arrived in New Guinea, and cannot say how long I may remain. I feel happier in work here than I did or could do in civilization. I missed my dear wife very much when in the colonies; here I feel she could not be with me, were she alive, because of the climate. She is safe with Jesus. 'Tis mine now to live and labour for Him, more entirely His than ever. There is a great blank in life now. God help me to bear patiently my lot!

'We were attacked the other day by the natives of Port Dudfield, and were nearly taken by them. To enable us to get to the boat, several shots were fired, and one poor savage was shot dead. I hope to be able to make friends with them.

'We leave here next week for Port Moresby, where I remain for inland work. It is possible I shall leave this end of New Guinea to others, and go to the west to break up new soil. We may say in this mission that one breaks up, another sows, and another reaps. Ever remember me in prayer, 'tis all I ask.'

Chalmers visited and encouraged the various teachers at the east end of the island, and then returned to Port Moresby, whence he wrote : ' I intend remaining in this district for some time, and, if possible, will try to get inland.' He never again resided at Suau.

# CHAPTER VI

## PIONEERING FROM 1879 TO 1886

In July, 1879, Chalmers made an inland journey from Port Moresby in the hope of finding healthier sites for missions than those along the coast. And in October of the same year he sent home the scheme of what later on, under the care of Lawes and himself, was realized—the plan for a training institution at Port Moresby where natives of New Guinea could be educated to become the evangelists of the island. Chalmers' plan differed from that attempted in Murray Island, in that he proposed to admit only those who had come under the influence of Christianity, and who were beginning to gain some knowledge of its meaning and power. Students who had begun themselves to realize the power of the Gospel were likely to become, he held, earnest messengers to the heathen tribes.

In November, Chalmers and Beswick went on a venturesome trip along the coast from Port Moresby to Bald Head[1]. In the Ellengowan, on their way to Thursday Island, they sailed in front of this great stretch of coast-line on both the outward and the return voyage. Already the costly nature of the mission, the ravages of fever which attacked Polynesians and Europeans alike, and the difficulties which seemed to stand in the way of white missionaries reaching New Guinea, rendered

[1] See *Work and Adventure in New Guinea* (1902), chap. iv.

the extension and even the continuance of the mission doubtful, not only to home authorities and friends, but also to those in Australia. Mr. Beswick retired from the mission in 1881. But Chalmers never wavered. In a letter to the Directors, dated April 10, 1880, he wrote: 'I do trust that not one station will be given up. Better that we all should live on native vegetables than that one teacher should be withdrawn. I consider Port Moresby the most important station we have in this mission, having the widest field. Seeing that teachers have lived there for seven years, I think a white missionary might too. . . . I do hope the Gulf will soon have teachers. I believe thoroughly in concentration and also in extension. "Go!" Christ says, and I do not think we should ever withdraw.'

In August, 1879, Chalmers visited the Kabadi district[1]. 'The Gulf natives,' he wrote, 'are a dreadful lot, rejoicing in murder and rapine. They have sent us word they will return next season and kill and plunder foreigners and natives alike. I have sent them word to come, and that we shall be glad to see them.' As a reflection on his visit to Kabadi, Chalmers wrote: 'If one only had teachers, what splendid openings we have for them! To-day's Gospel with the natives is one of tomahawks and tobacco; we are received by them because of these. By that door we enter to preach the Gospel of Love, and I wish it could be done now.'

Even the Directors were under serious misapprehensions at this time as to the facts and conditions of the mission, and as to the direction in which true and abiding progress could be made. Once and again Chalmers wrote home letters which urged suspense of judgement and deprecated hasty action. Here is an illustration.

[1] See *Work and Adventure in New Guinea* (1902), chap. v.

On December 28, 1880, he wrote: 'May I ask you still to wait awhile for a report on the mission. Sometimes in the boat I have found it difficult to say whether it was the first streaks of dawn I saw or not, so I waited a little, and if the streaks of light increased there was no room left for doubt. We are in that state here. I think it is morning breaking, but I want to be sure. Natives do many things like parrots—pray, keep Sabbath, and come to services, so that I would not put too much trust in these doings. We have all these signs of progress, and something more, I think—a few who really pray, and whose lives are working parallel to their prayers. God help us to be faithful, and by our lives and teaching to preach Christ continually!'

In January, 1881, Chalmers paid his first visit to the people of Motumotu, on one of the earliest and one of his most famous peace-making errands [1]. It had been the habit of these fierce Gulf savages to plunder and slay their weaker neighbours along the coast to the east, especially the Kabadi district. It is characteristic of Chalmers that he should have gone. It is a higher tribute to his magnetic influence that he should have been able to persuade a boat's crew of eastern natives to go with him. 'Our boat's crew,' he writes, 'were considered fools, rushing into the arms of death.' Yet with such a leader they went. Strangest of all was the extraordinary power he wielded over savages who had never conversed with him before. Arrived at Motumotu, he said to the chiefs, 'You must not again go to Kabadi, and all along the coast we must have peace.' This was practically telling them that the serious duties and fierce joys of life must come to an end. Yet they meekly replied, and what is more wonderful still, lived up to

[1] See *Work and Adventure in New Guinea* (1902), chap. vii.

their reply, ' It is right; we shall not again visit Kabadi.'
Certainly, at that time, no other mortal could have gone
to that tribe, spoken such words to them, and obtained
such an answer.   Chalmers, in speaking of their past,
says of this tribe, ' No enemy ever dare come near their
villages, and their houses have never been burnt down.'
In the eyes of these savages it was not the least of the
marvels connected with Tamate that he came to them
for this his first visit at a season when no native canoes
dare face the wind and the sea for such a voyage; he
came, moreover, in the teeth of the monsoon, urged on
by the stalwart rowers who formed his crew.   ' I want
you,' said the chief, ' to give me some of that medicine
you use to make your boat go '; ' I use no medicine,
only strong arms.'   ' You could never have come along
*now* without medicine.'

On April 12, 1881, W. G. Lawes returned to Port
Moresby, to receive the warmest of welcomes from
Chalmers, and to inaugurate a new epoch in the New
Guinea Mission.   Lawes wrote home to R. Wardlaw
Thompson, who had, in succession to Dr. Mullens, entered
upon the duties of Foreign Secretary to the London
Missionary Society:—

' We were welcomed most heartily on our arrival by
Mr. Chalmers.   He seemed overjoyed to see us, and
especially Mrs. Lawes, after his long, solitary life here.
It would do you good to see him.   He has done an
immense deal of work, especially in travelling, and
establishing friendly relations with new tribes and districts.   He is much thinner than when I left him here
three years ago, but is looking well and strong.   He
keeps everybody alive, and has an inexhaustible stock
of energy.'

Chalmers' first letter to his old fellow collegian,

Mr. Thompson, in his new capacity as secretary, warmly congratulated him upon his important appointment, and still more the mission upon the return of the European missionary who had been the first to make his home upon the mainland of New Guinea. The letter is dated April 20, 1881.

'A greater pleasure I could not have than the news of your having accepted the honourable and responsible position of Foreign Secretary of our Society. We shall ever pray for you.

'On April 12 I had granted to me the wish and the prayers of the past few years in meeting Mr. and Mrs. Lawes on their return to this mission. Mr. Lawes will reside at this station as the central station of the New Guinea Mission. I have travelled a little in New Guinea, and fancy I know more of the country and people than any other foreigner, and I know of no place where our head station should be but here, and no better workers to occupy it than those who bore the brunt of first opening it up. We all, missionaries and teachers, feel better and stronger for the work before us since the arrival of Mr. and Mrs. Lawes, and have now a good hope of a bright future.

'Since the massacre in Hood Bay, reported by Mr. Beswick, I have visited Hula, Kerepunu, and Aroma, and am only sorry we have no teachers to restation there at once. I should have visited Kalo, but was afraid of compromising the mission, as it is possible they may be punished for the outrage. I fear we are not altogether free from blame. The teachers are often indiscreet in their dealings with natives, and not over careful in what they say. We have also been niggardly with regard to expense at times. A very few pounds spent at a station like Kalo in the first years would, I believe, have prevented much trouble and probably these murders. The Kalo natives felt that Hula and Kerepunu got the most tobacco and tomahawks, and that their share was small indeed. Instead of our buying from the natives all the thatch required for the other stations, and only to be had at Kalo, we told the teachers with their boys to get it. We meant well, and did this only to save expense. My experience teaches me that it is wise to throw all I legitimately can in the way of natives not connected with our head station.

'I have heard with sorrow that it is intended to spend large sums of money in the setting up of an Institution on Murray Island. The world's end will have come, and New Guinea will be no better for the Gospel, if it is to be worked only from Murray Island, than it was twenty years ago. For ten years mission stations have been in Torres Straits, as "stepping-stones" to New Guinea, but New Guinea remains, in that part, the same as it did eleven years ago. For the Torres Straits Mission, which must ever be considered as distinct from the New Guinea Mission, Murray Island is useful; as a sanatorium for us and our teachers, it never has been used by us, nor is it ever likely to be.'

The massacre referred to in this letter was a savage deed of cruelty and bloodshed committed in March, 1881, at the instigation of the chief of Kalo, by which twelve persons lost their lives. This was for a time a terrible blow to mission work in that region, and it tended to deepen the public sense of the ferocity of the natives. Four native teachers, two wives, four children, and two natives of Hula, who were with the mission party, were all barbarously slain. One of the murdered teachers was Anederea, who had been a member of the first missionary party sent out to New Guinea from Rarotonga during Chalmers' residence on that island. Chalmers has left on record a sketch of this man, in which he describes the massacre, and furnishes a further illustration of the high quality of these Polynesian teachers.

' Anederea was a native of Titikaveka, Rarotonga. He was the son of a good man, who took a great interest in mission work. The son for a few years had led a wild, reckless life. He went to sea on board of a whale ship, and on his return home settled down to orange-beer drinking and to other evils. I had not been very long on Rarotonga when Anederea professed conversion, and was received into the church fellowship. His life became altogether changed, and he was a good worker in the church. Through his teacher he applied to be received as a student into the Institution of which I was then in charge. I admitted him, and during his six months' probation found him both earnest and willing. He got on well, and when his probation was over I received him as a student. He worked hard, and was soon the best scholar I had.

' In his spare time I employed him in the printing office, and there he soon developed into a good compositor, and an all round man in everything pertaining to printing. He began to fear that I meant to keep him always at printing, and that he would not be sent to preach Christ to the heathen. So he came to me and resigned all connexion with the printing office, and said that he would have nothing more to do with it unless I faithfully promised him he should certainly be sent to the heathen.

' When it was decided to send teachers from Rarotonga to New Guinea he was one of those selected. He was in great spirits, and started at once to inform his Titi-kaveka friends. As a preacher he was well liked everywhere, and during his last year he had preached often at the villages on the island. His wife was a good woman, but slow and somewhat untidy, whereas he was active and very particular about his clothing. He helped me much in teaching, especially with the first year students, and they all liked him as a teacher. He was one of the first band of those who left Rarotonga in 1872. In the first few years he suffered much from fever, and lost his wife. Some time after he married the widow of a teacher, a very capable woman, and a very suitable woman in every way to be his wife. She was a Mangaian, and in the New Guinea Mission the Mangaian women proved themselves to be excellent missionaries' wives, and good earnest workers.

'The year before I reached New Guinea, 1876, Anederea was placed by Mr. Lawes at Kerepunu, and he and his wife soon learned the language, and the people became much attached to them. There were no baptisms, but the few children who attended school were more advanced than those from any other station, and at our first competitive examination his school stood first. It certainly was only the day of small things, but it was a good beginning.

'In the beginning of 1881 I was at Port Moresby, doing what I could to translate the four Gospels, when one morning Taria, the Hula teacher, came in to tell me that Anederea was very ill, and to ask me to visit him or to send the proper medicine for him. He was suffering from fever, so I gave the medicine, and sent Taria back immediately, instructing him to proceed to Kerepunu, give the medicine, and tell Anederea to come on to Hula, and that next week I would send the boat there for him. The medicine which was sent he took, and he felt better, and a few days after Taria went in the whaleboat to bring him with his wife and children to Hula. They called at Kalo on their return to take Materua and his family on with them.

'That morning there had been trouble between the teachers' wives and chief's wife, and the chief of Kalo and his party determined to kill all the teachers. The boat going in to Kalo offered a good opportunity for a big massacre, one which the savages considered a deed worth talking about.

'Taria landed, leaving the others in the boat. Anederea, his wife and children, were sitting aft, and Quaipo, the chief, stepped into the boat and sat down beside the teacher. According to the report of the boat's crew the chief began to talk about Anederea's sickness, and other things. A great crowd gathered on the beach behind the boat, and most of the natives had arms. Anederea wondered what this could mean, but the chief assured him that it was all right. The chief had stepped out of the boat, and then the massacre began. He seized a tomahawk which he carried in his netted bag, and struck at Anederea, who looking at him said, " My friend, surely you are not going to kill us." The chief struck another blow on Anederea's head, and he fell dead. All the other teachers, with their wives and children, were massacred. So ended a life of great promise.'

This savage deed created such a stir that the British Government sent Commodore Wilson, in his flagship Wolverene, to secure the execution of the instigator of the murders, the chief Quaipo [1]. The missionaries were strongly against this action, and at first refused to have anything to do with it. But when the Wolverene returned a second time Chalmers yielded to the

[1] See *Work and Adventure in New Guinea* (1902), chaps. viii and ix.

commodore's plea that his presence would prevent much bloodshed. Quaipo had sent Chalmers the genial message that he would not be satisfied until Tamate's skull adorned his *dubu*. Chalmers' presence acted as the commodore anticipated. He was able to prevent what might have been a wholesale slaughter of the Kalo natives. Quaipo and his men resisted, of course, but in the first volley fired after the marines landed the chief and three of his men fell, and then it became possible to get on terms with the people, and to explain to them the reason of the commodore's action. Chalmers, in referring to his action, said : ' There was no looting, not a cocoa-nut touched, not a pig shot, and not a woman or child molested.'

Lawes, who had left New Guinea somewhat depressed and discouraged three years before, found upon his return new life and hope and promise in the work. This, so far as human agency was concerned, was entirely due to the clear sight, the courage, the perseverance and the faith of Chalmers and his heroic wife. A letter from Lawes, dated April 27, 1881, shows how fully he shared Chalmers' views at this time.

' I was glad to find a marked improvement in the condition of the natives here. They have become honest, and no longer plunder us. Many attend school and services. Some can read well, and better still, some have been baptized and formed into a church. The appearance of the place, too, is a good deal changed for the better. It has a more settled look, and we may reasonably hope has less malaria than in the early days.

' I am glad to find that Mr. Chalmers thinks Port Moresby the most important station we have. Uninfluenced and unsolicited by me he expresses precisely the opinions I have always held from the first about it.

It is the key to the interior, and a most important political centre. I am very glad that the District Committee has asked me to resume my work here.

'I hope you will be able to entertain our request for help, and quickly comply with it. If we do not soon receive it, the whole of the Maiva and Elema districts will be lost to us. We are threatened with Roman Catholics there, and if they come, Yule Island and perhaps Redscar Head will be the western limit of our mission. We are not playing " the dog in the manger " in opposing this Roman Catholic invasion. The whole of the district which they threaten to occupy has close and intimate connexion with this place. The Elema and Maiva people visit us here annually, and the Port Moresby people go there once a year.'

Chalmers in his own vein, somewhat later in the year, October 22, 1881, placed his views upon the general conditions of the work before the Directors:—

'I prefer any amount of hard work here, travelling or otherwise, to writing letters or reports. As to our work, criticize it gently from the distance. It is still only planting time, and who can tell what the full-grown ear will be ? As for dashing reports, they are to be decidedly deprecated. Why, if you wanted a report to startle or astonish our subscribers and the public, and I had only the pen of a ready writer, I could not only startle and astonish, but I could arouse the whole body of our supporters, so that for a time they could think of nothing else than New Guinea. The work done during the last nine years is quite sufficient for this purpose. But you must look through comparison glasses. We have gone only on the old lines of Pauline and South Sea work, and have aimed at true, successful work—living, preaching, teaching, and knocking around amongst the natives.

We believe that even a few years so spent are preferable to many years of many men and the constant stream of expense that will be needed, if the plan of Murray Island is to be followed.

'A few weeks ago our trading canoes went right down to Vailala, near Bald Head. There they are to remain for several months, and with them is one of our baptized natives, who will every morning and evening conduct service for the crowd, and observe the Sabbaths with three services and no trading. He will, I doubt not, use every effort to teach the Gulf and the inland cannibals the truths of Christ's Gospel so far as he knows them. I shall be really disappointed if, when I visit them a few days hence, I am not able to report that he has done good service.

'I claim the coast as far as Bald Head for this district, and with Lawes I am prepared to work it in personal contact with Christ's servants living amongst the people. We think morning has dawned and darkness is disappearing fast, and we hope that soon the children of the light will be carrying that light to other and distant tribes.'

In October, 1881, Chalmers made a long trip to Elema [1]. This was a journey full of interest and adventure, and one which did much to open up that whole district to missionary effort. His account has been printed in full, but the following letter, which accompanied the long report home, has not before been printed. It shows that Chalmers was quite as alive to the risks and dangers of the work he was doing himself and urging upon others at this time, as he was to the excitements and the rewards. On November 15, 1881, he wrote to Mr. Thompson :—

[1] See *Work and Adventure in New Guinea* (1902), chap. x.

'I am well aware that there will be trials innumerable,
sickness and death, many dark clouds to pass through;
but what are all these to the assured results? Only in
daring much can we hope for much, and the greater
our hope the greater our success. With thorough Christ
enthusiasm, and in true sympathy with Him in His
great work, we may hope for much in a very few years.
Why should we be so niggardly in enthusiasm, men,
and money, and so nice as to trials and hardships?'

Towards the close of 1882 Chalmers and Lawes paid
a visit to South Cape, the scene of so many exciting
incidents and of such tender and heroic memories. It
was impossible to avoid noting the extraordinary changes
which the four intervening years had wrought. The
contrast in the condition of the natives between 1878
and 1882 was a convincing testimony to the fact that
the Gospel has lost none of its ancient power for the
uplifting and deliverance of man from savagery, cruelty,
and sin. From Port Moresby, on October 28, 1882,
Chalmers wrote to Mr. Thompson, indicating the great
changes that had taken place at his old home:—

'The death of heathenism reigned when we landed at
the east end of New Guinea in 1878. Many who then
longed and laboured for the spring have gone home to
God, assured that the day of joy would dawn and that
some, though few, of that band would yet see the first
signs of life. Generations of superstition and cruelty
had produced a people sunk in crime, that had become
a custom and religion, a people to whom murder was
a fine art, and who from their earliest years studied how
best to destroy life. Disease, sickness, death, had all
been accounted for. They knew nothing of malaria,
filth, or contagion as causes of death, and traced death
to the action of an enemy. The friends of those who

died had to see that due punishment was exacted. These people had no idea of a God of love, but only of gods and spirits who were revengeful and had to be appeased, who fly about in the night and disturb the peace of homes. They lived in gross darkness and cruelty, brother's hand ever raised against brother. Great was the chief who claimed many skulls, and the youth was to be admired who could wear a jaw-bone on his arm, as a sign that he had slain his man.

'All these things were changed in 1882. For over two years there have been no cannibal ovens, no feasts, no human flesh, no desire for skulls. Tribes that could not formerly meet except to fight now met as friends, and sat side by side in the same house, worshipping the true God. Men and women who, on the arrival of the mission, sought the missionaries' lives, were only anxious now to do what they could to assist them, even to the washing of their feet. The change came about in the same way, by the same means, and on the same lines as in the many islands of the Pacific. In the sameness of the Gospel there is always a freshness of true life, by which the means used becomes fresh and living, and those amongst whom the work is carried on feel the power of the life and are drawn to it. The first missionaries landed not only to preach that Gospel of divine life but also to live it, and to show to the savage a more excellent way than his own. They learned the dialect, mixed freely with them, gave kindnesses, received the same, travelled with them, quarrelled with them, made friends, assisted them in their trading, and in every way made them to feel that only their good was desired.

'The natives thought at first that we had been compelled to leave our own land because of hunger. The following conversation took place, shortly after our arrival, between myself and the people. " What is the name of your country ? " " Beritani." " Is it a large land ?" " Yes." " What is your chief? " " A woman named Victoria." " What, a woman ! " " Yes, and she has great power." " Why did you leave your country ? " " To teach you, and to tell you of the great loving Spirit who loves us all." " Have you cocoa-nuts in your country ? " " No." " Have you yams ? " " No." " Have you taro ? " " No." " Have you sago ? " " No." " Have you sweet potatoes ? " " No." " Have you bread-fruit ? " " No." " Have you plenty of hoop-iron and tomahawks ? " " Yes, in great abundance." " We understand now why you have come. You have nothing to eat in Beritani, but have plenty of tomahawks and hoop-iron with which you can buy food."

' It was useless to tell them we had plenty of food different from theirs, and that want of food did not send us away from Beritani. We had no cocoa-nuts, yams, taro, or sago, and who could live without these ? Seeing us opening tinned meat, they came to the sage conclusion that we too were cannibals, and had man cooked in our our country and sent out to us !

' We had not been long at Suau before we translated into their language " Come to Jesus " and " I have a Father in the Promised Land." Singing greatly delighted them, and often, when paddling their war canoes, they might be heard droning these hymns. When listening to them I used to think of a broken home, of comforts given up, and of attached people left far away, for what ? For savages singing, shouting, and ridiculing the little they had learnt in these hymns. Would they ever come to know Him whom to know would be their life ? Were they worth it ? Would they ever receive the Gospel? Would the superstition and cannibalism of many generations give way to the light, love, and brotherliness of the Cross of Christ?

'Even then I thought it was worth all the toil and cost; since in time these evils would all yield to the Gospel. God is Love, seen in Christ; this was the life-word we brought them. Day after day in duty's routine, not in hymn-singing, praying, or preaching in public, as some imagine that missionaries spend their days, the work was ever going on. The Gospel was working its way in bush-clearing, fencing, planting, house-building, and many other forms of work, through fun, play, feasting, travelling, joking, laughing, and along the ordinary experiences of every-day life.

'Only four years after that anxious time we left Port Moresby, and visited all the stations. We arrived at Suau on a Sunday. Morning service was over, and from the vessel we saw a number of natives, well dressed, standing near the mission house waiting to receive us. The teachers came off, and with them several lads, all neatly dressed. After hearing from the teachers of the work, and how the people were observing the Sabbath, we landed, and were met by a quiet, orderly lot of men, women, and lads, who welcomed us as real friends. The first to shake hands with me was a chief from the oppo-site side of the bay, who in early days gave us much trouble, and had to be well watched. Now he was dressed, and his appearance much altered. It was possible to meet him, and to feel that he was a friend.

'We were astonished, when we met in the afternoon, at the orderly service, the singing of hymns translated by Pi, the teacher, and the attention when he read a chapter in Mark's Gospel, which had been translated by him from the Rarotongan into the dialect of Suau.

When he preached to them all listened attentively, and seemed to be anxious not to forget a single word. Two natives prayed with great solemnity and earnestness. After the service all remained, and were catechized on the sermon, and then several present stood up and exhorted their friends to receive the Gospel. Many strangers were present, and they were exhorted to come as often as possible and hear the good news, and then again others offered prayer. We found that numbers came in on the Saturday with food and cooking-pots, and remained until Monday morning. They lived with the teachers, and attended all services, beginning with a prayer meeting on Saturday night.

'Thus the Gospel shows itself still the power of God unto salvation, the life and light-giver to those in darkness. Before faithful preaching and earnest living Satan's strongholds yield. But it is evident that mission work can be done only by direct contact with the people. If the Gospel is to be preached throughout New Guinea, it will have to be by living on New Guinea, where the people can see, hear, and feel the glad news we have to tell them.

'I am astonished at the apparent fear and nervousness felt elsewhere concerning our climate and the natives. The natives are savages, and are often very cruel, but once get to know them, and you love them, and seek their good. The climate is as savage as the people, and to it many have succumbed. But others, notwithstanding many attacks of fever, have for years done good work. When once acclimatized little is thought of a shaking fever attack. In a few hours it is over, and then the sick man is up and at work again. We have Eastern Polynesian teachers who have been on New Guinea for ten years, who have done good work, and are as fresh

for work to-day as then.   Is it impossible to find
missionaries who will gladly dare all for Christ ?   Not
the "life in hand" business, or the "sacrifices I have
made"; but men and women who think preaching and
living the Gospel to the heathen the grandest work on
earth, and the greatest of Heaven's commissions.   We
want missionaries like the men Colonel Gordon defines.
He says, "Find me the man, and I will take him as my
help, who utterly despises money, name, honour, and
glory; one who never wishes to see his home again, one
who looks to God as the source of good and controller
of evil; one who has a healthy body and energetic
spirit, and one who looks on death as a release from
misery."

'Leave the twaddle of sacrifices for those who do not
appreciate the sacrifice of the Cross.   Let the church
give her very best in heart, mind, and body, for Christ's
world work.   The best and greatest of all works requires
the best and greatest men.   We want men who will
thoroughly enjoy all kinds of roughing it, who will be
glad when ease and comfort can be had, but who will look
upon all that comes as only the pepper and salt, giving
zest to work, and creating the appetite for more.   The
harvest ripens fast, where shall we look for labourers ?
The Master has said, Pray! May they soon be sent!
The light is being sown, the darkness is breaking, the
thick clouds are moving, and the hidden ones are
being gathered in.'

The years 1880-2 were a period of great development
in New Guinea, but one of considerable misapprehension
at home.   Mr. Macfarlane was in England from 1879
until May, 1882, and had the ear of the Directors.
Chalmers and he differed entirely as to the lines upon
which the mission should move.   But such were the

energy and resolution displayed by Tamate that in the end the Directors came to see and to admit fully the wisdom and promise of his plans. And time has justified him. To-day the hopeful parts of the mission in New Guinea are the stations which Chalmers laboured so hard, during the years 1878 to 1882, to found and to sustain.

But early in 1883 the divergence of view between Chalmers and Lawes, on the one hand, and Macfarlane on the other, as to the method of conducting the New Guinea Mission, reached an acute stage. The feeling was intensified by the fact that hitherto the home authorities had leaned rather to Macfarlane's views. Chalmers held that a missionary should live in the closest touch with the natives he was endeavouring to uplift; that he should visit the native teachers who were holding the hard places of the field frequently, and stay with them at times as long as possible. He did not conceal his view that to effectively work the New Guinea Mission from Murray Island was, in 1882, an impossibility, and that the methods advocated by Mr. Macfarlane, though possibly good in theory, were not capable of useful practical application in that stage of the mission.

Macfarlane had also raised an objection to what he considered an excessive use of tobacco in the work. And at first sight it must be admitted that it is hardly in accordance with the views of the average British supporter and friend of missionary effort to believe that tobacco can be an effective evangelizing agent. Yet this is only one of the many illustrations of how unwise it is to apply the views and habits of an old Christian civilization like our own to heathen and to savage countries, and to expect to find that what obtains with us will obtain equally well with them. To an official letter from home on this tobacco question Lawes, on February 6, 1883, wrote an instructive reply:—

'The quantity of tobacco used is large in the aggregate, but it has to be divided among twenty teachers and missionaries. Each teacher uses about one hundred and twenty pounds of tobacco a year. It is really the currency here; houses and churches are built with it, boats are pulled by it, gardens and fences made with it; it is our wood and water, our fruit, vegetables, and fish; it is the sign of peace and friendship, the key which opens the door for better things, and (as I so often stated in England) the shortest way to a New Guinean's heart is through his tobacco-pipe. You will, perhaps, regret that so much tobacco is used, and so do we, but you must not think of the short black pipes which adorn (or otherwise) the corners of so many English mouths, nor associate it with its accompanying English vices.

'I have no predilections in favour of the weed. I am a non-smoker, I have never had cigar or pipe in my mouth, and until I came here had never handled a piece of tobacco. But I entirely fail to see either the harm done by it to the natives, or the possibility of substituting anything else for it. If we dispensed with the use of it, the expenses of this mission would be increased at least twelve-fold. We should have to give a tomahawk which cost a shilling where we now give tobacco which cost a penny. And even then we could not manage, for you cannot divide a tomahawk as you can a stick of tobacco. When we first came small red beads were in great demand, and formed the small change of everyday life, but they will hardly take them as a gift now. The natives say that when they come home from fishing or hunting, tired and faint, a smoke is better than a meal. The oldest man here, one of the chiefs, who received the teachers into his house when they came ten years ago, is a great lover of his pipe. I have told him sometimes that tobacco was no good, but he always looks grave and earnest, and says, " Misi, if I had no tobacco I should die." I should be very sorry not to be able to gladden his heart with a piece of tobacco now and then. Of course I do not know whether all this about its soothing qualities is true, but no doubt some gentlemen on the Board can tell you from their own experience.

' It is better, we think, to get the supply of tobacco as we have done, and let the teachers have all they want. It is impossible for them to do without it. They can only raise a very small quantity of native food, but they need never be without it if they have tobacco. The people will work readily in fencing, building, and all kinds of labour, and the women will keep them supplied with wood and water for tobacco, when nothing else will induce them to move. Of course you understand the cost of what they have comes out of their annual salary of twenty pounds.'

A year later, February 11, 1884, Chalmers, in writing to the Directors, dealt with this same matter in vigorous fashion :—

' I have read Mr. Whitehouse's letter to Mr. Lawes, and I am astonished at the ignorance of our mission shown by the authorities at the mission house.

' 1. Long ago I wrote to Dr. Mullens that missionaries should come here as single men for at least two years, and I am now more convinced than ever that I was right. The sooner young missionaries are sent the better, so that they become acclimatized, and get accustomed to the work. If we two old stagers are left alone much longer, what is to be the future of the mission ? So far as I know you have no other mission, unless it be Central

Africa, circumstanced as we are. Believing as we do in direct contact with natives, and in sharing with our teachers the climate and all dangers of the work, you must get men willing for Christ's sake to endure, and look upon all that happens as pepper and salt to missionary work.

' 2. I would say, leave the tobacco question alone; we only can manage it. I use the weed myself, and have found it a good friend in many strange places and amongst very peculiar people. Mr. Macfarlane has been leading you astray in saying that at the east end the work was done without missionaries or tobacco. The statement is altogether inaccurate. No mission was better nursed by missionaries than the east end. When Mr. Macfarlane was living on Murray Island, and afterwards in England, your missionaries tended the teachers that had been placed by him at the east end as they had never been tended before, and the teachers themselves have said such things to me as I had better not report. Tobacco is and has been as much used at the east end as here, and perhaps much more. Mr. Macfarlane's own teachers have again and again said, "Suppose no tobacco, no man come church or come see us." I am chary, very much so indeed, of missionary reports which do not state all the facts, and I join outsiders in protesting against the way in which facts are sometimes dressed so as to look well in a report.

' 3. We are friends of the native race, and shall ever continue such, and you need not fear that flattery or abuse will turn us aside. The latter we are having in abundance, and I am now often stated by vile tongues to be guilty of every sin in the decalogue, the latest charge laid to my account being that of murder. The annexation is no bubble, but will soon be an accomplished fact.

The natives have from the beginning looked upon us as their friends and defenders, and have never doubted it, and we shall never give them occasion to doubt it, in whatever position we may find ourselves.'

Another matter of considerable difficulty in the early days in New Guinea was the rule of the Society that all matters affecting a mission are to be considered by a District Committee composed of all the missionaries at work in that field. From such a committee the Directors expected to receive suggestions and guidance as to the best way of doing the work; and to it, in order to receive its collective judgement, all matters of difficulty which arise are referred for consideration. This rule has always been found difficult to work in New Guinea, because the missionaries are scattered over a vast expanse, and because language and other difficulties render what is suitable to one region quite unsuitable to another. And it required little foresight to predict that a District Committee, composed of Chalmers and Lawes on the one side and Macfarlane on the other, was not likely to be unanimous. So far were they from agreement that after one meeting in June, 1882, they for years gave up the attempt to hold any others.

This was not in accord with home instructions and regulations, and consequently on May 3, 1885, Lawes sent home the following letter:—

'I am sorry, in some respects, that the two branches of the mission are not drawn closer together, but the divergence was greater in Mr. Beswick's time than now; and the separation was just as great between Macfarlane and Chalmers, Dr. W. Turner, Dr. Ridgley, Mr. Tait Scott, respectively, as between Macfarlane and myself.

'In reply to your question about the non-holding of an annual committee meeting, I have only to say that, except the one in June, 1882, none have been held since my return four years ago. At the Directors' request a committee meeting was held on the arrival of Mr. Macfarlane, to decide details about the Institution buildings. The committee decided unanimously on Darnley Island as the most suitable headquarters of the western branch; but Mr. Macfarlane began immediately to put up the buildings on Murray Island. He had, no doubt, good reasons for this action of which we knew nothing. I only mention it to show what a farce a committee meeting is, where the two missions are so distant from each other, and the members of a committee so few.

'All matters of importance are submitted both by him and by us to the Directors direct, and what is the use of our considering matters of detail, when we are entire strangers to the particular plan which necessitates them? Mr. Macfarlane and Mr. Scott are strangers to our mission here and its needs, while Chalmers and I are equally so to their mission. A compact mission, where the language, agents, and country are the same, even though very much larger than ours, may be worked by a committee; but we have nothing in common except the desire to serve our common Lord and Master. Language, teachers, climate, people, all are different. When each mission has four members, then you may work each by a committee; but until then it will only be a form and a farce, and any attempt to unite the two branches will for some years to come be a miserable failure.'

In later years, when the number of missionaries had increased, the practice of holding district committee meetings was resumed.

A series of excerpts from the private and official correspondence of Chalmers will illustrate his life and work from 1881 to 1886. His work and influence in

**the** proclamation of the Protectorate and the Annexation —unique services rendered freely to the Imperial officers which filled up a large part of his time during the years 1884 and 1885—are dealt with in the next chapter.

*November* 14, 1881.

'My dear Pastor: If the Directors undertake as I now suggest to them, you will see there is little chance of my soon being home. The work only gathers as time slips along. Often "my spirit takes a flight far awa' to bonnie Scotland," but what does it matter! The sun in its zenith might go down before the shadows lengthen, and in its strength we had better work. And I am better here. Love to you all!'

*January* 9, 1883.

'My dear Mr. Whitehouse: I thoroughly appreciate the kindness of the Directors in their pressing invitation that I should visit Britain, if practicable, very soon. Ever since I left England, seventeen years ago, I have experienced nothing but kindness from the Mission House, and should be sorry not to comply with the wish so kindly meant, but I do not see how I can possibly leave at present. We are beginning new work in the training of native evangelists, and have also begun work in the Gulf. We expect a reinforcement of native teachers from the South Seas this year, and I feel that I ought to be here to receive them, and to see them settled in their new stations. I did hope not to go home until the Gospel had been introduced as far west as Orokolo, and until in the east the line of stations from South Cape to Aroma met. Thus the present is, I think, a very unsuitable time for my leaving the mission. I am in excellent health, and as well able to undertake work as ever I have been. Would 1884 suit as well? I think I might then leave for a time.

'I am deterred from going home also by the thought of deputation work. I dislike public speaking, and I soon sicken of hearing myself tell the same story or stories over and over again. Rather than go home engaged to do deputation work I would risk climate, savages, and sea and land travelling; the former in open boats, and the latter carrying my own swag on New Guinea. All I ask is to be relieved whilst in Britain of regular deputation work, and to be allowed to return here as soon as possible. I might mention that, seventeen years ago, I left England expecting never to return.'

*March* 9, 1883.

'My dear Pastor: The work increases, and consolidates, and helps to keep us braced. We opened the New Guinea College in the beginning of the year, and have already twelve students and their wives. These are Christian men and women being trained as evangelists to their own people. The great work of the future will depend on such men and women, and I hope ere many years have gone we shall be able to do without South Sea Island teachers. We have at present many important openings. We are much troubled by the labour question, having heard that the Queensland Government have decided on visiting our coast for the purpose of securing cheap labour. They will get no natives honestly, and those they get dishonestly will be paid for by innocent blood being shed. It is a hateful traffic; nothing more or less than slavery.'

*May* 18, 1883.

'My dear Hutchin [1]: You wonder if we shall meet. I hope so. I often live in the past and try to plan the

[1] The Rev. J. J. K. Hutchin was Mr. Chalmers' successor in the care of the Mission on Rarotonga.

future—only the one plan. All the future I leave to day by day, and one hope is that I may some day visit Rarotonga, and see again the people I loved and love dearly. We were ten years to a day on Rarotonga; they were happy years. I know all her nooks and corners, her mountain tops and valleys, and most of her vices, and much of her goodness, and I can only say, " Rarotonga, I love thee still."

' During the last six years I have known little of home life, have spent much time in queer places and with as queer people, have had a good share of fever, several narrow escapes from spears and clubs, travelled many thousands of miles in boats, and many, many weary ones on land carrying my own swag, and have lost what to me was more than life—yet I have never repented leaving Rarotonga, and would even more willingly now do the same, notwithstanding all.'

*August* 17, 1883.

' My dear Hutchin : I am again asked home, but fancy myself too uncivilized for home society, being a kind of New Guinean, and more at home with savages than veneered humanity.'

Mr. Thomas Ridgley, who had been sent out in 1881 to New Guinea as a medical missionary, but who had almost immediately retired from the mission, writing from Townsville, Australia, on August 18, 1883, after announcing the death of Mr. Beswick, says, ' Chalmers has been on a visit to me, and has been bad with fever. He was looking shaky, and certainly ought to go to England for a good holiday ; but his whole heart is in New Guinea, and I fear his zeal may lead him to defer taking a holiday until he is worn out with these repeated attacks of fever, and by the rough work he is always doing.'

In October, 1883, Chalmers started upon what was, perhaps, the most extraordinary of his many remarkable New Guinea expeditions. The reader is by this time familiar with the eager desire Chalmers had long felt to secure footholds for mission work at suitable stations along the Gulf of Papua to the west of Redscar Bay and Cape Possession. He had been able to pay one or two flying visits to this district, which was all the more attractive to him because of the fierce nature of the natives, and because it was only by extending in this direction that he could get near to the cannibals of Namau. Every October the natives of Port Moresby, who are skilled in the manufacture of pottery, send large native vessels called *lakatois*, formed by lashing several canoes together into one large vessel, laden with pottery, which is exchanged for sago. The Elema district is famous for its sago, and this annual exchange was at the time the only great form of native trade. Chalmers on October 5 started upon a voyage to Vailala, upon a great *lakatoi*, formed of four canoes lashed together, named the Kevaubada, containing all told, crew and passengers, thirty-five souls. The vessel on which he sailed was one of a fleet all bound westwards for the same purpose.

This was the first time in the annals of New Guinea that such a voyage had been made by a white man, and only a man like Chalmers could have endured the hardships involved, and yet have looked upon them only as 'the pepper and salt of life.' He of course knew the language sufficiently well to get along with the crew, and there were included in its numbers some Christian natives from Port Moresby.  The voyage and all that it involved are fully described in chapters i and ii of *Pioneering in New Guinea*, so we can dismiss it here in brief space.  On October 10, after a voyage of five days and nights, he reached his destination and landed. He wrote of it, 'So ends my trip on board the Motu *lakatoi*; I enjoyed it much; it was unique, and I shall not soon forget the kindness of all on board.  I was more comfortable than I could have been on board the whaleboat, in which I have often to make long voyages.'

From Vailala Chalmers managed another matter upon which his heart had long been fixed—a visit to Orokolo, by which he secured the friendship of its cannibal chiefs. He was welcomed by Ipaivaitani, the chief of Maipua, and a great *dubu* was placed at his disposal during his stay.  'The temple is the finest thing of the kind I have yet seen.  The front is about thirty feet wide, and the whole length about 160 feet, tapering gradually down to the back, where it is small.  In each of the courts or divisions are skulls of men, women, children, crocodiles, and wild boars.  The human skulls are of those who have been killed and eaten.  The daintiest dish here is man.  The passage down the centre, which I walked along, had the appearance of glazed cloth, with figures carved on it.  It was carpeted with the outer skin of the sago palm, glazed by the blood of the victims so frequently dragged over it.'

Chalmers' two native helpers, Aruako and Aruadaera, preached in this huge temple to a crowd of savages, real cannibals.  'It was a weird scene, and it was the most attentive congregation of the kind I have ever met.  They listened well.  Soon after sunset it began, and when I sought sleep it was still going on.

When I awoke, and the sun had preceded me, they were still talking and listening. Looking at Aruako, who was quite hoarse, I said, " Have you been at it all night ? "   " Yes, but I am now at Jesus Christ, and must tell them all about Him." Yes, my friend had reached Him to whom we all must come for light and help and peace. When Aruako had finished, there was but one response from all their lips, " No more fighting, Tamate, no more man-eating; we have heard the good news, and we shall strive for peace." '

We resume the excerpts from the correspondence of this period :—

*April 12, 1884.*

' My dear Thompson : We shall soon have an intelligent band of New Guinea evangelists, but to do without South Sea Islanders entirely would, I believe, greatly interfere with the church life in the South Seas. I cannot see how I am to get away at present so as to visit Britain; next year I may. If the Directors are anxious I should have a holiday, I would prefer spending it in New Guinea in opening up the way into the great interior for the Gospel. With a few South Sea Islanders I believe I could cross from Bald Head to Astrolabe Bay, or even much west of that, and at little expense. I have travelled over much more of New Guinea than any other man, white or black, and have always, when travelling, enjoyed excellent health.'

*April 4, 1884.*

' My dear Pastor: Another thing that has hindered me from writing is that I became a " Special Correspondent " and an " Own Correspondent " for one of the Colonial leading papers; an unenviable business, and coinless withall. Friendship led me into it. I am now sending a paper, but think of giving up. My papers have not been unacceptable, as I have been asked to become a member of the Royal Queensland Institute, and to allow my papers to be collected, and reprinted in book form for the Institute. So much for egotism.

' Since writing you last I have had several attacks of fever, the last, so friends thought, about ending all. Now I am in excellent health, and, except my knees, strong and well, as of long ago. Some time ago we had newspaper correspondents doing New Guinea, and one of them got into trouble with the natives, shot one dead and wounded others. Well, I determined on making peace and friendship, and started for inland. Other tribes hearing of my visit begged for my assistance in bringing them together and making peace.

' It was a long, long, weary, wet walk, but I accomplished all, and returned in a week. I walked, say 170 miles, climbed in all about 20,000 feet, and in rain, crossing rivers and mountain torrents. My natives were dead beat, and I had to leave them a stage from Port Moresby. We preach the Gospel in many ways; one of our best at present is making peace between tribes.

' God is blessing His work, and one after another seeks to be taught. It would gladden your heart were you to see the church here, especially on Communion Sabbath, when many earnest men and women commemorate our Lord's death. Our college prospers. We have fourteen students, who are making good progress in knowledge. Mr. Lawes takes this department. I open up, and superintend outside—a kind of Bohemian. The school work does not flourish as I should like to see it; our teachers do not take kindly to school teaching. Teaching children A, B, C is dry, uninteresting work, but when faithfully done the results are good payment for the labour.'

*April* 19, 1884.

'Dear Hutchin: These deaths we feel very much, and more so that the others are sick, and are apt to think only of dying[1]. To keep them up needs more than praying and Scripture reading; they need constant rousing, and sometimes I have to say very hard things. Ezekiela was simply dying, two men and two women were in constant attendance—they turned him, bathed him, held water for him to drink. I simply stopped it all; told them he had some strength left, and must use it. He bathed himself, rose, and took his own medicine from me, sat up, went outside, and now is much better. Others are the same, only they have heard of what I said to Ezekiela, and they are on their guard. I know the feeling well—simply refuse to taste medicine and die. I have just had the women walking around the premises. No doubt they think it hard now, but afterwards they will be thankful.'

*July* 27, 1884.

'Dear Hutchin: We have had the man-stealers at the East End; but I hope their day is ending. They abuse me villainously, for which I am glad. One paper says I teach the natives that white men are cannibals. I could truthfully teach them that they are fiends incarnate. I shall keep at it with home and the colonies until the horrible traffic is stopped.'

*December* 24, 1884.

'Dear Thompson: It is with pleasure I can report having successfully placed nine New Guinea evangelists,

---

[1] This letter refers to sickness and death very prevalent at the time among the Rarotongan native teachers in New Guinea.

the firstfruits of our college. Before Lawes left for
Sydney they were ordained to the work, and the
services then held were certainly the most impressive
yet held on New Guinea. To all classes of natives they
were attractive and enjoyable, as being the first of the
kind ever held, and for the first time they beheld their
own children set apart to preach the Gospel amongst
themselves and the other tribes. Men and women came
in from the various villages round and spent several
days at Port Moresby. The young men and their wives
who were ordained had, before coming to college, spent
some years in their own villages with the teachers, and
came highly recommended. During the time they have
been with us, more especially with Lawes, they made
good progress, lived godly lives, and did good work at
neighbouring villages.'

*December* 17, 1884.

'Dear Hutchin: I shall not be long in England, as
I dread the winter. For some years before I left home
I suffered much from bronchitis, and at times it was
thought I should lose the number of my mess. Some
thought the Directors were making a grand mistake in
sending me out, and my dear wife's friends thought her
married years would be few indeed. Winter was cruel
to me, and I dread it. Even here our very cold weather
I dislike, but luxuriate in our hottest. A few family
matters I can settle in a month, see a few friends, and
then—back to New Guinea. Deputation work I detest
with all my nature, and only hope they will not press
me into it.

'I want you to send us young men who will gather
around them the youth and manhood of New Guinea.
This ought to be one of the greatest missions that ever
yet has been worked. We here, you there. Your best

in every way, representing you here, and carrying on
a work hitherto untried in our South Sea Missions.
Have centre schools thoroughly conducted, and a large
college receiving from these schools. Do not laugh,
brother; if I do not see it I shall not die happy, I do
not care where it is nor how it is—if by a club or a spear,
I shall feel it even then.'

*January* 16, 1885.

'Dear Hutchin: It is with great sorrow I have to
report the sudden death of our good teacher Mataio, at
South Cape, on December 20, a fortnight after I left
him. Brother, get the old father, Tukarakia, and for
my sake tell him kindly. I liked Mataio; though slow,
he was yet doing good, earnest, abiding work. From
many miles the once savage and cannibal came to his
funeral, and wept sincerely for him as for a father. The
doctor of the Raven [1] thinks he must have died of
typhoid fever.

'I am now on my way to Port Moresby, via Townsville and Cooktown, and hope to be at work again in
a fortnight. The Government officials say they cannot
do without me, and that I must accompany them, because
of the natives. Fancy Tamate's name known near Huon
Gulf. It must have travelled across country.'

*April* 3, 1885.

'Dear Hutchin: Some of the teachers (Tahitian) are
causing trouble. Because natives go fishing on Sunday
their canoes are broken up. I have made the teachers
pay for each canoe which they have touched. A more
serious charge, which I am now looking into, is that of
firing off a gun on Sunday to frighten the natives, and

[1] This letter was written whilst Chalmers was on board H.M.S.
Raven helping in the work of proclaiming the Annexation.

in doing so three small shot lodged in a woman. Would that our teachers could see the folly of force, and try to work as the Great Master Himself did. They look down upon the New Guineans, and bounce them too much. They know my horror of any bounce, and detestation of any force, and they pay the natives not to tell me. I shall likely send some back next time the John Williams comes. Tell the young men that it is by kindness, meekness, and humility in Christ that the best work is done, and may those whom you send come resolved to work in this spirit. God help you, brother, to a right selection.'

*May* 19, 1885.

'My dear Pastor: You will get a book on New Guinea[1], the most of which will be old to you. It is Mr. Gill's doing. He begged me to allow him to collect and publish some of my papers and reports. I have objected; still I fear I shall have to yield. The great Russian scientist and traveller, my friend Baron Maclay, writes saying that it will be a crime if I do not publish.'

The next two letters possess special interest. It was noted in chapter ii that a bosom friend of the first Mrs. Chalmers was Miss Elizabeth Large of Leeds. For many years correspondence had lapsed, but the publication of Chalmers' book led to its renewal. Miss Large had for a number of years been Mrs. Harrison, and her home was at Retford in Nottinghamshire.

*July* 3, 1885.

'Dear Lizzie: I have often wondered how I could get your address, so at last you send it yourself. You are the dear good lassie of old, and your charming letter has

---

[1] The reference is to *Work and Adventure in New Guinea,* the first edition of which was published in 1885.

done me good.   I got it when I came off a long tramp
(300 miles).   Eh, lassie, did you but know its good
refreshing effect you would have written years ago to
this lonely wanderer.   It is so good in you to write me
of your sorrows as well as your joys.   I really will not
write you a long letter just now, as I leave in the
morning in the schooner for the south-east end of New
Guinea.   I have never forgotten you, and there is still
that old love here for the dear little sister of Leeds.

'How I wish I had written you after Jeannie went
home, that is, since we parted, nearly seven years ago;
perhaps a wee letter now and then would have been
a comfort when those big sorrows were yours.   You
have had a long refining.   *He* was sitting by and saw
it all, and in the future all the questionings of your
aching heart will be answered.

'I hoped to be in England this year, but cannot now,
and at present cannot say when.   Had Jeannie lived we
should have been home long ago.   When she died in
Sydney I could not leave the mission.   My first intimation of her death was in a newspaper; she was then dead
four weeks.   I went and saw her resting-place, and then
went to her friends in New Zealand, and back here.
Lizzie, dear, in work for Christ I tried to forget my
sorrow; the wound remains, and will bleed.

'You ask for your old place in my heart—here it is,
and there it will ever remain.   Yes, teach your bairn to
call me uncle, and some day—soon, I hope—he will see the
old bronzed fellow, older than when you knew him, with
many grey hairs now, but, I think, with the old young
heart; at all events the same old heart to his sister
Lizzie.

'You would not know me, so some day when a very
unclerical, bronzed wayfarer knocks at your door, and

you ask his name, and he answers Tamate, take him in and just try and spoil him. For the last eight years my life has been a peculiar one—somewhat rough. I have had much fever, but always got over it. I have much to be thankful for; from everybody I receive much kindness. Savage and non-savage, white and black, all are kind.'

*February* 3, 1886.

'My very dear Lizzie: A thousand thanks for your kind and loving letter and for the home gift. Yes, I shall go to Retford, and perhaps sooner than you think. I am a queer mortal, always ready for a start, and why not some day start for England and say nothing about it? I am much of a Bohemian now, and I fear you will be terribly disappointed in me. I smoke as of old but not much. Port Moresby is my headquarters, and Mr. and Mrs. Lawes do their level best to make me comfortable; but for them, and long ago the cold earth was my bed, having gone on unnoticed and unwept except by my dusky Papuans and true, friendly Polynesian teachers.

'Before Jeannie left for Sydney, her last visit when she went to die, she left instructions with our teacher's wife here to look well after Tamate, to take care of him and his clothes; and faithfully did that poor woman carry out her trust, but it ended last Sunday night; after two days illness she died. She was a splendid teacher's wife, and a true woman—the best we had. I just returned on the Saturday, so was in time to see her die.

'I am getting very old and rheumatic, stiff as an old horse and lazy as one, and yet I must visit that land of damp, mists, and frost, that strange land wherein I shall be a stranger. I feel somewhat Paulish. I am in a strait, want to go and don't want to go. I should like to take you unawares, but I fear there is no chance of that.

'You know I travel a great deal over old ground and opening up new, a kind of vagrant, and few can tell where to find me. At times I am quite a vegetarian, at others nearly so, still, I enjoy life and good living occasionally. Here of course we have every comfort and luxury. Jeannie will have gone home seven years on the 20th inst., and since then I have not cared for home or a home, and have made home wherever I happen to be, still speaking of Mr. and Mrs. Lawes' home as my home.

'We are now in the middle of our north-west season, and have much sickness. During the last fortnight many natives have died and a great many are now ill, and I fear if the present close weather continues it will spread.

'Mr. Macfarlane has gone home. I was away when he was here, and so missed him, for which I am sorry. You say, you are plump and nearly forty. I am plump and over forty, quite the old youth. We are daily expecting new teachers from the South Seas, and on their arrival I shall be able to arrange for going " home." I do not expect to be long away from New Guinea.

'You will have seen in the papers that our new Commissioner, General Scratchley, is dead. I was with him a great deal, and knew him well and liked him much. To us he is a great loss. Had he lived I was to be with him this year, revisit old places and open up new country; that is ended, and so I am open for England. During last trip with the General I saw a good deal of the north-east coast as far as the German boundary, and we made some very interesting discoveries. Perhaps some day I may chat them over with you and yours.'

The proclamation, first of the Protectorate and later of the Annexation, postponed for a considerable time Chalmers' long-delayed furlough; and the services he was able to render to the officers of the Imperial Government form the subject of the next chapter.

# CHAPTER VII

## THE ANNEXATION OF NEW GUINEA

THE successive stages in the process by which South-Eastern New Guinea was formally annexed to Great Britain are clearly set forth in the correspondence of Lawes and Chalmers. Both men were deeply interested in this movement, because they had the welfare of the natives at heart. They were also able to render services of the highest value to the Government officials, because they were well acquainted with native habits and modes of thought, they had acquired considerable knowledge of New Guinea languages, and they were on terms of friendship with many of the chiefs. They were able, as no others could, to make fairly intelligible to the chiefs and their people the meaning of ceremonies that would, without their help, have appeared to the natives mere noise and dumb show.

The outlook was at first dark. The view that New Guinea was rich in gold, so situated as to be fairly accessible, led Queensland to cast a covetous eye upon her great island neighbour. The record of Queensland in regard to native races is very black. Everywhere in Australia the native has been treated with cruelty; but the most atrocious crimes against him have been perpetrated in Queensland. That colony's record in the matter of kidnapping Polynesians and exacting from them forced labour is also as bad as it can be. When, therefore, it seemed likely that New Guinea would fall under the control of Queensland the hearts of Lawes and Chalmers sank within them. They knew this meant either indifference to or absolute disregard of the human rights of the natives; the establishment of land laws wholly in favour of the white and wholly to the detriment of the black man; the tolerance and even the furtherance of the drink traffic; and a host of lesser evils. But happily this catastrophe was averted by the action of the Imperial Government.

A letter from Mr. Macfarlane, dated April 8, 1883, describes the first stage in the series of events which finally led to annexation.

'You will probably be surprised to learn that Mr. Chester, the Police Magistrate at Thursday Island, who has been for some time urging upon the Queensland public and Government the desirability of annexing New Guinea, left Murray Island a week ago in the Government schooner Pearl to take possession for Queensland (with the sanction of the Home Government) of that portion of New Guinea not claimed by the Dutch. He will probably be appointed to represent the Government there, and we may very soon hear of Queensland labour vessels on the New Guinea coast. It appears to be the labour question that has led to annexation. I fear that our mission will suffer.'

Mr. Lawes continues the record in a letter from Port Moresby, dated April 7, 1883.

'On Tuesday last, the 3rd inst., the Government cutter from Thursday Island arrived here. Mr. Chester, the resident Police Magistrate of Thursday Island, was on board, and soon informed us of the object of his visit. He had been sent by the Queensland Government to take possession of New Guinea in the name of the Queen. Mr. Chester is an old friend of ours, especially of Mr. Chalmers. He showed us his instructions, according to which the Queensland Government had telegraphed home offering to bear the expense of New Guinea for a few years if annexed, and had received a reply accepting the proposal on those terms. Mr. Chester was immediately instructed by telegram to come here and take possession.

'On Wednesday morning at ten o'clock Mr. Chester hoisted the Union Jack at our flagstaff, and it was saluted by the two guns of the Pearl.

'After the ceremony Mr. Chester made a present to the natives, and we explained to them as best we could the nature of the proceedings. We cannot understand them ourselves. Annexation we were in a measure prepared for, although we did not wish it. But that an Australian colony should be allowed to take this step is to us most surprising. Here is the largest island in the world, to which Fiji and even New Zealand are a mere nothing, annexed by a Police Magistrate who comes in a little tub of a cutter! There must be some mistake somewhere. We would much rather not be annexed by anybody, but if there was any probability of a foreign power taking possession of New Guinea, then let us have British rule: but as a Crown Colony, not as an appendage to Queensland. Nowhere in the world have aborigines been so basely and cruelly treated as in Queensland—the half has never been told—and are the natives of New Guinea to be handed over to the tender mercies of the men who have done these deeds?'

The report of this transaction, which Mr. Chester sent to the Chief Secretary of Queensland, is dated April 7, 1883. In it he states:—

'At ten a.m. on the 4th instant I took formal possession, in Her Majesty's name, of all that portion of

New Guinea and the adjacent islands not already in occupation by the Dutch, and read the accompanying proclamation in presence of about 200 natives and thirteen Europeans. A royal salute was fired from the Pearl, and at the close of the proceedings three cheers were given for Her Majesty the Queen. I then, in presence of the people, recognized Boé Vagi as head chief of Port Moresby, and gave the flag into his charge, until such time as an official should be sent to represent the Government. Mr. Lawes kindly explained the meaning of the ceremony to the people, and assured them that they would remain in undisturbed possession of their lands. A short impressive prayer by Mr. Lawes terminated the proceedings, after which about £50 worth of trade was distributed to the heads of families by Ruatoka, the Rarotongan teacher, in the name of Her Majesty. In the afternoon a long procession filed up the hill to the mission-house, each man bearing some small present, such as two or three spears, an armlet, a grass petticoat, or an ornament, and after this the Europeans present, the teachers and their wives, and Boé Vagi, were invited to a banquet, given by Messrs. Lawes and Chalmers, at which, after the usual loyal toasts, "Prosperity to the latest gem added to the British Crown" was drunk, and the health of the missionaries who had done so much for the civilization of the people.'

This event greatly exercised the minds of both Lawes and Chalmers. The former's view of the probable influence of Queensland government is shown in the letter quoted above. Chalmers was as fully alive as his colleague to the probable troubles in store for the native tribes he had so long laboured to benefit. On June 25, 1883, he wrote from Cooktown :—

'Having had a bad attack of fever in the beginning of May, it was thought advisable that I should take a change for a few weeks. I left Port Moresby on May 21 for Thursday Island, intending to proceed to Cooktown, and there await the arrival of the Ellengowan. Before leaving Port Moresby we thought that if I could manage a visit to Brisbane on the matter of the annexation and the labour question I might do some good.

'When at Thursday Island I found there was good time to go south and spend a week in Brisbane to see, if possible, leading men. A few days with my old friends Mr. and Mrs. Chester soon set me right, and a vessel coming in with Baron Maclay on board I took ticket for the south. On our way down we wrote a conjoint letter to Earl Derby on the annexation and labour question, expressing hopes that the native rights would be respected, spirits prohibited, and that strict orders would be given that no natives were to be taken away as labourers.

'On my arrival in Brisbane I saw the Premier, and spent a long evening with him. I found him a stubborn, good, honest Scotchman, anxious that justice should be done, and willing, if coolies could be obtained, that the labour traffic in natives should be stopped. I had an interview also with the Leader of the Opposition, and saw the editors of the leading newspapers, and many other men of more or less influence. I also addressed two large meetings, at one of which the editor of the leading paper took the chair.'

A letter written a few months later from Port Moresby, September 21, 1883, shows how rapidly the fears of Chalmers and his colleague were realized.

'Mr. Lawes will write you on the land swindle. Just

imagine an acre of fine sugar land bought for one penny!
No native understands what has been done, and when
informed what the transaction really means they look
aghast. We are quite prepared for any amount of
abuse, but are determined to oppose in every way this
land scheming. No native should be allowed to part
with an inch of land, and the British Government
should at once say so. Rather forfeit all we own than
permit the natives to be swindled by the glitter of new
tomahawks. I know natives, and understand their
politics, and I think no native or chief has any right to
part with his or her lands, and certainly not until there
is some responsible government on the island. Whatever you do, do boldly on Lawes' letter. Urevado
alone is chief, alone the landowner in this transaction,
and he never was seen, and received no payment or
present. Paru, the man who is supposed to have sold
the land, is no chief, holds no land, and has no right to
part with any, and all the other natives are in the same
position. I have written to a friend who has influence
with some in authority, and hope when all is tried the
land sharks will be ousted.

' Teachers are not only preachers of the Gospel, they
are also checks on these white spoilers. I do not see
how I can leave at present. I am called the " tyrant missionary," because the natives ever appeal to me, and
wish to act as I say. My tyranny is well liked by the
natives. I expect infinitely more abuse here than I had
in the South Pacific, only it will not affect me now as it
did then. I was then young, now am old, and accustomed to it. As then I will do the right, and take the
consequences, leaving all with Him whom I seek
to serve.'

In a letter written to Rarotonga the following day,

Q

September 22, Chalmers again refers to this land swindle :—

'Dear Hutchin: Let all who seek the good of the young men determine to stop strong drink, native and foreign.    Surely the fear of the white man has gone. Brother, prepare yourself for abuse; but never mind, do the right for God and man, and you must succeed. I like opposition, and I like hard knocks.    We are now entering into land troubles.    Two men representing a Sydney syndicate have bought 15,000 acres of splendid sugar land for one penny per acre, and have never even seen the real owner.    We are bringing the whole transaction to the light.    I am a "tyrant missionary"; I try to make myself King of New Guinea; the natives are afraid of me.    I must be put down.    Capital, I like the fight, and know that right must eventually win the day.    The people who sold the land have had no teachers, but have been frequently visited by me, and I certainly have great influence over them.

'It is impossible to say when I shall leave.    I have become sort of savage, and dislike meeting people; very unsociable, I am told.'

In the second stage of annexation development a prominent part was taken by Mr. H. H. Romilly, who had passed many years in Polynesia in different government appointments, one having been that of Private Secretary to Sir Arthur Gordon in Fiji, a good school in which to be trained for service among natives.    He had been ordered to New Guinea by telegram from Lord Derby in July, 1883, and arrived at Port Moresby from New Britain in November.    As there was no accommodation there for him, he went first to Thursday Island, and thence to Sydney and Melbourne.    Early in 1884 he was recalled to Brisbane, to give evidence

against two white men who had been arrested for
murder and outrages upon natives in the Laughlin
Islands. The men were taken to Fiji, and there tried
and punished. 'The government here,' he wrote, 'are
really making an effort to stop kidnapping. The result
is fury all round.'

Romilly knew Chalmers and Lawes well, and was in
constant intercourse with them during his stay in New
Guinea. His testimony is all the more valuable, since it
comes from a competent observer, and one not inclined
to take too sympathetic a view of missionary work :—

'I find Chalmers,' he wrote in 1885, 'a capital fellow
to live with. He is utterly unlike a missionary. I over-
hauled his wardrobe by force the other day, and found
that he had not even got a black coat and tie.

'Messrs. Lawes and Chalmers, whose names of late
have been much before the public, are the only people
who really have much knowledge of New Guinea; but,
in spite of their ten years' residence in it, their acquaintance is limited to the south coast. Even on the south
coast it is necessary to know three or four dialects in
order to get on with the natives.

'Mr. Lawes shortly after his arrival was joined by
Mr. Chalmers, and by their united efforts they began
a system of planting native teachers at various spots
along the coast, till they succeeded in establishing a line
of communication from the Papuan Gulf to the Louisiade
Archipelago. Many of these teachers were Rarotongans, who had been trained by Mr. Chalmers while
he was attached to the mission at that place. Of course
there have been some casualties among them; some
have died of fever, and some have been murdered by
the natives; but their general success in establishing
a firm footing and gaining an ascendency over the

natives wherever they have been, shows clearly that they are intelligent and courageous men. They certainly have a great aptitude for picking up dialects. Though it has been much the habit to laugh at and despise the native teachers, yet it is to them that the white man in difficulties always turns for protection, and it is always accorded him. They are furnished with serviceable whale-boats, and therefore anything of importance which may occur on the coast is known within a few days at the head station.

' The English missionaries have been always ready to supply visitors with information and assistance, and it is very largely owing to the influence they have over the natives that so many white men have visited the country without accident. Many of these in their subsequent writings have omitted to mention this fact, or to quote the source from which the greater part of their information has been derived. Of all the missions in the Pacific, there is not one which has done better work than that which is now firmly established in New Guinea [1].'

On November 11, 1884, Mr. Romilly wrote home : ' It may interest you to know that we have just finished hoisting the flag here, and a very imposing ceremony it was. I made rather an ass of myself, or rather other people made an ass of me, as I received a telegram from Lord Derby, giving me the limits of the Protectorate and other information about it, while I was kept in utter ignorance that the commodore was coming up here with orders to hoist the flag himself.'

The reference in this letter is to the fact that Romilly read his instructions in such a way as to believe that *he* was to proclaim the Protectorate, and he did so a day or

---

[1] *The Western Pacific and New Guinea*, pp. 241, 242.

two before Commodore Erskine's arrival, greatly to the astonishment of that officer when informed of the fact.

Commodore Erskine, by whom the official proclamation of the Protectorate was finally carried out, kindly placed at the disposal of the writer his report of the proceedings. This document fully recognizes the very important services which Lawes and Chalmers and the native teachers were able to render to the Queen's representative. The commodore's squadron consisted of the Nelson, Espiègle, Raven, Swinger and Harrier. It was evident that Romilly's action, referred to above, could not be recognized as either legal or authoritative. Moreover, it was the commodore's desire that the natives should be enabled to grasp the meaning and importance of the ceremony. It was in this connexion that the influence of Chalmers and of Lawes was so important. The most imposing demonstration took place at Port Moresby. On November 4, 1884, the Espiègle sailed eastwards to Round Head with Mr. Chalmers on board. The object was to induce all the accessible chiefs to come on board and be conveyed to Port Moresby to take part in the grand ceremony. Had not Chalmers been present to inspire the chiefs with confidence, and to explain matters, so that they could grasp something of their meaning, hardly a chief would have accepted the commodore's invitation. Meanwhile the Raven, with a native teacher, probably Ruatoka, on board, went west on the same errand, as far as Redscar Bay, while Mr. Lawes brought in the chiefs of the inland tribes. A large number of chiefs were thus assembled, and were all taken on board the Nelson on November 5 to enjoy a feast, and to hear an address from the commodore. When the feast was over Lawes translated for the chiefs the address, which

explained to them what the object of to-morrow's ceremony was, and what the results of the Protectorate would
be, so far as the chiefs and their people were concerned.
After this the chiefs descended to the main deck, and
each received a present from the hands of the commodore.

On the morning of November 6, in the enclosed
ground of the mission house the British flag was hoisted,
saluted with all due ceremonies, and the Protectorate
formally announced by the commodore.  On November 7
the Nelson and the Raven visited Hall's Sound and
Freshwater Bay, there also to raise the flag.  'The
missionaries,' the record of this trip runs, 'have been
in frequent attendance upon the commodore, who has
had to rely entirely upon them for information concerning the native tribes along the coast, and for getting
the chiefs and natives together.'

Commodore Erskine became deeply interested in the
mission work carried on by Lawes and Chalmers, and
his report contains an account of his visit to the school
at Port Moresby.

'Most of the children attend the mission school, and
an exceedingly interesting scene was witnessed in the
school by the commodore during his stay at Port
Moresby, after returning from the west.  It was arranged
that he would visit the school one afternoon, and the
ringing of the bell, which hangs from the branch of
a tree in full hearing of the village, brought together
about 120 children, the boys in the nude condition
usual with them, and the girls dressed in their fibre
petticoats.  The children were seated on the floor of
the schoolroom, a long, cool building, with walls and
a roof made of the pandanus leaf, and the floors of
boards from old canoes, the boys on one side and the
girls on the other; and behind the children were the

native teachers and their wives.   The children manifested all the interest and obedience expected from
European children, and were examined by Mr. Chalmers.
They sang, answered questions in geography, counted
in English from one to a hundred, and gave the English
for several phrases in common use spoken to them by
Mr. Chalmers in their own language—their knowledge
of the names of countries and their capital cities, of
oceans, seas, and islands, as they were indicated on the
different maps, was remarkable, and they were perfectly
familiar with the appearance and position of their own
country, which they know only by the name of New
Guinea.   They sang in their own tongue some hymns;
they also sang "Auld Lang Syne" and the "National
Anthem," and reverently standing, with eyes closed,
they repeated the Lord's Prayer.   There was something
very touching about this for the most of the English
ears that were listening; for although the words of the
dark-skinned children were unintelligible, their attitude
and earnestness showed that they had been taught to
understand the meaning of the beautiful words they
were repeating.   The whole scene was such as to rouse
feelings of sympathy, and to make one long to be able
to distribute a tin of lollies or a basket of buns amongst
them.   It seemed very much opposed to the English
idea of the fitness of things that fishhooks and sticks
of trade tobacco should be considered suitable gifts for
them, and yet the eyes of the little people, as they each
received the commodore's present of a fishhook, a
stick of tobacco, and a small paper of beads, glistened
with pleasure, just as the eyes of English children do at
school when they receive gifts or prizes; when they
were dismissed from school they bounded away with
just the same glee.'

On November 17, the Nelson, accompanied by the Espiègle, with Mr. Chalmers on board, proceeded eastwards to raise the flag at Kerepunu and other points. The Nelson had on board twenty-six natives who had been entrapped and carried off to Queensland under false pretences. Ten had proved unfit for the hard sugar work, and sixteen had run away. Part of the commodore's duty was to ascertain exactly how these men had been entrapped, and to restore them to their homes.

The ceremony at Kerepunu was quite imposing. 'The chiefs of Hula, Kamali, Kalo, Kerepunu, and Aroma, representing a large number of the villages and probably 20,000 natives, all of the Hood Bay district, were brought on board the flagship to receive presents, and to have the Protectorate explained to them. The principal chief among those brought on board the Nelson at Kerepunu was a great fighting chief, and one of the finest men we had seen. The missionaries said he was the finest chief they knew in New Guinea. His name was Koapena, and he was a chief of Aroma. He was well made, muscular and strong, and, notwithstanding his light copper-coloured skin and large head of hair, a handsome fellow. His features, slightly pitted with smallpox, were aquiline, his nose well arched, and his mouth and chin full of decision and firmness. His broad shoulders and arms were tattooed with blue marks, which represented the number of people killed by himself in fight; sixty-three were counted, besides many other marks which represented the enemies killed by his tribe. He wore armlets and small ornaments in his ears, and his hair was decorated with the scarlet blossoms of the hibiscus. In every respect he looked a splendid man; and his companion chiefs had more character about their features, and more bearing about them in their general appearance and in their movements, than any of the natives who had up to that time trod the Nelson's decks.

'They listened to what the commodore had to say through the interpreter, and then they began to deliberate amongst themselves. One old chief of Hula, who was somewhat doubtful of the new theory of life which the Protectorate was seeking to establish, asked, " In the event of Kapakapa near the neighbourhood of Hula attacking us again, are we to understand that we are not to pay it?" (that is, to be revenged). He was told, " Most certainly not." " Very good," he said, " but just tell me who is to do the payment." Then the commodore said that Her Majesty's officers would see that justice was done; but this did not appear to satisfy the chief until the matter was explained to him by Mr. Chalmers in a manner better understood by the natives, that payment in the way of punishment or revenge would be administered by the Queen's officers, and then the chief signified that he was content. "Now," he said, " there is to be peace for ever, and I am satisfied so long as somebody will punish those who do wrong." Mr. Chalmers put the question to him again and said, " Now, is it to be peace for ever and for ever?" " Yes," he answered, " it is peace for ever."

'After the ceremony at Kerepunu, the Nelson left for Argyle Bay, and the Espiègle for Toulon Island, in Amazon Bay. On board of the Espiègle was Mr. Chalmers, and Toulon Island was to be visited by the Espiègle alone, because it was not considered desirable to take the Nelson there, and the commodore instructed Captain Bridge to explain to the Toulon Island natives what was being done along the coast.

Toulon Island it not far from Cloudy Bay, and a short time ago an affray took place between the Cloudy Bay natives and the crew of a *bêche de mer* schooner, with the result that one of the white men received a severe spear wound, and several natives were killed or wounded.

'As the natives of Toulon Island belong to the same tribe as those at Cloudy Bay, it was thought by Mr. Chalmers that the islanders might regard the Espiègle as a man-of-war come to punish them for the affair at Cloudy Bay, and might resist any attempt on the part of the boats' crews to land. It was therefore decided that two boats should land, each armed, the first to convey Captain Bridge and Mr. Chalmers ashore, and the second, under the command of Lieutenant Ommaney, to lie off from the shore as a covering boat, until it was seen that everything was safe. Fortunately there were no signs of hostility, and the natives proved as friendly as they could be, and manifested much satisfaction when the Protectorate was explained to them.

'From Argyle Bay Commodore Erskine proceeded in the Nelson to South Cape or Stacey Island, to Dinner Island, the Killerton Islands, and Teste Island, proclaimed the Protectorate and hoisted the flag, with the usual formalities at each place. At daylight on the morning of Sunday, November 23, the Espiègle left Stacey Island in advance of the Nelson, bound for Moresby Island, and on Sunday afternoon anchored in Hoop Iron Bay. There was immediately a remarkable and affecting scene between the natives on the vessel and friends and relatives on shore. The seventeen natives had been given up by their friends for dead, and the relatives and friends were in mourning for them. In some cases so long had the returned natives been away that the period of mourning by their friends had expired, and their possessions had been divided amongst those entitled to share. The revulsion of feeling when it became known that seventeen of those who had been given up for lost had returned may be imagined, and as the Espiègle anchored, an old native, the chief of Moresby Island, was seated on a hammock gazing earnestly at the shore, and presently a canoe containing a man and a boy approached the ship. A recognition occurred instantly, for it afterwards transpired that the man in the canoe was the chief's brother; and when the canoe came close to the ship, and its occupants boarded the vessel, tears from the three natives flowed copiously, and rushing to meet each other, they fell one upon the other's neck, rubbed noses, gave expression to loud wailings, and manifested other signs of sorrow and joy.

'The natives said to Chalmers, "Where are the other boys? You have brought joy to some homes, but some are left in sorrow." They were told that they had better come to the commodore and see him personally about it. They were frightened, and refused to leave the island in any vessel. One native, who has a son in Queensland, implored Captain Bridge to bring the boy back to his home. "Now," he entreated; "go to-day, and we will fill the ship with pigs." Both Captain Bridge and Mr. Chalmers did all they could to induce this man to remain on the Espiègle, in order that he might tell his story to Commodore Erskine, but without success, and a movement of the screw of the vessel caused him to suddenly dart through one of the portholes of the vessel into the canoe, for fear that there was to be an attempt to take him away by force.'

Teste Island was the last place visited by the squadron, and early in December it returned to Sydney.

'The Raven received orders to convey Mr. Chalmers

back to South Cape, and the Swinger, for a few months, remained cruising on the New Guinea coast. Mr. Chalmers left the Nelson for the Raven shortly before the flagship took her departure, and he carried with him the good wishes of all on board. Just before leaving, the commodore, with some kindly remarks and thanks for the services he had rendered, presented to him a stick of office like those which had been given to the principal native chiefs. It was the only stick remaining out of six, and in Mr. Chalmers' possession it is an interesting souvenir of a period which will always be remembered and in which he played a prominent part.'

Commodore Erskine, in his official dispatch sent home from Sydney in December, 1884, fully and heartily recognizes the great services rendered by Lawes and Chalmers. It need scarcely be said that the Government paid no attention to the commodore's hope that some official recognition of their services would be made. The British Government has always been slow to recognize the great services constantly rendered to its officials by missionaries. Many difficulties would be averted, and not unfrequently bloodshed and expense avoided, if the officials of Britain, which is professedly a Christian country, could bring themselves to believe that missionaries are intelligent men who love their own country none the less because they are seeking to uplift the savages or the heathen among whom they live. But the average British official, both at home and abroad, is usually in crass ignorance about all missionary matters, has scant sympathy with religious work of any kind, and usually despises the men who can give the best and most reliable advice, preferring often the guidance of those whose only desire is to exploit British influence for their own selfish gain. There are, of course, indi-

vidual exceptions, and not unfrequently fine Christian
men are found holding office under the British Crown.
But there are not enough of these to leaven the service;
and Cabinet ministers can rarely discern any merit
in those who often, even as things are, save British
officials from very serious mistakes, and give most
valuable help in times of stress and of danger.

It is only fair to bear in mind that the last thing any
true missionary desires is government reward. In all
parts of the world missionaries place their services at
the disposal of the government when this can be done
without interfering with their proper work, and they
do this ungrudgingly and without the desire or the
expectation of any recompense. But the ordinary
Christian Englishman sometimes gets indignant when,
as recently in China, British officials make all kinds of
wild blunders, from which they could be saved if they
were as ready to consult the missionary as they are
the globe-trotter and the trader. Not for the benefit of
the missionary, but for the credit of our government, it
would be a desirable change if the high authorities of
our Foreign and Colonial Offices could convince themselves that a man who has given his life to the work, and
who knows the language and thoughts of the people, is
at least as good a judge and as sound an authority to
be consulted as the consul, who knows little about the
people and cares even less, or as the man who is living
abroad simply to make money and then depart.

Officers like Commodore Erskine often acknowledge
in the handsomest way their indebtedness to missionaries; but so far as the British Government is concerned,
in official action and official speech, missionaries are
considered nuisances that have to be tolerated, rather than
men of knowledge and common sense whose experience

should be turned to good account. Hence Commodore Erskine's recommendation was treated with contempt.

In his official report, dated Sydney, December 1884, he wrote:—

'It will readily be seen that it would have been impossible for me to have carried out this programme without the assistance of the Revs. Messrs. Chalmers and Lawes, whose acquaintance with the people and knowledge of their habits are well known and acknowledged. From the moment of my arrival these gentlemen have placed their invaluable services entirely at my disposal. They have been ready day and night to assist me in every possible way; they have spared no pains in translating and explaining the terms of the proclamation and addresses which I have made, and in collecting the numerous chiefs who, but for them, would never have come near the ship.

' These gentlemen, who first came and settled single-handed amongst these wild and cannibal tribes about ten years ago, have by their firm but conciliatory and upright dealings, established such a hold over the natives, as many a crowned head would be proud to possess. I have been lost in admiration of the influence which they command over these savage but intelligent people.

' During our cruise it has happened that a boat has been sent, in the middle of the night, to bring off a chief. When it is imagined what it is to suddenly surprise and wake up the inhabitants of a native village, to inform the chief that he is wanted, and must go off immediately to a huge man-of-war, and for that man to comply without demur, it will be understood what a magic effect is produced by a few words spoken by

"Tamate" or "Missi Lao," the native names for Mr. Chalmers and Mr. Lawes.

'Under these circumstances I desire to testify to the invaluable services which have been rendered to me by Messrs. Chalmers and Lawes, and to express the hope that they will be duly acknowledged by Her Majesty's Government. The wonderful confidence shown by the natives must be entirely attributed to their influence.'

After the proclamation of the Protectorate Mr. Romilly was left in possession of New Guinea as Acting Commissioner, pending the appointment of a Special Commissioner. His views in the main agreed with those of Lawes and Chalmers, and it is satisfactory that up to the present New Guinea has been governed in accordance with them. Nor can there be any doubt that our government policy has been very largely determined by the views and influence of these two missionaries. In 1885 Chalmers wrote a paper on the outlook for New Guinea, containing much valuable information and expressing characteristic views. The reproduction of some of these here will show how alive he was to the needs of the case, and how eager he was to secure the highest interests of the natives:—

'The fear at home is the expense on the taxpayer, but only in too much ruling can that expense be very great. It will be a grand mistake to send here a large force of officers, mere parasites for whom positions are made. Every office, from the Governor, or Administrator, down to the clerk of drudgery, should be shown to be a necessity before appointed. Every employé should have plenty of work that must be done, and there should not be one inactive member on the staff. With General Scratchley, Mr. Romilly, and a secretary each, there is a good start, and these gentlemen can fill up as required. Having a vessel at their disposal, they will soon get to know the extent of their work and begin to form ideas of its wants.

'One of the first things to do will be to teach natives the art of government, so that they may be able to govern themselves and relieve the British representatives as much as possible of mere tribal difficulties, so that there may be more time to devote to the general work. I think it would be quite possible to assemble the chiefs of the various districts once or twice a year at one or two central places, such as Port Moresby and South Cape.

'The chiefs could bring in unsettled disputes and have them examined, and the decision come to, with all other business, reported to the tribes on their return. The natives have a criminal code of their own, which, altered and enlarged a very little, would meet all present wants, at all events for some years to come.

'There will not, so far as I know, be any serious trouble about land. It all belongs to individuals, and each boundary is well defined. Nowhere that I am acquainted with is land held by a chief for the benefit of a tribe, and nowhere could a chief part with land belonging to another. Land being so held, there are no serfs, hence no one has the power to turn another or others off land, so that in planting there is no fear of any one being deprived of his or her produce; hence there should not be much difficulty in inducing the natives to plant or sow such things as would be useful for exportation. At first it will be necessary to encourage them by bounties to begin, these afterwards to be deducted from the produce either by an export duty or purchasing from the natives at a nominal price and selling to traders at a small advance.

'I fear I shall shock many of my friends and a large number of Christians in what I am now going to propose. The natives of New Guinea now under British rule do not wear much clothing, and it is desirable they should be encouraged to use only a very little. The women in many parts are clothed enough, and in others, where their clothing is scant, they should be encouraged to take to the petticoats and nothing more. Nowhere do the men want more than a loin-cloth, and every effort should be used to discourage anything more. Too little attention has been paid to the effect clothing has had hitherto on native races. Syphilis and strong drink have received the blame for the deterioration and extinction of native races, but I think the introduction of clothing has done much in this direction. A great mistake has hitherto been made in missionary work; the missionaries have reported "respectably clothed natives who once were naked savages," and the churches have applauded in the conversion of the savages. These clothed natives are, I believe, only hurrying along an easy and respectable road to the grave. To swathe their limbs in European clothing spoils them, deteriorates them, and, I fear, hurries them to premature death. Put excessive clothing with syphilis and strong drink, and, I think, we shall be nearer the truth.

'Retain native customs as much as possible—only those which are very objectionable should be forbidden—and leave it to the influence of education to raise them to purer and more civilized customs.

'One of the first things the Government will have to face at the very outset, if the government is to be for the benefit of the natives, is their education, and that should not be left to missionaries. At present the natives do not appreciate the blessings or benefits of education, but as soon as commerce is introduced and civilization advances they will become anxious to learn. Only by a thorough system of education will they ever rise above their superstitions and shake off for ever the fear of sorcerers and sorceresses. Earnestly taken in hand, and gradually educated, there is nothing to prevent the New Guinea natives so rising in the scale of civilization as to become an honour to us as a nation and to rise to a worthy national life. Looked upon as in every way inferior and not worthy of a place in the great human family, and treated accordingly, the present protection or annexation will be to them a curse, and an everlasting shame to us.

'Whilst I am writing, close to me a number of children are playing, and their noise of laughter and shouting shows they have little care, and their parents have not more. Life to them all is worth living, it is more than endurable; will it be so twenty years hence? I may not see it, but I trust others will, the blessings of Christianity and civilization everywhere in New Guinea, and children as numerous and happy as now, and parents thankful for Britain's care and full of intelligent hopes for a greater future.'

The British Government deemed it necessary (in December, 1884) to hoist the British flag along the north-eastern coast of New Guinea, and Chalmers accompanied Commander Ross in the Raven to do this work, rendering similar services to those he had given under Commodore Erskine. He refers to this, among other matters, in letters sent home, dated February 10 and March 29, 1885. In the former he states:—

'Thinking the Directors with yourself would wish us to assist the commodore, I have during the last few months been engaged flag-hoisting on each side of New Guinea and on the adjacent islands. Had I not been with them, their communication with the various tribes would not have been so pleasing. The commodore and his officers have done their work well, and I only hope that what has been done will prove to be for the good of all the natives. I returned only the day before yesterday, and leave to-night to inquire into troubles at Kapakapa, and then go further east, accompanied by Mr. Romilly, to make inquiries as to the massacre of a white man, his wife and crew, in Cloudy Bay. You must do your utmost to increase our staff.

'The Australasian Geographical Society, representing all the colonies, has asked me to take charge of an expedition to explore New Guinea. I wish to go home first, and meet you all, and then I could decide. If I go to Britain, I shall expect to return here in October. I dare not risk a winter. What frightens me and stands before me as a terrible scare is the deputation work.

'I hear you have appointed a missionary to help in the work. I hope he is a good all-round man without namby-pambyism, ready for all sorts of roughing it. I have as much zest to-day for roughing it or enjoying comforts as I ever had. I fancy this youth of old age not so bad. I am in better health all round. I think better able for work than ever I was.'

And in the latter, addressed to Mr. Meikle, he wrote:—
'Our Governor, General Scratchley, has not yet arrived. Mr. Romilly, his representative, is staying with me. We do not know what is to be done, what form the protection of the natives will take, or where the headquarters of Government are to be. We are daily expect-

ing men-of-war to punish natives who have committed murders on the coast. The teachers get on well with the natives, and at several stations there are inquirers. At all the stations schools are tolerably well attended, and many can read. We hope to extend east and west about the end of the year, and then to work inland to the mountain ranges.

'On the other side of New Guinea we found very few natives until we got to Rook Island, where we met a very fine tribe of natives, dark, well made, and intelligent. They practise circumcision, the first tribe I have met who do so since my arrival on New Guinea. They would gladly have kept me. Many splendid teachers could be had from amongst them after they have received the Gospel. It is impossible for us to begin a mission amongst them at present. We fear the Roman Catholics are on their way here now, and if they settle anywhere near to us it will be trouble from beginning to end. When I do go home I shall soon find my way to Inveraray.'

Lawes, a little later, May 8, writes on the same subject:—

'It is, perhaps, too late to say anything about the proclamation of the Protectorate, and the share which Chalmers and I took in it. I considered I was doing the best service to the people of New Guinea by assisting the commodore to make known his mission to them. He asked our help. We gave it willingly, and he has repeatedly acknowledged it. With the desirability, or otherwise, of the annexation (for such it will become) we have nothing to do. I have never by letter or word of mouth sought to bring it about. It would have been better for our work, and for the people, if they could have been left alone, but as this was impossible it is far better to have an English Government than any other.

'I have had several interviews and much correspondence with General Scratchley. I believe he is sincerely anxious to make his governorship a success, and that he will try his utmost to solve the difficult problem of protecting the native race and securing white men's interests. It will be no easy task, and I am more doubtful than sanguine of the success. It is impossible to bring nineteenth-century ideas and government into contact with the primitive customs of a barbarous people without much friction and trouble. We who at present are the only possible interpreters, and who alone have the confidence of the people, are sure to have plenty of worry, anxiety, and trouble, while others will have the honour and get the pay.'

The annexation of a portion of Northern New Guinea by Germany aroused some excitement. But Chalmers saw nothing to fear in it. He wrote:—

'In German annexation, on the other side, I think we have lost nothing, and the Germans have gained nothing. The natives are few and the country is savage, with mountains everywhere. What is really good of the other side we have secured, and our part contains most natives. I know that this is so, and I write from knowledge. I have been all round the coast, and say candidly that we have now quite enough territory, and ought not to want any more. Derby was right in leaving room for Germany. The colonies are angry from ignorance.'

Romilly's hope and expectation had been that he would himself receive the appointment as first Governor of New Guinea. But this was not to be. Sir Peter Scratchley received the post, and threw himself with

great vigour into the work of organizing the government upon a sound basis, and of making himself
acquainted with the territory he had to administer.

In trying to make the acquaintance of the people
whom he was to govern, he was most anxious to avail
himself of Chalmers' ability to introduce him to the
natives, and to make things easy and smooth. And
Chalmers felt that any services he could render would
react beneficially in the governor's attitude towards
the natives.

' Since the Special Commissioner's arrival,' he writes
to Mr. Thompson, 'I have been with him, introducing
him to the natives and interpreting for him. He is
anxious to be looked upon as a friend of the mission,
and as one with us in seeking the good of the natives.
I am now going with him to visit the north-east coast,
and on our return shall go to the Gulf. Then I hope to
have a few weeks' spell in Sydney, and then return here,
and in company with Lawes place the new teachers.
I do not think it would be wise for me to go home
at present. I am anxious to see the introduction of
English rule, and to help if possible; and so far we
have no reason to complain.

' There is not the slightest fear of my accepting a
position in the Government. I say this because of
a report current in Australia. I believe Sir Peter
Scratchley would be glad if I would consent to serve
under him; but I have given him to understand that
I am not open to an offer, and that a missionary I must
remain. I will help him all I can conscientiously, and
I will do all I can for the natives. He is very anxious
I should remain in New Guinea during his term, and
assist in the inauguration. I wish to go home and
report myself; still, if I can benefit New Guinea I will

remain. I am in excellent health and good spirits, and not much tamed from old days. H. O. Forbes begs of me to take charge of his expedition and do Mount Owen Stanley. Now that is a temptation and, I may have to own to you, a weakness. My Gulf trip must wait. No one is likely to run me out there, as it is a cannibal country.

'How I wish I could spend a quiet evening with you, chat over the present, and arrange for the probable future! I hope to see a great living church of New Guineans here, and to see go out from it a glorious band of native teachers.'

The concluding stages in the process of making British New Guinea a Crown Colony may be very briefly set forth. On October 27, 1888, British New Guinea was formally annexed and created into a separate possession and government, and Dr. (now Sir) William Macgregor, K.C.M.G., appointed the Administrator. The annexation took place at Port Moresby in 1888. Mr. Lawes, in a letter to Mr. Thompson, describes the closing event in this lengthy series of official acts :—

'The long-expected proclamation of British sovereignty was duly performed on the 4th instant. British New Guinea is now a part of the Queen's dominions, and the people of it are as much her subjects as you and I. On the morning of that day the Harrier, with Tamate on board, left for Thursday Island, so that, to our regret, he was not present at the inaugural function. There was not much display, and it was well that there was not, for flag-hoisting must seem to the natives to be a white man's amusement. The function of the 4th was the tenth at which I had been present on New Guinea. It is getting monotonous.

'The proclamation was duly read, Dr. Macgregor's appointment as Administrator, the Letters Patent containing his instructions, and other letters, and then the oaths of allegiance and office were administered by Captain Bosanquet of Her Majesty's ship Opal. The royal standard was hoisted, and saluted with twenty-one guns from the Opal, the marines fired a *feu de joie*, three cheers for the Queen were given by the white subjects, and the ceremony ended, so far as the official programme was concerned. But as soon as the English cheers died away a party of well-dressed New Guineans stood up behind the flagstaff and sang clearly and well a verse of " God save the Queen." It took the officers and men quite by surprise. Dr. Macgregor expressed his surprise and pleasure at this unexpected addition to the ceremony. Of course it was done by the mission young men and women. When I saw them grouped behind the flagstaff I sent a message to them which they obeyed very nicely.

' I think the bearing of this new order on our work will be for good. Dr. Macgregor is a man who thoroughly understands natives, and in his long Fijian experience has become well acquainted with the work of the Wesleyan Mission, and with the persons of the teachers. This is an enormous advantage, and one for which we may be deeply grateful. Any one who knows the misunderstandings and friction of the last three years will appreciate it. I am quite certain that the natives and mission have a good friend in Dr. Macgregor.

' Already laws (officially called Ordinances) have been passed, by which the land has been secured to the natives in a more stringent manner than we dared to hope for. Deportation of natives has been made illegal, and the introduction of intoxicants, opium, firearms, and explosives is prohibited.'

Here then end the transformations on New Guinea in her political relations, and long may she be administered in the way adopted in 1888, namely, in the determination to govern her, so far as possible, in the best interests of the natives, rather than in the interests of white immigrants.

We cannot better close this chapter in the life of Chalmers than by recording the testimony to his worth, and the exceptional value of the services he rendered to the nation, given by Vice-Admiral Bridge. In a letter to the *Times*, dated May 4, 1901, Admiral Bridge said :—

'I first met Mr. Chalmers in 1884, when the British flag was hoisted in Southern New Guinea by the present Sir James Erskine, who then commanded the squadron on the Australian station. I was at that time serving under Sir James's orders; and I am sure that my distinguished chief will be most ready to testify to the value of the assistance rendered him in a difficult operation by Mr. Chalmers and his colleague Dr. Lawes.

'Mr. Chalmers accompanied me in the ship I then commanded on an expedition to Kapakapa and Kailé on which I had been sent by Sir James Erskine. At my urgent request Mr. Chalmers again accompanied me, early in 1885, on a special expedition—in H.M.S. Dart, commanded by the present Captain W. Usborne Moore—to North-eastern New Guinea and Rook Island. His vigilance, cheeriness, readiness of resource, and extraordinary influence over native savages made his help quite invaluable. I can honestly say that I do not know how I should have got on without him. He had an equal power of winning the confidence of savages quite unused to strangers and the respect, and even love, of white seamen. Notwithstanding the great inconvenience and, I fear, not inconsiderable expense to which he had been put by giving his valuable services in the expeditions mentioned, he firmly refused to allow his name to be officially submitted in any claim for pecuniary remuneration, or even to accept the legitimate compensation to which he was entitled.

'It is difficult to do justice in writing to the character of this really great Englishman. One had only to know and live with him in out-of-the-way lands to be convinced that he was endowed with the splendid characteristics which distinguished our most eminent explorers and pioneers.

'In these days, in which fame depends on skill and audacity in self-advertisement, it will not, it is hoped, be thought out of place to offer even such a defective tribute as this letter is to the memory of a loyal subject and brave and self-sacrificing man, of whom his countrymen know nothing, because he did his noble work outside the sphere of influence of the newspaper correspondent.'

# CHAPTER VIII

## FIRST VISIT HOME, 1886

CHALMERS left New Guinea for England on May 11, 1886, and, travelling by way of Sydney, Melbourne, and Bombay, reached London on August 10. His furlough was about ten years overdue, and he reluctantly tore himself away from New Guinea in deference to the repeated and urgent requests of the Directors, rather than from any desire or need that he felt for rest and change. He had exaggerated notions about the extent to which life among savages had unfitted him for the restraints and the conventions of civilization; about the burden of deputation work, and his own special unfitness for it; and about his inability, after twenty years in the tropics, to stand the variable, damp and cold climate of Britain. Deep interest in him had been felt for years by the Directors, and by many of the churches. They honoured him for the noble work he had done, and for the varied adventures through which he had safely and successfully passed in seeking to plant the Gospel in New Guinea. Though unknown by feature or voice his fame had reached many who were prepared to give him a hearty welcome had he possessed far less magnetic attraction than he did. He was welcomed home at a meeting of the Directors held in the Board Room in Blomfield Street, in London, on Monday, August 30, 1886.

It was a memorable gathering. The room was

crowded with those who were eager to look upon the face and to hear the voice of the renowned pioneer missionary.   Honoured for his work's sake, he immediately won the hearts of those who felt for the first time the magnetism of his personality, and the intense force of his enthusiasm.   Who that was present at that meeting has forgotten it?   Mr. Thompson introduced him with the insight and the sympathy which are always the marked features of the speeches in which he introduces missionaries from the field to the Board.   There was also the brotherly love of the distant Cheshunt days acting and reacting upon the two men.   Widely sundered had their pathways been since in the sixties one went to the great Scotch city of Glasgow, and the other to remote Rarotonga.   Twenty-one years later they find themselves linked together; one bearing the responsibility of the world-wide foreign work of the great Society; the other adding to those responsibilities by the success and the restless vigour of his efforts to enter into new fields of labour, and to evangelize heathen tribes yet in darkness. No wonder there was deep feeling in Mr. Thompson's voice while he referred to Chalmers as an intrepid explorer, a friend trusted by many savage tribes, a faithful Christian missionary, and one who, wherever he went, was known as a man whose constant aim it was to secure the reign of peace and goodwill on the earth.

'When Mr. Chalmers rose to reply,' the records tell us, 'he was heard with the deepest interest.  His stalwart form and genial face, bronzed with travel and with toil in a tropical clime, the story he had to tell, and the message which he had at last come to deliver, and but for which he would not have come home at all, were alike impressive.  It was easy to see that, accustomed as the Directors were to the reception of returning missionaries, they were on this occasion deeply moved. Mr. Chalmers spoke modestly about himself; but he was emphatic in the delivery of his message. The work in New Guinea was growing fast, more labourers must forthwith be sent to enter in at the open doors, New Guinea wanted men, New Guinea must have men.' In this, his first utterance at home, Chalmers struck sharply, and with force, the note that was dominant in all his after addresses through the length and breadth of the land.

In the autumn of 1886 Chalmers began a long round of deputation visits to the churches in Britain which support the work of the London Missionary Society. Wherever he went he thrilled his audiences with the marvellous story he had to tell. His own burning enthusiasm, the love for his work and for the savages he was striving to uplift, which shone through every public utterance, his massive frame and head, his flashing eyes, his trumpet-toned voice, touched the heart of every gathering, great and small, and created in multitudes of breasts an undying interest in the evangelization of New Guinea. In a few weeks he became one of the most popular missionary speakers of the nineteenth century.

A missionary home on furlough, and the more if he happens to be in popular demand as a deputation speaker, has a hard time. There is sometimes more than a touch of irony in the occupations which fill up a missionary's season of rest and change. Churches and audiences think that the tired worker must be as eager to see and inspire them as they are to look upon the men and women who in the hard places of the field have been doing noble service. And the churches are not unfrequently wholly unreasonable in their demands upon the Home Secretary of the Society, and through him upon the time and strength and enthusiasm of a man like Chalmers. The day may not be far distant when missionaries will have to be protected from the rapacious demands of the home churches upon their nervous and spiritual energy and upon their physical power. Up to the full measure of strength, and sometimes even beyond their strength, our missionaries serve us in the home churches, and their reward is not always equal to their self-sacrifice.

Into a constantly increasing rush of engagements of many kinds Chalmers found himself drawn almost as soon as he reached England. One who soon became an intimate friend and correspondent has placed at the author's disposal a large number of letters beginning at this time. Extracts from these, and from other letters of this date, are the best exposition of Chalmers' life and thought at this time. It is Tamate among home influences as sketched by himself.

'Retford, November 11. I got here yesterday morning, and leave to-morrow night. After leaving you on Friday we got to town in rain, Mr. Blomfield going to the Bible House, and I to the Mission House. In the afternoon I visited Sir Robert Herbert, Under Secretary for the Colonies, and went over New Guinea affairs. He is anxious I should meet Stanhope, and I hope to do so, and may have to travel from Scotland, for that purpose. We had a splendid meeting at Hackney College, and I hope some will hear the Master calling them to foreign work. They have a fine lot of young fellows; it would be such a pity if they all stayed at home.'

'Retford, December 12. I am well, only my knees refuse much duty. I shall be right for next month. I have finished draft of my Colonial Institute paper, and start my Geographical Society one.'

TAMATE ON DEPUTATION WORK, 1886.

'Retford, February 2, 1887. I shall have finished my book work to-night[1], and then to another *Sunday at Home* paper. I find old age advancing from the worry of editors, and fancy I am getting greyer day by day. Next week I go to town from Wolverhampton. I have just had a note from Lady Spokes wanting me for the 22nd to dinner, and would I just come about five, as there is to be a ladies' working party for the Sevenoaks bazaar? Oh horrors! fancy me addressing a ladies' meeting! Yet I must go if possible. If you do not see the bronzed savage next week you may some time after. Well, I have bronchitis, and move about wheezing and puffing like an old engine.'

'Cheltenham, April 19. To-night Gloucester, to-morrow back here. Thursday Cambridge Heath. Friday Liverpool, also Sunday and Monday. Then Dundee, Greenock, and Edinburgh. The last engagement is on May 4, before the United Presbyterian Synod, on missions. 5th, Camden Town; 6th, Religious Tract Society. Not bad for a savage. I am well, and drink in this summer weather. This morning all over the moors after finishing my correspondence.'

'Northampton, May 5. I saw the Earl of Onslow; he only wanted me to know that the government of New Guinea would be very much on the lines of my books and papers, but he said, and here was the real reason why he wanted to see me, " I have heard you might take a government position, and if you would apply we should certainly give it immediate consideration." That was a feeler, and I replied, " I have never, my lord, hinted even that I should like such a position, and when spoken to about it I have always given a negative ; and if asked to now I should require much consideration."

[1] This refers to *Pioneering in New Guinea.*

They would like me to apply. I will have them ask me for a negative.

'The weather is deplorable, far more than " clean ridiculous." I have a grand host of bairns to address at Retford on Tuesday, and at night travel to the north. On my return to London I had better fix myself at the Mission House and pack, and visit Stratford, Woolwich, Maidenhead, and Rye. Then come the farewells, and it may be I shall join the ship at Plymouth.'

These glances at his correspondence show how the days and weeks of his stay in Britain were filled with manifold occupations. The numerous friends Chalmers made wherever he went were anxious to see all they could of him. There were relatives and old friends in Scotland and elsewhere to visit. Then he was engaged in seeing through the press his new book *Pioneering in New Guinea*, and in writing a series of papers for the *Sunday at Home*. He also read papers on New Guinea before the members of the Colonial Institute and the Royal Geographical Society. In addition to all this varied work he was preaching almost every Sunday, and speaking three or four or five times a week.

He took part in two of the great annual May meetings by speaking in Exeter Hall for the Religious Tract Society on May 6, 1887, and for the London Missionary Society on May 12. Both addresses were of exceptional interest and power, and like all his speeches uttered under deep feeling, and full of biographical interest. At the former meeting Chalmers bore testimony, in common with missionaries of all the great evangelical societies, to the help he had received in his work from the Religious Tract Society.

'As a missionary in the Hervey group I received from time to time very great assistance in my mission work from this Society. Books that had been translated into the Rarotongan dialect have been prepared at home here. The hymn-books used by all the natives were prepared by the Religious Tract Society. They have also occasionally sent out to Rarotonga bales of paper on which books were printed for the use of the natives; and it was through their help that for some time I was able to publish a newspaper; at first one number a fortnight, afterwards once a month. The object I had in view was to interest the natives in the outside world that they might know there was something away beyond them. Living in a small island like that, not only the natives, but even white men are apt to think that all the world is there. It was during the time of the Franco-Prussian war that this paper was being published. After giving an account of one of the battles fought, I remember, on a Friday, which was set apart for prayer for New Guinea, a chief present rose and said: "Stay! we are going to send teachers, I believe, to the large island of New Guinea; but I have just been reading in the newspaper an account of an un-Christian war that is being carried on in Europe, and what I propose is that we should send teachers to France and to Prussia. When the missionaries came here they taught us that fighting was bad, but we find that those nations that are called civilized still believe in fighting, although the Bible tells us it is indeed bad."

'Coming now to New Guinea, we have not yet received help from this Society in that island; but I sincerely trust that the day is very near when we shall be able to ask your committee to assist us in giving literature to the natives there. At present we have had one or two school books published in Sydney for the use of the natives. We have begun to teach them to read. People think we missionaries go out to those parts of the world, and from morning to night do nothing but preach sermons. It is quite a mistake. It is not the preaching of a sermon so much as the living the life that tells on the native heart. It is by living a divine life, by striving to follow in the footsteps of Him who came to express the Father's love, that we win the heart of the savage, and raise him up to become a true man or woman in Jesus Christ.

'We have to begin at the very beginning of things. We have to get the children and grown up people about us, and teach them the alphabet; and it is not so easy as in the schools here. For weeks you go over the five vowels, and then they come back to tell you they have forgotten all about it. It is the same in teaching them Bible truths. What interests them most is to tell them a story, say about Adam and Eve, or Cain and Abel. Noah and the Flood is a most charming story to them. Or we take one of our Lord's miracles, or one of His parables, and in a quiet conversational way we tell them about it. You cannot get them to stay long at services—sometimes only ten or twenty minutes— but when they begin to become interested, they will stay for an hour, but never beyond that. They would simply fall off to sleep if we continued for very much longer. I suppose people do not sleep at all at the services in England?

'I went down to Hall's Sound with a native to put up a mission house for teachers that we expected to be able to place there. The plan we adopt is to have short prayers every morning at sunrise, and every evening at sunset. When travelling on foot or on board a boat, or when living with natives ashore, we have prayers at sunrise and sunset. The rainmaker there, a native named Kone, whose acquaintance I had made on a former visit, became interested in these services. I taught him a little prayer, " Great Spirit of Love, give me light; save me for Jesus' sake." Again and again I had to go over it. He would go down to the village and, by-and-by, come back and say, " I have forgotten it "; but at the last he got hold of it, and remembered it. I left, and a few months afterwards I returned to the same place, and found the rainmaker had been killed. Thinking that because I had preached peace to his tribe, he had power to bring peace to all the other tribes, he sent for two Naara men to come, as he wished to talk to them about making peace in the neighbouring village. These two men were with him when the dancing began in the evening, and he saw the chief of the Lolo tribe, with whom they were at enmity, coming stealthily through the crowd with spears to attack them. He threw one, and would have struck a Naara man, but the rainmaker stepped in front of him, and received the spear himself; and they carried him home to die. When he was dying his one great wish was to send for me, but it was impossible, as the south-east wind was blowing too strongly. Every now and again that poor savage in his great darkness could be heard saying, " Great Spirit of Love, give me light; save me for Jesus' sake." He could not understand all that he was asking: I know that well; but I do think that the Great Spirit of Love stretched out the great arm of Divine strength, took that poor dark savage by the hand, and led him from the darkness and superstition and savageism of earth up to His own home in heaven. What we want, then, is this, that when the people become educated in a few more years you as a Society will take part in this great work; that you will come to our help and assist us to educate them still more; to educate a people worthy of the name of Christ.'

Chalmers' address at the Exeter Hall meeting of the London Missionary Society was the climax of his public work during this visit home. Exeter Hall was crowded, and although other able speakers were there it is no discredit to them to say that the main interest of the meeting centred in Tamate's unpolished but thrilling eloquence. We recall a few of the most striking passages.

'I have had twenty-one years' experience amongst natives. I have seen the semi-civilized and the un-civilized; I have lived with the Christian native, and I have lived, dined, and slept with the cannibal. I have visited the islands of the New Hebrides, which I sincerely trust will not be handed over to the tender mercies of France; I have visited the Loyalty Group, I have seen the work of missions in the Samoan Group, I know all the islands of the Society Group, I have lived for ten years in the Hervey Group, I know a few of the groups close on the line, and for at least nine years of my life I have lived with the savages of New Guinea; but I have never yet met with a single man or woman, or a single people, that your civilization without Christianity has civilized. For God's sake let it be done at once! Gospel and commerce, but remember this, it must be the Gospel first. Wherever there has been the slightest spark of civilization in the Southern Seas it has been because the Gospel has been preached there, and wherever you find in the Island of New Guinea a friendly people, or a people that will welcome you, there the missionaries of the Cross have been preaching Christ. Civilization! The rampart can only be stormed by those who carry the Cross.

'Recall the twenty-one years, give me back all its experience, give me its shipwrecks, give me its standings in the face of death, give it me surrounded with savages with spears and clubs, give it me back again with spears flying about me, with the club knocking me to the ground, give it me back, and I will still be your missionary!'

'How do we preach the Gospel? No, we do not go with a black coat and white necktie standing in the boat with a Bible in our hand. We go as man to man, to try and live the Gospel. The day before yesterday I was with some of my brethren at Cheshunt College, and I told them a story there that I think will do well here. I had been travelling away back among the mountain ranges for some time. I was away on that trip for three months. We had run short of food; we were travelling with our own kits; they call them swags in Australia. Mine was pretty heavy, but not so heavy as the others. We had very little to eat on Monday, and on Tuesday, and on Wednesday, and on Thursday we got but a few bananas that we could pick up; and I never want to see a banana again, except when hungry. It came to Friday—no bananas—and on Saturday I was dead beat, and at three o'clock in the afternoon I threw down my swag, and sat down on it. I was sore pressed. What was to be done? We never travelled on Sunday; but we could not starve. We had met with no natives. We were travelling through an unknown country. The natives were far away on either side of us, and we could not tell where to look for them. At last I said to the party: "Give one long loud shout, as loud as you possibly can; I cannot help you." Then there was one grand loud yell, and suddenly it was answered by another, and then there was another yell, and a man and a lad came out of the bush, followed by a woman carrying a baby. She came up, and my look of sorrow and want touched the savage heart. She stood and looked over me—we could not speak a single word to one another, but she indicated to me that I was to get up. She had a knitted bag, and she took up that swag of mine, and put it into the bag. I rushed to seize the baby—it was light compared with my swag—but she objected to that, and after placing the baby on the top, she signed that I was to follow. I followed, and the others came by-and-by. After passing through the bush, we came to a few houses. She motioned that I was to sit down. She went away, and shortly afterwards returned and placed food before me, and motioned me to eat. You know it was in that way that we begin to preach the Gospel. Her action was a gospel to me. Touch the heart of a man, let him be cannibal, savage, I care not what, give a look of kindness and sympathy, and you will get the same in return.

'Twelve months last December I visited South Cape, when I was left there by Sir Peter Scratchley, the first Special Commissioner appointed by Her Majesty to the new Protectorate. He left us to go to the Australian coast to die. A man full of interest and of earnestness in the work already undertaken, who thoroughly appreciated the position in which we stood on the island, and heartily thanked us for doing such great things for the Master and for the Government. Whilst I was there, on the first Sunday in December, I met with a large company of Christian men and women, and sat down and partook of the ordinance of the Lord's Supper, administered by a native pastor—one of our South Sea Islanders. There I was, united with and

shedding tears of joy with men and women who as
cannibals and savages had only a few years before
sought our lives. What did it? It is the old story
still of the Gospel of Christ!'

The great societies, specially interested for different
reasons in New Guinea, were not likely to miss the
opportunity of seeing and hearing Mr. Chalmers. On
the evening of Jan. 11, 1887, in Prince's Hall he read
a paper before the members of the Colonial Institute,
entitled 'New Guinea—Past, Present, and Future[1].'
This is a comprehensive title, and the paper was a wide
survey of the history of New Guinea, the facts about
the people and their life, and the right course for Great
Britain to pursue in the effort to rule them wisely and
well. There are in it many characteristic passages,
some of which throw light upon Chalmers' views at
this time both as to his past work and also as to the
future of his adopted home.

'Only by patient toil, only by many weary months,
perhaps years, of the old "open sesame" key will the
great unknown be opened and known. High mountains, dense bush, weary fetid swamps, hostile natives
may lie in the way, yet to every traveller I say:—Go
on; your little adds to the muckle, and by-and-by the
doors will be thrown open, and future travellers, entering by the doors you have opened, will laugh at your
troubles, your narrow escapes, your difficulties, and will
marvel at what they will suppose to be your highly-
coloured narratives of danger.

'We are constantly reminded that the natives of New
Guinea are terrible savages, and ought not to live, but
we who have lived amongst them think otherwise, and
will do all we can to preserve them as a people or

[1] See *Royal Colonial Institute Proceedings*, vol. xviii, pp. 88-122.

peoples. The only real attempt at Christianizing or civilizing them has been made by the London Missionary Society, at a great outlay of money and loss of life. That Society has held nobly to the work, and great have been the results. Others have borne testimony to the work accomplished, and it will scarcely become me to dilate upon it. Nowhere, except at mission stations, is there any appearance of civilization. I hold very strong views on what is called civilization. For more than twenty years I have been amongst natives. I know a little of New Guinea, have visited the New Hebrides, Loyalty Group, Samoas, Hervey Group, Society and Leeward Islands, Penrhyns, Humphrey Group, and Danger Island, and nowhere have I seen our boasted civilization civilizing, but everywhere have I seen Christianity acting as the true civilizer.

'In the inland villages tree houses are found, which are called *dobos*, and which are used in case of an attack. In every one of these *dobos* large bundles of spears are kept, and great quantities of stones suitable for throwing. Sometimes coming unexpectedly upon a village, an alarm was given, and the women and children would at once rush for the tree houses, followed by a few men, whilst others, seizing their spears and shields, rushed out to meet us and challenged our approach. My invariable plan has been to take very little notice, but holding up one hand to walk steadily, and apparently carelessly, on, calling *maino* (peace) and laughing at them.

'Give the native of New Guinea a chance, and I feel sure he can be what is called "raised." I wish I could plead for him that I might be heard; that I could feel sure that the terms of the proclamation would be faithfully carried out. I know, if that were done, the time would never come when it would be necessary to serve out blankets and flour to the Papuan. Teach our natives, encourage them in trade, and they will never want your charity.

'If, as a nation, we are anxious to learn from the past; if we desire to treat these Papuans differently and reserve for them their lands and rights, let us begin at once with ruling for that end. I believe Christianity alone can raise New Guinea, and make a people worthy of the name. It alone can civilize and lead aright its natives, and I therefore say encourage mission stations everywhere.'

An important discussion followed the reading of the paper, in which Dr. Doyle Glanville, Sir James Garrick (agent-general for Queensland), Captain Henderson, R.N., Lieutenant-General R. W. Lowry, C.B., Dr. Henry Guillemard, Mr. G. R. Askwith, and the chairman, Frederick Young, Esq., took part. Dr. Glanville had been a member of Sir Peter Scratchley's staff, and had accompanied him on his visit of inspection in the latter half of 1885. In his speech he bore testimony to the unique influence of Chalmers over the natives; and also to the civilizing influence of missionary work. 'Whatever work has been accomplished on the expedition could never have been done without his valuable help. His profound knowledge of the native character, his wide experience, and his great tact, placed us on a footing with the natives that otherwise would have been impossible. He taught us how to understand the natives, and their little peculiarities and ways, and he taught them to understand the members of the expedition, and what were the motives that prompted us to visit them.'

Captain Henderson bore like testimony. He was

commander of the Nelson under Commodore Erskine in the proclamation of the Protectorate. 'The name Tamate is talismanic, and gives one a safe conduct where but a few years ago it was unsafe for a white man to venture. Messrs. Lawes and Chalmers are supreme along the eastern half of the southern shore of New Guinea. Without their aid every stranger going there is helpless; he cannot communicate with the natives, and without their authority the natives will do nothing. By Mr. Chalmers chiefs were brought together on the quarter-deck of the Nelson who had never before met save to fight, and often the proclamation had to be translated through two and even three languages before it could be explained to them.' Lieut.-General Lowry, whose son had served on the Nelson at that time, also stated: 'I have a vivid recollection of my son's statement of the loving way in which Mr. Chalmers and Mr. Lawes ever referred to the natives, and of the effect of such converse on the men of the ships of war. Who can measure the amount of good to the inhabitants of such an island of having civilization, Christianity, and English character planted and exemplified by such men?'

The paper to the Members of the Royal Geographical Society was read on the evening of January 17, 1887, and gave a sketch of his exploration and travels in New Guinea from 1878 to 1885, with many details of the voyage on the lakatoi, Kevaubada, described in chapter vi, and his first visit to the cannibals of Namau[1]. In the discussion that ensued, Captain Henderson, R.N., Mr. G. R. Askwith, one of Sir Peter Scratchley's staff, R. N. Cust, Captain Wharton, Hydrographer to the Admiralty, and other speakers bore testimony to the invaluable benefits

[1] See *Proceedings of the Royal Geographical Society*, vol. ix, New Series, pp. 71-86.

of missionary work in New Guinea, and to the extra-ordinary personal influence of Chalmers.  Mr. Askwith said: 'Mr. Chalmers had mighty influence with the natives, whether as arbitrator, or friend, or religious teacher, or sorcerer, or as all of these, and it might be that he had taught some to believe in one Supreme Being whose influence was for good, rather than in a host of devils and ghosts of the dead by whom they were wont to believe that they were oppressed.'  Captain Wharton stated that when Captain Duru Stanley made the first survey of south New Guinea in the Rattlesnake he met with great difficulties everywhere because of the hostility of the natives.  There were now two surveying vessels in New Guinea, and their labours had been very much lightened by the missionaries.  He was glad to have this opportunity of thanking Mr. Chalmers for the great assistance he had been to those vessels.  He had just received a letter from the commander of one of those ships who owed his life indirectly to the missionaries.'

One of the most interesting incidents during his stay in Britain was the recognition by the home of his boyhood of the work he had done and the position he had achieved.  He was welcomed to Inveraray not only by those who remembered him as a lad and a young man, but also by the Duke of Argyll as the head and representative of the whole community.  On the evening of Sunday, June 5, 1887, Chalmers gave a stirring address in the Castle Pavilion, the use of which was cheerfully granted by the Duke of Argyll.

'The large and spacious pavilion was crowded, as many as 800 persons, including the Marquis of Lorne, from the town and district being present.  The address was chiefly confined to exploration and mission work in New Guinea—the speaker being unable for want of time to refer to his work in Rarotonga—the character and habits, the influencing power of the Gospel on the natives, many of the tribes being cannibals, and the suffering and danger to which he had been frequently exposed. At the close of his address, which was listened to with rapt attention, he in feeling terms referred to the few boon companions of his youth then present, for whom he cherished the liveliest affection; as well as for aged fathers and mothers also present, from whom he had received the greatest kindness in his tender years; but as long as he lived he would feel grateful to his old teacher, Mr. John Macarthur, schoolmaster, Glenaray, and to his beloved pastor, the Rev. Gilbert Meikle, of the United Presbyterian Church, from whom he had always received special sympathy and kindness. He thanked all present for their countenance and kind feeling towards him.

'On Monday last, before leaving Inveraray, at the request of the Duke of Argyll, who speaks of him as being a credit to his country, Mr. Chalmers planted a memorial tree in the Castle Park, near to one planted by Dr. Livingstone, the celebrated African explorer.'

Chalmers sailed from Plymouth on his return to New Guinea, in the steamship Orient, on June 15, 1887. He was, of course, entirely at home on board ship, and never more himself than when the sea was rough and the vessel lively. He sent home, for the amusement of friends, a diary of the voyage, which he wrote up from day to day. He had no idea, of course, that it would ever be published, but it is full of touches which reveal his lovable nature, his keen interest in life, his deep affection for children, and his readiness to pass from a frolic to a religious service, from a tug of war to a talk

THE TREE PLANTED IN THE GROUNDS OF INVERARAY CASTLE
BY JAMES CHALMERS ON JUNE 6, 1887.

(THE STANDING FIGURE IS THE REV. GILBERT MEIKLE.)

on the deep things of life. In this easy way we can make the voyage with him.

'Sunday, July 10. I slept on deck last night and enjoyed it much—simply and solely slept. I am now a masher in whites. Though hot, we had an interesting service—the captain read prayers admirably; the purser read lessons, fatigued; I preached, and enjoyed it. I felt homely on the first paragraph of John xxi. I do love Christ; He is simply, solely everything. You know, people speak about a religious life, and they mean going to church and prayer meetings. That is not it, surely. I feel it, and believe it. Christ everywhere, in all things. Means are good, but they are only bulrushes. It must be Christ all round, Alpha and Omega, end, between and beginning.

'July 12. Last night I was chairman at a concert with the seconds. To save nonsensical speaking in thankings I did it all myself, even proposing and seconding a vote of thanks to the chairman, and said nice pat things about him that were highly amusing to the audience.

'July 15. Last night I went aft to comfort the two parsons. They have also been very ill. I got them some sea medicine, got the Scotch parson and his wife on deck with the priest and others, all seedy. I told them personal sea yarns for over an hour, and they all forgot they were sick. The priest thinks—well, I won't say what, of me. He would like, I have no doubt, to see me a priest. I fancy he thinks I may get in at the last by some door. He looked aghast at my sea yarns —shipwrecks; careenings; upsets; waterless; foodless— a queer life, but I am glad of it. My father used to say, "Eh, laddie, ye're surely no born to be hung, for I'm sure ye'll nae be drowned."

'July 18. This morning we have had a fine time. All the children in the seconds thought a wedding would be a nice game, so I was to be married to a fine bright-eyed Irish lassie, and then we were to go shopping. Our barber keeps a sweet-shop. We assembled, but the difficulty was with the bride. All wanted that honour, even to the boys. We thought it best to do the shopping, and to the great amusement of the ship's company away we trooped from the quarter-deck to the main deck, then down companion, filling the shop to overflowing. We seized the sweets, and then took possession of a large saloon table and made equal divisions. That finished, I have been with them an hour telling them stories.

'July 21. Last night we were to have had a concert, but the weather became too rough; so I spoke for an hour to an interested company on New Guinea. To-day they want more.

'July 23. I was having a nap this afternoon when Powell came and roused me, saying the seconds had challenged us to a tug of war. Four of us were soon aft accepting the challenge. They selected their best four, and we set to; but they had no chance. I was anchor. They protest against me. I hear there is another challenge.

'July 24. We have had a splendid service; saloon full, Christians, Protestants, Roman Catholics, Greek Church and Jews, all present. I pleaded for the widows and orphans of seamen. Christ initiated the work of helping the widow; we carry on His work, and every Christian must say, "Do not weep," help the widow in every way possible, and that is His "Arise." Many wept, I trust honest tears of sympathy. I spoke straight to young men. I hope the fund for assisting widows and orphans of seamen has benefitted. I hope also some have realized Christ as the Life, their Life, and all have decided to live more for Him.

'July 25. We are to have sports this afternoon. They nearly fell through, so a meeting was called; I took the chair, finished the whole business in five minutes, and appointed a committee on which I am. Arrangements are completed, and so at 2.30 we are all boys and girls again. Jolly!

'July 26. The sports passed off well. Young Mr. Meikle did splendidly, he is quite an athlete. The tug of war is the constant cry. England and Scotland; the latter beaten. Three of England, three of Scotland; the former beaten. Now there is to be another struggle between five officers, and more sports this afternoon.

'The meeting with the thirds last night was a grand success. I spoke for over an hour on the main deck, and got three rattling cheers for thanks.

'July 27. A poor Irishman with his wife on board, after they had paid for their kit, pan, tins, bed, had one sixpence left. The Roman Catholic priest brought it before the seconds, and they made a subscription. I heard of it, and got the priest to give me the list, and in a short time returned it with £3 2s. 6d. The father could not express his thanks, he was so overcome. We left him to do the best for the poor couple.

'The officers beat us firsts; but in an open for seven passengers against seven ship we had two deadly pulls, and on each we won. I am sore, ache all over. Must have a pull to-morrow to put me right. Everybody seems pleased and the whole has passed off well.

'July 29. It is simply holding on by the skin of your teeth. Rough and cold. We are nearing the Australian Bight.

'July 30. Boxes, bags, boats, all walking, and will not keep still. Last night I turned in early to find a comfortable place, but the wretched ship would roll, and make all attempts at sleep futile. It is laughable to hear the varied experiences of the passengers.

'Aug. 1. We had a crowded saloon last night, several standing outside of doors. I spoke for an hour and a half, and felt tired. I think all were interested; at all events when I finished they sat looking as if they wanted more. I have consented to speak to-night, and so wind up my public appearances on board S.S. Orient. We leave results in the Master's own hand. Eh, lassie, but this is a thorough Australian winter day. A clear beautiful sky, a fine bright sun, and a strong WNW. wind, and we are dropping aside the miles at the rate of fifteen an hour. 'Tis charming, exhilarating—haven't the dictionary, so will stop adjectives. We had the thirds' bairns reciting this morning. They did well and were charmed with their prizes.'

Chalmers landed at Adelaide on August 3, 1887, and was at once greeted with enthusiastic welcome by many personal friends, and during his brief stay in the colonies was quite the great public man.

'ADELAIDE, *August* 4, 1887.

'Got here yesterday morning. The night before we had a fine snow fight in the refrigerator, where I tore my cut-away coat, and had to get it mended. Then we all met in the second saloon, and sang, "Auld Lang Syne," after which I was told to sit down, and an address was presented to me signed by all the leading passengers. After landing it was soon noised that I was in town. I had a pressing invitation from the Governor of Melbourne, or rather, Victoria, to luncheon to-day or to-morrow and a free pass for the railways. I cannot

Yours very faithfully
James Chalmers
alias Tamate

get away till next Thursday. Last night I spoke at a meeting in North Adelaide. To-night I was a listener at a lecture. To-morrow night a conversazione in the Exhibition. To-day an invitation to dinner from the Chief Justice. On my arrival yesterday I was interviewed, and the result appeared in to-day's paper. I am staying with my good friends the Searles. People are all very kind. On Sunday I have three services, on Tuesday two, on Wednesday two. It is not all play.'

Chalmers was heartily welcomed back to Australia at a public breakfast in the Victoria Hall, Adelaide, at which the Rev. Samuel Hebditch, the Chairman of the Congregational Union, presided. The meeting was attended by representatives of all the churches. In addition to sermons and speeches Chalmers also gave a lecture before the South Australian Geographical Society on Explorations in New Guinea.

From Adelaide he went on to Melbourne.

'MELBOURNE, *August* 16, 1887.

'We left Adelaide 3.30 p.m. and arrived here at 9.50 a.m. I was met at the station by representatives of the Press, the Geographical Society, and clergy. I am staying with Mr. King, our agent, being quieter with him than in any of the big houses to which I was invited. I preached twice on Sunday, and last night I was received by the Geographical Society.

'To-night I am to dine at Government House; to-morrow I go to Queenscliffe; Thursday I am at Harthorne; Friday with Dr. Bevan. Sunday I preach twice, and on Monday there is a public meeting, and on Tuesday I am off to Sydney.

'There has been a young fellow exploring in country near to Namau, and he has renamed many

T

of my places. It will be all right, seeing mine are
charted, even in Germany.'

At the reception of the Geographical Society Baron
Von Mueller presided, and in his address of welcome
said :—

' Mr. Chalmers has spurned all worldly gain, and has
brought his extraordinary talents and gifts to bear in
developing the history of New Guinea, and such is the
position he occupies that we feel honoured to welcome
him. The council is glad to meet Mr. Chalmers,
because it is anxious to be advised as to his proposals
for future research, for he is one of those divines who,
while devoting his life to the cause of Christianity, still
has done a great deal in aiding the knowledge of
geography. The council hope that it will fall to Mr.
Chalmers' share to scale the steep and lofty heights of
the Owen Stanley range.'

In his speech acknowledging the compliment, Chalmers
stated clearly his position with regard to exploration.
He said :—

' The Society has on three occasions done me great
honour : first, when three years ago I was asked to take
command of an expedition, which I declined, for Captain
Everill ; secondly, when the offer came again, and when
Mr. Lawes, my colleague, was in Australia, and I was
unable to leave the mission ; and thirdly, for this last
favour. I was in England at the time, and when I found
that arrangements could not be made with Mr. Forbes,
and Sir Henry Barkly came to me stating what the
Society wanted, I was very glad to undertake it, and
more pleased later on when I heard that Mr. Cuthbertson
had been dispatched to precede me. My advice is to
leave him entirely unfettered. Seeing that he is now

at his work, I think it would not be just if I disclosed to you my own plans, as they might hamper him in his intention.  As soon as I return to New Guinea I shall write to the Society, and explain my arrangements, but at present I think it only right that Cuthbertson should have a fair field, and if he be willing I shall assist him so far as I am able.  When his present task is completed, I would recommend that he be returned to make further investigations into the interior.  With regard to myself, I shall continue my mission work while I am carrying on the exploratory tour.  That I cannot give up.  In the past nine years my exploration has been entirely associated with the mission, and I can only say that the success I have met with is due to the fact that I was a missionary.'

It was at this time Chalmers hoped and intended to get further inland in New Guinea than any white man had hitherto gone, and also to be the first European to stand upon the summit of Mount Owen Stanley.  Had he chosen to accept the flattering offers made to him while in the colonies, had he been willing to subordinate the missionary to the explorer, he could and would undoubtedly have gratified this ambition.  But he chose the path of duty in preference to that of inclination, and his feet never trod the summit of New Guinea's great mountain.

During his stay in Melbourne there was also a great public meeting, at which both Sir Henry and Lady Loch were present.  Missionaries in general, and Chalmers in particular, have reason to be grateful for the countenance given to them, and the help afforded, by those in high official position in Australia.  And while there, as else-where, masses of the people are indifferent or hostile to missions, yet large numbers of the Australian people have been hearty and liberal in their support of missions, and enthusiastic in their reception of such men as Chalmers and Lawes.

From Melbourne Chalmers passed to Sydney on his return to work.

'SYDNEY, *August* 31, 1887.

'We had a splendid meeting in Melbourne, and Sir Henry and Lady Loch were delighted. The Geographical Society steer clear of me because I will not tell them my plans. There are many expeditions out. One now here has been on old ground of mine, and renamed many of the places first discovered by me. Still, they have made good discoveries.'

In another letter of the same date Chalmers draws an amusing picture of the awkward corner in which a man sometimes finds himself when he is unwilling to give to others the full credit which they deserve for work done honestly and well.

'SYDNEY, *August* 31, 1887.

'I have steered clear of all the Geographical Societies. They have been dubbing me in all the colonies, and are extremely anxious to know what I am going to do, and anxious to assist me, secure me, do anything for me. But I have kept my counsel, and mean to carry on as I have formerly done. The Directors have always treated me well, and I feel sure they will see me through in my next trips.

We have four teachers and their wives here. I do wish I could take them in to Glenhurst, that you might hear them sing. Yesterday I took them to Rookwood, where Mrs. Chalmers rests, and they were much moved with past memories. Eh, it was a living past in a dead present.'

'COOKTOWN, *September* **17**, 1887.

'The Sydney branch of the Geographical Society wired me yesterday to know if I really did state in Melbourne that nearly seven years ago I had named much that Mr. —— has now named, or was it a mistake of the newspaper. I wired back, "Quite correct," and then referred them to authorities. I wrote by this morning's mail, saying, that if Sydney geographers were so far behind the times, I did not think it my place to right them, and saying I was astonished they should leave inquiry until after I had left, seeing I made the utterance in public.'

In this connexion we may quote the testimony of one supremely competent witness. Sir W. Macgregor states [1], 'The principal addition that should be made to Sir Clements Markham's paper is the discovery—really a very important one—of the mouths of the Purari river by the Rev. James Chalmers in 1879, and his subsequent visit to that place in 1883. Mr. Chalmers makes no pretence to having ascended the river, or even to an examination of the delta; but a reference to his books, *Work and Adventure in New Guinea* (1885) and *Pioneering in New Guinea* (1887), will clearly establish his claim to be the discoverer of the Purari outlets.'

Towards the end of September Chalmers was back again in New Guinea. The 'bronzed savage' had sojourned in the dwellings of civilization far longer than he had deemed possible when, sixteen months before, he had sailed away from his field of work. He had in several senses discovered himself. He had found that the deputation work he had so feared had

[1] *British New Guinea*, p. 4, edition of 1899 (John Murray).

become in his hand a mighty power for good; he had left behind hundreds of friends who were thinking of him, and praying for the work of himself and his fellow workers. It was to a wider horizon, a larger outlook, and yet to the same work, that he came back with renewed energy, zeal, and faith.

'PORT MORESBY, *September* 22, 1887.

'We had a good passage across, made comfortable by our good captain. The excitement on landing was great; one dear old lady through excitement cast her arms around me and rubbed, to her with great satisfaction, my face all over. It was a grand ovation, to be written on more fully hereafter. We had to pay our respects to the admiral this morning, and dine with him to-night. Mr. and Mrs. Lawes are as good as ever, and did give me a good welcome back again. I paid my respects to the governor also this morning.

'24th. I had a very enjoyable evening last night. To the great amusement of the admiral, his officers and I went over old scenes, and he thinks he will return and have me if possible to run him round. On the deck smoking I had a most appreciative reception. Old hands gathered round, and would see and hear Tamate.'

# CHAPTER IX

## LIFE AND WORK AT MOTUMOTU

FOR some time after his return to New Guinea Chalmers remained at Port Moresby with his old friends Mr. and Mrs. Lawes. He had returned more enthusiastic than ever in the prosecution of his plan to extend the mission westwards up into the Gulf of Papua and among the strong tribes of Elema and Namau. The death in 1887 of the brave young Samoan teacher whom he had stationed some years before at Motumotu, or, as it should more correctly be called, Toaripi [1], was a great blow to him personally, and a serious hindrance to the work. Tauraki, the teacher in question, was the son of Elikana, a native of Rakaanga, one of the islands of the Penrhyn Group. This man, in a series of adventures among the most romantic and striking in the history of the Pacific, was the agent in introducing Christianity into the Ellice Islands [2]. Tauraki, his son, had been educated at Malua in Samoa, sent to New Guinea, and duly stationed at Toaripi. Chalmers, in a letter dated September 28, 1887, tells the story of his end, and in so doing adds another to the long series of examples of the self-

---

[1] Toaripi is the native name, Motumotu the name given to it by the Port Moresby natives.

[2] See my *History of the London Missionary Society*, vol. i, pp. 422-429.

sacrificing bravery of the Polynesian teachers in New Guinea :—

'Tauraki, who was murdered, his wife and child and ten natives, left their homes one Sunday night about ten o'clock, and went down some distance to an island just at the mouth of a river, and slept there, so as to be ready for an early start in the morning. They wished to ascend the river, and collect the bulb used in making the best arrowroot. Monday and Tuesday were spent in collecting this bulb. They returned down the river on Tuesday afternoon, and when approaching a bend they saw a large number of canoes, each with the fighting wisp in front. They tried to get back by another route, but that way was also blocked. They then just drifted down the stream, and the canoes closed on them. Tauraki's wife begged him to fire a shot from his fowling-piece or rifle, and thus to frighten the natives, but he would not. There was a contention amongst the enemy—some pleading that there should be no fighting, others declaring that they would murder the whole party. Hoping to make friends, the wife distributed some tobacco ; but soon the arrows began to fly. Tauraki's child was wounded by an arrow. His wife was also wounded, and two natives fell dead. She had the fowling-piece in her hand, and fired, and the shot scared those near. Tauraki's party had two canoes lashed together, and some of their natives sprang overboard and got between the canoes. His wife with the child followed, and the husband stood up with several arrows sticking in him, and began firing his rifle. This scared the enemy, and they all plunged into the river. Those with Tauraki who were still alive, and his wife and child, got into the canoe, and paddled away. It was then getting dark, and they were a long way from home.

Their great want was water, but they kept on, and about midnight got to the beach near their own house. On landing the child expired. The teacher and wife were helped up to the house of Mr. Edelfelt, resident at Toaripi, who with his wife did everything possible for them. But on Saturday morning Tauraki died, the wife recovering.

'Five natives of Motumotu who had been in Tauraki's canoe were dead. The attack was really made in order to kill the natives with him. If Tauraki would have consented to go on board one of the enemy's canoes, with his wife and child, all would have been well for them. But that he nobly refused to do, saying that he would stand by his friends, and if need be die with them. Eh, 'tis a sad, sad story. He was our very best teacher, and from him I hoped much. I leave next week to begin again our Motumotu work.'

In a subsequent letter of this time, Chalmers wrote:—
'We had another teacher and his wife at Motumotu. In January of this year the husband died from fever, and a few months later the wife followed. Yet there is light in the darkness—lives given to Christ and man. Following in His footsteps, they count not their lives dear; as He went to Calvary, knowing all, so do they, trusting in Him, and following His example. Christ shows us how to live, and also how to die, and there are still Calvarys with their grand life ending.

'We have had a most enjoyable time at Port Moresby. At the meetings there were New Guineans from Milne Bay, South Cape, Aroma, Kerepunu, Hula, Boera, and Port Moresby; and there were Tahitians, Rarotongans, English and Scotch, all united as one—one in Christ. I spoke in Motuan, and Pearse in Tahitian. Ruatoka addressed those who had not yet decided for Christ, and pressed them to accept Him as their life. The deacons

who served were four New Guineans. What cannot the
Gospel do when blessed of God?'

Here is Chalmers' own picture of his reception at
Motumotu, drawn in a letter to the lady who became his
wife:—'We left Maiva on Sunday evening, and got
a jolly wetting going through the surf. It is disagreeable to get drenched when one has to sit long in a boat.
We had to pull nearly all the way, and did not get off
Jokea until midnight. A shout was given, and the
people ashore, recognizing the voice of Turia, their
teacher, were soon astir with lights on the beach. It
was a weird sight, the boat at sea outside a long line of
white breakers, and on the beach a crowd of natives carrying dry, burning cocoa-nut leaves. A hard pull, a long
pull, steady—again a hard pull—there she goes, over and
through everything into the hands of the savages, and
away she is carried right on to the dry beach. What excitement in meeting their teacher! And then there arose
a terrific roar when they found that I was in the boat.
The poor old chief heard it in his house, where he has
been confined for some time, and he too must come to
meet Tamate. Nothing would suit him but rub noses.

'Yesterday morning we got out through the surf
again, and had to pull against the wind for nine hours
in a broiling sun. Getting a slant of wind we sailed up
to Motumotu, but the sea was breaking so fearfully we
could not land on the beach. So we had to sail away far
beyond the village, until we got to a quiet entrance into
the river, where in crossing the bar we shipped two seas
and got a drenching. On landing here just after sundown,
I was met by Mr. Edelfelt, the government representative, and he insisted on my going to his house. His
wife was down with a terrible attack of fever. I am
sorry for her and for him too.

'After a good night's rest I went out to visit, and to look over all the mission property. Eh, 'tis sad. When I began my journey home I left here two teachers and their wives. I had great thoughts of future work. I now return, and all are gone. God knows best, and He does move in mysterious ways.

'The people are hearty and kind. There is enough wood sawn here to make a large house, so this may be your future home. There is fever everywhere, but it is not worse here than in other places. After Tauraki's murder the government sent an expedition, and five of the natives were shot, a few others wounded, and a splendid village burnt. I resolved to visit these people, and to make friends with them.

'I left in a canoe with four natives from this place, and paddled up the river to Moveave. We smoked and chatted on the way. The chatting was done with difficulty in pidgin English. Of course there was danger, and I might be received with suspicion so soon after the punishment. When near the first village we came suddenly upon a canoe with a husband and wife and two bairns in it. Poor things, they had a terrible fright. The husband flew to his bow and arrows, and the mother and bairns were about to spring into the river, when we shouted, and assured them that we were friends, and that I was Tamate. The bow and arrows were put down, and they paddled near to us. Then a little tobacco helped to soothe them. The bairns were crying piteously, and the husband and wife trembled dreadfully. We got them to go on ahead, and to warn the people of our approach. We paddled on and into a narrow creek, where if attacked it would have been impossible for us to escape. We landed in the bush some distance from the village. One of my party shouted, and soon a large number of armed natives came rushing along. They were told who I was, and that they must not approach armed, as I was quite unarmed, not having even a knife with me. They put away all their arms, and came in a crowd to meet us. They were glad, I believe, from the very depths of their hearts that I had come to make friends with them.

'My four native friends who were with me, having arms with them, delivered them up, and away we went to the village. They would not let me step in a damp place, but insisted on carrying me over every little drop of water. A few new houses had been put up. On the way up the river I cut up about ten sticks of tobacco into very small pieces, which I gave to a chief, one of my four, and he distributed it. Men, women, and children hailed us with delight. We went through the bush to another village, and had the same kind of reception. On our return to the first village I found a large shade erected for me. It was made with cocoa-nut leaves, and underneath a crowd sat, and we conversed as best we could on the misery of war and the blessings of peace. They gave me presents of cocoa-nuts, betel nuts, and other treasures, and in return I gave them knives, looking - glasses, tobacco, and jubilee medals. It was a good time. We stayed only a short while with them, and then returned to Moveave, our first village.'

After a brief stay at Motumotu Chalmers returned to Port Moresby to look after his heavy baggage, which had been delayed on the voyage.

'We got here yesterday (Oct. 20) from Motumotu, and set to at once to open cases. What pleasure there is in opening boxes! To-day I have been arranging presents for students and wives, teachers and wives, and servants and friends. No easy matter when there are so many to receive them.

'It is well I did not start on any long journey at present. The weather beats description—thunderstorms, heavy rains, hot and sultry; not such as needed for long land journeys. My visit to Motumotu was well timed. I was able to make friends with the people up the river, and they are now all returning to their villages with confidence. I wish we could place teachers at both places. As soon as the new teachers become a little acclimatized two will be placed at Motumotu, and I think I shall put up a shanty for myself there at present. I must keep on the move amongst the stations, and prepare for more new teachers who come to us next year.

'To-day our captain, who is a bit of an electrician, has been busy with the telephone[1], which has come all right, except the carbons, which are all broken. It is fairly successful. The natives are astonished, and frightened. A boy who has been to Sydney says, " I now can understand those wires overhead."

'At our morning service one of the speakers gave an account in thorough native fashion of Jacob's deceiving his father. I felt intensely interested when he spoke of the wild hunter chasing the kangaroo, while the sneaking brother was at home with the ambitious mother quietly killing and cooking a kid. I don't like Jacob. He would have been a prominent, mean, calculating Christian under Christianity, for ever trying to get to the windward of every one else.

'Sunday night. This morning I took an English service, and spoke from Esther vii. 5 and 6; and in the

[1] This was a telephone, long enough to connect with a distant house, which a friend in England had presented to Chalmers.

afternoon a native service, and spoke from Mark vii. 37. I find my native somewhat heavy, but with use it will come all right.

'Oct. 28. To-day a party was formed : Mr. and Mrs. Lawes, Captain Hennessy, H.M. Special Commissioner, Mr. Douglas, and his Private Secretary, and this youth. We went to Valrikori, a village four miles from here, and in charge of a native teacher born and bred in the land, and educated at the college here. He had a catechumen class of six men and three women which Misi and I examined, and were pleased with. We then called a meeting of all the people, and in their presence baptized the nine, and thus formed the Church of Christ there. It was a most interesting occasion. God is blessing His work, and the light is being sown in the darkness, and Christ is being loved by the once savage. The picnic was also a success, and on our return all felt that a profitable and pleasant day had been spent.'

After unpacking his goods Chalmers was soon back at Motumotu, and in the Ellengowan visited Vailala and Orokolo. Later on several new teachers were selected for the Gulf stations, and placed there by Ruatoka in accordance with the wishes of Chalmers. But Mr. and Mrs. Lawes being absent on a furlough in the colonies, Chalmers had to take charge of the college and routine work at Port Moresby. Here he lived and worked until his second marriage in October, 1888.

From this period onward there is in existence a large mass of Chalmers' private correspondence. Hardly any of this has ever before appeared in print. It covers in detail from week to week, and almost from day to day, his actions, his plans and his thoughts. Moreover, in these letters the real man appears, and very frequently he unveils his innermost purpose and his deepest desires. The letters were written for the most part without any belief or desire that they would ever come under any eyes but those of the correspondent. It has been a great privilege, and also a great trust, for the author to have had such full and unrestricted access to a correspondence which constantly opens the door into the very heart-life of both the writer and the recipients of these letters. And the closer they are studied the nobler does Tamate appear in his enthusiasm for work, in complete consecration to Christ, in self-denying labours, and in lofty ambitions. It is true also that from time to time the letters prove him to have been very human, and that he was perfect neither in life nor thought nor achievement. But because they exhibit a very lovable and strong personality, and at the same time do not conceal many little human weaknesses and failings, they are all the more precious. We shall from this point onwards largely ignore official and formal documents, and allow the reader to share the life and opinions of Tamate as his close friends and intimate correspondents shared them.

In a letter dated January 4, 1888, he outlines his life at Port Moresby as soon as he had once again thoroughly settled down to New Guinea conditions. Until August he was alone there, Mr. and Mrs. Lawes being in Australia.

'I have to superintend certain duties every day. Now some women are washing, others are weeding, and a few girls are sweeping up. I have men repairing gates and strengthening houses, for this north-west monsoon has no mercy—others are washing boats. We have our week of prayer now. May we be greatly blessed and others through us!

'13th. Last night we had a grand row in the village.

A few days ago a great many natives, alarmed at the small quantity of rain falling, determined to try a sorcerer who happened to come in, and get him to procure rain in abundance. The sorcerer consented on payment, so a collection was made consisting of arm shells, toma-hawks and sago, and two dogs. He went through his mummeries and cleared, and no rain coming the natives who gave no payment made fun of the others, and last night it resulted in a fight. Nothing serious happened.

'My plan with a row is not to interfere, only laugh and tell them to go on with their bit of fun, and this they very much dislike. When bows and arrows are rushed for, then we separate the opposing parties.

'I am getting the boys a little into shape. Insist on smart attendance immediately on bell ringing, and insist on a thing being done on one telling. I do like smart-ness in class and everywhere. A new teacher who did not know me except from hearsay thought he would do as he liked. I called him once, I knew he heard; he took no notice. I called again, the same result. His bringing up was bad. He is all right now, and he knows me better than he did, and I know he likes me. May he long live for Christ's work!

'Canon Taylor's remarks will do good. There is something wrong in our mode of working. We look too much for individual cases of conversion; these are chronicled and made much of. Do not you think the Gospel is for mankind, and that it ought to influence whole tribes? We potter away with one or two converts; good, but strike for the higher—assert for the nation or tribe. Our statistic system is all wrong. They will keep the statistics in heaven, I feel sure, and I would leave them in their hands.

'Have had another very bad shaking. I must cave

in and lie down a bit. All afternoon I have been very
ill. Mueller wants me to go over Cuthbertson's ground,
take more extensive angles, and make a large collection
of botany. I cannot do it now. If I get across to
other side, might do it on my return journey. I am
out of sorts. This morning I felt splendid.

'17th. Bad fever. Must close.'

'January 31, 1888. I have another application from
the Australian Geographical Society, but I cannot at
present reply. Our real mission-work requires me for
the present. I begin new stations next season, extending our work further into the Gulf. When I speak
of West and Gulf I mean the district to the west of Cape
Possession. At present Motumotu is our largest village
and most important station. Two new teachers went
there at the beginning of the year, and I must visit them
in March. If you have a chart or a map, you will see
Motumotu, and beyond it Karama and Uamai and
Kerema, Vailala and Orokolo; well, all these I hope to
occupy soon. If I can make an exploring trip or two
between I shall, but my real work must be first.

'I have a Chinese cook, but he leaves me soon.
When ill I had nothing to eat, not fancying anything
the natives could make me. One day I staggered to
a bookshelf and got down Mrs. Beeton, but, alas, she
was complicated, and I had to give it up. Since my
Chinese cook has been here, loaned from young Lawes,
I have been faring sumptuously every day, and feel as
strong as an African lion.'

'February 1. I dearly love working Christians, and
like to see all native converts doing something for Him
whose they profess to be. Last Sunday was a high day
for us at Tupuselei. We began with a morning service,
when the church was crowded, only four with any

U

clothing. In the forenoon I had a children's service, and afterwards met twenty-seven catechumens, twenty-five men and two women. I left them unbaptized for the present, preferring they should still wait, and be prepared. In the afternoon there was another large gathering, when, after I had addressed them, I threw the meeting open and invited any one to speak. It was a strange sight to see one naked man after another rise, give a short earnest address, saying, " Let us love God, let us listen to the teacher, let us keep the Sabbath and remember Christ loves us," and so on, and so on, and then sit down. But the address of the occasion was the following. A young man got up and said, " Friends, if we do evil, Jesus weeps—is pained; if we do well, Jesus is well pleased. I have finished." He was naked. He was intensely in earnest, and his voice had a pathos that made one feel the reality of his words. I think that address is unique, and would tell well in a home audience. It is short and pointed, and needs no commentary. To hear a native in earnest prayer is refreshing. He praises like a child, he pleads like a child, and you feel he expects to get a blessing. Would that we were more like this!

'I am just getting into the old swing of classes, and enjoy it as much as ever I did in Rarotonga, only I want a help for the women. They all read beautifully, better than their husbands. I will have a writing class with them once a day. I wish I could teach them to sew. All the teachers' wives have machines, and the girls are not taught sewing.

'It will take some time before my students and children will get into the way of learning at home and coming prepared—they are finding it hard work. They must succeed, and will soon, if only their patience is as lengthy as mine.  Don't laugh, I am very patient with children and natives.'

When Chalmers left England in 1887, through the influence of a friend and the courtesy of the officials of the Eastern Telegraph Company, he was allowed the privilege of sending home free telegrams.  This privilege had to be suspended because, it was said, at the time of the Colonial Exhibition visitors who possessed it abused it.  But on January 20, 1887, Chalmers sent home a telegram which to the uninitiated certainly presented an alarming appearance, and finally crept into the press, originating considerable innocent amusement. It ran, ' Had several attacks of fever.  Now well. Getting in trim for next season.  Ask Jones, Devonshire Square, send one gross tomahawks, one gross butchers' knives.  Society pay.  Inform Dr. Muirhead going east try make friends between tribes.  Chalmers.' It must be admitted that this message had a somewhat sanguinary quality about it, and many were the jokes in the City about Chalmers' method of promoting friendship by means of tomahawks and butchers' knives. But as these articles happen to be the most serviceable currency in the wildest parts of New Guinea, the telegram was simply a request for the replenishment of his stores of barter, in anticipation of projected journeys. In a letter from Port Moresby, dated May 26, Chalmers acknowledges the receipt of these weapons.  ' Tomahawks and knives were all right, and already some gone to a tribe on my route inland to make friends and peace. Capital way of getting stuff quick.'

' May 1.  Since writing last I have been on the move, been west and visited all the stations.  We had very rough weather west, and difficult landings at some places.  At Kivori, near Cape Possession, we got chucked out of the boat. There were heavy seas, and the boat swinging on one capsized. At other places we got drenched and swamped. We had services and school examinations at all the stations, and where least I expected it good progress has been made. At Naara, where my queen Koloka is, there is a good earnest work begun. Koloka seeks baptism, but I advised waiting. Several children could read.

'Having finished with the west I visited all the stations to Hula, where the schooner overtook me, and we proceeded to Kerepunu. Mr. Pearse joined us, and we continued our voyage to the east, calling at Aroma and Mailiu (Cloudy Bay). At the latter place my old friend Gidage came off and renewed friendship. He wants a teacher, and promises to treat him kindly. We were anxious to visit Toulon, but the wind was unfavourable, and we continued on to here. Since then we have been to Teste, Killerton, Vagavaga, Dinner Island, Leocadie, and back here. At the Leocadie the people were pleased we visited them. We have only an evangelist there as yet. Years ago the natives gave me for the London Missionary Society the large island, Delina, and yesterday confirmed it by reminding me that the island and all on it was ours. It will make a good head-station, better than any other place we have at the east end. The people some years ago murdered a number of Chinamen. Now they are really friendly, and anxious to be taught.

'We are likely to have some little trouble with the government about Dinner Island. I wait until I meet Misi and Douglas. At Vagavaga it simply poured all the time of our stay, so that we could do nothing. Two Loyalty Islands teachers were there a short time some years ago; being very unhealthy they were removed, and since then a Dinner Island native has occasionally visited them. We were anchored close by the mission-house. About four in the afternoon a deputation of clothed natives came on board, saying they belonged to the mission. Children sitting under a house for shelter were singing hymns. There is a change seen even in the appearance of all the natives. They were a wild cannibal lot a few years ago. One of the natives who came off spoke a little English. Pearse, who certainly would make a fine feast, asked him if they eat man, and was answered, " No. No eat man now, all fellow missionary now." In the evening at seven a bell rang, and soon hymn-singing was heard; they were having evening prayers. You cannot realize it. Savages, cannibals, murderers, now seeking to worship God. It was strangely pleasing to hear an old hymn-tune in such a place.

' Had good time at South Cape and visiting stations. I was refreshed in visiting the stations with New Guinea teachers. At Savaia, where only a short time ago there were cannibal feasts, there are three catechumens and six who can read well, and all the people friendly. The teacher is a Suau lad, and his wife from here. She is a mite, good and clever, keeps a clean house, teaches in school and has singing classes, holds more than her own with the savages.

' At Navaapou quiet, steady, gentle Hari of Suau is making headway, and the people really love him. He too has three wishing baptism, men who already take part in services, and who speak a word for Christ when they can. I always like to see all who desire to profess Christ by baptism showing their love to Him by working for Him.

' A New Guinean, preaching last Wednesday, said:

" The time has come for us to be up and doing. Foreigners have brought us the Gospel, many have died of fever, several have been speared and tomahawked. Now let us carry the Gospel to other districts, and if we die 'tis well we die in Christ; if we are murdered 'tis well, 'tis in carrying His name and love, and 'twill be for Him. Motu, let us do it." He knows only a little, so very little; yet he loves, and he is willing to endure for Christ. I saved that lad a few years ago from being attacked, perhaps murdered, by his own people.

' Did I tell you, at Vabukori near here there are forty-three catechumens, and at Tupuselei fifty-six? The prayer of faith is being answered. The greatest power of the mission-house is that monthly prayer-meeting.'

On June 4 he wrote to Mr. Wardlaw Thompson: 'I am in excellent health, and should like much a run to the mountains, but I cannot manage it now; I must keep at my post on the coast. What think you of five hours' teaching daily for this wanderer! I like it, and I like t'other too. I have only two sick folk on hand. Do not trouble about me; alone or with friends I am perfectly happy. I must do that Gulf this year, and get as far as Vailala with new stations. The house at Motumotu, a wooden one, is finished. It will be a splendid bungalow, built of cedar, and will cost the Society about twenty pounds or less. My houses have not yet cost much; and I don't mean that they shall. I want to be at Motumotu as much as possible to watch over new stations. I must travel. I feel it in my bones.'

' July 7. A week ago I went to Kabadi. Mr. Romilly hearing I was going, he having a party travelling inland thereabout, decided to go with me, so the Government cutter took us to the Skittles (Kekeni), Redscar Bay, and there my whaleboat met us. About four p.m. we left the cutter, eighteen all told on board the boat. Mr. Romilly was against landing until the morning. I was anxious to spend as long a time as possible with the teacher and people and visit all the villages, hence the hurry ashore. I had a trusty native at the oar steering. We were very deeply laden. On nearing the bar it did not seem to me as *very* dangerous, so we stood on. The first bar sea sped us on, the second one caught us, we shipped water, the steer oar got jammed, the boat swung and went over. It was deep and the seas heavy, and for a short time it seemed some of us must go. It is a terrible place for crocodiles, but I suppose so many of us frightened them. The smashing in the surf was enough to kill. The boat's crew of native students did nobly. We got ashore. I feared at one time Romilly was drowning. I felt somewhat exhausted myself. I fancy Romilly must have been struck with an oar. The boys got the boat in after a good hour's hard work. I got three times on to the boat's keel and each time was swept away. At last got an oar, and assisted by a native I got to a sandbank—resting a little, then ashore. A fire was lighted, around which we all gathered, when one of the students engaged in prayer, and with full hearts we all joined him in thanksgiving. During the night things were washed ashore and amongst them my swag. Intending to stay until Monday, Mr. Romilly had two guns and two rifles for birds and crocodiles. All were lost. My loss was small, chiefly food. I took a supply for the crowd. To-day I have made good the crew's loss. We remained by the fire all night. The teacher on hearing of what happened brought us a change each, but being a small man there were difficulties. The next morning we pulled through the surf, and got on board the cutter, and ran to Manumanu, where we spent Sunday. We all felt sore and unfit for much exertion. I spent the Sunday ashore at the teacher's and had two services.

'Don't moralize on the foregoing and say, "Rash man." Yes, I am, and have been blessed and successful in all kinds of hazards for the last eleven years in this land. No use, will do it again, and must, hoping to get through all right. I am exceedingly cautious, especially when others are with me; but there is such a thing as excess of caution.

'Thank God for bairns' prayers. I like best the prayers of the children. Eh, lassie, wha kens when it is most needed? When in battle with the sea lately, it may be some of you were speaking then for me.

'I have to destroy all my letters. Anything happening to me, my spirit would grieve when seeing others reading my correspondence. A party might return without me some day—a boat might come back flag half-mast high, no Tamate; so I take precautions.'

'SOUTH CAPE, *August* 7, 1888.

'I accompanied H.M.S. Opal to Kerepunu, and there got three of the Kalo bigwigs to come on board. They were terribly frightened, but being told I was waiting their arrival they got into the boat. On getting on board they were quite unable to hide their fear. The captain had them in his cabin, spoke kindly to them, shook hands with them, and they told him never to fear they would again do any foreigner an injury. He gave them each a present, and in return they gave him their marked lime calabashes as tokens of peace and friendship. I got them down into the stokehole, and on one of the furnaces being opened they thought their end had come. On getting on deck they had quite enough of man-of-war life and made for the boat. I spent Sunday with Mr. and Mrs. Pearse, and on Monday returned in the Ellengowan to Port, arriving on Tuesday afternoon, to find that Misi and wife had landed the day before. I was sorry they should tumble in, and no Tamate to receive them.

'The Harrier was anchored near[1]. She is a pretty schooner, and wonderfully comfortable for all hands. She is the fastest vessel that has ever been here. We left at six a.m., went outside, and for the first time in many years I got sea-sick—consoled, sailors also sea-sick. Reached Hula next morning seven a.m., got teacher and wife on board who were going for a change—arrived at Kerepunu three p.m. We left Kerepunu on Thursday and arrived off Cooktown on Saturday. The captain and crew of Ellengowan were paid off. We did not get away until Saturday, August 4.

'To-morrow I go to the west, to Farm Bay. One of our New Guinea teachers is very ill, and I fear will not recover. He came to us shortly after our arrival here, nearly eleven years ago, and in after years followed me to Port Moresby, where he entered the college. The year before I went home I placed him in Farm Bay, and since then he has been blessed in his work. I feel depressed when I think of him, so young, and giving such good promise of doing great work for Him whom he loves and who loves him with a Saviour's love.'

The government had for some time been anxious to secure as their chief station at the east end of New Guinea, Samarai, or Dinner Island. This had in the

[1] This vessel had just been purchased by the Society.

early years been purchased by Chalmers, and was the Society's property. But the Directors raised no objection to the exchange which the government offered.

'We have parted with Dinner Island, feeling it better to do so gracefully than being forced to do so by government emergencies. We could not carry on our work either in a place where all that is bad may congregate. We get in exchange an island near by called Kwato—much larger than Dinner, and although not so central yet may be as suitable for our work. It is all our own, and no others are to be allowed to put houses on it. On Monday I go to arrange for the removal of the teacher and his people, and also to secure ground on Hayter Island in Stanley Bay for another station.'

Three important events took place about this time. The first was the demonstration of the fact that the Murray Island Mission had practically collapsed, and that if any effective work were to be done in the Torres Straits Mission it could only come to pass by beginning again, and upon a new foundation. Mr. Macfarlane had left the mission in 1885. Mr. Harry Scott, his successor at Murray Island, arrived there in December, 1883, but was compelled by ill-health to retire from the mission in 1886. Mr. Savage was appointed in 1885, but in six years withdrew altogether from missionary service. The Rev. A. E. Hunt reached Murray Island in 1887, but found the mission in such a state that there seemed no prospect of successful work there, and in 1889 the Directors decided to close it for a time.

In September, 1888, Chalmers' heart was rejoiced by the arrival of two new missionaries, both of whom had been trained at Cheshunt College. They were enthusiastic and active, and during Tamate's visit home had come under his spell.  The sight of them refreshed his spirit, and some of his long-cherished plans for the uplifting of New Guinea appeared to be coming within the sphere of the possible.  The two new members of the staff were the Rev. F. W. Walker and the Rev. H. M. Dauncey.

The third important event was Mr. Chalmers' second marriage.  He has himself, in his autobiography, sketched the steps which led to this event, fraught with so much blessing and help to himself and his work.

'My first wife was a schoolmistress in Leeds, and lodged in the house of Mrs. Large—Lizzie's mother. At one time they were well off, but lost much during the cotton famine in Lancashire.  Visiting my sweetheart, I stayed with them and got to know the lively Miss Lizzie, then about seventeen years old.  We became very friendly, and continued so through the years.  After marriage, we visited them and spent several days.  We arranged that Lizzie should come to us, and help us in work at Rarotonga.  My wife and Lizzie constantly corresponded.  But a few years after we left she was married to Mr. Harrison, a very excellent Christian gentleman, and for nearly twenty years they were very happy.  Several children were born, but only one lived, Bert.

'After my Jeanie's death correspondence ceased, and I lost sight of Lizzie altogether until after the publication of my first book, *Work and Adventure in New Guinea*, when I received one of her old delightful letters.  In 1886 I went home, and after spending a few days in London, I went to Scotland, breaking my journey at Retford, where they were living.  I spent two days with them.  Mr. Harrison was ill, suffering from heart affection.  I went to Inveraray, and when in Edinburgh on my return I received a telegram saying Mr. Harrison was dead. I hurried to Retford, and did all I could to assist the widow and her son.

'During the stay in England I saw much of them. We became engaged, and after my return to New Guinea I spent a year alone. In 1888 she came out, and we were married in Cooktown. Arriving in New Guinea we spent a month at Port Moresby, and then went east visiting the mission-stations. On Christmas Day we left Port Moresby for Motumotu, where we were going to settle. We pushed on so as to be in time for the New Year meetings. We had a good passage until near to Motumotu, when it blew hard, and a very high sea got up. She had a very rough life at Motumotu, but entered heartily into all work, and got to like the natives much. I was much away, and she felt being alone. I remember once being away for many weeks, and on my return I found her very ill, and gone to a mere shadow. Recovering she again took up her work with zeal.'

Mrs. Harrison reached Cooktown on October 6, 1888, whither Mr. Chalmers, on board the Harrier, had gone to meet her. He describes the events connected with the wedding in characteristic vein.

'Expecting the Jumna in before her time, we got to Cooktown, as we thought, in good time. We anchored on Friday night (5th), at eight o'clock, about two miles from the wharf, ready to go in the next morning. At half-past five on Saturday morning the watchman called out to me, " Mr. Chalmers, mail he come in this morning half-past three, he anchored no far off." Decks were soon washed down, anchor weighed, and the Harrier sailed close under the Jumna. The captain, thinking we were going alongside, called out that the doctor had not been on board. Lizzie was nowhere to be seen. We went on towards the wharf and met the doctor, who came on board and passed us.

'The pilot boat with the doctor was bound for the mail steamer, so I got a passage, and was soon on board. Lizzie looked well, and had thoroughly enjoyed the passage. The captain was very good. I remained for breakfast. Our own boat with Captain Hennessy came off, and by half-past ten we were on board the Harrier. No use losing time, especially as I was anxious to get back to Port very soon; so I saw the parson and arranged the wedding for twelve same day—just an hour away.

'It was capital fun to see the state Lizzie got in when told to get ready; the bride was rushed. All ready, and away we went to the parsonage. Present—the Rev. and Mrs. Canon Taylor, Miss Henriques, Captain Hennessy, Mr. Mowbray (police magistrate), and Mr. Hely, of the New Guinea Government. In a few minutes it was all over, papers signed, and we away to Great Northern Hotel. The Canon called on me to return, and we two poor old " gowks " went back to be drowned with rice and old shoes. We thought some paper was left unsigned, although we had done four, but it was only rice.'

The voyage across from Cooktown to Port Moresby was a trying experience to Mrs. Chalmers, even after her long voyage in the Jumna. The Harrier was a comfortable vessel, but greatly addicted to rolling. Mrs. Chalmers, in her journal, has given a graphic picture of the trip across the Gulf and of the welcome at Port Moresby.

'I do not like sailing vessels, I must say. With the Harrier it was one incessant roll and pitch all the time. I was very sick, and did not leave my berth except for a little while on the Sunday night, when Captain

Hennessy anchored under lee of an island, so that I might have a quiet night's rest. I did enjoy the brief rest from the weary tossing and rolling—felt very weak and ill, but not sick. It was a lovely night. A view of Queensland coast and several bush fires in the distance. Pretty well wooded island close by. Just a soothing rocking motion of the vessel, bright stars above and moonlight, and we two alone to chat and enjoy it all thoroughly.

'At three a.m. on Monday we started once more, roll, roll, roll. Poor me a prisoner in my berth, unable to take anything except soda-water. We got outside the reef about one a.m. Tuesday, but could not get through until daylight. When inside the reef, at 5.30, I had my first sight of New Guinea, and, what is not always to be had, a grand view of Mount Owen Stanley away inland. I cannot tell with what a curious mixture of feelings I gazed on the country which was to be my future home.

'Very soon we sighted Port Moresby: with the aid of a glass I saw the mission compound. Flags were flying gaily, and soon we could distinguish natives about the hill-side. Then we saw a boat being put off from the station, and sundry white helmets waving a welcome. We could not land, and they had no business to come before the government boat had boarded us. However, they reached us first, and Walker and Dauncey sprang on deck and gave me the first hearty greeting. Then came Misi and Misi Haine, with a warm welcome. The boat's crew, six fine bright-looking fellows, shook hands with a grip, and beamed upon me in a most friendly manner, talking and laughing, and telling Tamate their opinion of me in free fashion. Every one so kind, and all looking bright, well, and happy.

'After chats all round we got into the boat and were

rowed across the lagoon; how lovely it all looked!
Before us the two native villages, built in the water, and
above on the hill the mission compound. As we near
the beach, here come troops of friends to meet us.
Foremost comes Ruatoka, of whom I had heard so much;
then came several native teachers and their wives, who
are in Port from their various stations, and some who
have only lately come from the South Seas in the John
Williams. All in white or nice bright print dresses, the
men in light or white suits, and all wearing large native-
made hats. The girls belonging to the mission were
mostly in white.

'A crowd of natives were there from several villages;
the men have just a piece of string round the waist, but
all the women wear grass petticoats; the children are
quite naked. Somehow, as Tamate beforehand told me
I should, I felt it quite natural to see them in native
style, and did not feel any inclination to shrink from
them—which was fortunate.

'After getting through the lines of teachers and
mission retainers, I went through the midst of the
natives, shaking hands right and left, and only afraid
of nose-rubbing, which, however, no one attempted.
What a noisy excitable crowd they were to be sure!
And all seemed glad to see Tamate and his wife.'

Mr. and Mrs. Chalmers, soon after the latter's arrival
at Port Moresby, paid a coasting visit of a month's
duration to the stations in the direction of East Cape.
On their return they remained at Port Moresby until
the close of the year. Here Mrs. Chalmers began to
make the acquaintance of the natives and to become
familiar with their appearance and habits.

'Various people from inland and coast tribes keep
coming in. Just now there are four or five big naked

fellows leaning on the verandah rail, and having a good
look at me and my surroundings; heads like mops,
some with feather and flower ornaments, beads, shells,
and also bone too.

'To-day again there are a lot of natives about, great
fellows, with such mops of hair. They like to nod and
shake hands and look at me. I wish they wore even
a loin cloth. The women do not look at all bad in their
nice grass petticoats.'

Chalmers had determined to make Motumotu his
station, have his home there, and from that point make
continual journeys along the coast and also to the inland
tribes. He had a high appreciation of the Elema
natives, and was anxious to bring them under the
influence of Christianity. He thought too that from
Motumotu as a base it would be easier to take the
needful steps to secure the great desire of his heart,
namely, the establishment of mission-stations upon
a permanent and good working footing at suitable
points in the delta of the Purari and the Aird
rivers.

Mrs. Chalmers threw herself with great spirit and
courage into this new work, and it was upon her that
the brunt fell most heavily. Chalmers had for long
years been roughing it among savages, and was inured
to any possible experience that could befall him. But
Mrs. Chalmers went to Motumotu with but a very
inadequate notion of what life there would mean. What
contrast could be greater than for an English lady to
come from all the comforts and customs of our civilization and suddenly find herself planted in the midst of
a tribe of fierce savages, of whose language she was
ignorant, and whose customs outraged every sense of
fitness? Her husband was the only other European

nearer than Port Moresby, 170 miles away, and he was often absent for weeks at a time. This made the life at Motumotu a trial of no ordinary kind for his wife, and no one can read the story of her first year's residence at that station without feeling that she was a woman of remarkable bravery, devotion to duty, and of high Christian principle. She trod a rough pathway faithfully and uncomplainingly. And possibly one of the hardest trials in her life was the fact that Tamate, although he had a deep, strong and true affection for her, seemed hardly able to realize how grievous a trial many of the ordinary details of the life were to her, and especially during those not infrequent periods when she was left at Motumotu alone.

Tamate and Mrs. Chalmers left Port Moresby on Christmas Day, 1888. He was anxious to reach Toaripi in time for the New Year gatherings of the natives. The journey was made in a whaleboat, and any one who has made a twenty or thirty mile run across the Atlantic swell off the west coast of Ireland in an ordinary Kerry boat can appreciate the discomfort and downright hardship of a voyage of this kind. We will let Mrs. Chalmers tell the story of her home-coming, and first impressions of Toaripi.

'A week ago we got here after a long, tedious voyage in the boat. We landed at three a.m., and I was too ill to walk to the house, so Tamate sent for something to carry me on. The scene was fine. Two boat-loads of us landed, pitch dark. We could not land on the beach, owing to heavy seas and surf; so we entered the river some miles further on. We knew there were alligators in plenty. I declare I hardly dared get out on the banks. At last in answer to our shouts came answers from the natives and the teacher, and on came a lot of wild fellows with blazing torches. They crowded round me and gave me an excited welcome.

'I was ill and worn out. I had been twenty-six hours in the boat, and during that time had only had a few biscuits, and some cocoa-nut milk to drink. By-and-by four men came with a sort of rough sofa from the teacher's house, with some pillows and a mat on it. I got upon this, and six men carried me shoulder high, others leading the way with torches. There was great excitement. I wanted them to put me down at the gateway of the fence, but no, I was lifted over, then on to the verandah, and into the house. I wanted to go to bed, but there was none; no furniture, only just a mat or two on the floor. There were no doors or windows. All our cases of stores were piled up in one corner of the room. I could not stir; but the teachers' wives we had picked up on our way were equal to the emergency. They got our mattress spread on the floor in the end room, and soon a comfortable bed, with mosquito netting stretched across to nails in the wall, was ready. Native mats were nailed up to the doorways, and I retired. Tamate had boiled some water, and I took some cocoa, biscuit, and marmalade. How very queer it all seemed! The waves roll up with tremendous force, such a rush and roar, all the time. We are about fifty yards from the breakers.

'The house is made of rough planks with high thatched roof, quite open to the top. There is a ten foot verandah all round, over which the roof comes down low, making it nice and shady. The one large room has been partitioned off into three rooms, a doorway back and front to each. We mean to have doors some time. We brought some folding chairs and two cane chairs also. The sofa is of wood, with

plaited cocoa-nut fibre for the bottom, and it is like
a spring mattress.    A native mat and plenty of pillows,
stuffed with the silk down they get off the trees here,
make it quite comfortable.    A lot of mats, pillows, and
a pretty patched cover were given to me by the teachers
on my arrival.    One of the teachers has made a good-
sized square table, on which I have my crimson table-
cloth, that, with a rough wooden cupboard with three
shelves above, a piece of furniture which belonged to,
and was made by, poor Tauraki, the teacher who was
murdered here, completes our furniture for our one
living room.    This is twenty-one feet by eighteen feet
in size, with native mats at the doorways, looped back
in the daytime to give light (there are no windows).
We brought one iron bedstead and mattresses with us,
and netting, so we sleep very comfortably.

  'The natives are a very wild lot indeed, and very
powerful.    The men fine-looking and independent;
they are very fond of dress, and ornament themselves in
all sorts of ways.    Their heads are beautifully decorated
with leaves, feathers, and shells.    One man I admired
very much.    I thought he had a gaily coloured net over
his face, the pattern was quite artistic.    I was surprised
when Tamate said it was stained on the skin.    There
are always a lot of these men about.    They come to see
me and shake hands.    One chief wanted to kiss me at
first, but I objected, and now they are all satisfied to
shake hands.    At Lese, where we called on our way here,
I was introduced to a great cannibal chief and his
followers, also two of his wives.    None of them wore
any clothing at all, and they had just come in their
canoes from a great cannibal feast.

  'When Tamate went up the river the other day,
and left me alone, except for Meraka, the nice old

widow of a teacher, who is to stay with me for a few months, I felt funny. The teachers' houses are a good way off. A score or two of big natives came round the verandah. Tamate told me they would not enter the house whilst he was away, and they did not offer to do so. I went and sat out amongst them, and made myself as agreeable as I could, let them touch me, and shook hands, and they were quite pleased and let me examine some of their precious armlets and necklets. One man brought me some fish and another some young cocoa-nuts, and I gave them in return a bit of tobacco. I do not feel at all afraid of them, and I do not think I shall be afraid to be left with them when Tamate goes inland for a week or two. But I shall be terribly dull, for I cannot talk even to the teacher's wife.

'We had thirteen teachers here for New Year's Day. Most have gone, but two are staying to make us some doors; but I want Tamate to pack them off, for it has taken three men just five days to make the frame and cut the wood for one plain door. They are busy with it now, and may possibly get it nailed together to-day, but not put up.

'January 11. This morning, at five a.m., Tamate pulled the blanket door aside, and there, a long way out, was the Harrier. We think they have been at anchor most of the night, and it has been a fearful one; thunder and lightning and very heavy rain. We expect Messrs. Walker and Dauncey are on board, and they will stay with us whilst the Harrier goes on with the Hunts and Savage to Thursday Island. We have hoisted our flag, and Tamate has gone to the river to go off in our boat to the vessel. There is no possibility of landing here during this season; these tremendous rollers would swamp any boat. Sometimes the waves look wild and strong, and as if they might come over the boundary, and swamp our shanty altogether. So the Harrier must go some miles further up the Gulf and enter the river, and then they can land near the back of our house.

'We have begun school work here, and I gave my first lesson to two or three boys yesterday. They are learning their letters and to count in English up to 100. We are going to put up a school-house and build a church close to our house. At present they have just a sort of shed. In the far village the teacher is using Tauraki's old house as a school. There are a number of villages, and all built close up to our boundary fence at the back and sides. We have not much ground, so Tamate built the house as near high-water mark as he dare, so that in front, at least, I should have nothing but pure sea air. The native houses here are miserable affairs, and packed close together, so that the villages are very unhealthy; for they bury their dead close to the house. We have planted in front and round the house about 300 cocoa-nut trees, and if they survive the strong winds in a few years there will be nice shade and something green to look at, instead of sand. At present the trees are from twelve to twenty-six inches high, but in four or five years they will be pretty tall palms. Even now they rest the eyes from the glare of sea and sand.

'I have three boys as servants: Barnaba, Tamate's boy from Port Moresby, is about sixteen years old, and understands household ways a little; Naimi, a Maiva boy we got on the way, twenty-four or twenty-five years old, very good for boating, and a very strong great fellow; Bamuri, about thirteen years old, is really Meraka's servant, but as long as she stays with me he is to be

ours. Tamate is very strict, and even when I feel pretty
well he will not let me do much, and makes me lie
down for a couple of hours every afternoon, although
I cannot get into the habit of sleeping. I wish I could, it
would do me good. I have fever on and off, but have
never been quite laid up. I am so watched and doc-
tored that the fever cannot get the upper hand, but it is
a nasty feeling. I am much thinner, but no worse for that.

'The natives are running and shouting in the village,
so I think the friends from the Harrier are coming at
last. Here come two captains, Mr. and Mrs. Hunt and
baby, and Jessie, Mr. Savage, Mr. Walker, and Mr.
Dauncey. Nine extra people—we are in a fix, because
we only have half a dozen of anything here, so
nothing goes round. Mrs. Hunt and I are going to
sleep together, and the gentlemen in the other rooms on
the floor, with a pillow each and their rugs.'

A letter to the author from Tamate, dated January 21,
1889, gives his views and hopes with regard to the
mission at this time.

'We are here extending west, and working this as the
central Gulf station. I have long been anxious to get
right west to Orokolo, and did hope to do so now; but
other places require teachers, and except Rarotonga
all South Sea missions have failed us in supply. You
will hear about Murray Island. It seems impossible to
work it on Macfarlane's lines. Only Christian young men
should be received for training, or intelligent lads from
the mission schools, such lads to be returned home after
four years. If anxious for further education and considered suitable, they should be received into the college
for the training of native evangelists. The taking of
*heathen* lads away from their homes and returning them
once or twice a year has failed everywhere.

THE HOUSE IN WHICH MR. AND MRS. CHALMERS LIVED AT MOTUMOTU

'Yesterday a native here engaged in prayer. It was short and comprehended much—"Lord Jesus, I am dark, we all are very dark; we want light, give us light, and save us." We have two teachers here, who are getting on with the language. I am doing my best, but years make it more difficult. From twenty to twenty-eight, or perhaps thirty, are the best years for getting a thorough hold of a new language. We have lost Piri, our very excellent teacher. We all loved him, and by the natives he was loved and greatly respected.

'This Harrier business troubles me much. I cannot think we are worth so great an expense. The Ellengowan was too small, but the Harrier is too expensive. Within the last year or two our opportunities of getting about have increased. The purchase of the Harrier startled me somewhat. She will require another great outlay immediately.

'We have good signs of good work. There are quite a number of Christian men anxious to be trained as evangelists. Walker and Dauncey are well, and will go to their stations a few months hence. Two more wanted, one for this place, and one for Hall Sound.'

The fever soon laid hold upon Mrs. Chalmers, and in spite of all her husband's experience and watchful care she suffered very severely. But through it all she bore up bravely, and in her letters enables us to realize what the hardships of life in a savage district are like.

'I am just beginning to feel alive after my last bad dose of fever. I do wish you could see this house. Tamate thinks it a delightful place. I am not quite so much in love with it. The walls are of very roughly sawn planks, which overlap each other; so inside there are ledges innumerable from floor to thatch, every ledge a nice accommodation for all kinds of insect life.

I should think the house is fifty feet long, and divided into three rooms; the partitions are the height of the outer walls only, and leave the very high, pointed, thatched roof open from end to end.    At night it is *too* lively, rats, mice, and, on the roof, lizards all over in armies.    I do not object to the latter : they are very tame, and make a cheery chirp, and best of all they hunt the spiders, tarantulas and others, big and little, cockroaches and crickets, and beetles of all kinds.    Ants and mosquitos abound, and they like me very much.    I am bitten all over, and my only time of peace is under the mosquito netting.    If you look down on the mats and floors, you perceive they are covered with life, and even this paper is continually covered with tiny moving things which I blow off.

'There are about 3,000 wild savages here, big, fine, handsome men, got up in truly savage style.    Tamate says he believes I would rather face a crowd of them than the insects in the house, and I would too.    At night the bats fly in between the walls and roof.    We are close to the sea, high tides come nearly to the fence, and the sunsets are grand—I do enjoy them.    From 6 to 7.30 p.m. I have a good time of enjoyment.    Every day about 5 p.m. some of the swells come up fully got up for conquest.    They look very fine, hair in a great bush, and beautifully dressed ; some have plumes a yard long made of tiny white feathers, and leaves and flowers tucked into their belts and armlets ; faces, some beautifully painted in various designs and colours like fine network, and others horridly smeared with paint— bodies greased and polished to perfection.    The tight belt round the waist is the only clothing the men wear.

'The girls wear a very scant bit of grass back and

front, some not more than six or eight inches in length, and the women wear less still, often nothing at all, They are not nice-looking; we have not seen one bonnie girl since coming.   At the East End some are very pretty. I do think it strange that the men are as a rule good-looking, and the women so ugly.

' The life here is altogether different from that at Port Moresby.   You would be amused at some of Tamate's methods of getting the people and children together. One Sunday morning he went through the village, and wherever he saw a number of people on the platforms, he shouted and gesticulated, and made a row until some of them came after us to service.   It is wonderful how he is picking up the language; already he has a list of nearly 200 words.

' In the midst of all our sickness and worry, it is impossible to feel dull where Tamate is.   The natives appreciate fun, and if you heard the hearty laughs which I hear just now, you would think we were jolly indeed. Tamate gathers them round and has lessons from them in the language, and they roar at his mistakes, and tell him again and again the different words.   They like to hear English words, and remember them well.'

From the earliest days of their life at Toaripi Mrs. Chalmers had to get used to being left alone.   The trips taken by Tamate, in the prosecution of his work varied in length from three or four days to six or seven weeks.   They were for him seasons of hard work, exposure to storms and difficult landings.   To his wife they were times of loneliness, often of vexation and difficulty with her boys and girls, and sometimes, in the early days, of extreme danger.   But she always bore them bravely and uncomplainingly, as the following record of one of the earliest shows :—

'Toaripi, Motumotu, *March* 8, 1889.

' Here I am, all alone. Tamate left this morning. I think I should have gone with him, but since my attack of fever three weeks ago I have been so weak and ill that I did not think it advisable to venture.    Tamate said not a word about going until after breakfast, and then suddenly, at nine a.m., " Lassie, there is a good wind and sea, so I must away."    Naimi sought up a crew, and by ten a.m. they were really off, bag and baggage.    The wind has been favourable, so I hope all is well with them.

' I have been very busy, and the day has passed quickly away.    I had all our boys for lessons, and *they* enjoyed it.    I could not hear reading and spelling, but we had counting tables, and sums, and then writing.    We make each other understand somehow, and they think it fine fun all round.    I shall take them every day if I keep well.    Many natives have been round to visit me, and to tell me there is a good wind for Tamate.    Really they came to beg tobacco, but I only gave to our old pensioners.

' Seven p.m.    Mosquitos terrible again—there is nothing for it but bed.    Very often lately I have been obliged to draw the mosquito-net and sit on the bed to sew or write.    We have fires lit on the verandah, and in the middle of the room floor.    I am almost blind with smoke and my eyes are so painful.    It is a choice between two evils, mosquitos or smoke, and certainly the latter is preferable.

' Last night I thought I would shut the doors, but it was so very hot, and there are no fasteners on them, so I fell asleep with them wide open, and found myself and the house all right in the morning.    Turia and wife in from Jokea; he is ill, and so I have turned doctor.

Another of the new teachers down with fever too. We have had prayer-meetings here as usual. I do not understand what they say, but I like to have them here. All were here except Uapari. Meraka is going to sleep in the house to-night. I do not want her, but she thinks I am lonely. Barnaba is a good boy, and my right hand in everything, though he is only about fifteen years old. I brought him up from the east end in May last year, and it is wonderful how he has got on in school work, and everything else since then.

' 10th (Sabati). Very much disturbed in the night. About nine p.m. a native drum commenced—it is most monotonous. Fortunately the feast and dance were at one of the villages furthest away from us. They kept up without a break until 4.30 a.m., and though distance softened the sounds I could not get to sleep, and so heard all the frisking about of rats, bats, and lizards.

' At 4.30 I heard a man outside trying to attract my attention by various noises and coughs. I called out that he must go away at once. I got up and looked out, but could only distinguish a dark mop above the verandah. Soon after he knocked at the other end door, and Meraka was terrified. I thought they had come to kill us, knowing we were alone. I think it was one of the villagers come to see that all was right— perhaps just called on his way home from the drum affair. We cannot find out who it was.

' 12th. Tamate home unexpectedly about two a.m. Never heard a sound until some one's head popped in, and a voice said, " Are you awake, dear lassie ? " I am very glad and happy to have him back. Every one on the station up to welcome him, and many natives came too. I am glad the rooms were finished before he came. I got on very well, and was not afraid at all. I like these people very much, but I am sure they could be very nasty if they got angry.'

For some months Mr. and Mrs. Chalmers persevered steadily in their work at Motumotu. But the fever had so grievously injured the latter's health that in May a visit to Port Moresby became necessary. The journey had to be made in the whaleboat, and was one of the worst that even Tamate had ever made. It also illustrates his skill in handling a boat in the wild Papuan surf and his nerve at a critical moment. 'The long journey in the boat,' writes Mrs. Chalmers, 'was terrible. The first morning we were nearly upset, and shipped a big sea. I was drenched. Everything was wet through and completely ruined; most of our provisions were spoilt too. Well, Tamate wrapped me in a blanket, and there I had to remain till sundown. All day there was a rough, nasty sea, and very heavy swell, but the wind and current fortunately were in our favour. I thought at times that the waves must engulf us, but the little boat rose to them splendidly; sometimes she seemed almost perpendicular, and then down into a deep trough, with waves as high as a house behind and before.

'Arriving off Maiva we were warned not to land— the boiling surf looked dreadful right along the beach. Two splendid fellows swam out to us and said we could not land in safety. Tamate nearly lost his life here some time ago, when he attempted to run the boat ashore in such a sea. It was sunset, I was ill and wet, we had had nothing all day but biscuits and water, the wind was now right ahead, and the boys would have to pull to Delena, fifteen or twenty miles off. Tamate said that it looked like a stormy night, and so he determined to risk it, especially as we now had two fresh men

to pull. I sat straight up and threw off the blankets.
I think the excitement cured my sickness and headache.
Before turning the boat for the boiling surf, Tamate
said : " Now, Lizzie, in a surf like this, the boat, if she
goes at all, will turn right over, so do not cling to, but
keep clear of her if possible. The boys and every one
will think first of you : and if we get ashore alive,
never mind if all goes, the anchor will fall out and keep
the boat."

'Then we faced it. The men were so excited, but
Tamate and Naimi timed the pulling well. We got
over the first line of surf all right, and there was a great
shout from shore ; then a second and third line were
crossed successfully ; in the last line we were a little
too late, and should have been washed back, and,
meeting the next breaker, have been swamped, but
dozens of the natives rushed in up to their necks and
dragged us on to the beach—we were pretty wet,
but thankful. I went to bed. Some tea in a canister
was dry, so we could have some hot tea and some
biscuit.

'We stayed from Friday night until early on Monday.
Tamate had four services, one at Maiva, and three
inland. Four young men were baptized.

'On Monday we set out on the next stage, had a fair
wind, and got in earlier than we expected. The sun
was fearful in the middle of the day ; and though we
had as much shelter as possible, I had sunstroke and
fever, and yet feel pain from it at times. One night
we spent at Delena, one at Boera, and then on here
to Port Moresby. Tamate says that what with
putting right out to sea to catch wind, and then
coming in to the stations, the distance travelled would
be about 250 miles. It seems like coming back to

civilization to get here, where they have many comforts and plenty to eat. The beds at the various stations are horrid—especially after sitting or lying in a boat all day—wooden planks covered with native mats, sometimes a sort of mattress made from the cotton they gather from the trees. My bones have felt so sore and stiff at times. The teachers themselves always sleep on mats on the floor, but they all have a bedstead, and sometimes two, for the use of the white missionaries.'

In June Mr. and Mrs. Chalmers returned to Motumotu, and soon after his return he learned that Mount Owen Stanley had been ascended, and that one of the keenest ambitions of his life could now never be fulfilled.

'You will have seen the telegram that Macgregor has had Mount Owen Stanley under him. 'Tis done, wish I had done it. I am glad Macgregor has succeeded. He knew I was going for it in August, and that may have hurried him. I intended leaving last week for the inland, but not being well I had to remain. I shall not be able to keep really well until I have had a good walk. Victoria would have given me £500 for Mount Owen Stanley. Macgregor's expenses must have been quite that, not including his own and surveyor's salary.

'You remember I told you Misi wanted to finish his translation of the Scriptures, and I offered to take the college. Since returning here, pondering, praying, seeing, I fear—no, not fear—I feel it our duty to remain here—so I think. This is our most difficult field, largest population, most isolated, and considered most unhealthy. I began the work, pressed it on, and am eager to carry it on. I am extending fifty miles further along, have new teachers, and we both feel we ought not to leave them, and the work grows on our hands here—so what is to be done? Well, here is the solution. Hunt goes to Port Moresby, and we remain where we are. Or a young missionary is sent out at once from home to take up the college work at Port Moresby. It may be the Directors will clearly see their way to send us another one or two for the west. I might be able this next north-west to open up to the west of Bald Head on to Fly River. It must be done in a whaleboat.

'Tamate Vaine would remain here if well. Altogether, I think she has stood the climate so far very well. We now have a really nice home here. The house has been greatly improved by giving it a coat of whitewash, painting the posts blue, and sticking pictures all about. What transformations a lady can perform! Ugly pine boxes become splendid seats. 'Tis marvellous.

'I fancy you would like our home now it is decorated and has a woman's notions all about. Our next move now is to have it enlarged two more rooms, so if angels or non-angels come along they may find a place to stretch themselves. We have a new school-house built in the compound, and hold school in it daily. We teach in English and Motuan, and are learning Toaripi, so as to teach in it also. In our school we have classes in the following languages—Suau, Motuan, Maiva, Toaripi, English. It is a school for the descendants of Babel. I feel nearly confident that unfortunate tower must have been built near here, somewhere in New Guinea, at all events.

'Our great difficulty with the village schools is the irregular attendance of the children. They cannot see any advantage in being taught, and it is only by making it lively and having some fun that they will come. Only a few of our teachers like school work; they dislike the continuous drudgery of teaching A, B, C, and I confess it is heavy, dreech work at times, especially on hot, close days. I teach a little English, and the bairns rather like it, laughing heartily at their own mistakes. I am at present engaged preparing a short Scripture catechism in this language, and when finished will have it taught, say, one question a day.'

Mrs. Chalmers, in her Journal, gives us further glimpses of the hard but happy life at Toaripi.

'We had the ordinance service on Sunday, and a good congregation of natives to witness it; they were very attentive and interested, and Tamate tried to explain it to them. We have no church members here yet, but with teachers from other stations, ourselves, new teachers, Naimi, Ikupu, and one of the Hanamoa crew, some four natives from Pari, we made a goodly number. It was a solemn and strange service in this wild place. I could not help contrasting this service with the one at home: here the bright sun outside, and on one side the dazzling sea breaking in heavy waves up to the very steps of the church; on the other, a portion of sandy beach, some native houses, looking like haystacks on high posts. Cocoa-nuts, palms, and little peeps in between, and underneath the houses, of the wide river beyond; plenty of dogs and pigs running about. Inside, my table covered with white cloth; and on it a jug of cocoa-nut milk, and two glasses, and two plates of bread. Tamate at the table, a teacher on either hand. I sat at the right hand, and on the floor at my side the native members; on the left hand the teachers and wives; in front a gathering of orderly, interested-looking natives, many gorgeously painted, and befeathered, and dark faces peering in at the six doors.

Can you picture it at all? The church is built by the natives—walls of nipa palm spines, and thatched roof of palm leaves, floor of bark—two *doorways* on each side, and one at each end, and plenty of square openings for windows. We have no church members here yet, but we think of the Moffats, and feel encouraged. They were fifteen years working at one station, and not one member, and yet she asked a friend to send her a communion service, and directly after it arrived they needed it.

'These people are very quiet at present, but there has been fighting at Maiva and Kivori, and very cruel spearing to death. The other day Tamate started up, saying, "Listen, there's the death wail." Again and again it sounded, such a weird mournful sound, and then two women, the wife and daughter of the dead man, came out of the house, quite nude, each heading a procession of women; they went in opposite directions, taking the paths he was most accustomed to tread, each leader chanting a sad solo, and now and again at various stopping-places all the women joined in chorus. It was a strange sight and sounded most mournful. We have lost three teachers here in less than six weeks; two were confined and fever at the same time, and one fever alone. They are most difficult to manage when ill, and do not give themselves a fair chance of recovery.

'There have been two fights here lately—some were badly hurt. The last was unpleasantly near the mission house, as one party were in the bush close to our fence. I was on the verandah, and some shells and one or two sticks came over close to me, so I retired. Tamate and Ka went out and sent off one party (I should think there were 200) to their own village, and then Tamate went into the bushes and routed out the other side; they were angry at the interruption, but eventually cleared off. They will, I expect, fight it out some time, and go further away to do it. It is a quarrel between the young men of the different dubus, and formerly would have led to a desperate fight between the tribes, but now we are here the chiefs will not join in, and they try to stop the fight. The young men have been shut up in the dubus for eighteen months, only coming out on very rare occasions, and at night to get a little fresh air on the beach. They are most of them fine strong fellows, and anxious to try their strength on each side. They have just come out this month, and freedom makes them rather wild. I think I never felt myself amongst savages as I have done this last week, the excitement has been so great. The feast to " Semese " has been held. It is only held, I believe, at intervals of many years, and now we are here and getting an influence over the people, it will most likely never be held again in all its wild savagery. I am glad to have seen it, for from description one could not possibly imagine it.

' 10th. Yesterday we went inland. Tamate thought he would like me to see Moveave in its wild state. It is tiresome to get there in a boat—the canoes go a short cut through some winding narrow creeks; we went in the boat up some splendid streams of water, tributaries of the large river. It was very pretty indeed; the banks were covered with nipa, sago, and cocoa-nut palms, and the mangrove swamps look pretty, though they are so deadly. We disturbed two crocodiles on the way, one twenty feet long at least, but they slid so quickly into the water I could not get a real good look. I am so anxious to see one close to. They are wonderfully quick in their movements, and being the exact colour of the muddy bank one can't get a good look at them.

As we got further inland, we heard plenty of parrots, and saw a few, and many wonderful insects, lovely colours.

'One creek Tamate wanted me to see, and with some care and trouble we got through it; it was one continual wind in and out—in some places the men had to lift the leaves and push them on one side to get the boat along. Swamp lands on each side covered with dense vegetation. It was such a pleasant rest and change for my eyes after the constant glitter and glare of the sun.

'After an hour or two, sometimes on the broad stream and sometimes in winding creeks, we turned suddenly into a grand stretch of water. It really was lovely; we met two canoes going down, but they turned back at once when our boys shouted, "Tamate is coming." Soon we saw houses, and thought we were at our destination. The way was quite new to Tamate. On landing we found we should have a tramp of two miles through thick bush. I was not well, and quaked at the information. The boys said, "Not far," but Tamate had a notion of his whereabouts when landed. It was my first experience of tramping through thick bush. The native path was just wide enough for a native without any clothing to walk along, single file; tall grass, ferns, and bush plants hid the path, which wound in and out and round about in most eccentric fashion. In the little hollows it was ankle-deep in mud and boggy green stuff, and sometimes knee-deep, and in the deep places the *thin* trunk of a tree was thrown across. The natives spread thick palm leaves over the shallow places, and I got over without much discomfort—some places I was carried over. I managed to cross the genuine rustic bridges with a native to hold on to; the wood was very slippery, and the long grass had twined round and round in some places.

'Ka and some teachers who had come in to buy food had gone the short way in a canoe, and given notice of our coming, and halfway through the bush we were met by a number of natives. At the first little village, I was so hot and tired, we had a halt. Huari carried my folding chair, and I sat down comfortably, as I thought, to rest, while the chief sent a boy up a tall tree for fresh nuts. The milk was delicious, but the rest was not; the chair was low, and the natives crowded round in a circle, men, women, and children, so that I could not feel a breath of air. I gave up the notion of having anything to eat there, and was glad to move on soon.

'It was very hot in the bush, and I was glad to reach Moveave and know I could rest and eat. It is very much larger than I expected, and the houses are built on a nice open plain, which felt airy after the close bush. The first sight was a sad one. An old chief died a fortnight ago, and we had to halt at his place; in front of the house was the grave in an enclosure, nine feet square, and inside this the whole family—widow, children, and grandchildren—are living, sleeping, cooking, and eating. The widow does not come out at all for three months, but she came to me, naked and daubed with clay—so wretched, and *so dirty*, for they do not bathe during the first mourning. We left them and went on into the village.

'There were quite a large number of dubus, some of them much higher from the ground than any Tamate had seen before. I longed to get up, but did not think it at all possible. The steps are just tree-stems tied across, two feet apart (sometimes more), to two long slender poles, and they are not as a rule very straight across. I was terribly tired, and hot, hungry, and thirsty. There were a great many strangers in the village, as

a great feast was in progress. The houses were half
hidden by immense quantities of food; splendid bunches
of bananas hung round the platforms, and piled high on
the platform were taro, sweet potatoes, yams, cocoa-nuts
in all stages of growth, and bundles of sago. A great
amount of cooking was going on in front of the houses,
and there did not seem one place to rest and cool off.
On a dubu we saw some of our people who had come
by canoe.

'Tamate, to please them, walked with me round the
village; such a scene of noise and excitement it is impossible to describe. They crowded round me until
I felt stifled. Out again in the centre, which is rather
open, we were near a large new dubu, twenty-two or
more feet from the ground, and my chair was placed
underneath for shade and coolness; but it was no use,
they would stand round me and keep away the air.
Ka and Naimi and some of the men set to work and
put more strands across the ladder, and I determined to
venture. I shall never forget the ascent as long as I
live; but at last I was safely landed, and it was delight-
fully cool and shady—so far above them all. I unpacked
the food, and we had cocoa-nuts to drink.

'The getting down was dreadful; and there was a
sudden misunderstanding between some of our teachers
and the natives. In a moment every one seemed armed—
bows, arrows, and those dreadful clubs. Fortunately
I did not see the quarrel, and when the natives suddenly
appeared armed and around us, I thought it was part of
the show for our entertainment, and I had only just time
to realize danger before it was over. We had a narrow
escape, and five minutes might have seen the end of us
all, and no one left to tell the tale. Tamate seems equal
to any emergency, however, and everything was made

right. It was want of tact, and nervousness, on the part of one of the new teachers which caused it all.'

We interpose a letter here from Tamate himself.

'TOARIPI, *October* 3, 1889.

' Tamate Vaine has had a severe attack of fever. We spent a week at Port Moresby for our committee meeting, and a day or two before we left to return she complained ; on board it became severe, and now she is quite down. We got in here yesterday morning. At Delena a teacher we had on board for health landed, and during the night died. A number were present, and he told them to be active and strong in Christ's work, that he hoped to have done many years' service, but God says two is enough. Poor fellow, his wife was at Motumotu. I would not allow her to leave with us as she was nursing one of the motherless bairns. No one thought he was so ill. The teachers, seeing he was dying, prayed he might be spared a little longer. He said, " Why ask so for me ? Why keep me back ? I am going home. He says 'tis enough." Yesterday when we landed we were met by the wife with her child on the river bank. Eh, it was a sad, sad scene. We are being tried as by fire. God help us to be faithful even unto death.

' I intend visiting the Fly River. When at Port the governor came in. I met him, and had a long chat with him. He has asked me to accompany him in his Fly River trip—try and get right away inland and begin a mission there. If possible I shall accompany him and report to Directors. Should I not be able to go with him because of sick teachers or sick wife I shall visit it when able. I do not leave unless all are well. Should I be long away, Tamate Vaine would go to Brisbane. Next year I hope to visit with Tamate Vaine

New Zealand and the South Seas. I fear the enthusiasm is not so great as formerly. There is something wrong.

'We shall begin at once to get accommodation for eight couples. We must face a future when we may have to look to New Guineans alone.

'Walker goes east alone. I do hope the Directors will send him help soon. Dauncey is not strong, and remains at Port. He will be a great help to Misi. Wood for a house at Delena we shall begin to cut now. The next three years will be our most trying ones in the Gulf. This will be a grand mission, once established. It is considered very unhealthy; it may be, and cannot be helped. Christ's command must be obeyed. We have had the great Semese's feast. Many of the young men for whom it was held made light of it and kept away. Will there be another? I hope not.'

'TOARIPI, *November* 18, 1889.

'You will wonder how I get on. I am very weak and poorly; have not got up my strength since the last bad attack, and Tamate would like to send me away. But there are no means of going just now. My great hope is that we may be able to hold on here together until the place is fairly started and working, so that we might be able to leave it in the teachers' hands awhile, with Mr. Savage to come and go and generally superintend matters. We have still a great deal of sickness. We white people stand the climate and fever much better than they do. For one thing they lose heart at once, and say, "We shall die like the others." They will not take medicine unless made to do so.

'I always get up as soon as possible. Even if I am lifted for an hour on to the verandah, and then back again, I feel the better for the effort and change. You may guess I feel like shaking them up occasionally.

Tamate says I shall never understand real native laziness. I rave, and hurry up the boys, who creep round as if they had all day in which to do five minutes' work, and my right-hand boy, Barnaba, says, "Oh, Tamate Vaine, *do horo*, *kava kava*." *Do horo* is "after a while," or "plenty of time," and *kava kava* is "foolish." *Do horo*, as they say it, sounds like *no hurry*, and I feel wild. Poor boys! they never bustled about so much in their lives.'

The close of 1889 and the first few days of 1890 found Mrs. Chalmers at Port Moresby, where she was joined by her husband on January 3. On the seventh they returned to Toaripi in the whaleboat, accompanied by Mr. Savage, but had a stormy and difficult passage, and did not reach their destination until January 13. At this time Chalmers hoped and believed that in Savage he would find a colleague who could efficiently aid him both at Motumotu and also in the work of the Fly River. But this hope was finally disappointed, and in 1891 Mr. Savage withdrew from the mission. The work at the station was consolidating. The children were being trained, the students were gradually coming under discipline, and services were being regularly held both Sundays and week-days.

On January 21 the Merrie England with Sir W. Macgregor on board suddenly appeared. Chalmers went off to her, and in a short time Mrs. Chalmers received a note from her husband, saying, 'Get all ready; she leaves in a few hours.' This meant that before sunset he would be off for a long trip to the Fly River with the governor. Mrs. Chalmers had known for some time that this expedition was probable; still we can hardly wonder that she writes in her diary, 'I was in a state of mind, Tamate leaving in an hour or two.

I felt dreadfully bad.' The steamer did not leave until the next morning, and she writes, 'The last little prayer-meeting together comforted me, and left me brave and hopeful.'

Tamate was away for nine weeks, and although for some of this time Mr. Savage was at Motumotu he rather added to than lessened Mrs. Chalmers' anxieties. She really had the whole burden of the work and its responsibilities upon her shoulders; and she had to meet them with very imperfect helpers, with only an elementary knowledge of the language, and at a time when she was subject to, and often prostrated by, severe attacks of fever. But she rose to the occasion, and did her part right bravely. Tamate hoped at the start to be away only a month, and also expected that Savage would stay at Motumotu until his return.

Mrs. Chalmers' journal for this period, which has been preserved, stirs the sympathy of the reader on her behalf in her loneliness.

'February 9, 1890, Sabati. Terrific storm during the night. Every one awake, and students and boys all up. Natives shouting and blowing the shell, which sounded most unearthly between the peals of thunder. The rain poured into the houses, and all their mats were wet through. It rained into our house in some places. I never did hear such thunder or see such lightning in my life. I did wish my husband was at home. Houses were blown completely over in the villages. Sabati as it is, they are obliged to do a little repairing, and from all appearance we may expect another storm to-night. This morning cold and rainy, and all services very late. I jumped out of bed, and ran out to fasten a door, and the wind and I had a trial of strength for it; in a minute I was wet through, and I feel cold and feverish to-day.

'I am teaching my boys two new tunes, and they are very pleased, and look forward to singing them as a surprise to Tamate. One is, "Nearer, my God, to Thee," and one, " Rest for the Weary." The hymns are in the Motu book which we use.

'February 6. Been with the girls at washing—the women left them to do as they liked, and when I am not there they let them mix the things any way. Could not eat any dinner, and lay down all the afternoon. Another bad night, I'm afraid. I do wish my dear husband was here; I feel very much alone when I'm sick.

'March 2. Roused all up, and saw them off to service. I feel very poorly this morning, and did not sleep. Terai and Ka a little better, and all out for forenoon service. I went to the Motu service and stayed in all the rest of the day. Sent sick folks a mug of soup each at dinner-time. Tipoki very poorly; Ola is to take students in the morning. I have been obliged to rest to-day and take quinine.

'Eleven p.m. Just ready for bed when it seemed as if bedlam had suddenly broken loose on the beach and close to the house. I put on a dressing-gown, and went out to find about fifty young fellows hiding behind our fence, and a crowd coming along past the church with torches, dancing and yelling like maniacs. I knew there would be no sleep for me if I could not stop them, so out on the beach I went. There was poor me in the midst of those fellows, scolding right and left, and turning them off the fence. I made them understand that the whole beach was their own to make a row on except the small portion between the end of our fence and the boat-house. I left them talking the matter over, and went with Boari at my heels to meet the advancing host; really they looked formidable, but before I could reach them I was joined by about twenty older men from the village. I addressed them in a mixture of English, Motuan, Toaripian, and many signs, all of which I hope they appreciated. I am sure I did myself, and could have laughed heartily at the ridiculous figure I cut. One good old fellow patted me on the shoulder in a most paternal manner, and told me to go and sleep, and they would see I was not disturbed any more.'

Chalmers returned on March 25, greatly to the delight and comfort of his wife, and to the benefit of work at the station. The reason for his visit to the Fly River was the need for reorganizing the whole of the Western Branch of the New Guinea Mission. The Directors had fixed their thoughts upon Chalmers as the only man strong enough for the work. He himself went to see exactly how matters stood, and to form his judgement after inspecting the stations, and also getting as far up the great river as possible. In this enterprise Sir W. Macgregor was anxious to help him in every possible way :—

'I got back last week from my nine weeks' western trip with the governor. Tamate Vaine was left alone. The first few weeks Mr. Savage was here, but he had to leave, and then she had all the work on her shoulders, and right well did she bear it. You know she is yet what is called a " new chum," but she carried on every branch of the work quite in " old chum " style. She has been very ill with fever, but on my arrival was better. If we could agree to part, I suggest she takes up a central station and out-stations for herself, but I fancy we can get on better together. She and the savages hit it well, and they gave her no trouble during my absence. I believe we shall leave this part of the mission and go west to the Fly River and Western District. The

Directors want to rebegin the Fly River work, and they are anxious it should be carried on vigorously lest another should step in and take our crown. I cannot say much of what I saw of the mission. A good feeling has been created, and we have something to work on. The country is everywhere low and swampy, and I fear will be a bad fever district. We must have a successor here to carry on the college, station, and out-station work. Were Britain only nearer we should run home and confer, but we are too far away. At present we are enlarging our house here, and will continue all our work as if remaining.

'I hope we shall be able to leave soon for a trip to the South Seas and New Zealand. I want to spend next Christmas with the Dunedin folks, if at all possible. Lizzie is afraid it will take too much time. She will likely go to England while we are getting things straight in the Western District. There will be a good deal of roughing it for a few years. She is not afraid of that, but the no house won't do for a "new chum," and in a region where I fear there will be plenty of fever.'

Chalmers' view of his wife's power to get on with the natives is confirmed by her own statement at this time:—

'I am quite attached to these wild people. Indeed I always did like and get on much better with wild rowdy folks, than tame quiet ones. Some of the wildest here will do anything I ask them, though they don't profess to like or have sympathy with the mission of peace yet. But when Tamate was away and they began to work at canoe-making, and have skirmishing on the beach, I asked them not to do these things on the Sabati, and at once they gave them up, and were quiet and orderly for the rest of the day.

'The place begins to look like a little town, and all

the people gather about us in a free and easy way. I encourage them round always. Our house and lives are open to all eyes.'

In the middle of the year 1890, it became evident that Mrs. Chalmers must have complete rest and change. She had been brought so low by fever that at one time hope of her recovery had almost entirely gone. Chalmers himself was anxious to reinvigorate the missionary enthusiasm among the students at Rarotonga and Samoa. Hence it was decided that he and his wife should pay a visit to both groups of islands. Chalmers, who was ever on the alert to utilize even health trips for the benefit of his work, hoped also to raise money enough in the colonies to get a fine steam launch for his new work on the Fly River. In his letters, and those of Mrs. Chalmers, we can follow them on this attractive and useful and health-restoring journey :—

'BRISBANE, *August* 15.

'Been travelling, and have got this far on our way south. The weather is cold, and we are afraid to move on until really necessary. We are staying just a few miles out of Brisbane with the Scotts, right good friends. Tamate Hahine [1] is better. At Cooktown she was very ill, but improved a little before leaving. On the way down she got much better. Since coming here in the week I have addressed six meetings. This afternoon we have an invite to a garden party at Government House, to meet Lord Charles Scott, the admiral of the Australian station. I suppose I must go. One day we had tiffin with the bishop. We intend remaining here until it is time to go further south and meet the Samoan steamer. It is too cold in Sydney for Tamate Hahine.'

The voyage to Samoa, and the pleasant friendships

[1] An alternative (South Sea) form for Vaine.

there formed and cemented, are set forth in a letter written by Chalmers from Samoa shortly after his arrival there :—

'MALUA, SAMOA, *September* 26.

'After twenty-four years here I am again in the same house, in the same room. As soon as Tamate Hahine was able to travel we left Brisbane. We arrived in Sydney on Saturday, August 30, and left again for South Seas on September 4. In Brisbane I had several meetings, which I trust will lead to a greater interest in mission work. In Sydney I had three minutes with the parsons, and spoke straight, which they appreciated. We called on no one. We met the Hunts in Sydney, and accompanied them in the German steamer to Samoa. We had rather a rough passage here, and were thirty hours behind time. Louis Stevenson and his wife were on board, and we enjoyed the trip well. They have bought 400 acres of land behind Apia, and are going to squat. George Brown, of the Wesleyan New Guinea Mission, with his wife was also with us, and you may be sure the smoking-room, the best place in the ship, was well patronised. We called at Tonga, but did not see the old king, now ninety-eight years old. We visited the college, and were much pleased with the students and work. A long way off, in somebody's time, New Guinea will, I hope, have the same.

'We got here on the 15th inst. at night, and found the John Williams at anchor. She was disabled, and had to return from Niue here. Clark and Claxton soon boarded us in the John Williams' boat, with a Rarotongan crew. Tuesday was a day for reception and memories of the past. Twenty-four years ago we came here " distressed British subjects," not a cent in the world, and with borrowed clothes on our back. Marriott and

Newell and Mrs. Newell came in. On Wednesday we had a meeting of all the clans in and about Apia. A "May meeting" it was called. 'Twas a large meeting. King Malietoa and Tamate addressed the meeting, and the three consuls were present. Newell interpreted for me. On Thursday night I gave a lecture to "whites," Louis Stevenson in chair, and had a crowded house. On Friday I came here, leaving Tamate Hahine at Apia, she not feeling well enough. I spoke at prayer-meeting that evening. On Saturday I went to Leulumoenga and addressed Hills' schoolboys. On Sunday I had two services, Newell interpreting. On Monday we had five hours of it, and on Tuesday the same. Monday was given to the students, and they made right good use of it by asking questions that seemed to comprehend everything. On Tuesday the pastors had their innings, and they made the best of it. On Wednesday I went to Savaii, and stayed with Davies. Yesterday, Thursday, I gave three hours, and in the evening left for here, arriving 12.45 a. m. Tamate Hahine not so well. We leave to-day for Apia. To-morrow night another lecture or talk to white folks. Sunday, native service in fore-noon and English service in new hall at night, and on Monday away in the Richmond to Tahiti and Rarotonga.'

Chalmers, in the sketch of his wife, part of which has been quoted already [1], gives a fuller account of this meeting with Stevenson :—

' We spent some time in Sydney and then were off to the islands. We had as fellow passengers Mr. and Mrs. Louis Stevenson on their way back to Samoa. We had a very rough passage, but the smoking-room was well patronized, and we spent many happy hours in it with our new friends. Dr. Brown and Mrs. Brown of New

[1] See page 315.

Britain were also with us.   Oh the story-telling of that
trip!   Did that smoking-room on any other trip hear
so many yarns?   Brown surpassed us all, and the
gentle novelist did well.   His best stories were personal.
My dear wife often said, " How gentle and lovable he is!
just one to nurse."   He was in very bad health, and was
well nursed and cared for by his clever wife.   We became much attached to one another, and hoped to meet
in Rarotoṅga, and afterwards in New Guinea; but we
never met again after Samoa.'

Chalmers thus made the acquaintance of Robert Louis
Stevenson and his wife.   It was inevitable that such
a man as Tamate should possess great attraction for
the brilliant novelist.   To hear Chalmers in the quiet
chat of social intercourse describe the many thrilling
adventures of his past life was an experience, once
enjoyed, never to be forgotten.   And this Stevenson
enjoyed to the full.   It was a happy accident which
thus brought the man of letters into contact with the
man of action, and he a missionary not at all after
the type depicted in modern fiction and agnostic
journalism.   Chalmers was in many respects an exceptional man, but he would have been the last to claim,
or to admit, that he was exceptional in either his love
for his work, or in his devotion to that Master from
love to whom he gave up his life to the hard and
dangerous toil of evangelizing the savage natives of the
Papuan Gulf.   He was richly endowed for the life-work
which he so splendidly accomplished; but he would
have scorned to accept any appreciation of his own
work if accompanied by depreciation of his fellows from
all churches also seeking to evangelize the heathen
world.

Chalmers was a man after Stevenson's own heart.

Then he was a fellow Scot, and had for twenty-five years been living through and experiencing adventures by flood and field of the very kind which possessed the most attraction for the author who was afterwards to write the *Beach of Falesa* and the *Ebb Tide*. A man who had been able to exert some restraining influence over the fierce ruffian 'Bully Hayes,' who, when the lives of all in it depended upon his nerve at the critical moment, could steer with the skill of the best natives a boat through the mighty Polynesian surf; a man who had visited nearly every part of Western Polynesia, and who numbered among his friends the chiefs of many a ferocious New Guinea tribe; a man, moreover, who, in the explorer, had never for a moment lost sight of his great mission, no other than that of his Master, to seek and to save the lost— such an one was indeed likely to be grappled to the heart of R. L. Stevenson as soon as they had looked one another in the face. Would that the smoking-room of that steamer in which they met could have recorded the brilliant talk that passed within its walls!

Nor was Stevenson slow to recognize and reluctant to acknowledge the value of the friendship thus begun. In December, 1890, he wrote, 'Christmas I go to Auckland to meet Tamate, the New Guinea missionary, a man I love[1].' Mr. Graham Balfour in the *Life of Robert Louis Stevenson* states:—

'His personal relations with the Protestant missionaries in Samoa were most pleasant. He was a loyal and generous friend to every man and woman among them, told them quite plainly whenever he disagreed with them, or disapproved of their line of conduct, and was a most stimulating and liberal influence on their

[1] *Letters*, ii. 212.

work . . . for Mr. Chalmers, Tamate of New Guinea, he felt a kind of hero-worship, a greater admiration probably than he felt for any man of modern times except Charles Gordon [1].'

At Apia, on September 18, 1890, Chalmers gave a lecture on New Guinea, at which Stevenson took the chair. In the course of his speech Stevenson said, ' There are some men who never need introducing, and Tamate, as I prefer to call him, is one of these. It has been my good fortune to steal a march upon my fellow townsmen, and to anticipate many of you in the privilege of acquaintance with Mr. Chalmers, for I travelled with him from Sydney here. This intimate intercourse has resulted in my having the highest admiration for Mr. Chalmers. And I am sure that all present will not only enjoy listening to his narrative, but will also very heartily wish him God-speed in all his future endeavours as a pioneer of civilization and love. I believe we shall all be stimulated to greater courage in taking up the cross that all heroic souls have taken—the cross of light and progress.'

Stevenson cherished the hope of visiting Tamate in New Guinea, but this design proved, unhappily, impossible. But for some years a correspondence was kept up, and we are able to quote here three hitherto unpublished letters from Stevenson to his friend, letters as characteristic and striking as any that even that brilliant letter-writer penned.

'VAILIMA, APIA, *November* 5, 1890.

' My dear Tamate.—I wish I could tell you how pleased I was to get your note. I shall never cease to rejoice I had the good fortune to meet you ; and whatever you are good enough to think of me, be sure it is

[1] *Life*, vol. ii. pp. 126, 127.

returned with interest. I cannot come on the Richmond; our presence is very needful, and work pressing;
the most I can do (and in that I do not mean to fail) is
to go by the next Wainui, and meet you, and arrive
about the same time with you in Auckland. My wife,
who is tired and dirty and rheumatic, and embittered
by bad yeast, and yet (like myself) interested beyond
measure by our hard and busy life here on the mountain, bids me send all things nice. "I cannot think of
anything nice enough," quoth she, " to Tamate and his
wife."

> ' The same from
> ' Your affectionate friend,
> ' ROBERT LOUIS STEVENSON.'

(Undated. Late in 1890 or early in 1891.)

' My dear Tamate.—I had looked forward to meeting
you with a pleasure that I should find it hard to exag-
gerate. The kindness of your letter, which encourages
me to suppose that you yourself had looked forward
to the event, makes me the more sad to-day. Yet I am
very sure you will approve me altogether. I have my
work well forward, I have never done so much in so
short a time before. I am pretty tired. I looked forward to a change, and here is the state of affairs; my
wife has been working and over-working; cutting,
planting, digging. All the time she has never heard
from her son; and has not the usual consolation, for
Lloyd has never neglected to write to us. Doubtless
the post office is at fault, so we think, so we know,
but this scarce mitigates the strain of waiting and the
annoyance of receiving disappointments. I was practically packed up to come away, and I have given up.
My wife is not fit to be left alone with all this work and
all these workmen. It would be base in me if I dreamed

of leaving her. You must go without my farewell; and I must do without the inspiration of seeing you.

'I am a man now past forty. Scotch at that, and not used to big expressions in friendship; and used on the other hand to be very much ashamed of them. Now, when I break my word to you, I may say so much; I count it a privilege and a benefit to have met you. I count it loss not to meet with you again.

'"Just now," I make haste to add. If death spare us, and the junctions of life permit, I mean to see you, and that soon. If things oppose, accept the expression of my love and gratitude, my love for yourself, my gratitude for your example and your kindness.

'I hope Mrs. Chalmers will not mind if I send also my love to her; and my wife's. How often have we talked of you both; how often shall we not think of you in the future! I ask you as a particular favour, send me a note of the most healthy periods in New Guinea. I am only a looker on. I have a (rather heavy) charge of souls and bodies. If I can make out any visit, it must be done sensibly, and with the least risk. But oh, Tamate, if I had met you when I was a boy and a bachelor, how different my life would have been!

'Dear Mrs. Chalmers, you say (and very justly), "Tamate is such a rowdy"—your own excellent expression. I wonder if even you know what it means, to a man like me—a very clever man, no modesty, observe! a man fairly critical, a man of the world (in most of the ill senses), to meet one who represents the essential, and who is so free from the formal, from the grimace. My friend, Mr. Clarke, said, "I wish I could have him for a colleague to keep me up to the mark." So I; I wish I had him for a neighbour to keep me human.

'Farewell! Forgive me my failure. I think your

Master would have had me break my word.    I live in the
hope of seeing you again.    I pray God watch over you.
                    'Your sincere friend,
                        'ROBERT LOUIS STEVENSON.'


                                'VAILIMA, *May*, 1891.
  'My dear Tamate.—Your photograph is on my
chimney-shelf as large as life, for I am in my new house,
more betoken as the head of me is in, and the tail still
out in the bush. It's a change any way; and my
mother has just come two days ago, and I am on the
mend, and my wife is far from well, mainly overwork,
I still hope, to pass away when we come to some kind
of a bearing.
  'The trouble about the photograph is this.    It was
sent to me enclosed in a very kind letter from a lady[1]:
what was her name?    Eh, man, I canna tell ye!
Whaur's her letter?    Weel, nae doubt, but it's here,
but ye see there's a routh o' paper a' round me, and it's
got in mixty-maxty in the lave-o't, and I canna just pit
ma hand upon the bit.    I am really much vexed; for
I had meant to express my obligation to the lady
properly—and I will too, in case I get hold of the
missing note before an unreasonable lapse of time;
and meanwhile my only hope is you may send on this
screed to Tamate Vaine, who is far more of a business
man than either you or me, and has far more gumption,
and will do the right thing for a man whose heart is in
the right place, although his correspondence is terribly
mixed up with flittings.
  'What ill-fortune we had, not to meet!    I am sure

  [1] This refers to a special photograph of Chalmers which Stevenson had desired to possess, and which had been sent to him at
Chalmers' request by a friend in England.

I missed you at last by a narrow margin. My hunt for you while I was in Sydney brought me in a very funny predicament. I was told there was a Mr. —— from New Guinea in the hotel, and immediately collared him for news of your movements. My reception was so strange, that I withdrew. Presently comes Mr. —— to say he had not caught my name. I said that made it the worse, and I had no desire to enjoy the acquaintance of any one who could be so rude to a stranger. Then he said it was your name that made the trouble. All the more reason that we should separate, said I. Chalmers is a friend of mine. And then, I am bound to say, —— made rather a favourable impression on me; said he had had all kinds of rows with you; admitted you had cause of complaint, from your point of view, I think, he said, but must not prejudice the man from memory. Made no complaint himself, said that his difference with you had brought him many disagreeable interviews, and he thought mine was another, &c.; and I came to a sort of armed peace with him. I know it's no use asking you what the trouble was; but I still cherish the hope this may go on to Tamate Vaine, and *she* may answer me.

'My dear Tamate, I wish I could go with this letter; but it's no good talking. All I can say is, my most sincere affection goes; and when you have done your day's duty, may we both live to meet and have a crack in the evening. I wish there were more like you. You are the man for my complaint: you do me good: I wonder if I am of any use? None, I fear, or so little. Well, you have been of use to me.

'The house, as I have said, is inhabited and pretty habitable. By desperate efforts we got a room ready against my mother's arrival; and a sort of a rough sketch of a dining-room to live in; it nearly murdered my wife, but it was done, and the old lady arrived looking as bright as a dollar, and about as young as my battered self, to find a tabernacle and her husband's portrait over the chimney. It nearly murdered my wife, I say; and that is why you hear from me only: she had meant to write, but has been in bed all day, sick and faint, and a pure wreck, and I doubt if she will be fit to wag a pen before Captain Turpie heaves anchor.

' I wish you from my heart good strength, good spirits, a good courage, and a blessing on your endeavours. Go on, my dear man, in God's name, the right man in the right place, and may you see the reward of your success.

' Your sincere friend,
' ROBERT LOUIS STEVENSON.'

Mr. Graham Balfour has also kindly supplied from Stevenson's letters in his possession two characteristic extracts bearing upon this episode.

Writing to his mother in September, 1890, ' s.s. Lübeck, between Sydney and Tongatabu, three days out,' he remarks, ' We have a very interesting party on board, three missionaries and their wives: Messrs. Chalmers and Hunt of the London Society and Mr. Brown of the Wesleyans. Chalmers and Brown are pioneer missionaries, splendid men, with no humbug, plenty courage, and the love of adventure; Brown, the man who fought a battle with cannibals at New Britain, and was so squalled over by Exeter Hall; Chalmers, a friend of Mrs. Hannah Swan's. . . . I have become a terrible missionaryite of late days; very much interested in their work, errors, and merits: perhaps it's in the blood, though it has been a little slow of coming out. No, to be sure, I am wrong: I remember I always liked the type. Chalmers, a big, stout, wildish-looking man, iron grey, with big bold black eyes, and a deep straight furrow down each cheek: aetat. forty to forty-five.'

Writing to his mother from Vailima in October or November, 1890, he speaks of going to Auckland. 'I want to see Sir George Grey. I shall meet Tamate once more before he disappears up the Fly River, perhaps to be one of "the unreturning brave"—and I have a *cultus* for Tamate; he is a man nobody can see, and not love. Did I tell you I took the chair at his missionary lecture; by his own choice? I thought you would like that; and I was proud to be at his side even for so long. He has plenty faults like the rest of us; but he's as big as a church. I am really highly *mitonari* now, like your true son.'

Robert Louis Stevenson is the most striking example of a literary man of high class, coming into close contact with missionary work and workers in one of the great modern fields. He saw this work, as he himself tells us, at first with unsympathetic eyes. But he did what no other man of his training and standing has done in this generation. He came to know missionary work not in the superficial and often supercilious manner of the globe-trotter and of some government officials. He learned its true nature through living among Samoans who had been trained under missionary influence; by watching their daily life; by the knowledge he gained of their language and modes of thought and aims in life. He was strong enough to lay aside his prejudices, and to number among his intimate friends several of those missionaries at whom occasionally Cabinet ministers gird, and whose advice diplomats seldom seek. He looked beneath the surface, he saw missionaries and missionary work as they are, and not as the modern pagan *littérateur* often imagines them to be. Thus to large numbers of Christian people the most interesting references in his life and in his letters are those which have to do with his attitude towards the Christian life and towards missions. In Sydney in 1893, to a gathering of missionary workers and helpers in that city, Stevenson gave an address which may be commended to those who can see nothing more than 'rice Christians' in the Chinese who died by thousands rather than deny the Saviour whom they loved; in the Hindus who, under the light of the Gospel, submit to all the suffering involved in breaking caste; or in the Polynesians who forsake idolatry, and who are slowly but surely rising to higher levels of life under the teaching of the New Testament. 'I had conceived a great prejudice against missions in the South Seas, and had no sooner come there than that prejudice was at first reduced, and then at last annihilated. Those who deblaterate against missions have only one thing to do, to come and see them on the spot. They will see a great deal of good done; they will see a race being forwarded in many different directions, and I believe, if they be honest persons, they will cease to complain of mission work and its effects [1].'

Chalmers was greatly pleased with his visit to Malua. He aroused there immense enthusiasm for mission work in New Guinea. He rejoiced to know that many of them would become his helpers in the Fly River Mission. Summing up his impressions at this time, he wrote:—

[1] *Life*, ii. 193.

'I am glad to feel the Samoan church, as seen from pastors and college, is a living one, and holds firmly to Christ notwithstanding the many storms. *We* have been greatly blessed and refreshed, and I trust missionaries, pastors, students, and churches will be as greatly. I have asked for six teachers now and a constant supply to follow, and I am confident both will be forthcoming.'

During Tamate's intercourse with the native pastors and students at Malua he allowed them to question him freely. He sent home a representative list of the questions asked him. From them some notion may be formed of the intellectual and religious development of these students, all of whose ancestors, only a generation or two since, were fierce and degraded heathen. Here is a portion of the list he sent home :—

' 1. What is the root of the difficulties in the work?

' 2. What is the best method of winning the New Guineans to Christ?

' 3. Are they as tribes in customs and physique alike?

' 4. Are those who come as candidates clothed or unclothed, and are they exhorted to be clothed?

' 5. Are the people much scattered, or do they live in large villages?

' 6. Which is the part of New Guinea for Samoa, and the teachers who leave next where will they go?

' 7. How many Samoans do you wish for now?

' 8. Is the language difficult to acquire? and give examples.

' 9. Are there many foreigners, are there stores?

' 10. What about Romanists and others, have they got to New Guinea?

' 11. What are the New Guinea students taught?

' 12. What about German New Guinea, and are there missionaries there?

' 13. Where did the first missionaries come from?

' 14. What about Romanists in days to come when we have enlightened the people?

' 15. How many missionaries are wanted to evangelize all New Guinea?

' 16. Can long journeys be made in New Guinea?

' 17. What do you think about Mr. Brown's action in New Britain?

' 18. Do the people of New Guinea poison others?

' 19. Do the animals of New Guinea dance like men?

' 20. What are the occupations of the people?

' 21. Suppose I go to a place and the people wish to kill me, what am I to do?

' 22. Are the islands of Torres Straits inhabited?

' 23. Is the translation of the Bible complete?

' 24. Are there villages on mountains?

' 25. Do you understand New Guinea fever?

' 26. What is the prevailing wind?

' 27. What about the snakes and crocodiles?

' 28. What about the tailed and big-eared people?

' 29. Why don't you ask for a larger band of men?

' 30. How many years should we spend here before we go?

' 31. Will there be an English missionary with the Samoans?

' There were many other questions asked, the above were leading ones. They are building a new public hall, and Tamate is to open it to-night. Our vessel is not in, though due, and it is possible she may be detained by the strike. If only we knew that she was not coming for some weeks I should be off to all the stations and mountains. I am greatly pleased with the earnest desire

on the part of the Samoans for better education, and
what is just as real, the thorough aptitude of the
missionaries to meet it. Newell is the mainspring of
this mission, and he is quite abreast of all that is needed.
They certainly know how to spend money here, and as
they certainly know how to work.'

On leaving Samoa Chalmers sailed for Rarotonga, the
island of happy memories and of successful work. It
was dear to his heart not only because of the blessed
memories of his early wedded life, and because of the
love, and zeal, and toil he had there thrown into the
duty placed upon him. But the bonds of affection had
been strengthened by the fact that during the thirteen
years which had passed since he left it many earnest
and faithful native teachers had come from its Institution
to co-operate with him in the New Guinea Mission, and
many of these, both men and women, had laid down
their lives in this great enterprise. It is easy, then, to
imagine the joy with which he contemplated revisiting
its scenes of beauty.

'On the evening of September 30 we left Samoa,
wishing we could have stayed a few weeks longer. We
had a very pleasant trip here, arriving on October 4,
about 6.30 p.m. Fancy travelling in the South Seas in
a splendid steamer. The John Williams left Samoa for
here three weeks ago, and has not yet turned up.

'October 13. Yesterday was a red-letter day. The native
services were large and enthusiastic, and the English
service was also well attended. A great sorrow awaited
us on our arrival here. A young pastor lay dead, to be
buried the day after we landed. As a lad I taught him,
and afterwards he joined the college, and when finished
was elected as pastor of the Avarua church. As a baby
he was adopted by Queen Makea, and brought up by

her. He was a very loving, thoughtful laddie, and we all loved him. In coming along I often thought of him, and hoped to have many pleasant meetings with him— but not yet awhile. We anchored about six p.m., and no one expecting us we landed, and in the dusk walked up through the village. The majority of the people were at Makea's to comfort her in her great sorrow. It was soon noised abroad we were coming along, and the people began rushing about looking for us. Guess the excitement was great. Hutchin hearing came on, and together we walked to her Majesty's. She is changing much. We stayed there a short time, and then up to the old place, the mission house. On Sunday I preached, baptized, administered the ordinance, and helped to bury the dead, and in the afternoon took another service.

'During the week we went to Ngatangiia, Matavera, and Arorangi. All is changed, we travel in buggies now. When at Matavera the people insisted on our staying that they might give us a present, and so be the first to do it. It is the smallest of the villages but the most pronounced in wickedness and kindness, and ever determined to go contrary to chiefs and laws. There is a good teacher, and I was glad to meet several who, when I left many years ago, were a wild, godless lot, but now are changed and members of the church. A few months ago Isaia died at Arorangi. He was teacher there for nearly thirty years. He was son of the first teacher landed on Rarotonga[1]; father and mother

[1] This was Papeiha, the man who accompanied John Williams in 1823, and who, taking his life in his hand, landed alone on Rarotonga, lived there alone for four months, and was largely instrumental in converting the island to Christianity. See my *History of the London Missionary Society*, vol. i. pp. 261, 275, 276.

will remember him as being in England with William Gill. He was a good man, and did good service. He has a son in the college preparing for the work. The changes amongst the people are very great, many, many are dead, and what I am sorry to see is so many youngish people. There are a few very old folks left— two or three about ninety. The white man's spirit and clothing are doing havoc.

'To-morrow I am informed is to be a great day here —presents for Tamate and wife. In the afternoon after fun is over we go to Ngatangiia for meetings, and then back on Saturday or Monday to go round the group.

'I do wish you could see this island; it is the loveliest in all the South Pacific. If ever I grow old, and should have to retire, I think I should come here. This climate is, I believe, perfect. I wish Stevenson had come here, it would be better for him than Samoa.'

To Mrs. Chalmers also, this visit was full of tender associations. The first Mrs. Chalmers had been the friend of her girlhood. She herself had intended to take part in the work. In a letter written under the spell of first impressions she enables us to realize the welcome his old friends gave to Tamate, and to her for his sake.

'AVARUA, RAROTONGA, *October* 11, 1890.

'Doesn't it seem strange to you that I should be writing to you from this place? Here I sit in dear Jeanie's old parlour which she described to me so long ago. It is all just lovely. Tamate felt it much returning to the old home, where so many happy years had been spent. Never shall I forget the reception. The Consul came on board the steamer and lent us his boat to go ashore and take our luggage. The crew shouted to some one ashore, " Tamate, Tamate Vaine." Directly we saw a commotion, and first some women hurried to meet us. All through the town the crowd gathered until we met Mr. Hutchin, the missionary, followed by a large number of old and young. Two women who had lived with Jeanie as girls took possession of me, and at the head of the crowd we marched. At every house people came out to join us, many old people embracing us, some throwing themselves at Tamate's feet, embracing them with tears rolling down their poor old faces, saying they had never thought to look upon his face again on earth. These people seem to worship him, and even the little ones know all about Tamate, his name is a household word. There never has been and never will be anybody like him to them. Poor Tamate was quite overcome at times. His memory is wonderful; he remembered their names, and could inquire after the various families. Younger men and women who had been his scholars were delighted when he said, " Why, you must be so and so's son or daughter."

'We were met by sad news on the beach—Makea's (the Queen's) adopted son was dead, and to be buried the next day. She was in great trouble. We went to her residence first, the crowd followed. The house is handsome: two storeys, verandah, a balcony above, and furnished in European style. There is an avenue of trees from the gate to the front entrance. As we approached, the Queen and her women came out of one of the French doors and met Tamate at the head of the steps. She put her arms round him and kissed him, then keeping her hand on his shoulder put him back, and examined his face; with tears in her eyes she spoke a few words. Tamate did not speak, but drew me forward and put my hand in hers, and she kissed me and introduced her husband. He took my hand and led me

into a nice large drawing-room.  It was dusk, and the
servants brought in lamps, so now we could see each
other distinctly.   There were two couches and several
easy-chairs, a table in the centre and side-tables, also
pictures, two French windows opening at the verandah.
Tamate was put in an armchair facing the doors, the
Queen and I on one couch, the other two gentlemen
on the opposite couch, and the Prince Consort next
Tamate.   Then the room filled as well as the verandah.
One poor old lady turned eighty forced her way through,
sobbing and crying, threw herself at Tamate's feet, and
clasping his legs would not leave him for some minutes.
Tamate's heart was full.  I said, " Do say something to
them."   He got up, then sat down again, saying,
" I cannot."

'Mr. Smith, Mr. Hutchin, and myself went up the
drive past the churchyard, and into the mission grounds.
It is a paradise for position.  I don't know how they
made up their minds to leave this most lovely spot.
Tamate had gone to the place where the poor young
man was lying in state.  He would not allow me to go.
When I heard Tamate's voice, I met him on the verandah.
I knew he must feel sad entering his own old home.
It is a grand house built of coral, the walls two feet thick
and plastered with lime and cement.  The house stands
a little way up the mountain side, there are flights of
wide stone steps, and the ground is laid out in terraces
in front.  At the back a piece has been dug away and
made level about thirty feet in width, and the mountain
rises precipitately, clothed to the summit with trees and
bush, oranges in abundance, most delicious when they
are fresh from the trees, cocoa-nuts and many other
kinds of fruit.'

At the close of his visit to his old home and his well-remembered and deeply loved flock, Chalmers summed up his impressions of Rarotonga and its prospects in a letter to one of his friends at home deeply interested in mission work :—

'RAROTONGA, *November* 3, 1890.

'I must write you a wee letter from this old homeland of ours. Thirteen years and a half since we left it, and what changes! The enemy has been busy, and many, very many faces are not. The people were glad to see us, and all gave us a right good welcome, so that we found the affection and kindness still remain.

'We have had right good missionary meetings here, and I have visited other islands, viz. Mangaia, Atiu, and Aitutaki, and at these we had enthusiastic meetings. Our visit, we pray, being blessed to us, may be abundantly blessed to all the people, and that the blessing through them may extend to New Guinea. They are all very anxious we should remain with them, but I cannot consent now. I have undertaken the Fly River work, and shall continue it for some years. When old, this would make a good resort. The climate is perfect, and the scenery a lovely picture.

'Isn't it sad that a people so free, kind, and truly attractive should be dying out? Strong drink is a fearful agent, but it cannot alone be blamed for the sad decrease. I blame clothing, change in housing, and introduction of foreign food as much as strong drink. I feel persuaded that were these natives to return to the manner of living of their forefathers they would again increase. The introduced changes are too great. How pleased you would be with their pretty churches, the work all done by themselves. They build or repair their own schools and churches, and pay their own pastors.

'They are a people easily led, and with a thoroughly religious nature. Their one great failing is drink, but from it many have been saved and are leading true lives. We want a Maine liquor law, worked by a thoroughly honest white man. The chiefs are not able to contend against the whites, and although anxious to stop drink, cannot. They feel like Khama, and plead like him, that the fearful curse of drink may be stopped.'

The following extracts from the correspondence of this time enable us to accompany Mr. and Mrs. Chalmers on their return journey to Motumotu:—

'AUCKLAND, *January* 20, 1891.

'I have addressed fifteen meetings in ten days; last Sunday I had four services. We leave on Thursday for Wellington, thence Lyttleton, Christchurch, Timaru, Oamaru, Dunedin.'

'MELBOURNE, *April* 27, 1891.

'Here we are on our way north. I find it very difficult to move on. We were a fortnight in Tasmania, but they pressed hard for a month. Could not be done. We got over £90 in Tasmania for steamer, and all independent of churches.'

'NEAR KEPPEL BAY, *May* 17, 1891.

'Since July I have only been idle two Sundays, that is, on each of these Sundays I had only one address. Last Saturday night I addressed young men in Sydney, and on Sunday evening had a splendid meeting of men.'

Chalmers returned to Toaripi with the knowledge that his main work was now to lie elsewhere. This having been decided, it was his nature to be restless until the change of field had been effected.

# CHAPTER X

## THE FLY RIVER, 1892-1894

MR. AND MRS. CHALMERS reached Port Moresby in May, 1891. 'Since our return to New Guinea,' he writes, 'we have had a varied experience. After our arrival we remained at Port Moresby until the new teachers came by the John Williams. There were twenty in all, viz. two young women from Mangaia to be married to teachers; five teachers and their wives from Rarotonga; five teachers, four with their wives, one left his wife at home, from Samoa; and two teachers and wives from Niue. There was also one old teacher returning from Samoa with his newly married wife. We all had a right good refreshing time during the week we spent together. They were a very fine body of men and women, and all seemed full of real earnestness.

'In a week we missionaries had to go to Kerepunu for our annual committee meeting. At the committee meeting it was decided that I should visit Cooktown, and arrange for a vessel to visit our eastern stations during the absence of the Harrier in Sydney for repairs.

'After being a week away I returned to Port Moresby. We all spent a few happy days together, and then those of us for the west went on board schooner and sailed away.'

Mr. and Mrs. Chalmers left Port Moresby for Motumotu on June 30, 1891, but did not get off their home until July 6. In her journal Mrs. Chalmers describes the trying experiences connected with her landing:—

'July 6. We left Delena on Saturday morning. There was heavy sea, and the rolling about was bad. When fairly out of the lagoon we made way, and in the afternoon had a fair wind and spun along at a fine rate, hoping to reach Motumotu by nightfall. It was a very rough sea, and we had to hold on all the time to something. Fortunately the wind was in our favour, but I was very sore and bruised with bumping about so much. Before sunset we sighted the dear old place: it is dear to us, though I must say it looks anything but inviting as a place of residence from the sea. A low flat stretch of land with a grove of palms here and there, and not a bit of rising ground to be seen. How we hoped and longed to land; but no use, there were tremendous seas, and no boat could get through such a surf. We had to keep well out and cast anchor. There is no good anchorage here either. What a terrible night we had for discomfort, to be sure; the ship swung a little and got nearly broadside on the seas, and with every roll she shipped a sea one side or the other. The men lashed me firmly to the seat, which is bolted to the companion-way, and I just rolled with the ship, feeling every time she went down on my side that the great wall of water must come over us. I never passed such a night; and there opposite was our own home, and every time the ship came right side up I caught a glimpse of the lantern which our people kept on the flagstaff. Of course no one slept. Tamate and Savage stayed down below. They could not stand on deck, and they could not keep in the berths either. Tamate struggled up and peeped over at me two or three times. I was fast enough, but could only move with the ship.

'Next morning (Sunday) the two boats left the river before daybreak, but it was 6.40 a.m. before they got round to us. Then the difficulty was to get into them. Tamate thought it would be impossible for me to manage it. No ladder could be put out, and the boat rose and fell to a great height and depth. Of course I was anxious to land, and did not want to wait, no one knew how long, for the sea to behave better. Our students were in the boat, and I said to Naimi and Ola, "Stand ready to catch hold of me, boys, and when she rises again I'll spring." Tamate said, "That's the only way, but I'm afraid you won't do it in time"; but as he finished speaking I landed safely in the boat, feeling rather shaky and dizzy. By-and-by our boat got off with twenty on board. The swell was heavy, and it was provoking to be opposite our house and yet have to go miles away from it and into the river. The boys managed splendidly, and we only shipped one sea crossing the bar. I was very sore, and sick too, for want of something to eat, for we did not stay for breakfast or anything on board.

'What a crowd to meet us! the river bank was lined. Our house boys were all out at the very end of the sandspit, and ran on the bank alongside us to the landing-place, and the dogs swam in to meet the boat. All the teachers were there—the girls and their blessed babies all looking bright and happy, and so glad to see me especially, for none of them expected to see me again when I left. Truly it was a home-coming, and one to be thankful for in every way.'

On July 10 Chalmers left Toaripi in the Harrier for Cooktown.

'On the Friday morning I went on board of the
Harrier, and with a light wind we did not arrive at Port
Moresby until the Monday. There we had the sad news
that death had already been busy with our new band of
teachers. Of the four men and women from Niue or
Savage Island, one man and woman were dead, and of
those from Samoa, one man and woman had also died.
'Tis well for us the Master knows best what to do with
His servants. It was a terrible blow to us all; but far
worse to the remaining new teachers. On Saturday we
left for Cooktown.

'We called in at Kerepunu, and then we crossed the
Coral Sea, having very dirty weather all the way over.

'On Thursday, at three p.m., we entered Cook's
Opening of the Barrier Reef, and began beating down,
hoping to be in Cooktown the following morning. No
such good luck, the stormy night was against us. All day
Friday we kept at it, carrying away several head sails and
forward stays, and had to anchor under Three Islands to
repair damage. About four p.m., up anchor and again
started pile-driving against a heavy sea. It is not often so
heavy a sea is met with inside the Barrier. At eight p.m.
we rounded ship and stood away on the starboard tack,
expecting when we again went about we should fetch
Cooktown. Several of our sailors, including our captain,
have their wives there, and some of these were singing
" Homeward bound." The night was wet and dirty, and
wind and sea very high. Some time before nine I turned
into my bunk. A passenger we had on board got to
his before me. I was nearing the land of unconscious-
ness, and fancied I was dreaming of rocks—hallo!
a grate! a bound! a bump! I was up, on coat and
on deck. It was 9.15. All hands were on deck, head
sails were soon off her, followed by mainsail, a boat with

a kedge anchor sent away. The kedge was dropped in five fathoms of water, and the hawser made fast to the windlass on the port side. A long steady, heavy, near breaking heave; but no use, she was fast. When the tide went out she was on her bilge and very uncomfortable.

'On Saturday, July 25, we were getting ballast on deck ready to throw overboard if she righted with the night tide. The kedge was sent out right astern, and the hawser passed in over the starboard quarter and on the windlass, to be ready for another attempt. Signals of distress were flying all day and that night; hoping we might be seen from Cooktown, we fired rockets, blue lights and tow soaked with kerosene. We were not seen. At 10.30 ship righted, and overboard went the ballast placed on deck, and then all hands to windlass. No use, she had no go-off movement in her. She had been making water, but the pumps kept her dry. Wind and sea now increased, grating and bumping worse than ever, and now hopes of saving her were lessened.

'On Sunday morning there was a fearful sea breaking on her starboard quarter, the pumps no longer were of any use, and the deck on the port side was beginning to rise. The sea was flowing in and out; she was leaning much more over on her side, and it was evident something must be done to prevent her, if possible, going over altogether. It was sad, but necessary, and instructions were given to cut away masts. The lee sides of the masts were cut, and then the port rigging, all stays, and finally the starboard rigging—a big sea, a fearful bump, and away went the sticks; she laboured easier. There seemed to be no chance of our being seen by passing vessels, so the whaleboat was got ready to go to Three Islands, and there try and intercept a vessel.

The prospect on board the wreck was not inspiring, but that of going in a gale of wind and a heavy sea running was much less so.    There were three teachers on board, going to Cooktown for change, and Mr. George Belford, so well known as accompanying our governor in many of his expeditions.    Belford did splendid service from the striking on the reef until leaving.

'The whaleboat was got up under the jibboom, and in charge of the second mate, Mr. Macdougall, of Stornoway, was well managed.    A few provisions and a few things belonging to the passengers and crew dropped into her, then we followed, just holding on to a rope to be ready when she rose to let go.    When leaving, I saw a sailor emerge from the hold, and I said to him, "What are you up to?"    He yelled, "Looking for the poor old cat, sir, we must save him if we can"; and Tom was also thrown into the boat.    We had a young cockatoo also on board, and that one of the sailors got hold of and dropped with it into the boat.

'We were eleven all told, and, with provisions and effects, far too heavy.    We got over the reef to leeward, and stood away under reefed mainsail.    They were to those who knew the danger two very anxious hours.    Macdougall did splendidly, and kept his presence of mind well.    We had to bale out all the way.    We landed on the lee side of Three Islands, took possession of a beche-de-mer station, and began our look-out for passing ships.    We fired the grassy part of the island, so that it might be seen by the five we left on board of the wreck, and inform them that we were safe.

'Some time after we landed, a lugger passed, but took no notice of us.    Before sunset another vessel, which some knew to be the Government pilot boat, Governor Cairns, was bearing down, and we hoped would come near enough to see us, but she kept well in towards the mainland; the sun set, and soon darkness, and we saw no more of her that night. We burned two blue lights and fired one rocket, and kept a large fire burning all night. Soon after sunrise we saw a small vessel coming towards us from the north, and shortly after another vessel running clear full for the lee side of the island. The latter was the Governor Cairns; our signal the night before had been seen. By eight a.m. we were all aboard, and, through the kindness of Mr. Saville Kent, we were enjoying a good breakfast. Mr. Kent had been out on the reefs, and was returning to Cooktown.

'Captain Cole, of the Governor Cairns, hearing the captain and four others were on the wreck, at once weighed anchor and beat up towards the reef, under the lee of which we anchored, and soon had all on board, and by four p.m. were under way for Cooktown, where we arrived at 11.10 p.m.

'For some days some of us were stiff and sore, but we are now getting right. The sick teachers have had fever, but are now better, and I am glad to say Belford, who is over for his health, is much better.

'I deeply sympathize with our good captain, to whom no blame can attach, and who, from the time of striking until leaving the wreck, on Monday afternoon, did splendidly. He has been a good servant of the Society.'

The above is Chalmers' official account of his fourth shipwreck. In a letter to a friend from Cooktown dated August 7, 1891, he gives some of his inner thoughts about his terrible experiences:—

'Well, yes, been and got wrecked. Some of the papers have it that when the Harrier struck I called all hands aft to prayer. Utterly false. I believe in prayer—have good reason to believe in it—but to call all hands aft then would not be prayer, but simple stupid fear. Every one on board was engaged getting sails in, and afterwards heaving on the hawser.'

Chalmers never relished the task of writing elaborate reports of his movements and his doings. As a matter of fact, there are a large number of such reports in existence, but over the vast majority of them he groaned and toiled unlovingly. One influence only could move him to write with real care and interest, and that was the hope and belief that those who read his words would be stirred up to show an active interest in the work always nearest to his heart by praying for it and doing all in their power to help him in its prosecution. Among Chalmers' dearest friends in Australia were Mr. Searle, of Kew, Victoria, and his family. He kept up a close and intimate correspondence with them, and they have kindly placed at the author's disposal numerous extracts from Chalmers' letters. In August, 1891, at the request of Mr. Searle, Chalmers sent him a letter to be read to a class of young men. As it is the best record of his life at this time, we quote a part of it here:—

'Having arranged with the well-known Queensland firm, Burns, Philp & Co., to visit our eastern stations from Port Moresby once in two months, I felt anxious, after the wreck of the Harrier, to get back to Toaripi as soon as possible, but could find no boat or vessel suitable. In my extremity I made application to the colonial treasurer and the port-master at Brisbane to have the loan of the Cooktown pilot schooner, Governor Cairns, and it was granted; the London Missionary Society to insure the vessel, put captain and crew and provisions on board, and take all risk. In a few days after getting the vessel we were ready for sea, and soon slipped away from the wharf. We had a fair wind and good weather, and made a splendid passage across to Port Moresby. There we found all well; but not a bit of news from the west. I felt more anxious than ever for those I had left, and spent as little time as possible at Port Moresby. When I had left New Guinea for Cooktown some teachers were dead, and others were ill, and I had left my wife and several new teachers and their wives in the Gulf at a not over healthy place. So naturally I was anxious to get back. Sailing on a Tuesday, we were at Toaripi on Wednesday, and ashore just after dark. All were well. Tamate Hahine had had no fever, and the new teachers and their wives, although they had been very ill, were much better. Our Father in Heaven had cared for all, and our songs were those of thanksgiving.

'I feel deeply grateful to the Queensland Government for the loan of the schooner. No rent has been charged. The kind act was for the Society, and not for me personally, and I hope the auxiliaries in the colonies will take notice of it, and duly thank the Colonial Treasurer of Queensland, Sir Thomas McIlwraith, for his promptness in granting my request.

'During my absence Mr. Savage had made arrangements and built houses at the following places for our new teachers, viz. Orokolo, where two are to be placed who are to be supported by friends in Dunedin, New Zealand; this is a very populous district, and has, I think, the largest number of children in any district I know: at Vailala, where there is a village on the eastern bank of the Annie River, and another on the western; the latter has been occupied by a teacher for more than a year, and now there is a good house in the former which a teacher will soon occupy: and at

Kerema, which has an eastern and western village; the former already occupied, and now a house is being built in the latter, and a teacher is ready to be placed there.

'I want you to pray, just here, for these men and women; a special prayer, that they may soon know the language, and be made wise to turn souls, that their lives may be spared in holiness and honour to a real good old age, without any looking back. I don't like the looking back.

'I have not been able yet to visit the old stations, but Mr. Savage has done so during our absence, and he reports good work at some, whilst at others the teachers are too vagrant for successful work.

'At this station the following is our order of work:—

### CLASSES AND SERVICES.

6 a.m. sharp.    Bell rings for morning prayers.

6.30 to 8 a.m.    Bible class.

9 to 11 a.m.    Boys' class.    This frequently goes on to twelve.

3 to 5 p.m.    Men and boys for arithmetic and writing; women for reading and sewing.

5.30 p.m.    Evening prayers.    These must be in daylight on Sunday, Wednesday, and Saturday; prayer-meetings at which all attend.

7 p.m.    Evening service in house.

### SUNDAY.

6 a.m.    Morning prayers.

6.30 a.m.    Services in villages.

9 a.m.    Students and boys assemble in class-room, and after prayer march to church.

11 a.m.    Service in class-room in Motuan, and a quarter of an hour given to catechism study.

3.30 p.m.    Assemble in class-room, and after prayer march to service in village.

5.30 p.m.   Prayer-meeting.
Fridays and Saturdays there are no classes, these being
        the days devoted by the students to food-getting.
From 9 a.m. to 1 p.m. are the "students'" working hours.

'Toaripi has an eastern and a western village, and each
has now a teacher who have their daily work, teaching
and preaching and doing all the work required to be
done at a station.   As everywhere, the life we live is
the greatest influence for good, and far the most telling
sermon we can preach.

'In a comparatively new station such as this, where the
people are just emerging from savagism, we have many
queer experiences.   On my return I was told that some
of the natives in the eastern village were rather troublesome, and threatening the teacher because he claimed
certain land and cocoa-nuts for the mission, which they
said belonged to them.   These had really been bought
by the young teacher Tauraki, who was murdered a few
years ago by the Moveaveans.   I never threaten, and
I dislike threatening, and always feel disagreeable myself
when threatened.   So yesterday I finished my classes
earlier, got my cane, ordered some of our lads belonging
to the village to accompany me, and with the teacher
went on to the disputed ground near to the cocoa-nuts,
on one of which there was a tapu.

'A crowd gathered and I ordered the boundaries to be
cleared, and walked round, and giving a tomahawk to
a youth ordered the tapu to be cut down.   This was
done.   We then marked the trees in dispute, since
they really belonged to the Society, and no one inter-
fered.

'I spoke a few words to the point, and then left for
the western village, there to make inquiry for a dress
stolen from a student's wife.   A good deal of feeling

was shown at the accusation; but I wanted them to know that I could not let thieving pass. We did not get the dress. While I was waiting for evidence a wicked-looking fellow with a tomahawk came down from a house close by. I had my eye on him. He came near to where I was sitting, and seated himself behind me. I pretended not to be noticing, but in an offhand way turning round I ordered him to move to the front, which he did. In the morning, just after breakfast, I had to disarm of his bow and arrows a man who came into our grounds to attack or frighten the students. In the evening I sent for him, and on returning his bow and arrows spoke firmly and kindly to him and we parted good friends. Such scenes would be leaves for an autobiography, but I dare not make anything sensational of them, as I can see no sensation in them.

'I am anxious to visit all our stations before going to the Fly River. I feel sure you are praying for us, and I know we shall not be forgotten by you in the future. Do not expect too much. Forced work is unhealthy and manufactured converts do not last long. Let the work grow with our lives, and in God's own good time there will be a temple worthy of His praise.

'To us here it is intensely interesting and strengthening to know that so many of you at Kew take such interest in Christ's work. We think every Christian man and woman, young and old, should be one with Him in that which is so dear to Him, the world's salvation. Let our rallying cry then be, " The world for Christ," and for that let us ever strive. I am intensely gratified with the interest shown in China and India, but is there not some danger that the savages and heathen of Australia and New Guinea, which really belong to you, may be forgotten by the churches of Australasia? To God we are responsible for those nearest to us. 'Tis a fearful thing to think of the long, long time that these poor savages have been neglected. The devil has been busy enough, whilst we have been careless.'

During Tamate's eventful voyage Mrs. Chalmers had been left alone at Motumotu. She was a woman of great spirit and energy, and devoted heart and soul to the work. Her health was far from well, and the burden resting upon her was almost too heavy for any woman. But she loved the fierce natives of Toaripi quite as deeply as her husband did; she was willing to sacrifice herself on their behalf, and she exerted all her powers to see that the work of the station was properly attended to during Tamate's absence. It was a strain few women either could or would have endured. Nothing but her love for the Saviour, for her husband, and for the savages around her could have carried her through. But her faith was strong and sustained her hopefully and successfully under trials and disappointments and difficulties that would soon have utterly crushed a weak or an unspiritual woman.

She kept during the last half of 1892, and until she sailed for England, a daily journal. It is full of clear and striking sketches of the station routine, and, being intended for none but intimate relatives, often reveals her inmost thoughts on life and its trials. It is well for us, through such a medium as this, to be enabled to realize what the wives of pioneer missionaries have to endure. Chalmers was away on two occasions: the first was this visit to Cooktown when the Harrier was lost; the second was a visit of inspection to the islands and the stations about the Fly River and in Torres Straits, whither they were soon to remove.

'July 10.  Tamate left early this morning.  They had a fair wind, and were soon out of sight.  I have been putting things straight in the store, and going over the students' houses.

'July 21.  It has seemed a tiresome day somehow, and very wearying.  I could not get the girls to the washing till late; and as for the boys, they have had their own way so long, and gone so much to the village, that they are quite demoralized and do not care to do any steady work at all.

'July 23.  Two boys away again last night without leave, and I determined to catch them.  So I sat up on the verandah without a light, and between twelve and one p.m. saw two dark forms stealing in through the bananas.  Of course I pounced on them, and we had a small rumpus.  They are little more than savages after all, poor boys, and don't understand being under any rules or restraint.  They try to take advantage of me when alone, and I have to be very spry, but it is very disheartening sometimes.  I do not know how to speak very freely to them either.  Still have bad attacks, once or twice a day, and often in the night, but I think not so severe as formerly.

'Last night I really thought the house would be carried off, the furious waves seemed to break so close, and with every thundering crash the house shook. I got up to see if it really had come under the house; it was at the gate and washing inside, the whole of the bank had gone, and for miles along east and west, and far out to sea as eye could reach, was wild surf. It certainly looked grand and brilliantly white in the moonlight, which shone fitfully between the great black clouds.  I was glad to pop back into bed, for, grand as the sight was, it made me feel desolate and lonely.

I wondered where the Harrier and her precious passenger might be, for I had a very nasty creepy dream
about them.

'August 25. No time to write since the 9th, so much
has happened. I was sitting on the back verandah
when I heard a great shouting on the river bank; soon
a boy rushed in very much excited, with a travelling-
bag and a lady's satchel, saying, "White man, he come;
Tamate, he come." It was a very dark night, but looking round I caught sight of a slim, white figure flitting
across the raised platform from the school-house, and
it proved to be Fanny Baildon[1]. Then came my own
darling husband, followed by Harry Baildon and Dauncey. I felt altogether dazed for a while. Getting them
into the house, I had immediately to look after a substantial meal for the whole party. Then what a tale
I had to hear of shipwreck and danger! Tamate says,
in all his varied experience, he never had such a boat
journey as that from the wreck of the Harrier to the
island.

'Fanny and Harry were down the coast at Cairns, and
Tamate wired them to come on and take the chance of
going over to New Guinea. So here they are; but unfortunately we have had most wretched weather, and no
one remembers such a continuance of bad weather and
such dreadful seas for so long together. They had only
four days with us, which we enjoyed very much indeed,
though I should think two of the party never roughed it
so much in their lives, and never wish to do so again.

'August 29. The boys are really tiresome, and one
needs a lot of tact and patience. Even Tamate finds
them difficult to manage, and wonders how I have got
along alone. He has had trouble in the village. One

[1] The Baildons were distant connexions of Mrs. Chalmers.

or two excitements which would work up into very
sensational stories; but Tamate only laughs, and no one
could persuade him to dress up and moralize about such
incidents.

'September 5. I have just paid my boys, and bought
a quantity of food for them; extra cocoa-nuts must be
got in, for to-morrow is Ordinance Sunday. Sesevi and
Naimi's wife both wish to be baptized, but Tamate
thinks they must wait a while longer.

'September 7. The people are rather tiresome, and
on the station I find they have done exactly as they
liked out of class hours, and are consequently inclined
to rebel against any kind of restraint and steady work.
Of course it is wearying work, and a constant worry,
but it must be done in a place at this stage. They
must feel that you are very much alive, know all that
is going on, and will not let any breach of the rules pass
unnoticed.'

Mrs. Chalmers was once again left alone on the
station while her husband was visiting distant stations.

'November 14. Just three weeks since I wrote last.
I am only beginning to walk a little. Tamate did not
get back until the sixth, and found me, as he did once
before, almost at death's door. I had a terrible fortnight alone. No one who could get me any medicine
or proper food. One day they carried me into the
store to the medicine shelf, and touched all the bottles
until I nodded at the aconite one. Then how to get it
dropped was the question. I signed them to steady my
elbows until I dropped the quantity. I was tenderly
carried back to bed, and, after the aconite, I slept and
awoke feeling much less feverish. One of the women
tried to make some gruel, but it was all burnt to the
pan bottom. They baked some bread too, which

could not eat—too heavy. For more than ten days I just kept alive on tea, and badly made barley-water with a little brandy in it. Of course I was reduced to the lowest state, and could not have held out much longer.'

In September, 1892, Mr. J. E. Liddiard visited Chalmers at Motumotu. He enjoyed the very rare pleasure of seeing Tamate at work amid the surroundings of his daily life. He has gladly supplied a page or two from his notebook.

'One night about nine o'clock there was a great disturbance in the village, and we heard the noise of many loud and angry voices, and, as Tamate said he must go and see what was the matter, I determined to accompany him. As we pushed forward in the darkness many of the wild natives rushed past us with their weapons in their hands, and shouting defiance. We made our way to the large dubu or men's club-house in the centre of the village, and there ascertained that one party wished for a great dance, and another party objected on account of the death of a native. This dubu had only recently been erected. Its opening was put off by Tamate from time to time until he could obtain the promise that there should be no sacrifice of life in connexion with the opening, as it has always been considered necessary for the dubus to be consecrated with blood, and that until lives have been sacrificed it could not be regarded as fit for occupation.

'Having made peace between the parties, we climbed up the rough ladder to the platform on the front of the dubu. The only lights in the interior of this large building were given off by the fires which in several places were burning on clay hearths, and it was truly a weird sight as the figures and faces of the members of

this club, with all their strange decorations, were brought
into prominence as the light fell upon them.

'We were well received, and after a long talk we
gathered on the platform with a fire burning in the
centre, and the natives crowding round. Tamate then
offered prayer, all reverently bowing their heads and
repeating the "amene" at the close. Bidding all good-
night we descended the ladder again, and, attended by
a large crowd who were waiting below, we returned to
the mission house.

'I esteem it a great privilege to have been permitted
to see so much of the wonderful island of New Guinea
and its people, and especially to mark the changes
wrought by the Gospel among the savages. I am also
thankful that I was able to spend so long a time with
Tamate. It had been a great pleasure to know him as
a friend at home; it was a much greater pleasure to be
with him in his work. Tamate is an ideal missionary;
bright and cheery, brave and fearless, brisk and energetic in all his movements, and intensely in earnest.
Tender, yet firm; as bold as a lion, but as gentle as
a woman; a real friend to the natives, and untiring in
his efforts to do them good. Truly devout, yet
thoroughly practical, alike physically, intellectually, and
spiritually—a strong man.'

Mr. Liddiard's visit was closed by the arrival of the
Merrie England, which carried him to Thursday Island
on his return journey to Australia, and carried off
Chalmers for the trip, the object of which was to choose
his new home. Mrs. Chalmers was again left alone,
and for so long a time as to arouse the active sympathy
of one of the Toaripi chiefs.

'One day I was laid on the native couch whilst my
bed was being made. I heard some one come gently

behind me, and soon felt a hand stroking my hair and forehead. I was quite helpless, and could not turn to see who was there; but I soon found out, for suddenly Lahari's voice broke out into great abuse of my Tamate. I could not understand half Lahari said, but made out, "Tamate very bad, very bad husband indeed; he was no good to leave his wife for so long when she had a big sickness and no one to cook her 'Beritani' food, &c." I tried to expostulate and explain, but I had not strength to make him understand. I felt quite upset, he got so excited. I made out that he meant to meet Tamate to do something to him, but what, I could not find out. Tamate said afterwards, "The first person I saw on landing was Lahari, who seized hold of me and told me everything he thought about me for staying away from you so long."

'Dear, fine-looking, savage Lahari, the great warrior chief of Motumotu, he is always my dear friend and champion. He always comes to our services, and never lets a day pass without making me a call, and staying awhile at the house, and he has given up his fighting raids. Tauraki was the means of the fighting being stopped. He made Lahari promise not to go fighting and murdering, and above all not to avenge his (Tauraki's) death. This was a tremendous sacrifice for a noted warrior chief, a thoroughly brave, fearless savage, to make, but he promised his beloved teacher and friend, and so far his word has been kept. Tamate was nearly six weeks away, and said he should have been another ten days at least, but he felt impelled to come back at once—an impression he could not put on one side made him sure he was needed much here. Light winds delayed them a little too. I was thankful to hear the natives shout, "Sail ho!" and then, "Tamate, Tamate!"

' Nov. 22. Good attendance at all services. On the Saturday night Tamate sends the students in couples to the dubus in each village, with a short Gospel message to the men gathered in them, and a reminder of the next day being " Sabati." The students are not to sit down, gossip, or smoke, during these Saturday night visits. They just give their Bible message as clearly as possible, sing a hymn, and come away. We are so glad that since Tamate had the special meeting with all the elder men of the villages, and spoke and reasoned with them on the subject, that the Sabbath has been really well observed.

' Dec. 5. Tamate is here very ill indeed. Has had fever three days, but would go on with exams and visiting the stations. Has had no food for four days, was carried to and from the boat, and three men helped him into the house here. He does look dreadful. When got to bed he said, " Eh! lassie, I am bad indeed; but I care not now I am at home, dearie."

' 14th. More than a week since I wrote. I have had no time. My dear husband has had a hard time, but now, I am thankful to say, has got a turn. He is weak as a wee baby, but to-day I have managed to get him up and partly dressed for the first time, and he looks so thin and ill, cannot take food yet, and I wonder how he keeps alive at all.'

Chalmers had a great contempt for the custom in some modern missionary books of exaggerating the risks run and the dangers passed through in savage parts. He had no patience with one or two conspicuous cases in which he knew that in the hairbreadth escapes described imagination and a dread of the natives played far too large a part. The narrators believed that they had passed through many dangers which existed nowhere save in their own over-active brains. On December 17, 1891, he wrote a long letter to a gathering of old Cheshunt students, and he has sometimes in conversation told the incident described in it as an example of the way in which he could have worked up harrowing pictures of peril had he desired to do so.

'We are glad to know that this savage land is not forgotten in the old home, and that there are new fellows being equipped and looking forward to soon joining us. We want all-round men, just such as we have been getting, don't care men, you know, who like anything that may come, on shanks, their own or others; in a boat bowling along before a stiff breeze, or flying on the top of a sea to be chucked out, lose everything, and get to shore by the skin of the teeth. It is grand work this: a quiet, steady time at the central station of the district, teaching A, B, C, preparing teachers, preaching God's love, superintending house-building, road or bridge making, giving out medicine, killing or curing; and then away to out-stations on horse, foot, or boat, or to new places to select stations, and prepare the way for teachers.

'In some places it is, at first, very uncertain how you are to be dealt with, spear and club, or friendliness and food. We are now so well known that the chances of the former are very few, although there is so much of the animal in the savage that he is apt to forget himself and do things for which he is soon after sorry. Knowing that He whom we serve is ever near us, we need fear no evil. Often things look serious that may be turned into a mere fiasco.

'Our people here are a wild lot, and have long been the terror of the coast and inland. Some time ago we were holding our Sunday forenoon service, and had a very good congregation, amongst them many youths, one of whom was particularly troublesome, especially at prayer-time. When the last prayer was concluded, I got up, caught the youth, and made him sit down by me, so that when all had gone out I should speak to him alone. Some went out hurriedly, others lingered. Waiting for all to leave, I was looking out through a window on to the main street, when I saw a number of excited men, armed with clubs, bows, and arrows, rushing along towards the church. The leader carried a large wooden broadsword. I sprang to the door just in time to meet him as he ascended the steps, and wrenching the sword out of his hands, I shouted. He sprang back, and the others, seeing me armed, betook themselves in all directions, rushing helter skelter into the bush close by, anywhere they could get. I cleared the house, spoke to the youth and let him go. My own boys were sure it was a case of murder, and they got away at the back, through the bush to our house, informing every one that I was murdered. It was suggested to me I should get quietly away by the back, but that would never have done. So, getting my few boys and young men together, we marched through the village home, I carrying the broadsword, to the great amusement of those who had taken no part in the affair. The braves had a bad time of it from the others. They were coming to release the boy by force.'

Tamate and his wife paid a visit to Port Moresby at this time, and on the return journey experienced very bad weather, even for that stormy coast. They landed on January 29 at Oiabu, and on attempting to get through the surf and regain their boat, which was beyond the breakers, they had an experience both exciting and dangerous.

'At two p.m. we thought it might be possible to reach the boat, so the large canoe was again launched. It was very hot indeed, and I dreaded the sun. However, start we must, and now came a new experience for me, and anything but a pleasant one. Tamate and I got into the middle of the canoe, natives pushed us out and swam on each side, raising the bow to meet the rollers. So we got over two lines; then the men paddled their hardest, but could not ride the great waves which broke in turns over us, under, and all around us; every time the wave broke over us the men sprang into the sea, holding up the canoe and then swinging it high on the advancing wave and letting it be washed back on it; this was to empty the canoe of water. We two, seated on the connecting plank with nothing to hold on to, were anything but comfortable. I held on to a stalwart native who was in the water on my side, and with the other hand clung to Tamate. I never had such a time, swinging backwards and forwards, every other moment just enveloped in white surf. We were of course drenched at the very first start, and we were out in the midst of that surf for nearly an hour. No one can imagine the more than strange sensation of seeing an immense wave all white with surf, which one feels must come over you, and then suddenly the bow is raised, the men give one swing in unison, and you are on the crest and washing back before you have time to feel nervous. I got quite accustomed to it, and quite as excited as the men; I believe I shouted as they did as the rollers came thick and fast. The natives on shore were in a great state of excitement. Tamate thought we should have to try and get back, which would have been almost as bad as getting forward. There was a very heavy swell beyond the breakers; the boat had come in as near to them as she could with any safety, and was pitching and tossing in a frantic manner. Even if we got through I thought it would be almost impossible for us to get into the boat. Our Toaripians are good surf swimmers, and four of them had reached the boat. All at once there was extra shouting and commotion on shore, responded to by the men with us. We saw a man swim out with two others. The leader was a grand swimmer. Tamate said, " I believe that's the great sorcerer; they've fetched him to subdue the waves." He came on right across our bows, and we saw he had a half cocoa-nut shell in each hand. The men made a desperate effort to follow him, and paddled for dear life. We should have been washed off but for the men on each side, and for a moment or two could see nothing—we were in the midst of it. Then the surf settled, and Tamate said, " Look! the fellow's got oil in the shells; fancy their knowing that trick." We did get through eventually by the aid of the sorcerer or the oil. The natives were triumphant, of course. Their sorcerer had more power over the waves than Tamate. I don't know how I got into the boat, but it was managed, and we were away, wind ahead still. Our men strained every nerve to reach Jokea before sunset, and we got there just after. Tamate insisted on keeping me wrapped in a blanket over my wet clothes. I felt miserably hot and uncomfortable. We landed pretty easily, and were all and everything safe inside and the boat up before the storm came which we had been dreading for the last hour or two.'

At Thursday Island, early in March, Tamate and his wife parted, she to return to England, he to enter seriously upon his new work. On March 5 Mrs. Chalmers wrote :—

'How I dread this parting, when I know that months may elapse before I get any letters from Tamate; sickness and death may come and I know nothing of it for long. My dear one says, "If I too fall by the way, can I, or can you, wish anything better than to die in the field about the Father's work to the last?" Well, it is good and comforting to know that everything is arranged for us, and for the best.'

We have now reached the point where the autobiography again takes up the record of Chalmers' life. It is unfortunate that he appeared to tire of writing about himself as he drew towards the close, and consequently he has given us far less in the way of detail than could be desired.

'We had settled at Motumotu, and had extended to Orokolo, and we were settling down to steady work, when I was asked by the Directors to undertake the Fly River and Western Division of our mission. The work was certain to prove more difficult than that in a new district. My hope also was to extend inland by the Mai Kasa, and go west to the boundary of British New Guinea, and if possible get to know the Tugeri. I resolved after much prayer to settle on Dauan. My wife continuing to suffer from the climate, we decided that she should go home until I got established in my new field. For the Fly River I decided on Saguane as a central station. I had Maru and his wife to place, and concluded to put them on Saguane.

'My wife left Thursday Island in March, 1892, and I arrived a few days after at Dauan, the Government station, where Maru and his wife were awaiting me. They had the whaleboat, and the same afternoon we started for Mauata. There I chartered a small vessel, and so lightened the whaleboat. The following morning we started, and two days after we anchored in the whaleboat, at nine p.m., in the creek near to Saguane. It was an anxious night, as we did not know how we should be fixed in the morning. I did not know the creek, and there was only swamp land about, and I wondered where the sandy land was which I had seen the year before. We had prayer, and I told Maru and his wife to stay by the boat, and that I would go and look round. I was very cast down. When walking along I heard a voice very distinctly say to me, " This is the way, walk you in it." I sat down on a log close by, and said, " If thine, O Lord, is the voice, teach me to hear and act," and I heard, " Fear not, for I am with thee ; neither be thou dismayed." I thanked God, and took courage. I walked on until I came to the village, but found no one there, only two dogs to greet me. I passed the village and turned in off the beach, and there I saw a nice piece of ground, very suitable for a mission station. I know of no place in the Fly River drier or more suitable. I determined to make this my own headquarters. I selected a spot for our house and returned to the boat, where I told my discovery and prayed.

' We then came to the village and selected a house, praying all the time to be guided aright. During the day the schooner came in, and they told us that at this season all the natives were up the river at Iasa for *muguru* [1]. That afternoon the schooner went up the river, and the following day the canoes came down. I felt rather anxious, as we had slept in a house, and I knew not how they would take this action. I walked down the beach to meet the people coming from the canoes. The first man I met seemed a decent sort of

[1] This was an initiation ceremony for the young men of the tribe, at which indescribable abominations were practised.

fellow, and I tried to explain to him that we were occupying the end of one of the houses, and that I would pay for it. He was excited, and kept saying, " *Wade, wade, wade!* " (good). We got to the house and found it was his own, the one of which he was chief. He then gave us to understand that we should have it all, and that he and his people would go elsewhere.

'After arranging about the house we all went to look for a site for the mission house, and having decided on one I selected twelve young men to assist Maru in the building. On the Monday we began work, whilst all the people left us but the workmen and returned to Iasa. During the week I visited Iasa, and found a very large population, and all very happy. It was the season of the great annual festival, when the young men are initiated into the tribe. The dancing and feasting continue for months. There must have been over 2,000 people; but the real Iasa population does not amount to 200. The various villages have their houses, and the friends from far away live there with them. The houses are very long; some at Iasa were nearly 300 or 400 feet long. The one at Baramura, up the river, I measured, and found it to be 692 feet in length. They are about forty feet broad and very high. Families sleep in divisions along both sides, and a chief or headman sleeps at each end. When travelling we always occupied an end. The main entrance is at the ends, and there are small openings along both sides.

'All the dancing is done in one of these houses. For the dances they dress very elaborately. The head-dress, some of them twelve feet high and three feet broad, is one mass of feathers, chiefly the bird of paradise. It rests on the head, and has a piece of wood running down the back which is fastened with a string round the middle. There are also long streamers of white feathers attached, and the whole is so springy that every movement of head and body makes the head-dress move gracefully. There is also a very finely wrought band of various colours round the waist, and beautiful garters with tassels and dried nuts to make a noise, and anklets like a ruff of fine silk, also with dried nuts attached. Men, women, and children dance and sing and beat drums, and continue the whole night through. The women wear new petticoats made from the young frond of the sago palm, and dyed various colours. The young men who are being initiated wear great streamers from their ears made of the same stuff as the women's petticoats. They look very demure, rather depressed, as if something terrible had happened, or was going to happen. From December to the end of May the feasting, dancing, and sago-making continue, and all school work had to be suspended during this period.

'By the middle of May our house was finished, and I ascended the river to visit various places. At that time my district extended from Cape Suckling westward, so that I could not settle in any particular place. The Directors having decided to send me help, I resolved to divide the western branch of the mission and have two central stations, one at Jokea and one at Dauan; the latter so far west in order to be near the bush tribes and the Tugeri. I tried when at Saguane to hold a school, but only for a few days could I get two children to attend, and then they left for Iasa.

'In 1894 I received a cablegram, "The Directors want you home," and I thought I ought to leave as soon as possible. I made one visit all round, ascended the Fly to Howling Point, and was well received. Every previous expedition had to use their rifles to get through. On May 20 I left Thursday Island, and arrived in London in the first week in June. Lizzie, who was ready to return to me in March, was advised to remain, and so met me at the docks. I remained at home until November, 1895, when I left London, having been instructed by the Directors not to proceed further west, but to confine myself at present to the Fly River. My wife remained in England for the present.'

Before we accompany Chalmers to England on his second visit, it is needful to look a little more closely into his work from 1892 to 1894.

Chalmers felt the instruction of the Directors to take up the work in the Western District of New Guinea as a call to new but most serious and even dangerous duty. The man being what he was, this fact only led him to enter upon it with strenuous vigour and confident hope. In a letter of May 17, 1892, he writes, 'I feel quite young again in this new work, and quite fit for any amount of it.' But the darker side was also present to his mind, for a month later he says, ' This Fly River work I look upon as my last and perhaps greatest work for Christ, and being always with Him I fear not. God knows there will be many Gethsemanes, and it may be Calvarys ; but all for Christ, and it is well.'

'June 23, 1892.

'The people of Saibai and Dauan are greatly delighted at the prospect of having a white missionary settled amongst them. From Dauan we went to Mabuiag, and then on to Thursday Island. We had terrible weather, and all of us felt ill after it. I took the Sunday evening service, and proclaimed war against giving drink to natives or allowing boats to take it to the islands in the Straits. Mr. Douglas, the Government Resident, says I must now carry on the war. Yes, I am all ready ; 2 Chron. xiv. 11, 12.

' When at Kivori I saw the Motu New Testament, and am delighted with it. Thank God Misi has been able to give us that. There had been so much sickness and so many deaths, that we had a special prayer-meeting, and I read passages concerning death, resurrection, and the home yonder. The people were thrilled. I read without comment, and when I had finished one man said, his voice trembling with emotion, " Oh, Tamate, those were good words and we were astonished."'

In July Chalmers was back at Port Moresby to attend the committee meeting of all the New Guinea missionaries, except Dr. Lawes, who was away on furlough. The meetings were held from July 20 to July 23. Chalmers was in the chair, and the resolutions adopted were of great importance to the future working of the mission. It may give the reader some insight into the local working of an important mission like that of New Guinea if the main resolutions adopted at this business meeting are given ; and it will serve as an illustration of the nature of all these District committee meetings. There were present, in addition to Tamate, the Reverends A. Pearse, F. W. Walker, H. M. Dauncey, and C. W. Abel.

' That the New Guinea District committee take this first opportunity of welcoming the members of the Wesleyan Missionary Society, who have recently commenced work in this country, and of heartily congratulating them on the success which has attended their settlement on the islands of the Eastern Archipelago. They pray that God's richest blessing may continue with them in their work, and that they may achieve the highest success in the gospel of Christ.

'That having heard the further report of Mr. Chalmers on his recent visit to the Fly River, we feel that the work should be proceeded with without delay. We also feel that to meet the requirements of that district it would be necessary to have a steam launch for navigating the Fly River. We unanimously express our hearty sympathy with the continuance of the Society's work in the west of New Guinea. At the same time we are of opinion that the Elema district should not be left permanently until two new missionaries are sent out to take over Mr. Chalmers' present work at Motumotu and Delena.

'That we regret to state that after careful investigation, and a wider experience of the various tribes outside the Port Moresby district, we are convinced that the Motu language can never become the spoken language of the people, and we propose to rescind the previous resolutions regarding the Institution based upon this theory. We therefore consider that translation work in the other districts should not be discontinued. Meanwhile we are anxious to avail ourselves of the splendid services rendered to our mission by the Rev. W. G. Lawes, and urge upon the Directors to make adequate provision at Port Moresby for the training of our students in the Motu language until such time as we are in a position to give them the Scriptures in their own tongues.

'That we endeavour to arrange a conference with the members of the Anglican and Wesleyan Missionary Societies, to be held at Kwato after the District committee meetings next May, and that if possible a conference should be repeated for Christian fellowship whenever our committee meets in the east end of the Possession. That a copy of the above resolution be forwarded to the representatives of these Societies.'

It is neither possible nor desirable to enter upon any consideration of the large questions involved in these decisions.  But we may indicate the chief results which have followed.  Dr. Lawes and Chalmers both believed that Motuan might be made the literary language of New Guinea.  In this view their colleagues at first acquiesced; but the resolution given above marks the reversal of this opinion.  The language difficulty in New Guinea is enormous, and at any rate the die is now cast.  Each European missionary provides literature for his people as best he can in the vernacular.  This seems natural and fitting, but in New Guinea, under the influence of the London Missionary Society alone, there are spoken at least seven different languages.

Another result was the transference of Dr. Lawes from Port Moresby to Vatorata, and the institution there of a new and enlarged training college for native teachers.

It also led to the Rev. H. M. Dauncey making Delena his headquarters, and the transference of the Rev. F. W. Walker from Kwato to the Gulf Mission.  Mr. Chalmers' work at Motumotu and the stations in the Gulf was consolidated and extended by the Rev. J. H. Holmes, who was stationed first at Jokea and then at Orokolo.

After leaving Port Moresby Tamate went on a long trip to the stations, including another visit to his old Namau [1] friends.

In September he was back at Toaripi.  'Yesterday,' he writes on September 12, 'was a day that will be long remembered here.  I baptized eight natives, after they had given good public testimony for Christ before their countrymen.  There are others waiting.  My only sorrow is there were no women, and until the women are got

[1] See *Pioneering in New Guinea* (1902), chap. x.

for Christ we cannot expect any real living church.
A change for the better is coming over the people, and
neighbours formerly afraid of them speak gladly of the
change.'

From 1887 onwards, friends in England were very
kind in forwarding, among many other things useful for
the work, books likely to be helpful and entertaining to
lonely missionaries. Many of the letters of Mrs. Chalmers and Tamate show how greatly they appreciated
such thoughtful consideration. A case arrived at Toaripi
at this time, and Chalmers writes :—

'I thank God for Gilmour. What a grand fellow he
was. Lovett has given the world a good picture of
a good and great man. How small some of our lives
feel in the presence of Gilmour. To-day I went to hear
Dr. Reynolds, and had a feast. *A Window in Thrums*
I am enjoying; it is real life. Spurgeon I shall hear on
the voyage, and also reserve *Little Minister* for that
time. *Tim*, too, will then be read. What can I say for
all the loving thoughts these books convey ? '

Chalmers returned to the Straits towards the close of
the year.

'MURRAY ISLAND, *November* 19, 1892.

'Many thanks for the letter written when voyaging
amongst the Fjords of the Land of the Midnight Sun.
In the land of stewing and frizzling 'twas refreshing
indeed to have the "God bless you" from the land of
coolness and grandeur. I should like to see that
wonderful country, just to have been a fellow-traveller
with you all. I can imagine your feelings somewhat
when amidst that grandeur of nature. I was brought
up among the mountains, I loved them, and now love
them more than ever. When far inland in New Guinea,
and amongst the stern sentinels of Mount Owen Stanley

on the rugged rocky mountains of the east end, I have often spent hours alone with them, the everlasting hills, and been awed at their presence, as they reflected the grandeur and fervour of their God and my God.

'I too have been travelling lately in new country, but how tame and flat to where you three have been. The highest thing we saw was a cocoa-nut tree. There were some high temples and in them many curious things, such things as only savages could appreciate.

'You will know our latest plan, a steam launch for the Fly River and neighbourhood. That will help us much, and enable us to carry on the work better for Christ and the New Guineans. I hope to hear next week that she will be in Thursday Island soon. I shall meet her and clear out immediately for the scene of operations.

'The launch arrived here on January 5, 1893, in a deluge of rain. On the way up they had very dirty weather, but she proved herself a splendid little sea-boat. I like her much and think her most suitable. The only alteration I shall make is to use a tiller instead of the wheel amidships. She has a very pretty little saloon, and the cockpit aft can be made with canvas a very comfortable place for the crew.'

The first trip in the Miro is fully described in *Pioneering in New Guinea*[1]. Unhappily the steam launch did not equal the high anticipations with which she was received, and did not prove powerful enough for the work required.

The field at this period under Chalmers' superintendence was of enormous extent, and involved constant travelling between the Straits and the Gulf. He was

---

[1] Edition of 1902, chap. xii.

expected to attend committee meetings in New Guinea once or twice a year. He had to supervise the native teachers over the whole of New Guinea west of Hall Sound and through the Straits to Murray Island. It was inevitable that with such duties he should be always on the move and not unfrequently in perils among the heathen and constantly in perils of waters. But he loved the work. He could never have settled down at a station and carried on steady work year after year, no matter how attractive or how fruitful. The man of settled habits and methodical life was apt to think his life easy and his labour to some extent spent in vain. The truer estimate is to look upon him as a man magnificently endowed by his Maker for the work he did, and the work he loved. He was the pathfinder through the New Guinea wilderness. He did that which no one else could have done so well—he opened innumerable doorways into savage districts. Through these for a generation to come those who are to consolidate and extend the work will enter. That this task was after his own heart he ever gladly acknowledged. On December 6, 1893, he wrote :—

'I am in excellent health and have all the youthful ardour I ever had, more, really more. To be away and finish visiting my stations and then on to new work— opening up new places has a strangely wonderful charm for me. I dearly love to be the first to preach Christ in a place, never mind though it has to be through an interpreter.'

'NEAR JOKEA, *May* 26, 1893.

'Having no other means of travelling I came here in the Niue and since then have been storekeeping, undoing things and giving out the needful stores to the teachers. We also have had some really good prayer-meetings, real soul-stirring ones, and God knows we needed them much. I have had to return one teacher for neglecting work and trading, and I may have to do so to another. I may not be careful enough of Mr. Mammon, but some of these men are certainly too careful and forget all else. Once I was terribly stranded so far down that I felt it really and truly, but I can remember no other time when want of money bothered me. I have often been without it and been happy enough, and did not care; but that once I wanted a stamp for a love-letter, and could not get it, and I really felt the pinch of poverty, and was envious. Never again. Money I do not think is my temptation; if I have it, it must go.

'A teacher has just been carried in sick, and he tells me I must go to his village as there are several who wish baptism because they love Jesus, and he has been teaching them well. I cannot go now. Such is our experience, dark clouds and then light. We have all been greatly blessed in our study of Exodus xxxiii. 12 to end, and xxiii. 20 to end. I want all of us to go over it every Sabbath and make it as our covenant with God, using our own names instead of Moses. When I get a chance of seeing Moses, I shall want to know what he really saw, but I fancy he will not be able to describe so great a glory even in the Glory itself. What a time we shall have asking questions and solving many things!

'You would be pleased with Kwato and the work accomplished in the few years. Their practice is to have all sorts of games with the lads, and, being a lad, I had a go at football and suffered from stiffness for days. They have plenty of land to make the whole pay, and so save the London Missionary Society's funds. The largest bit of land we have on New Guinea is here, and it is big enough to support a large population, at least 100.

'I want to get to Motumotu, but cannot yet. A vessel is anchored off, and we are in communication with it only by swimming. Two strong youths who seem to think it fine fun undertake to go to and fro, and do it well.'

'FLY RIVER, SAGUANE, *July* 7, 1893.

'I am kind of storm stayed and am writing up. I have been visiting a short distance up the river and down the left bank, and found the Miro really a comfort. When wet and dirty it was pleasant to get on board and have a change and rest and a comfortable meal. We found the majority of villages well in from river bank, and had to wade through mud and water and cross creeks on saplings to get to them. The villages consist generally of one big house and two or three small ones. The largest house I have seen was 690 feet long. It was all divided into compartments or stalls down each side for each family, and down the centre a large open space where they dance. It must be a strange life they live there, but it is home, and that is everything.

'We had meetings at each place, and for the first time many heard that " God is love," and of Jesus His beloved Son who came to make Him known and to bring us to the Father. I had a teacher from Sumai with me, and he interpreted for me and also gave addresses himself. At some places we had large meetings, advising them to give up some of their customs at once; and they have promised to do so. I hope they will soon give up *all* useless and bad customs; but some we must insist upon their giving up at once, as they interfere much with our work. I think their promise is good.'

'DOMORI, *July* 13, 1893.

'Bad weather sent us up the river again, and I have
visited several, to me, new places. They call them
villages, but they have only one house, divided out
into portions for families. There is no privacy whatever, as these divisions are all open. Everywhere we
had a good reception, although at most places the
women and children were all stowed away in the bush.
I have just now returned from a village, and on entering
saw only one elderly woman, and gave her a present
of beads. We were some time in one of the houses
holding a service, and getting curios, and on leaving
for the boat I was surrounded by all the women and
children they had, and to all I gave a little present. Wherever we go in this part it is through mud
and water. You should have seen me the other day
after a hard day's visiting—guess you would not have
known me. I must go to Thursday Island for supplies, and new articles, and may be to meet a new
missionary. At Bampton I had a grand Sunday, though
very sad also. In the forenoon I buried one of our
teachers. In the afternoon I baptized thirty-eight men
and women who professed faith in Christ, the first
converts from our Western District. The work grows,
light spreads, and Christ is glorified. We may all rejoice
therein, you in Melbourne and we in New Guinea.'

'DAUAN, *September* 22, 1893.

'A few hours ago Holmes [1] and I arrived here in the
whaleboat from the Fly River. That word, river, has
been the bane of my life since I came here. Every-

---

[1] This was the Rev. J. H. Holmes, recently appointed to the
Mission. He was for some time at Jokea and then at Orokolo,
where he has carried on work in the way Chalmers so eagerly
desired to see it done.

body seems to think of a splendid stream of fresh water gently flowing through tropical countries and falling into Papua Gulf. I myself, until this last season's experience, thought it might be a little boisterous at the mouth, but up the river a large, calm, peaceful stream. I now know it to be a fearful place for gales of wind and heavy seas, and up it a dangerous bore during spring tides.

'At Domori I got the chief on board, and, anxious to get him right away, cleared out for the island close by where I have been before. He could introduce me to each place, and amongst the places was one that gave trouble to Macfarlane's and the Governor's expeditions as well as to D'Alberti's. Crossing to the island we were carrying one fathom good all the way, when suddenly, "five feet," "stop her," we were on a mud-bank fast enough.

'Fearing we should break the stern post I would not back her but just waited the rising tide. About 6.30 the tide rose a little, and we pulled on a kedge I had got out astern. We were off when we heard a peculiar express train noise, and soon were on the bank again, and all on board thought clean over and all up with us. It was a big bore that tore down on us and carried us bodily, anchor and all, on to the bank, and away across it. We simply were torn over it, and although we gave her the bow anchor that too went with us. We pulled up in six fathoms of water to find the rudder would not work. Next morning we kedged her ashore on to a bank of the mainland, and when the water left her high and dry we found the rudder post bent and cracked, and the stern post carried quite away on the under part. For two nights we remained on that bank, but had to clear out into better quarters.

'There is no one to blame for the weakness of the engines and boiler. Had I been in Sydney, not knowing the Fly River as I do now, I should have thought her powerful enough and been an anxious party to her purchase, she being such a pretty boat and her small saloon so comfortable.

'The word "river" has done the mischief. No use burking it, we want more powerful engines and a different boiler, and a protracted keel to protect the propeller and strong enough to hold the rudder. There are banks innumerable and unknown in the river, and we must be prepared for them. No one *knows* the Fly River, and only now are tribes and villages coming to light, and to each one of these we want to bring the Gospel. No use finding fault with any one, the Fly River is a river, but a bad, bad river, unknown to any one. I think, and am troubled about the expense, but I look through glasses beautifully clear, and I see savage tribes now unknown sitting and being taught of Jesus.

'SUMAI, *September* 13, 1893.

'We had visits from many natives when up the river, and had frequent services with them. I taught them to pray, "Jesus Christ, Chief, give me inward light. Amen." It was a trying time, but a good one. Mr. Holmes is with me, and has stood it well. He is a fine young fellow, a man of prayer.

'When we were in difficulties the chief of Domori came to us with native food, saying, "Tamate, this is a real present, and I want no pay." The man is a savage, and a very frightened one, and it is only now he comes to see me with a look of pleasure. A native who is with us prayed at a service. When he had finished, Araua, the chief referred to above, said, "Tamate, by-and-by when you teach me I too can pray like him." He came to see us every day. He will accompany me up the river, and introduce me to new places on both banks. The work will have to be done by constant visiting of the people, and on every visit something taught.'

'JOKEA, *Jan.* 1, 1894.

'I have been much struck and pleased with the prayers of many of our recent converts, especially the Motumotuans. Have you ever heard heaven named as the "place of laughter"? One prayed for help to live a holy active life here for Christ, and hereafter "the place of laughter." After a good day's work, and there has been a good supper, often the natives sit in the street or on a platform, and shouts of laughter, screaming laughter, may be heard as story after story is told of the day's doings and sayings. All are happy and thoroughly enjoying themselves—hence the simile.

'The great New Year Feast has passed quietly by. No difficulty here to find guests, and never such a thing as a refusal. The New Guineans must think those mentioned in the parable terrible fools to beg to be excused. They are now rushing in uninvited, and being sent back.

'It is now all over, and a memory for them, and much to speak of for many a day. *He* has been looking on, and is also pleased. The influence of to-day will go on widening, and extend a long, long time. On Saturday we had all the children, and they were made happy, and their Friend and our Friend was happy too, I guess. Can there be anything to give more real pleasure than the feeling we have made Him happy through helping His own little ones? and though they are children of savages (?), yet they are all His, and He loves them. There were five languages represented, but all joined in His own prayer in the Motuan.'

The Centenary celebrations of the London Missionary Society began in 1895. The Directors, in view of that great event, deemed it advisable to secure the magnetic and heart-stirring advocacy of Tamate at the great meetings which were to be held all over the country. On reaching Thursday Island in March, 1894, he found a telegram awaiting him, brief but to the point; ' Directors want you home.' By the middle of May he was on his way to England.

# CHAPTER XI

## THE SECOND VISIT HOME, 1894

CHALMERS returned to England in the belief that he would be used by God to stimulate and deepen the missionary enthusiasm of the churches at home. In this endeavour he was prepared to exert all his influence and to tax his energies to the uttermost. He had been separated from his wife for over two years; he was deeply concerned about the future and well-being of his stepson, Bert, whom he loved with a strong affection; and the delight of reunion with these, his nearest and dearest, was a strong attraction. He landed at Plymouth in 1894 with very different feelings from those which dominated him in 1887. Then he felt himself a stranger, more at home in a canoe than in a train, far more at ease in a dubu than in a church. He dreaded the duty of addressing audiences, and he contemplated a speedy return flight from the restraints of civilization. In 1894 he looked forward to renewed fellowship with hosts of loving friends, he had tested and knew his power to move vast audiences, his enthusiasm for his life-work was even more fervent than in 1887, and he felt that God had a work for him to do and would give him grace and strength to perform it. 'I have come home,' he wrote, 'for good hard work, and, God helping me, I cannot get too much. I have a feeling in my soul and all through me that we shall have great blessings this autumn and winter.

'My dear old Dr. Reynolds writes, "Our difficulties will vanish (they are not mere financial deficits) before a new outpouring upon us and infusion into us of the spirit and mind of Christ." He has hit it straight, and we must have it. The less we talk about the money and the more we are filled with Christ, and so talk of Him and His kingdom the plentiful supply of the former He will see to. We need to see *all* the professing servants of Christ revived and quickened, and not the comparative few only who are concerned about His affairs.'

After his many years of strenuous work in the tropics Chalmers found the home climate trying, especially during the winter months, and once or twice he was threatened with a serious breakdown in health. His old enemy, the New Guinea fever, was ever ready to attack him the moment his health suffered. And when later on in his furlough friends urged him to work less and rest more his reply was the same, 'I am in excellent health, but want a "rest awhile" very badly. Tamate Vaine of course agrees with you, but I shall do the appointed work in Ireland. When coming home to Britain, and after my arrival, I said if health is given me it is for His purpose, and it shall be used accordingly. Since coming home you know how I have been blessed, and I cannot now go back. I would listen if only I were sickly. I feel power has gone out of me, and I need a little while apart, and I am in hopes of getting it after Liverpool. We are not our own but His.'

Dr. Griffith John had been expected home to take part in the public work connected with the centenary work of the London Missionary Society, but he could

not tear himself away from his loved duties at Hankow.
Could he have come he would have shared the duty of
speaking at great meetings. But by his inability to
come Chalmers was left to bear the main burden. No
matter who the other speakers might be, at every great
assembly, and at multitudes of the smaller meetings also,
the one indispensable orator was Chalmers. And so
from Dan to Beersheba, throughout Britain, he travelled
unceasingly, speaking, preaching, kindling into burning
flame of love and zeal alike the individuals who were
fortunate enough to come into close touch with his
virile, sympathetic, Christ-possessed humanity, and also
the great assemblies that were enthralled by his rugged
eloquence and unquenchable enthusiasm for the uplifting
of humanity. Multitudes who were gripped by him in
the public gatherings will treasure as long as life lasts
the scenes he enabled them to see, the object-lesson he
gave them in entire consecration to the Master's service.
No missionary speaker of this generation more nobly
utilized the great opportunities granted to him of influencing his fellow men. Possibly no one had the
power of so deeply stirring the heart as Chalmers when
he told his famous 'let us walk and pray' experience, or
how he almost grew impatient for the cannibals to kill
him and end his terrible suspense at East Cape; or how,
moved by some inward impulse, he turned upon the
following savage just in time to wrench from his grasp
the club that in another moment would have crushed in
his skull.

Chalmers on the platform and in the pulpit was
great; but in the quiet home, after the day's deputation
work was over, in congenial society—it was then that
the simplicity, the single-heartedness, the consecration,
the Christ-likeness of the man shone out most brightly.

There come to us as we write evenings spent long years ago with one who has long since greeted him within the veil—an English lady nearly a generation older than himself, whose life in its duties was the diameter of being away from that of the great pioneer. That which linked them together was love to the one Saviour, a life of prayer, a deep desire for the salvation of souls. On these occasions Chalmers, in the most simple and natural way, feeling the presence of a kindred spirit, opened his heart as he never could in public. As he talked you saw the wild, fierce face of the cannibal soften at the story of the Cross; you trod with the intrepid missionary across the beach to the chief's hut, not knowing whether you would return alive; you sat at the Lord's Table with men and women who but a few years before had eaten their enemies; you clung to the boat as she swung backward and forth on the surge until the wave came big enough to float you over the reef and into the lagoon, beyond the reach of the thundering and dangerous surf. To have spent even one such hour with James Chalmers was a blessed memory and an uplifting inspiration for a lifetime.

It would be only wearisome to detail even the largest meetings he attended, and the most important centres he visited. His services were eagerly sought, not only by the Congregational churches, but by all the evangelical free churches, and he became undoubtedly the missionary most widely known in all these circles. But his correspondence, although the letters of this date are the briefest of the brief, is full of self-revealing glimpses.

'September 18, 1894.

'I came here last Friday. We are having good refreshing times here. I attended an intensely in-

TAMATE IN 1895.

teresting prayer-meeting at Stapleton Road after the service on Sunday evening, and last night at Urijah Thomas's place there was the largest prayer-meeting I ever saw, and the feeling was solemn and earnest. Funds leap up here without difficulty, because of much prayer for His kingdom. Bristol sustains its traditions. I wish every missionary who comes home could attend these Bristol meetings, and get his soul warmed and fired to white heat.'

'WEST HARTLEPOOL, *December* 18, 1894.

'We drove out yesterday and had a sniff of dear old briny, and I heard voices calling me away. Watching and hearing the long swish on the beach created a great longing to leave, and be with my own New Guineans on that south-east coast. I want to hear the music of the breaking seas there.'

'*January* 16, 1895.

'There was a splendid gathering at the City Temple, but —— did not turn up in time for his speech, and so Berry had to lead, and he did it splendidly. I was in hopes —— had forgotten the meeting, and felt equal to an hour; but just before Berry finished he came in, and after singing got up, and instead of twenty-five minutes took three-quarters of an hour, and had a lady soloist that he wished to sing, and Johnson had to announce the lady, so that I had five minutes left. I protested against speaking at all, but Berry persuaded me, and I spoke. I had a splendid reception, and could not but say something. Had Berry not been there, I should have only bowed and sat down.'

In January, 1895, a meeting of the members of the Cheshunt Union was held at Cheshunt College. The main objects of the meeting, which lasted three days, were to renew old college fellowship, to cultivate the spiritual life, and to consult with and to encourage one another in ministerial life and work. A feature of touching and pathetic interest was the fact that, as Dr. Reynolds was on the point of resigning the Principalship, this was the last gathering of the kind over which he would preside. The old students gratefully and lovingly commemorated this by a presentation. The presence of Chalmers greatly heightened the interest and helpfulness of the meetings. None of those who were fortunate enough to be present will forget those meetings. Chalmers entered into the fun and frolic with all the zest of his old student days; and he also in no small degree intensified the spiritual uplifting of the serious meetings.

'THE COLLEGE, CHESHUNT, *January* 22, 1895.

'At the station yesterday I met a large host of Cheshunt men, and they gave me a hearty welcome to travel with them. We had noisy, hearty receptions for one and another all round. In the evening there was a sweet, hearty, happy meeting. Mr. New presided, spoke splendidly, and administered the ordinance of the Lord's Supper in a grand spirit of love.

'The dear old Doctor was present. We sat up until morning. The Doctor looks better, but is very feeble. He engaged in prayer this morning. There are about fifty present. The missionaries have all spoken and done well.'

'*January* 23, 1895.

'We had an inspiring meeting last night. The subject was "Ministerial Work." This morning's meeting will never be forgotten. The speakers were Dawson, Thomas, Thompson, and Whitehouse, who were filled

with the spirit and spoke from the heart to the heart.
Then came the grandest of all, the dear old Doctor, in
response to a present of an album beautifully got up and
containing the greater part of our names. He spoke as
very near to God and brought us into the very Presence.
His old self frequently flashed forth, and we again saw
and heard him as in the days of old. His very soul
touched ours, and we were lifted up out of ourselves.
We burned with fire, and we sobbed, and then at the
close we stood, clapped, stamped, cheered, and felt 'twas
grand to be Christ's. These meetings were worth my
coming home for. We were on the mount, and could
have wished for tabernacles to remain there.'

Immediately after this helpful break in the routine of
life, Chalmers resumed his laborious round of deputation
work. The winter was severe, and the intense cold was
a trial to him.

'*February* 6, 1895.

'I feel bad, and if I get worse I shall make for home.
It is only a cold in the head and chest. I ought to be
thankful it is not worse, and it may be considering this
Arctic weather. Arnold Thomas of Bristol and myself
are the guns to-day. Griffith John is not coming home.
I am sorry for it, as he could take many of my places.
He is so well known, and such a capital deputation
that the change would please the folk. Here is snow
again. New Guinea is paradise after this. I agree with
the natives who have learned a little pidgin English,
and who say, "My word, no gammon, he cold like hell."'

One of the most notable gatherings which Chalmers
addressed was a centenary gathering on behalf of the
London Missionary Society, held in the Free Church
Assembly Room, Edinburgh, on the evening of March 11,
1895. The gathering differed little from the many

great meetings then being held, save that Sir William Macgregor was in the chair. He had been Governor of New Guinea for seven years, he knew the country as no other living man, he had seen with his own eyes all parts of the Mission, and he was a keen-witted, competent man, well fitted alike by training and experience to form a sound judgement. Hence his testimony to the value and the influence of Christian Missions in New Guinea is worthy of the most careful consideration, and may well outweigh that of some omniscient modern editors, correspondents, traders, and globe-trotters.

From Sir William's speech as chairman, which was extensively circulated at the time, two or three paragraphs deserve the careful attention of all who are concerned for the evangelization of New Guinea. How well worthy of study the whole of it is these passages show.

'Let me now, looking at the subject from the Government point of view, tell you what, in my opinion, has been and is the value of our missionaries.

'First of all, the London Missionary Society has done a considerable amount of exploration work that has fallen to the others only in a much smaller degree. Their greatest explorer has been the Rev. James Chalmers. This gentleman has been the first European to travel over large distances, and is the original discoverer of the great Purari River. I am bound to say that I never knew of one single instance in which his explorations did any harm. They have undoubtedly been productive of much good at very many points. I have seen him called in an official report, " The Apostle of the Papuan Gulf." There is nothing strained in the definition.

'As a teaching body the London Missionary Society, in the teeth of great and many difficulties, has effected much good in New Guinea. Its stations are as yet practically confined to the coast line, and even on this they are sometimes separated by great intervals, which leave numerous populous tribes totally unprovided with teachers. There are certainly many hundreds of tribes living inland from the coast stations who have not heard of a missionary, and who can never be taught from the posts now established. To reach these a great accession of strength is required, and a different and more extended plan of campaign will be necessary. Native teachers born and reared in coast villages will never take kindly to residence inland; the boys and youths of the interior will not as a rule remain long enough at the coast to acquire the training of efficient teachers. European Missionaries must therefore leave the coast and take up permanent stations among the tribes of the interior and educate the future inland teachers on the spot. It may be said at once that New Guinea must be taught eventually by native teachers.

'Let me say a word for the coloured teacher. He, poor simple soul, leaves, at our call, his own little world and warm-hearted friends in the South Seas to devote his efforts to his fellow men in an unknown country. I believe some eight of the Society's teachers have been murdered by our natives. How many of you ever heard of those eight men? Had they belonged to our own race we should all have known much more about their career, their suffering, their martyrdom. Scores of them have died splendidly and silently at their posts. Let me remind you that often less courage is required to perform a brave and daring deed on the impulse of the moment than is needed in the man that remains, as the native

teacher does, at an obscure and difficult post for a pro-
longed term, especially when he knows that he will get
no credit of any kind for his performance.   The work
of the South Sea teacher has the misfortune of not
appealing to the imagination.   Only those that see his
work, and understand him and his surroundings, can
appreciate him and sympathize with him.   Any missionary
will starve himself to provide hospitality for his guest—
I have known it done often—and the poor coloured
teacher is certainly no less hospitable than the white
missionary.   Now what, except the promises of the
Gospel and the approval of his own conscience, has
the coloured teacher to look forward to as his reward ?
In a month or two after he ceases to work his very name
fades like an echo.

' It would not be proper for me to speak of the work
of spiritual conversion.   That for some time to come
will probably have to be waited for in New Guinea,
where there is a singular want of development of the
religious instinct, of the kind that can be readily converted into enthusiasm.   Missionaries will for some time
yet have to be content with a decent demeanour in
church, and a formal compliance with religious observ-
ances.   Their teaching will eventually touch deeper
the hearts of their hearers.   Another great drawback
to a rapid development of mission work is the absence
of chiefs or men of influence.   We have in New Guinea
no Vladimir to command baptism; no Clovis to lead
the way on which all must follow.   The missionary
must study the personal character of each individual
Papuan, for he will find each one a separate undertaking
on an independent footing; and he will not meet with
any religious fervour.

Let me assure you that there can be no finer mission-field in the world than that now held by this Society in British New Guinea. There is a large population of people without any trace of literature, with no religion, without an alphabet, living in the stone age, and of good intellectual qualities. What has been already done there proves that the mission can make Christians of that interesting people; and that you can also lend important aid in making them valuable economic subjects of this empire.'

Early in June, while in Birmingham, Chalmers had a severe breakdown, and was for a time quite seriously ill. The strain through which he had for months been passing was greater almost than any man should be called upon to bear. Yet his own eager desire to do all that he could, and the imperative demands for his presence that would take no denial, combined to produce the disaster. Happily rest and his own vigorous constitution speedily brought him back again to his working level. Genially he himself placed the responsibility upon our climate. 'This Laodicean weather is what upset me. In the winter I knew where I was, but feeling uncomfortable in heavy things I went into lighter, and then another change came, or I entered a cold belt between Sheffield and Birmingham, and so, not prepared, I was thrown over. On Sunday I was truly ill but got up to show myself at Carr's Lane. My voice was quite gone, and I was in a raging fever (105°), and my friends here would not let me out, so I quietly collapsed and got somehow to bed.'

Inveraray by this time was so impressed with the greatness of her son that the burghers of that ancient town determined to confer upon Chalmers the highest honour in their power—the freedom of the city. Early in

August he made his way there to fulfil numerous engagements. On August 1 the Duke of Argyll had written to Mr. Meikle (Mr. Wylie has forwarded me the letter), 'I shall be delighted to give the Pavilion to Mr. Chalmers. So glad to see him again, he is a man to be proud of.' But though the Duke honoured him, the climate did not. On August 12 he wrote from Inveraray :—

'We got here on Saturday, and had a very fine trip, all the Meikles are well. On Saturday night the rain descended as it knows how to in Inveraray, and kept on until eleven. It remained fine until 7.15 when it forgot it had rained a deluge all night, and began in greater earnest than ever, continued, I suppose, all night, and is now (10.30) hard at it, just as if it had done nothing for the last six months.

'It was dry for the clan gathering yesterday afternoon, and there was a great attendance. I go to the Castle by request this afternoon. They were very affable yesterday after the service. Many came in from long distances. The town is as it was in the beginning, unchanged, but the people have changed.'

The presentation ceremony took place in the Inveraray Court-house, and was attended by a considerable number of townspeople, and also by many visitors. The Council minute deciding to admit the Rev. Mr. Chalmers a free burgess and a guild brother in recognition of 'his career as a missionary and his eminent services in the cause of civilization and the spread of the Gospel among the heathen' was inscribed on parchment, and was presented to Mr. Chalmers, enclosed in a silver roll casket bearing the burgh seal and Mr. Chalmers' monogram, and richly chased with Celtic ornaments and a design of Scottish thistles.

The local papers thus reported his speech on this occasion :—

' Mr. Chalmers said he had had many honours in his life-time. He had been initiated into the tribes of New Guinea, and received by them as a brother, in which connexion Mr. Chalmers gave an interesting description of the rites of the tribes. He had also had a recognition of his work as an explorer—although he had never claimed to be an explorer; his object had always been to be considered a Christian missionary—a bringer of real civilization to savage and cannibal tribes. After the most important of his travels his services were recognized by the Geographical Society of Germany. Then followed recognition by the various societies of the Australasian colonies. When he returned to this country nine years ago, the Royal Geographical Society did him the honour of presenting its diploma—which was also held by their great countryman, Dr. Livingstone—and of making him an ordinary member. But considering even all these things from societies, literary and scientific, nothing gave him greater pleasure than the act which had been done that day in making him a free burgess of their royal burgh. He thanked them sincerely, and trusted that his future career might be even more brilliant—if there had been any brilliancy in the past—than it had been. On an occasion of that kind he could not but look upon the past and remember the days of his boyhood in that old town. When he looked round he saw many who were boys with him. It might interest the younger members of the town to know that he was one of the first volunteers in Inveraray. He was also a member of the first cricket club established in that part of the Highlands, and he was considered one of the first-class football players of the district. Indeed, at that time there were few things, bad or good, that took place in Inveraray that he did not have something to do with. Remembering the past he had a feeling of joy—he did not wish to be egotistical, but one could not help feeling it now—at their recognition that day. It was done, he believed, not merely because he spent his boyhood in the town—although but for that the casket would never have been put into his hands—but because he had tried in the past to do his duty, the duty that God gave him to do. He had never been able to look far ahead, but he had tried every day to do every day's work as well as ever he could.'

'INVERARAY, *August* 19, 1895.

' 'Tis over and your humble friend is now " a burgess, freeman, and guild brother " of the royal and ancient burgh of Inveraray. The ceremony was short and sweet. The Provost presented, and Tamate replied. I am greatly pleased with the honour and am now sorry I did not give a much better reply, but it was Inveraray, and I feel more nervous speaking here than anywhere else. Mr. and Mrs. Meikle and old friends are greatly delighted. Yesterday I spoke to Free Church friends, and in the afternoon addressed my old Sunday school, descendants of my own chums many of them.'

Chalmers during his stay in Britain had several interviews with Mr. Arthington of Leeds. Of these meetings no record is extant save a reference to the fact that Chalmers could obtain from him no direct help for his work in New Guinea. It is not impossible, however, that this intercourse may have been among the influences that induced Mr. Arthington to bequeath so large a sum as he did to the London Missionary Society.

Chalmers left England on his return to New Guinea on November 13, 1895.

# CHAPTER XII

## THE FLY RIVER, 1896–1901

THE closing section of Chalmers' autobiography briefly summarizes the work and experiences of the last stage of his New Guinea life. This section is printed here; and then, as in previous chapters, the narrative is supplemented from the private correspondence of Mr. and Mrs. Chalmers.

'I arrived at Saguane on Jan. 20, 1896, and started houses at once, having determined to make our central station there. We took down the Dauan house, and shipped the material to Saguane. Maru was of the greatest possible help, being a carpenter, and willing, and he carried through all the work, and did it well.

'The school was a poor affair, and for a long while the roll went up and down between two and fifteen; yet I felt sure God had something for us to do there, and we plodded on. By-and-by we got over thirty scholars, and my heart rose with the numbers. We built a good schoolroom, and a boys' house, and took in boys from all round. It was dreech uphill work, teaching A, B, C to wild, sprightly savages, and for long it seemed as if they would never settle down to it. How terribly irksome was the discipline of the boys' house and schoolroom! Time passed, and with changes in the lads the irksomeness passed away, and the majority took pleasure in the school.

'My wife joined me, and took great interest in the

work. Her class went ahead, and all seemed to aim to get to her. After her death there were five that we made pupil teachers; in fact we could have done the same with her whole class. The greatest punishment we had was to send a child away out of school; but we had not to go to that extreme often. Our highest average was one hundred and nine, and continued at that figure for nearly two years.

'We had frequent visits from strangers, but especially at New Year time, when as many as 2,000 would assemble at Saguane for nearly a week, and attend all the services, in many cases returning home to hold services in the same way. At many places the service morning and evening amounted to no more than striking for some time a piece of angle iron, not a word being spoken, for they knew not how. How my heart aches for them! Ah well! He sees it all.

'The sea was encroaching, and as this continued year after year there was nothing for it but to move to Daru. Having received from the Government, for building purposes, a piece of land on the south end of the Government ridge, I decided to begin in September, 1901. I had a good man for the work in Anana, a South Sea Island teacher, settled at Iasa. We feel that all kinds of work belong to Christ, and he, believing the same, willingly undertook to put up all the houses.'

Thus abruptly ends the narrative of the autobiography.

A careful consideration of the map will enable the reader to appreciate the nature of Chalmers' field of work. Since the settlement of Dauncey at Delena, and of Holmes at Jokea he had been relieved of the prime responsibility for the mission work from Port Moresby as far west as Toaripi. The ambition that now possessed him was twofold. He longed to establish in the delta of the huge Fly River a firmly established base whence missionary evangelization could proceed up the river, thus gaining access to wild tribes at present entirely unknown. He also believed that in time this might prove a way into the heart of New Guinea. Then from those early days when he had discovered the Purari Delta, and made the acquaintance of the splendid but ferocious savages of Namau and the Bald Head district, it had been his great desire to make friends with the untamed and fierce skull-hunters of the Aird River. By securing a foothold there he felt that the conquest of the coast-line would be complete, and then right round from Daru in the west to Kwato in the east the chain of stations would be unbroken.

But his first work at this period was the superintendence of the stations scattered over the Torres Straits on various islands, from Murray Island in the south to Bampton Island in the north. These communities were small in numbers and widely scattered. To visit them repeatedly—and only by this means could the work of the native teachers be rendered effective—involved constant voyages in either the tiny mission schooner, or in the still smaller and more cramped whaleboat. The whole region is one in which navigation is of the most difficult order; stormy weather is frequent, and the squalls exceedingly violent, and the task of landing on the different islands toilsome and dangerous. To pastoral visitation of this nature the last years of Tamate's life were devoted.

Saguane, on the island of Kiwai in the very jaws of the Fly River Delta, was chosen as his base, on Chalmers' fundamental principle of always stationing himself as near as possible to the strategic point for work. And if the doing of this involved hardship and the excitement of danger so much the more he liked it. Probably no less inviting spot in the whole region could have been found. It was low, desolate, swampy land, only a few feet above the sea level, and it finally had to be abandoned because of the encroachment of the resistless waters. But here at Saguane, when not off upon his visitation voyages, Chalmers spent days and weeks, patiently instructing savage children in the rudiments of know-ledge, and conducting simple daily services of prayer and praise with handfuls of natives who came but slowly to any comprehension of the meaning of the actions in which they took part. He was ever seeking and ever gaining more and more hold upon the savages who, attracted by his residence there, and by his irresistible personality, came in the first instance to see what they could either get or steal from the white man, and ended by being compelled under his constraining influence to surrender all the worst features of their savagery. It would be hard to find in the whole mission field a more striking instance of surrender to duty than that of Chalmers, the intrepid explorer, the man who was never happier than when keenly reading the faces of hitherto unseen savages, the man whose services were sought by learned societies all over the world, who could thrill vast audiences by the power of his personality and the burning force of his en-thusiasm, patiently giving himself to the work of an infant school teacher with the savage children of Saguane.

The correspondence of himself and of Mrs. Chalmers for the years 1896 to 1901 illustrate the work they did, and the experiences through which they passed.

'SAGUANE, *February* 17, 1896.

'Rob Roy (Sir William Macgregor) was here last week. His first hail was, " I am glad you are back,

Chalmers, you are much wanted." He looks well, though much thinner, and he says not so fit for work. Since he returned from Britain he has only been three weeks at Port Moresby ; on the go all the time. He wanted me to go with him, but I could not, I am required here, I fancy.

'I am struggling with the language, and fancy I can crawl, if not toddle, between chairs. We get a fair service on the Sunday, but our schools are poor, wretchedly poor. Yesterday a chief prayed, and he was very particular about " we much want tobacco, calico, and tomahawks, and knives." The teachers are always in a hurry to have baptisms, and I have myself yielded too easily to them, finding out my mistake afterwards. Better far wait until those who wish to be baptized have received the Holy Ghost.'

'SAGUANE, *July* 29, 1896.

'I have been travelling for the last three months, visiting stations. I ought not to be here now, but got tired of knocking about in boats and small vessel, playing captain, mate, and pilot, and doing mission work, without much comfort, and often wet from morning to night. Now I am only squatting a bit before carrying on my visitation to finish. I am greatly pleased with the evident progress of the last few years, and remembering the past and the introduction of the Gospel my heart is filled with thankfulness, and I am strengthened for all future work.

'We are beginning to be felt here. There is a yearly snake-worship (*Kina*) here, and people come from all parts to it. It is a regular gathering of the tribes. The worship is indescribably filthy, beats anything I know of or have ever read of. The two last gatherings were times of much sickness and many deaths, and the old men and sorcerers have met and said that it was because many were forsaking *Kina*, and coming to us. They are calling for a rally round their ancient faith, saying also that we are only vagrants, and will soon be gone, and warning all against us. They urge that none should come to our services, and no children attend our schools. The effect is none came to services, and the school was forsaken.

'On my return here I heard all this, and then I spoke: "The Gospel has come to stay, and it will give light and life by leading men to Christ; the filthy worship of *Kina* will soon be forgotten, and all who knew it will be ashamed of it. I expect services to be attended by all, and all the children to come to school."

'We have had well-attended services, and the children now come to school with great avidity. They fancy my style of teaching, and think the play just capital fun. These old sinners and sorcerers are calling for another turn of *Kina*, but I say "No, it must not be."'

On August 7, in reply to a letter from the author, in which he had been urging Chalmers to leave on record his own sketch of his adventurous life, he wrote:—

'I do, my dear friend, remember your request as to my autobiography, and I will attend to it when I can swallow enough egotism to put it on paper. I have really got as far as noting down the main points, but grew tired of myself, and so put away the notes.'

'SAGUANE, *December* 18, 1896.

'Last Wednesday I came in from a ten weeks' visitation of all my stations, and those in Elema belonging to Mr. Holmes, who has had to go away for his health. At many of the stations a good work is being carried

on, and the schools are well attended; at others they
need more life, more go. We had some uncomfortable
experiences in our voyages. The worst was at Vailala,
when coming out of the harbour at the mouth of the
river. The wind was light, and there was a heavy
swell on the bar, but there was enough wind to take us
through with the strong current running out. I took
the precaution to see the ports closed and sky-lights
down, as I expected to have some heavy seas on board.
As we neared the bar the wind fairly dropped, and
before we could anchor we were taken on towards the
west point, where a fearful sea was breaking, and the
current sweeping round it. Seas and current drove us
on to the bank, and for a short time it looked as if
vessel and all on board must go. The anchor was of
no use; it rather increased the danger, so orders were
given to slack out every inch of chain and so let the
seas drive her in over the bank and through the outer
lines of breakers. It was hard work holding on to the
rigging, as sea after sea swept, smashed, and crashed on
our decks.

'We were seen from the shore, and a whaleboat,
manned by natives paddling in charge of a white trader,
worked their way out, and we being now in better
water, got us off. A large double canoe also came to
our assistance. To make a long story short, we got
ashore all right, and when the tide went out, returned
and landed everything movable, picked up the anchor,
and on the next tide about 100 natives got her into
a kind of a lagoon. It took a week to get her into
deep water, and as time was getting short I took to
canoeing and did about seventy miles.

'The natives have it that all the trouble occurred
because of some gods I had obtained from an old

sorcerer and had on board. The natives say they are the ancestors of all other gods, and that their wrath was great for my having been allowed to have them. Before we were taken off the vessel, so sure were the natives that we were all done for, that east and west the news spread, "Avea's gods have destroyed Tamate and his vessel." Poor Avea is in the border land, betwixt light and darkness, and gave me the gods, saying he knew I would look after them, as he wanted them no more.'

In a letter to one of his most intimate correspondents, under date of July 14, 1897, Tamate describes in his own style, and in full detail, one of his voyages of visitation in Torres Straits. It may be taken as typical of scores of similar voyages, and enables the reader to follow very closely and clearly the nature and quality of the work, and the conditions of his missionary life at this period. The discomforts of this particular trip appear to have been somewhat lighter than usual.

'Some years ago I used to wonder what sort of a place heaven would be without sea; now I am glad, at all events at present, "no more sea." I have had quite enough of it lately. Come, let us have a trip. We have done with the east, but Torres Straits and the Fly River have yet to be visited. Wood and water are on board, the morning is fine, so down to the beach and on board the whaleboat. The tide is running strong, and it is a hard pull to get alongside of the Niue. Here we are! just step on deck when the boat rises. Bob of Aitutaki is our captain, a good old salt, and our mate is Lui of Samoa, a very good fellow and a good sailor. The crew, two lads from Saguane, who now do very well. We have with us two boys to cook and steward for us, and this helps to keep them out of mischief. Jimi, the elder, is a half-caste Torres Straits lad. His father was a Scotsman; a nice lad, very willing, and very clean. Agere is from Saguane, a smart, passionate youth, who ran away from me last year, and came back some time ago, begging me to allow him to return.

'The Niue is fifteen tons, has a very comfortable cabin, but no cargo room. She is a very wet boat if there is much of a sea on. There is about forty fathom of chain out, so "Heave short. Enough, now up mainsail and back again to windlass." "Anchor up," "Up jib," "Up staysail." "Give her the foresail quick." We are away and standing across the mouth of the Fly River. Just a little sea, not unpleasant.

'On the other side, as I want to visit one of our stations, we try to get as near land as possible, and so save the long wading through mud. "Down foresail and try the lead." We are about a mile and a half off. "One and a half," and that keeps on for some distance. "One fathom." "Go round." We cannot anchor here, for when the tide is out we should be ashore and on our beam ends, a most uncomfortable position. We stand away now to our anchorage off Neva Pass, and as the tide is too far out, and would necessitate a long wade and a long walk, I shall defer my visit until the early morning.

'At six in the evening the teacher comes off in a canoe and gets his supplies—trousers, shirts, undershirts, white calico, unbleached calico, prints, tobacco, soap, rice, flour, knives, tomahawks—about £5 worth altogether. The anchorage is good, and so for a good sound sleep.

'There they come, dashing forth from the east, just a little after five, the sun's steeds, and we get ready. "Bring the dingey alongside." Jimi and one of the crew pull ashore. The tide is well up, and we land beyond the mud. There is a walk of about two miles, but we get to the village before the people have shaken themselves together. " Ring the bell," and a piece of old iron is struck with a large spike nail. The queerly built church is soon filled, and we have a service and then school. We adjourn to the mission house, have a talk and then a meeting with the people who have been baptized. Several pray. I am now ready to return to the vessel so as to catch the tide, but must wait a little as the people are anxious to give me a small present, and they bring me yams, which are very acceptable, as the crew have only rice on board.

' We get to the vessel and soon have breakfast. It is too late to visit the station on Bampton Island unless you would like a wade of three miles through slush and mud. I don't care for it, so put it off until I return. " Heave away, my lads, and let us get through the Pass." I call this place Purgatory because of the mosquitoes and the time occupied in getting to the other side. The tide is low, and we cannot cross the banks between Bampton and Daru, so must anchor on west of Purgatory and wait for tide. At six we up anchor and stand across the sandbanks, with just enough water to float us over, and at eight p.m. we anchor in a snug anchorage under the lee of Daru. As we are going into Queensland waters I must have a permit for my boy Agere and a clearance, so ashore and secure these to be ready for an early start.

' At six the following morning we are away, and it is now blowing hard. To make comfortable weather of it we shall to the leeward of the Warrior Reef. Blowing fresh, yet it is very comfortable, so have a big read and as big a sleep. We want to pick up Moon Pass, and go through, and then beat over to Damuth, where we hope to anchor to-night. We have left one pass behind,

and here is another, and this must be Moon. We beat
in and are on the other side, but can find no opening
out, so take an opening more to the south, and find we
are going back and eventually out, having only cut
a bit of the reef. We continue on close hauled, but
come to no other opening.

'It is now five o'clock, so must get ready to anchor
for the night. "Try the lead." "Three fathom, sir."
"All right, keep on." "Two fathom, sir." "Down
foresail, down jib, down staysail," up in the wind and
away goes the anchor. Just at sundown all assemble
and we have service. Very few days pass that we have
not morning and evening service.

'We have had a good night and a good sea sleep. It
is now 5.30, but we cannot see the reef, so wait for
sunrise. Have had coffee and service and now away.
We had better keep right on to the end of the Warrior
Reef, and go between Tut and Dungeness. The tide is
running out against a strong south-easter, and there is
a nasty sea in the Channel. By three p.m. we are fairly
through and standing up for Damuth. At sundown we
could not see the island, and the weather is not agreeable and looks as if it might be much worse. We must
find an anchorage, so beat up to that small island,
Rennel, ten miles off. It is a stiff beat, but we are at
anchor by nine. It is dark, and in getting near the
island we had to be cautious, for in the dark it is impossible to say how far off it may be, and the anchorage
will be close to the shore reef. "Down foresail." The
lead is going, "No bottom at twenty." "Down staysail," "Luff her right up," "Now take a cast of the
lead." "No bottom at twenty." "Keep her away
a little." "Fourteen fathom, sir." "Anchor in ten."
On we go. "Twelve," a little more. "Ten fathom, sir."

"Down jib, hard up, pull in main sheet." "Let go," and we are at anchor.

' We look very near to the white shore, but the wind is blowing off, so all right. Now to sleep, and not a sound is heard all night on board. All hands on deck at 5.30, a dull, dark, windy morning. There is Damuth, so we weigh and stand across. At 8.30 we anchor close to the small village. Having finished breakfast, I land with Jimi, my boy, who has relatives here and who all want to embrace him, but he is just that age he doesn't like it and turns away his head. The whole population numbers twenty, and the services during the week and on Sabbaths are conducted by Johnnie, a native of the island, who can just read but no more. The piece of iron is struck and all assemble, and we have an interesting meeting. There is no school, Johnnie could not do that. He is an evangelist, and has £2 worth of things to get, which he receives with great delight.

' By eleven we were away. Blowing a gale, so we had to reef down everything. I want to call at Ogar (Stephens), but there is too much sea on, so we beat up to Darnley. Eh, it is a beat against a gale of wind and heavy seas. At ten we anchor on the lee side, where there are about a dozen pearl-shelling boats at anchor. All are glad to turn in and enjoy the sleep which refreshes; I am very glad indeed.

' The next day is Sunday, so our mate lands early, and after breakfast and a short meeting with the crew I land, to get a wetting by slipping off a stone into the water. Never mind, I want to take the forenoon service, so hurry on over the two miles to the village. We have a good gathering and a good service. I find the Murray Island teacher and his wife and bairns here on their way to Saibai, so I need not visit his island. We have a good prayer-meeting in the teacher's house. I sent Lui off to bring the vessel round to the village anchorage, and so save a long walk in the evening. The afternoon service was also a good one, but I was not satisfied with the school. I got on board by 5.30.

'At noon we weighed and stood away for Ogar. Three p.m. anchored, and although tide is out, into dingey and ashore. Old boots on for a long reef wade, and then walk on soft coral. There are twenty-two people on the island, and of these seven are church members. The church is down, and we had service under a banian tree growing near the village. Jack, the chief, acts as evangelist. He says they are going to put up a new church very soon. Church building is in the air at present. In Jack's house we had a meeting for prayer. I said, "Jack, no many man stop along Ogar now, before he all the same." His face became sad, then lightened up, and he answered, "My word, no gammon, true, good true, no man stop along here now, before plenty, plenty man, big village, he stop along here," and then I felt sorry, as he added with a feeling voice, "All he go, all he dead." I brought him on board with me and gave him things. The Darnley Island teacher often visits them.

'The next morning we are away just after sunrise, and in a few hours are at Masig. Into dingey and ashore, and have meeting with people, and spend a few hours with them. The tide is now out, so we must get the boat carried out into deep water, and then wade out. We give the evangelist his things and up anchor and away. Before sundown we anchor off Cocoa-nut Island, but no people on it. The boys all land to get firewood and look for turtle eggs. The latter not to be had.

'Another day with an angry sky and now blowing

great guns, and outside a big sea running. Never mind, let us away. Reef her down, weigh, and off. Roughish, not pleasant, but by 9.30 we are anchored at Waraber. Only five people ashore, with whom we hold service on the beach. All the others, sixteen in number, and chief are on Yam.

' On board, up anchor, and now with a fair wind stand over to Yam. Fine seas are rolling up behind us, but we ship none. At 1.30 we drop anchor near to shore-reef off Yam Island. Ashore, where I find a teacher who formerly was at Mauata, but had to leave because of blindness, and who for some months has been on Darnley and got better, but not sufficiently so to return to New Guinea. We have an interesting service and then a meeting for prayer. I have decided to place the teacher here, where there is good land for building and planting; and being central he can take charge of all the small islands, gather their children in, and teach them in English, which he can do. He is a Lifuan, and a very good fellow.

' I go on board for a bit, and at 5.30 land for evening service. The chief, Maino, is evangelist, and delighted that he is to have a teacher, saying, "You see, all children grow up now, no savee nothing." I feel for the children.

' That night we had a proper rocking, but did not sleep well. Six a.m. away for Moa, and at twelve we were off the village, but not a soul, not a living thing to be seen, and no intimation stuck up as to where the people were. Up anchor, and away to Badu. " That water looks queer; try the lead." "One and a half, sir." "Keep her away." We are on a sand-bank I knew nothing of. All right, we are soon in deep water, and stand in to the Badu reef. Strange, not a living being about. Run down again, stand up, no use, so shape away for

Mabuiag, and there we anchor at four p.m. Not many men at home, out on the Orman reef looking for shell, and our teacher also.

' Things are askew, and the cat is thought to be far away, and the mice are having a game of their own. I am vexed. In March I came to Mabuiag and arranged with the teacher, a Samoan, not to build the church at present, but prepare for it by cutting wood and collecting money gradually, as the famine is great, and the people will require rice and flour and will have to pay for it in shell. A few weeks after I left, he, by hard pressure, got £215 together, started for Thursday Island, arranged to have a church put up. Many of the people, and the chief, want delay; oh no, my lord must have his own way, and when I arrive a church is up, built of cheap soft wood and not what we wanted. I am vexed, but more so to find him away, and to hear that for a long time there has been no school.

' Saturday comes, and I have a serious talk with him and inform him that he will have to leave. A change will do him good, and he can come to my part of New Guinea, or join the Samoan contingent in the Port Moresby district. No, he will go home. Right, but do not decide now, think about it, pray about it. The bell is rung and there is a large gathering, as all are now ashore. We have a good service, and at the close I propose opening the church to-morrow (Sunday), and it is agreed to. I feel doubtful, and fancy they will change their minds. I sleep on board.

' Sunday morning early, Jimi brings my coffee, and says, "Plenty Mabuiag men come now." I know what is up, a deputation from the people to put off opening until October, that having spent so much money they may have a grand occasion. "Well, yes, I will try and meet your desire," and so October 16 is fixed. We had a grand day ashore, and in the afternoon quite a field time; many speakers. Many have been to me asking me to remove the teacher at once, but that I cannot do, and it would be cruel not to let him have part in the church opening.

'On Monday morning we got away, and out by the Brothers, and then up to Dauan, but not a soul at home, then across to Saibai to find many natives in from all quarters, and all Saibaians busy preparing for church opening on Wednesday. Up until midnight, boats and canoes are coming in.

'On Tuesday many more arrive. I am ashore arranging programme, and have a visit to new church. It is a fine building, built and paid for entirely by themselves. They gathered together £111, and have £9 left. These people were savages when I came to New Guinea, and a couple of years before inveterate skull-hunters. Now they have the finest church in all the New Guinea and Torres Straits Missions, and all their own. If that is not evidence of the Gospel's power, what can be?

'Wednesday morning at nine I land; at ten we form in procession in front of mission house and march to church, when, the keys being handed to me, I open the door, and in a few words pronounce the church open. It is soon crowded, and then we have prayer and singing. Then I pray Solomon's prayer at the dedication of the Temple, again sing, and a short address. Sing, and two minutes' addresses are given. Thirty have spoken, with singing interspersed. The collection, £21. Another hymn and prayer and all away to feasting.

'The largest feast I have seen since I left the South Seas. Cooked and uncooked food in great heaps, and forty-six cooked pigs and nine uncooked. I do not know anywhere in New Guinea where such a feast could be had. The dividing was a complicated puzzle, but in a few hours unravelled. I left them to finish. When in church we had severe wind and rain. The Saibai youths were dressed in dark Norfolk jackets and knee-breeches, with long white stockings, no boots or shoes. The women were dressed in Turkey red dresses, black hats, with red binding as ribbons. The whole was a great success.

'On Thursday morning, after taking the Kunini teacher and his wife and Parama and Wigi teachers on board, we weighed anchor and stood away to the east; fortunately the weather moderated and we were able to stand in near shore. At one we landed the Kunini teacher and wife, and at 5.30 we anchored off Daru. The Niue has to go east, and I landed and got a coast clearance. A wet night right through and a dark tempestuous morning. Never mind, let us away. When out in the passage it was blowing a gale, and dark and wet, and looked bad, so we put back to our anchorage and remained until the following morning.

'The weather is better to-day, so we up anchor and away. We anchored in two fathoms to wait for high water to get over the banks, and at six were away again, to stick fast for about half an hour, and then into the Pass, Purgatory. Our progress was slow and the mosquitoes were bad, but there is an end even to Purgatory, and at nine p.m. we anchored on the eastern side. By eleven the teachers were landed.

'We had a good night's rest. Service with crew, breakfast; and meeting for prayer with captain and mate. Now ashore, it is a long pull, and we may get stranded. A mile from the village we have to leave the dingey, off boots and socks, buckle up and into mud and water. Not a bit pleasant. We are late, the pull was long and the wading was longer. In mission house meet many of the people, then prayer-meeting, and arrange for afternoon service, and Ordinance of the Lord's Supper. We had a good time. I got on board by 6.15 p.m.

' By six a.m. Monday morning we are bowling across the mouth of the Fly River, and shortly after nine drop anchor off house at Saguane. Thank God for all His goodness and mercy.'

In August, 1897, Mrs. Chalmers reached Saguane, more than three years after she had left Toaripi. ' I did look round the house,' she writes, ' in despair when I came. I look round now, just one degree removed from it. I am feeling very languid and weak; it is the change of climate, I expect. We have only unpacked three cases yet, but I must have two more done to-day. They arrived last Saturday, and had to wait of course until Monday to be landed. It rather worries me to do things in a perspiring crowd, but I shall soon get accustomed to it again. I have not the heart to send the natives off, they are so curious and interested. At present I can get no one to help, and the washing done at the teacher's needs a revolution, but I must have patience and do little by little.'

Mrs. Chalmers found both place and people at Saguane very different from the stormy beach and the wild savages she had learned to love at Toaripi. But she soon set herself, for the Master's sake, to the duty of loving and caring for the degraded children and natives around her. On Dec. 1, 1897, she wrote :—

' My children are a handful, perfect young savages, and if anything goes wrong, they fight tooth and nail, the former being the favourite mode.   Sometimes I hear screams and yells, as if some one was being murdered, and I find that a boy or girl has made her teeth meet in the flesh of another.   They are terribly passionate; and we cannot do much, for they would set off, and not return.   Tamate says the work went on here a very long time before any one came about to stay.   So we are glad to have the boys and girls round us.

'We get good attendance at school, although most of the parents discourage their children from coming.   The attendance at church is fairly good.   I look round and long to see some sign of real interest.   It is early days yet, and we must just work on in patience.   I want you to pray that I may grow to *love* these people.   I do not feel to love them as I did my Toaripians.   They are a much lower type than the latter; they are so mean, and dirty, and selfish—but Jesus loves them all, and oh, how they need His love, and they need ours too. Tamate, bless him, seems to like them well, and shakes hands, and puts his arm over their shoulders, and never minds dirt or disease.'

At this time Tamate met with an accident that might have been fatal, and the results of which troubled him for a long time.

'SAGUANE, *February* 9, 1898.

'I have been out of sorts for a bit, and had to give in quite for a few days.   When getting better, and at translating again, I had a bad fall.   My study is approached on a bridge from the house to the study verandah.   Before stepping on to the house verandah there is a narrow bridge to the store, one side of which has no rail, and from the study bridge there is one step on to it and then turn sharp to the right.   The night was very dark, and thoughtlessly I marched on and stepped over and had a drop of nearly twelve feet. I got shaken and my right side and my leg badly bruised, and for three weeks have been doctoring. I seem all right now and in full swing.

'I am reading the "Sixty Years' Reign" copy of the Bible, and have got to the Psalms. I read from Genesis to Job as I would history, and when I have time in the mornings. The devotional parts blow sometimes gently, sometimes in gales. I get caught sometimes by a prophet with a perfect hurricane and drive on furiously, sometimes it is a firm, steady breeze, and then again it is a quiet, gentle breeze wafting one along in a dreamy, easy, restful kind of way. May we ever just be in touch with Christ, His will our all.'

Mrs. Chalmers took great interest in the school work at Saguane, and her next letter enables us to realize some of the heart-breaking difficulties and trials of such work.

'*March* 7, 1898.

'The people are not a nice lot, even for savages; they are terribly deceitful, and will not help us in any way; it is difficult to get them to do any work, though we pay them well, and often we cannot get them to sell us any food. Now and again, if they are very anxious for clothing (which they like), they will bring in food and want exorbitant payment. I told you how well the school was doing; well, now there are only a very few children left. All have gone to the great *moguru*, and they go for from four to six months. The children on the station have also decamped—just bolted in twos and threes during the nights. The immorality, from our standpoint, is fearful. The girls here all take the initiative. If they fancy a man or boy they just go and fetch him, or persuade him to go off to the bush with them; it is terrible to deal with. Parents here have no control and never correct their children. Young children of six or seven are quite independent, and go off in canoes to distant dances or feasts, and say nothing to any one. No uneasiness is felt, as every one treats them kindly and feeds them.

' I could weep for my class of children, who could read so nicely and write and do sums—if they come back in a few months' time everything will be forgotten. This vile *moguru*, with its dancing, feasting, and abomination. Most of the boys are going in for all the excitement of their first initiation ceremony. The people do not want us, but Tamate says, for that very reason, we must stay, and give them a real chance: we must not give up too soon. It is strange we cannot seem to get into real friendly relations with them. Tamate says they are the most difficult to make friends of that he has met.

' I want you to join us in our special prayers for this people—who harden their hearts, and will have none of the blessed Gospel, but give themselves up, for half the year, to terribly evil practices, impossible to write about. We want the young ones for Christ, in them lies hope— our only hope—for the future.'

In May, 1898, Chalmers started on the Niue to visit his teachers in the Straits, and fortunately, as it turned out, Mrs. Chalmers accompanied him. They had hardly started when one of the worst series of gales ever known, even in that region, overtook them. They were compelled to take refuge at Thursday Island, where first Mrs. Chalmers was laid up, and then Tamate himself had a dangerous illness, due partly to the fall described above, and partly to the exposure, fatigue, and drenchings occasioned by the terrible weather through which the

Niue passed. Mrs. Chalmers, on June 13, wrote home an account of this time of peril and suffering.

'We left Saguane May 19, and had a most terrible time in these Straits. They are dangerous at all times, anywhere out of the big ship channel, and every island is reef-bound—besides the sunken reefs, and many sand-banks. For over a fortnight we were out, and battling with awful seas and constant squalls night and day. The little Niue is always what we call a wet boat, but during this time she had seas over her from stem to stern—and often the water came into the cabin, and our mattresses, pillows, and selves were soaked. We were beating and tacking the whole time—anchoring at night under lee of islands or reefs, and pitching, rolling, and dancing the whole night; only twice we had a quieter anchorage. Tamate was on deck nearly the whole day long, wet through and through, but obliged to be there in such stormy weather.

'We visited Yam, Masig, and Darnley Islands, and I managed to land, under difficulties, at the two last named. We could not sleep ashore on any of them, as there was no good teacher's house, and the natives said the sand-flies and mosquitoes were very bad. It was a choice of two evils, and I chose the restless anchorage. Three times we put out to go to Murray Island, and had to run back before the wind on a tremendous sea. I shall never forget our experiences.

'We had to run close-reefed, and Tamate said if we were driven on one of the reefs in such weather ten minutes would leave no one to tell the tale. At last Tamate decided to try to get here, and we started once more in a different direction. We anchored after a stormy day at Masig, and had a rather quieter night. Next day another bad time—peak halyard carried off, and squalls following

each other every fifteen minutes or so. The poor little
ship was so battered and strained by the big seas, that it
seemed as if she must split up. She must have sprung
a good bit, for the water began to rise in the cabin, and
the boys had to work the pumps often to keep it down at
all. Anchored at Cocoa-nut Island. Tamate landed.
I was too ill to do so, but from the deck I could see the
whole of the few inhabitants and the few houses. There
is a poor man there who knows only that God is
our loving Father and Creator of everything, and that
Jesus, His Son, is our Saviour, and died for us, and
that it is wrong to lie, and steal, and murder, and
he gathers the twenty or thirty people together each
day, morning and evening, to pray and praise, and
he tells them all he knows, and they pray for more
light. He tells me that when he was a boy plenty of
natives lived there, but now some have gone, and many
have died.

'At one place, on a rather large island, there are just
sixteen people left. They live happily together, and
one, who knows a little of religion, acts as their leader.
He has quite a pretty little church, with nice shade round,
and there they meet every day for morning and evening
prayers. We could not get over the reef until evening
in the boat—and our service was held by firelight.
Afterwards we all sat round a big fire and talked. It
felt so strange to think we were all alone on the island.
I asked them if they did not feel lonely sometimes—for
they are out of the way of boats. They have a boat in
which they go to dive for shell: it belongs equally to
all, but they can only go near home. Tamate talked
to them a long time; they all understand "pidgin
English" more or less; then I had to be carried over
part of the reef, and we had a dangerous journey over

F f

the rest—sometimes bumping on the sharp rocks; it was starlight, but no moon, and cloudy.

'Next morning away from here, and a fearful time. Tamate says he never, in all his twenty years round here, encountered such winds and seas. We almost despaired of making Thursday Island; when at last we got in we found a great many boats in for shelter. Tamate was obliged to rest a few days, and then he would go on, but Dr. Salter forbade my attempting to do so.'

'THURSDAY ISLAND, *July* 8, 1898.

'Tamate returned on June 21, very ill indeed, and had to go at once to bed. Doctor pronounced him suffering from rheumatic and malarial fever, and also from the effects of his fall. We have had a very bad time.'

Chalmers was, for him, very slow in casting off the effects of his severe illness at Thursday Island. In a fashion quite his own, writing on August 19, from Saguane, he longs for a disturbance in which he might intervene as a desirable tonic for him.

'I am out of sorts, and as lazy as they make them, though I do my school for four hours a day, but lack zest and push. I ought to be up and joyful, for it is dawn with us. I have a good deal of nausea, and no appetite. Tamate Vaine preaches give in, but if I do that I might go out altogether. She is not over bright. The season is a wretched one, cold and wet, and much sickness about. I intended writing you a long letter, but I fear " no can do." An attack, a fight, a jolly big row, might rouse me.

' Some months ago I had run down a bit, and one morning there was a big row in the village, and I was soon fetched. Getting my favourite walking-stick I went over, and before me the combatants fled, and I pursued some distance, overtook the leaders, and talked fatherly to them. Some had nasty cut heads, and others bruised bodies. It was all about a girl who ran away from her friends because of her dislike to the youth they wished her to marry. I hoped it was over, and had the bell rung for school. Shortly after we had begun I heard them begin again with their fiendish howlings and screamings. A friend fetched me, saying they had got the girl, and she was likely to be murdered between the parties. I seized my stick, and felt militant. The arrows were flying, but I hurried on to the centre, where there was a fearful scrimmage, and heavy sticks at work. Holding my stick above my head for defence, I got to where the girl was pulled every way by arms and legs, and in a faint. One flourish of the stick, and a proper shout, and I had the girl in my left arm. They attempted to close round me, but I warned them as they had never been warned before, and I carried the girl triumphantly inside of our fence, and delivered her to the charge of friends, and gave orders that no outsider was to be allowed in. Poor girl, she was " close up gone." Now, the whole business was quite refreshing, and I felt much better after it.

'The church is crowded. Three services on Sunday, and three have come inquiring. At Ipisia, near to here, there are over twenty church members. I expect soon we shall have students. We have thirteen nice lads staying here, who are getting on well. Throughout the district there is a moving as of the Spirit of God, and an anxiety to know of Jesus.'

In the closing sentences of the same letter he says, 'I should not like to become a shelved missionary in Australia. Far better, like Lewis [1], when the time is, to

[1] This refers to his friend the Rev. Edwin Lewis, of Bellary, who had died suddenly when in full active work.

go hence from the field. Busy, at work, and away—
guess that's perfect.'

During 1898 a scientific expedition was at work
in Torres Straits. It was under the direction of
Dr. Alfred C. Haddon, who had visited the Straits on
a similar errand in 1888. Chalmers knew Dr. Haddon
well, and was able to be of service to the expedition in
several ways. The members of the expedition visited
him at Saguane. He was also never averse to exacting
in return, if he could, aid for his own special work.

'SAGUANE, *September* 21, 1898.

'We have had the scientific party here. They stayed
a few days, and then on to Mabuiag, leaving Ray the
philologist at my request. He goes with me next week.
He is quiet and entertaining, with a marvellous memory
for languages, and great aptitude in getting to know
them thoroughly.

'We got Ray to talk to the children this morning.
He is a London schoolmaster, and he drilled them
thoroughly; put them through their facings in real
style, and the bairns are delighted.

'Ray is getting all sorts of songs on to phonograph
cylinders, and some come out very well. The natives
fancy it is a ghost, but how it works cannot make out.'

During 1898 there was considerable uncertainty as to
the future of the western mission of New Guinea, and
the work and station of Tamate himself. Affairs were
not going well financially with the London Missionary
Society. The expenses connected with the Fly River
work were heavy. Not a few competent judges held
the opinion that the same energy and money spent elsewhere would yield more fruitful results. The furlough
of Mr. Hutchin on Rarotonga was due, and a plan

was mooted for sending Chalmers there for two years, partly because it was thought that this would benefit his health, partly because there was no one else so well qualified to take Mr. Hutchin's place. But fortunately, although these changes are referred to from time to time as possible, and even probable, none of them came to pass.

'SAGUANE, *October* 29, 1898.

' I had a good inland mission in the beginning of the eighties, but had to leave it for many reasons, chiefly no help. It was considered too costly, and the young men do not care for inland work. No new missionary has done anything for inland. If no one else can, then I will gladly, but this place must be supplied.

' Day is dawning with us, and we expect great things, and to leave this post now, when the battle is nearly finished, would be cowardice. I mean the tough fight of a new station. Only those who have tried it know what it is.'

'SAGUANE, *December* 1, 1898.

' God is blessing our work very abundantly, and many are seeking baptism. Last month I baptized at Parama sixty-four, and at Geavi thirty-two, and at each place hosts of children. Last Sunday I baptized fourteen here and seven children. We need more teachers at many places; they hold services and do their best. The Master sees it all, and will bless them. Now that the hard up-pull is easier, the long, dreech waiting over, I would gladly give up to a younger man.

' I fancy our school is the best in the mission. Our average is fifty-three, and knowledge is *much* more than in any other school. Fancy leaving all to flow back again to chaos. A young man has material here for a grand up-river movement in a few years. We want no namby pamby youth, who, when he arrives, begins thinking of the time to go home, and counts the months as they pass as so much less to serve. If you know a good all-round manly fellow, inform Mr. Thompson and have him sent this way. No nonsense, dispatch him straight away, and we will then go wherever desired.'

'SAGUANE, *June* 1, 1899.

'There is a great giving up of idols and charms in the district. The Bull Roarer is one of the most formidable things in the native cosmogony. They must never be seen or heard by women or children. A few days ago there was a feast at Ipisia, and the Bull Roarer was going, and women and children in bush. I allow no native teacher to disturb any feast except by teaching, service, prayer. Yesterday the men with women and children in the village began using the dreaded symbol, and invited all to come and see it, and that it was no more of use but for children to play with. It is deafening all round here, and I have had to order my boys on to the beach if they use it. Fancy, for centuries, innumerable generations, the Bull Roarer was the most dreaded symbol they possessed, and to-day it is the plaything of the children.

'There are many anxious for baptism, but I prefer waiting. May they grow in light and love! May they all belong to Jesus truly! I long for a quiet time with earnest Christian folk of my own kind. More real, true, burning love to Christ I want. Just to be His altogether.'

Mrs. Chalmers' health, which had begun to fail steadily, necessitated at this time a visit to Australia. There Tamate joined her towards the close of her stay. He was ever alert to utilize such visits and the opportunities they afforded for stimulating assemblies

and for consulting friends and officials so as to benefit
his work.

'I was able when south to assist the London Missionary Society somewhat. We had wet weather all the
time. We had to go overland to Brisbane to meet the
Home Secretary and arrange about English schools in
Torres Straits. He is delighted with our mission work,
but is astonished at no-English in our schools, and so
will appoint a *Marm* to Darnley, Mabuiag, and Saibai
to train the young in English only. We could not do
it, so I acquiesced. Had I not been south I should have
had to go from here to meet him, as it is a most important move. He is anxious to work with us and do
everything to assist us.

'Queensland is repenting or suffering with remorse,
and is now anxious to whitewash the past by doing all
she can now for the living aboriginals.'

Soon after his return Chalmers was off up the river
attempting to consolidate friendly relations with the
natives.

'I think I told you of our visit to Baramura, a village
of one house, nearly 700 feet long. The people were
suspicious, and if they meant mischief we did not give
them much time to think about it. We bought some
bananas, and held a service, and then to the boat. Now
there is a sequel. Baramura is some distance up a creek
off the river; we get to it in a boat, anchoring the Niue
in the main stream. When we run short of food here
the teacher ascends the river, holding services and buying
food at several villages. I sent the Niue up last week,
and they had the whaleboat accompanying. They
anchored the Niue off the right bank, near to the mouth

of the Baramura creek, then landed in the whaleboat.
The Niue's captain, anxious to see a one-house village,
landed with two of a crew in the dingey. As with us
a month before, not many natives were met with, and no
women and children. We met only one woman and
no children.

'They had bought bananas, and were about to hold
a service, looking at an idol some distance up towards
the roof, when arrows began to fly, and they rushed for
the boat, but could not sit to the oars. The teacher
had his gun with him. He shot a pigeon the night
before, and there was left one cartridge. He fired in
the air, and the noise astonishing them they stopped
firing arrows for a few seconds, to begin with more
vigour again. In the cessation they got the boats near
to the opposite side of the creek, and as the bank was
lined with natives with bows and arrows, and so impossible for them to pull, they abandoned the boats and
took to the bush, and made for the river bank, where
they plunged in and swam off to the Niue. One man
got an arrow in his left arm.

'Our friends at Sumai, hearing the boats were left,
formed a large party, and went to Baramura determined
to get the boats, even to fight for them. On arriving
there not a soul was to be seen, and the boats lying in
the creek all right, so they took them and have brought
them here. God truly did deliver our party. I hope
soon to give them a teacher.'

The gatherings of the New Year in 1900 passed off
successfully and hopefully, and with many tokens that
the people were beginning at last to respond to the
power and attraction of the Gospel. Mrs. Chalmers
wrote on Jan. 28, 1900 :—

'Our New Year's gathering was not so large as last

year—two or three parties came much too soon, and
had to go back, and one contingent came too late. We
had over 1,700 visitors though. You may be sure it was
a busy, tiring time. I was not able to be about much.
I kept up till all was given out to our own people, and
all arranged for the feasts and sports. We had just
grand hearty meetings. We sat down 300 at the Communion Service, all from this district. After the large
open-air service the church members joined in communion in the church. In the afternoon another large
gathering under the palms; at this service 136 adults
were baptized, these from various places.

'It was wonderful to think of these people of various
tribes meeting together in unity, and enjoying themselves.
Savage strangers here for the first time were much
interested, and made many inquiries, and were taught
many and wonderful things of the Great Father, and
His Beloved Son, and so the Light spreads around.'

In April, 1900, Chalmers was greatly relieved and
encouraged by the arrival of a young colleague, the
Rev. Oliver C. Tomkins, who was to superintend the
Torres Straits Mission, and thus leave Tamate free to
explore the Fly River and to attempt to extend the
mission eastwards from that river. He was a colleague
after Tamate's own heart, a man of fine physique, of
beautiful spirit, of a missionary enthusiasm akin to
Chalmers' own. From the first Tamate loved him.
'He will do; send us two more of the same sort,'
was the message the veteran sent home about him.
Through the trying scenes of the last illness of
Mrs. Chalmers he was as a son to his elder colleague.
'What can I say of him who was the sharer of his
martyrdom,' said Dr. Lawes, at the great meeting in
the Albert Hall in May, 1901, 'except that he had won

all hearts, and that we expected great things from him for many years to come? A man of faith and prayer, mighty in the Scriptures, he was a great help, comfort, and joy to Tamate. He was to him what Timothy was to Paul, his "dearly beloved son."' Such was the man who joined Chalmers in the work in 1900.

'SAGUANE, *June* 25, 1900.

'The bell has arrived, and is already calling to services and school. It only came last week, and was fixed up two days after. It is now ringing, calling to school. Great interest is attached to it by all because it was the bell that called Tamate to church and school when he was a boy.

'We have been in Torres Straits for eight weeks, introducing Mr. Tomkins and handing over the work to him. He is a fine fellow, and does not fear work, of which he will have an abundance.

'We have to leave here because of the sea encroaching on our bit of land and eating it all away. The governor has kindly given us land on Daru, near to the Government station, and we are now busy getting the frames of houses ready. We hope in a few months to remove hence. It is a big job, and will be a little expensive. This station has cost the London Missionary Society nothing. Your cousin's handsome gift to me when at home, and a smaller one from Mr. Allan, Belfast, has covered all expense. I hope the present removal will be done as cheaply to the Society. Pray with us that the money sufficient may be provided, as well as sufficient to get a new vessel suitable for river work.'

The bell referred to was that which used to hang in Mr. Meikle's church at Inveraray. The lease had fallen in, the church had been given up, and the Duke of

Argyll, at Mr. Meikle's suggestion, allowed the old bell to be sent out to New Guinea. The sounds of the old bell, which carried Tamate's recollection back to his earliest boyhood, were now used to summon the natives of Kiwai to service and the children to school.

In July, 1900, Mrs. Chalmers became seriously ill, and as week after week passed without improvement, it gradually dawned upon them both that there was only one possible end to her sufferings. As a complement to his own autobiography, Chalmers prepared, during his last lonely months at Daru, a sketch of his wife's life. The first portion of this has been given on pages 315 and 316. The latter portion tells tenderly the story of these last sorrowful weeks:—

'Lizzie came out to me in 1897, and enjoyed Saguane much at first. She had mellowed much, and had become much more spiritual. With the old spirit she threw herself into teaching, and her bairns made progress. In the beginning of 1899 she suffered greatly from small boils, and went to the colonies, where she soon recovered. I went to Sydney to meet her, and stayed four weeks, when we returned to Saguane. Towards the end of the year the boils began again, and she suffered a good deal internally. In 1900 she still carried on her classes. In May we went to Thursday Island, where I left her. I visited the Straits, introducing Mr. Tomkins to his work.

'On our return we found her much better, and anxious to get back to work, and especially to prepare for our removal to Daru. Soon after our return she and the boys packed away all her small things. She carried on her classes, and on July 23 she had her evening class, and on my going to her she complained of feeling very poorly. I got her to bed, from which she never again rose without assistance. After returning from Thursday Island she often complained, but not very seriously.

'For fourteen weeks she was ill, but steadily growing in Christ. She longed much at first to see her boy ordained and married, and then as time wore on she felt less, and said one day to me, "It is strange, dear, but I have no longing now to see Bert, and I feel it is all right. How good our Father is!" She was thankful for her long illness, notwithstanding the great suffering, as it gave her time to understand better, to get a clearer view and a stronger faith. Often she could be heard in praise, and saying, "Peace, perfect peace!" "In my Father's house are many mansions." "Jesus is near, very near." She loved to hear the children sing.

'One thing she feared was that she might die at Saguane, and so would have to be buried in the swamp, and earnestly prayed she might be spared to reach Daru and be buried there. On October 24 we carried her on board the Niue. We had a very fine run across, and at 10.30 we anchored off Daru. I said when the anchor was going down, "Daru, dear," and with great satisfaction she replied, "Yes." My hope was to get her to Thursday Island and on to Sydney. But that night she became much worse, was sometimes unconscious, slept a good deal, and was evidently soon to pass on yonder. She knew me until 9 a.m. on October 25, and at 10.40 she quietly went home. She rests in the native cemetery. The few whites were all exceedingly kind and sympathetic, and helped me in every way. The teachers were as sons, and did all they could. Thank God for sympathy and love! The world is full of both as it is of God.

'During her last stay at home she came a good deal in touch with two very excellent ladies, one in the North

THE SECOND MRS. CHALMERS.

and the other near to London, and their quiet, earnest
Christlike lives had a wonderful influence on her life,
and she often spoke of them and their real Christ
devotion.   She did a good deal for the London
Missionary Society in speaking.   She did not like it
much, but considered that she was serving the Master
Christ in it.   Christ was very dear to her.   She often
said, " The teachers do not make enough of Christ."
When she began to get a little knowledge of the
language, and I had been away, on my return I would
find in the journal she kept during my absence such
remarks as this : " I, *you* must speak to the teachers to
preach Christ, more of Christ, always Christ."

'She was for long greatly distressed about the
Society's difficulties, and prayed that relief might come,
and that all the work might be carried on increasingly.
The week before her death I was out in the kitchen one
afternoon, and on coming into the bedroom I found her
sitting up and in visible distress.   On my inquiring
what was the matter, she said, " Oh, James, dear, I am in
great trouble, and don't know what to do—a great, a very
great sum of money has been left, and I am ill and weak,
and I cannot see to it.   It has been left for the work,
and for me to arrange."   We had often spoken of
a vessel suitable for the Fly River, and I said, " We
shall get our vessel now, dear."   She replied, " That is
nothing, merely nothing ; the money left is thousands,
and thousands, and thousands, and whatever am I to
do ? "   I said, " You have only been dreaming, dear, so be
quiet."   " No," she replied, " I am not dreaming, but
wide awake ; and it is all right, but what am I to do ? "
" Well, dear, if the Master has given you all that money
to arrange for Him, you may be sure that He will give
you health and strength and grace and wisdom to

arrange it." "Of course, He will," she replied, "how very stupid I am not to remember it. I am so tired. Lay me down, dear." And I laid her head on the pillow, and she went off to sleep. The following evening she told Mr. Tomkins all about it, and asked us to pray that she might be rightly guided. Months after her death we found that Arthington of Leeds had died about that time, and had left the London Missionary Society a quarter of a million, and that a Scotch minister had left it £20,000. What revelation had my beloved?

'She was a good, true, loving wife, a faithful, earnest follower of Christ, ay blithe and hearty, and seldom looked on life's dark side. If she could not speak well of any one she certainly would not speak evil; and she ever sought the good in all. Scandal she detested, but willingly listened to anything good. She had a wonderful knack of making herself at home, and of making friends.

'A few days before her death I said to her, "We shall all soon meet over yonder." Then hesitatingly she replied, "Yes, but I am so tired. I want a long rest first with Jesus, and then I shall be waiting for you all." Another day she said to me, "You know, Tamate dear, you are always in such a hurry, you make people feel very uncomfortable. Now at your time of life try and take things a little easier, and all your friends will feel more comfortable." '

A few days after his wife's death Chalmers wrote to the lady with whom Mrs. Chalmers had so long as she could kept up a most intimate correspondence :—

'THURSDAY ISLAND, *October* 29, 1900.

'What a grief it was to my dear one she could not write to you during her somewhat long illness. Some

time after being taken ill, when the Niue returned to
us from the Straits, I proposed going to Thursday Island
and away to Sydney, but she very decidedly opposed
it, and the weather being very bad I did not press it.
When again we had the Niue it was too late.   During
her illness she frequently thanked God for sparing her
from day to day, as her light was brighter, her faith
stronger, her love greater, and she had good opportunities of much communion with Jesus before she went
to His home.'

After this sad bereavement Chalmers found solace
in but one thing—the strenuous prosecution of his
work.   This spirit runs through all the remaining
letters.

'THURSDAY ISLAND, *November* 14, 1900.

'It is well with Tamate Vaine; she is at home with
Jesus, and He is nearer and dearer to me, but I smart.
I return to loneliness, but to work, and all is well.
What a blank there is in each of your lives, father gone
home, followed mother.   You know it is well with
them, you rejoice in their reunion, in the blessedness
of their lives in His presence, and yet there is a big
vacancy, and life has changed.   God will fill it up to
us all.

'We want a flat-bottomed vessel badly, and I am
afraid to ask the Directors in these trying times—the
whaleboat Tamate Vaine gave, it is now being built.
About a fortnight before her death she said, " Tamate,
I know what you are going to do; you are going to
give yourself to more visiting in the river, and you
must have a suitable vessel.   Well, He will give it to
you if necessary in His sight.   You cannot now knock
about in a whaleboat and a canoe." '

'DARU, *December* 21, 1900.

'There was a sad pleasure in breaking up the old home. It will take some time ere we get all our houses up here, but we are getting on, though slowly. The majority of our boys have accompanied us, so we will make a fair beginning. We have got a very fine position here, about a mile from the village and about thirty feet high. I think it will be healthy. It can make a very pretty station, and we shall do our best that it is so.

'We left Saguane on the Saturday, and on the Thursday previous the church members from up the river arrived. I sent for them. They speak in grateful terms of their reception by the people everywhere, and many are the places where they have spoken of Jesus and introduced services. The people were greatly disappointed at their leaving, and cried bitterly and pleading they should return soon. We shall try and carry on so that Jesus may be known far and wide. I have another £12, and that will support eight evangelists for some time. Next month we go up the river and begin at Gaema. I have got the frame of a good house sent there. I shall make Gaema the centre of work for some years. I cannot rest and so many thousands of savages without a knowledge of Christ near to us. More than that, we were compelled to carry on by the Holy Spirit. Two things I am afraid of: (1) Our running before (ahead) of God; (2) Our dropping so far behind that I lose sight of Him.

'I feel sad and thankful about China. How fearful the sufferings of some of the martyrs, but what a grand pouring in to the Saviour's presence. Our missionaries have conducted themselves splendidly; they are grand men and women. I should like to visit China and grip

their hands.   For years to come China will be first and
foremost in the home churches, and rightly too.  We
shall all joyfully take a back seat.'


'DARU, *January* 25, 1901.

'Thanks, cousin dear, for that invitation home, but
I fear I am too much attached to New Guinea.   I am
nearing the Bar, and might miss resting amidst old
scenes, joys, and sorrows.   No, I am in excellent health,
only a stiffness of the legs at times, a great loneliness,
and a gnawing pain at the heart-strings.  I know it is
well, and He never errs, and is never far off.  I must,
God sparing me, see this work through.'


'DARU, *February* 15, 1901.

'We have seen that Arthington is dead, and has left
£250,000 to the London Missionary Society.  I fancy
my old friend sold much property in Leeds, and lived
on about three shillings a week, and so the money was
got to be expended in Christ's work.   My fear is that if
it is true the subscriptions will fall off, and so will the
prayers.   I told you of Tamate Vaine's trouble over the
thousands, and thousands, and thousands.   Her trouble
was how to dispose of it all well for the Master, and she
so ill and weak.   When did Arthington die?   Tamate
Vaine's vision would be about October 14 to 18, or
a day or two earlier or later.   I know the spirit world
is about us.'

The following letter was written to the wife of the
Rev. A. T. Saville.   Mr. and Mrs. Saville were fellow
passengers with Chalmers during that eventful voyage
in the John Williams, which ended with shipwreck on
Savage Island.

G g

'DARU, *March* 8, 1901.

'VERY DEAR TAVIRA VAINE,

'God bless and reward you for your kind, consoling words. He has not erred, yet it is strange, and to be explained hereafter. We had dreams of a little rest together in a cottage out of London somewhere, before we crossed the flood. We shall dream them no more; she waits on the other side, as she said, "I shall be waiting for you all." I like dreaming, never mind though they are never realized. Another dream was to visit China and Japan and cross America. Perhaps in the other life we may do it and with ease.

'I have just been thinking yours will be a splendid mansion yonder for us to visit. There will be much visiting in heaven and much work. I guess I shall have good mission work to do, great, brave work for Christ. He will have to find it, for I can be nothing else than a missionary.'

'DARU, *March* 6, 1901.

'We have just heard from Saguane. Services are being conducted by the deacons, and three of Tamate Vaine's bairns carry on school vigorously morning, evening, and night. The children's prayer-meeting keeps up in interest and earnestness, and we trust many of them will become teachers. We continue our services and school on the verandah back and front, and do from five to six hours a day at teaching.

'After committee meeting Mr. Tomkins will be chiefly in the Straits, and I shall be alone again. For some time I hope to be in the River, visiting and opening up, and then west to stations to arrange for new ones. I shall keep the teachers moving into bush districts and preaching Christ. My time may be short, and there is much to be done, and I certainly do want to help in it.

'The whaleboat is launched, and she is a beauty, pronounced the best ever seen in these parts or any- where in the north.   She is now London Missionary Society property, all paid for.'

The whaleboat referred to in this letter was a gift to the mission by Mrs. Chalmers.   It was the one in which Tamate left the Niue on the fateful morning of April 8, 1901.

It is almost certain that during these lonely months at Daru Chalmers completed his autobiography, and also the sketch of his wife's life given on preceding pages.   He gave much thought to the growth of the New Guinea Mission, and to the methods of work pursued.   He was greatly troubled at the expenditure necessarily involved in such a mission, and anxious to do all in his power to keep this within narrower limits. The closing paragraphs of the autobiography deal with this subject.

'The work in the Fly River will for years to come be chiefly done by travelling evangelists holding services wherever they go, teaching all they know, striving to live holy and blessed lives.   My whole soul is greatly troubled at the slowness of the Gospel advance, at our indifference in preaching repentance and remission of sins to all the people, in bringing the Bread of Life to all hungering ones.   The temptation to settle down quietly and act the very respectable missionary is very great.   Whole-souled devotion to Christ and to His work would soon be more abundantly blessed.   Mad for Christ's sake, cast out for Christ's sake!   Where is the offence of the Cross?   I fear we have departed far from the Spirit of the Cross.   Hundreds of our brethren at home have difficulty in making ends meet, and live in small houses and yet have a missionary deputation once a year and a collection; and the deputation has in the foreign land a good house, servants, and many comforts. How my heart has ached when on deputation, and how shame has burned within me, when I have known and seen the struggle of many of my brethren at home! Will the young missionaries revert more to the originals? Will they have pluck enough to be men of the Cross, willing to bear the offence of the Cross? I can only say, *Peccavi.* I have great respect for all my brethren in the mission, but I feel sure we must confess that we have sinned greatly.

'There is a great danger of settling down to an easy, comfortable life, and leaving outstations and new places unvisited. I was once so situated that I settled down at a station, and got so to enjoy the ease and comfort that boating, canoeing, and walking became so uncomfortable that I did it as seldom as possible, and really began to think I had plenty to do at the station, and need not go out to other work. To do really true mission work in New Guinea requires roughing it somewhat, and to have many unpleasant experiences by sea and land. The home churches think we have terribly trying experiences, many discomforts, and much to endure. I fail to see these, and contend that our position is vastly superior to the hard-working city missionary, and that we are princes compared to the brethren in small, poor churches. Our brethren, the city missionaries, have hard, trying work, and do it with a smile. The hard-working country pastor in his wide and varied work puts us to shame. Let us be done for ever with the cant about hardships when there are none, or comparatively few; the trials of mission work, when they cannot be compared to those of the home pastor

or city missionary.  Let us do earnestly the work set
before us.'

The following letters, certainly the last he penned,
were written only the day before the Niue left Daru
on that trip from which so many of her passengers
were never to return.  The first was written to Miss
Searle, of Kew, Melbourne, the daughter of one of
Tamate's oldest Australian friends; the second to
Mrs. Arthur Edwards.

'DARU, *April* 3, 1901.

'We leave to-morrow for the east, Risk Point, and
Cape Blackwood, and I shall be away for over a fortnight.  Our work here gets on very slowly.  Last week
the schoolhouse collapsed.  I hope, when we return, to
get into my new quarters next to schoolroom.  The
mission house will not be begun until May or June.
Sometimes the greatness of the work oppresses me, but
He keeps saying, "Be strong and of a good courage,"
and I know He is with us, so all is well.

'We had the John Williams here a fortnight ago, and
held committee meetings ashore on this verandah.  Oh,
it was a good time.  Next year we meet here, and
I shall have to cater for all, and arrange for all sleeping
ashore; it will be a big, pleasant bit of work.  I have
promised them taro, sweet potato, and perhaps turtle
or pig.

'I keep well—a slight touch of fever about a fortnight ago, just after the John Williams left.  I have got
very lazy and must break it off, and so will be on the
move for the next six weeks.'

'DARU, *April* 3, 1901.

'Just a wee note to leave for any chance there
may be to Thursday Island.  We leave to-morrow for

the east, as far as Cape Blackwood, and expect to be away more than a fortnight.

'Many years ago I used Law's *Serious Call to a Devout Life*, and am again at it. We are apt to get so formal and lukewarm and need occasional stimulus.

'Night before last Tamate Vaine's pet collie was shot dead by a Government officer, for what, no one knows, and that has caused us much sorrow. We buried him yesterday morning in the compound.

'The sun is shining, and a south-east wind has come up, and I feel cheered. For more than two months we have not had such a day. Ah me! how I long to have all the houses up and be done with the worry of them. Would we could communicate just now and I knew of your well-being.'

The next day the Niue left Daru for the voyage which ended so disastrously at Goaribari Island.

# CHAPTER XIII

## THE TRAGEDY AT DOPIMA

THE annual committee meetings of the New Guinea Mission were held at Daru from March 18 to March 20, 1901. Chalmers, in the brief diary which he made up every day, remarks under the 20th, 'Finished meetings. Been good time.' There is nothing in the minutes of these meetings which throws light upon subsequent events. Chalmers was far from well. In the entries between March 22 and April 4 there frequently occur references like these: 'been lying down all day,' 'not feeling fit,' 'been ill and in bed.' On March 31 the entry runs, 'Fine morning, looks like rain. I am much better. A very good day. Only three to the English service.' This is the final record of a Sunday's work penned by his hand. The last entry in the diary is under date of April 4. Each day Chalmers invariably noted the wind at six a. m. The full entry runs, ' 6 a. m. SE. strong. Heavy showers. 8.40 a. m. Blowing and showers. Hope to leave. Will go down and see.' Later that day the Niue sailed on the fateful trip, the last Chalmers was ever to take in her.

Chalmers had intended making a voyage up the Fly River, but the letters just quoted seem to show that he had resolved first to visit the region of Goaribari Island. His health had been below par, and this may not have been without influence in the critical hour on the morning of April 8. He may have been less keen to detect signs of danger, and less equal to facing, with the promptitude and commanding influence of old, the crisis of life or death. It had been for long years the desire of his heart to make friends with, and to gain the confidence of, the savage tribes in the Aird Delta. When in England in 1895 he told the writer that he had set his heart upon establishing stations all along the coast from Cape Blackwood to the Fly River. He spoke in the highest terms of these savages, said they were splendid fellows, and if he could only get hold of them they would make fine missionaries.

We shall probably never know exactly what happened until a mission is established on Goaribari Island, the language mastered, and some of those concerned in the cruel deed tell the native teacher or the missionary what they did, and why they murdered those who were really their best friends. But whatever brought them there on the evening of Easter Sunday, April 7, the Niue was at anchor off the eastern end of Goaribari Island. What followed is known only from letters and reports written a month later. The following letter, by the Rev. H. M. Dauncey, tells all that at present can be known about the terrible events of that day:—

'MERRIE ENGLAND, OFF CAPE BLACKWOOD, *May* 4, 1901.

'The news I have to send is terribly sad. On Sunday morning last the Lokohu came in with flags at half-mast, and in a short time a note arrived from the doctor with the terrible news, " Passed the Niue yesterday. The captain called out, 'Tamate and Tomkins both dead.' We were out of hearing so soon that I could hear no more." What to make of the message

I did not know, nor was I any the wiser when, a little later, the doctor arrived. About four o'clock we knew that something grave had happened, and that there had been foul play, for the Merrie England came in with the governor on board. The doctor and I went off, and heard from the governor and Hunt as full particulars as they could give. They are summed up in the statement made by Bob, the captain of the Niue.

'He reports: "Left Daru, on April 4, with Tamate and Tomkins, Hiro, a Rarotongan teacher, the chief of Ipisia, and a party of ten mission boys. Made for Risk Point; arrived there April 7, at four p. m. Directly the vessel anchored the natives came off, and stayed on the vessel till sunset, when Tamate persuaded them to go ashore, and promised to visit them in their village the next day. At five a. m. the next morning a great crowd of natives came off, and crowded the decks so that there was no room to move. The canoes in which they came were filled with bows and arrows, clubs, bamboo knives and spears. They tried to persuade the natives to go on shore, but they refused. Tamate then decided to go on shore himself, thinking he might thereby induce the natives to leave the vessel. On announcing his intention of going ashore Tomkins at once said he would accompany him. They got into the whaleboat with the mission boys and the Ipisia chief, Hiro remaining on board to help the captain. Tamate said he would not stay more than half an hour, and would be off again to breakfast, after which they would make for another village. They watched the boat go away, followed by about half the natives, the rest remaining on board. When the boat neared the village they saw it go in, then come out again, and then in again, after which they could see nothing more of it.　About seven o'clock a breeze sprang up, and the Niue was got under way and taken to an anchorage right opposite the village to which Tamate had gone. Waited there till noon, but saw no signs of the party. Went on a little further, but could still see no signs of either the mission party or the boat.　Waited till sunset, but still no sign.　The Niue was then taken outside the island, and anchored for the night.　Next morning they went along the coast for some distance, but could see no sign of them, and at eight a. m. on April 9 left for Daru to report the matter to the governor.　The natives who had remained on board when Tamate and Tomkins went ashore, looted the vessel, taking all the barter goods and the clothes and stores belonging to Tamate and Tomkins.　They had no stores of any kind with them when they went ashore."

'The governor was going with a large force to the scene of the massacre.　I decided to go with him, and then on to Daru.　Early Tuesday morning the Merrie England started, and on Wednesday morning we were off Orokolo.

'Three of us went in the boat to see if we could communicate with the teachers, and send them as far west as they dare go, to search the coast.　Unfortunately the sea was too heavy.　We could not land, and they could not come out in a canoe.　We returned to the Merrie England, and just then the smoke of a steamer was seen. She proved to be the Parua, with ten men and an officer from the garrison of Thursday Island, sent over by the Queensland Government in case our governor needed help.　She came after us as we steamed away for the Aird Delta.

'On Thursday morning the captain began to feel his way in, and his ship, so far as I know, was the first

vessel of any size to come here. The governor did
not wish Hunt and me to go in the boats, so we went
on board the Parua as ambulance men. He started
with the steam launch, with six boats in tow. We
followed in the Parua, with the small launch ahead to see
that we did not get into too shallow water. When near
Risk Point we could see men gathering there, with their
arms, and, what looked worse, the women making over
to the mainland in canoes. Off the village of Dopima
two of the boats were cast off, while the governor with
the other four went about a mile and a half further up
to the second village, Turotere. He no sooner got
abreast of the village than the natives rushed down, and
opened fire upon him. Not till then did he hold up
a white flag (the signal to fire). A few rounds were
fired, the whole party scrambled ashore through the
mud, and in a short time had possession of the village.
At Dopima the attack was not made till after that on
Turotere had begun. Leaving two boats at Turotere,
the governor went round the north end of the island to
a village on the mainland. Here again he was attacked.
Heavy rain came on as he and his party from Dopima
joined those at Turotere. In the dark and the wet they
went ashore and camped in the dubu. For hours the
most violent thunderstorm that I have ever known
raged. Despite this the natives made two attacks on the
dubu, and wounded one of the native police.

'On Friday morning the governor went away to
Aimaha with four of the boats, leaving two others to
destroy the war canoes and the dubus. He had given
orders that none of the family houses were to be touched.
This order was obeyed, except in the case where the
wind carried the flame to other houses, and best part of
the village was burnt. One of these dubus was fully

300 yards long, and the shortest would not be less than
150 yards long.  At Turotere four of these dubus were
fired, and no sooner did the smoke begin to rise than all
along the mangrove edge was lined with men in very
small canoes.  Some few of them tried to cross, but they
vanished into the mangrove the moment the small launch
tried to capture them.  The governor had given orders
that there was to be no more firing except in case of
need, and this order was in keeping with the spirit in
which the whole affair was carried out.

'During Friday and Saturday ten villages were visited,
and the fighting dubus in each destroyed.  Saturday
morning, Hunt and I went ashore at Dopima and stood
upon the spot where they landed, and where they most
probably were killed.  One's thoughts were sad, but
after all I could not help thinking that it was the kind of
ending to the chapter that Tamate would have chosen
had it been left to him.  With Tomkins it is different.
Young, with any amount of "go" in him, one cannot
help wondering why he should have been taken.

'When all were on board again the governor addressed
the men from Thursday Island.  This is a summary of
what he said: "I wish not only to thank you for your
ready assistance, and for the willingness you have shown
throughout the expedition, but I wish also to thank you
for the humane manner in which you have carried out
my orders.  Mr. Chalmers came to New Guinea in the
interests of peace, and he gave his life for that purpose.
I believe that we have seen the last serious fighting in
British New Guinea.  The news of this expedition will
spread, and will, I trust, put an effectual check on
massacres and fighting of any serious nature.  If that
be so, and I trust it will, it will serve to crown the life-
work of that noble man."

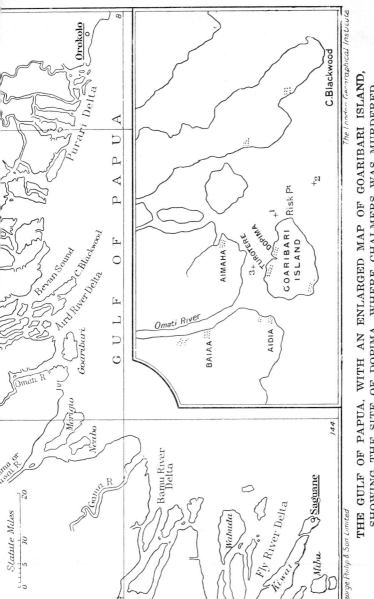

THE GULF OF PAPUA, WITH AN ENLARGED MAP OF GOARIBARI ISLAND,
SHOWING THE SITE OF DOPIMA, WHERE CHALMERS WAS MURDERED.

1. WHERE THE 'NINE' ANCHORED. 2. WHERE THE 'MERRIE ENGLAND' ANCHORED.

3. WHERE THE 'PARUA' ANCHORED.

George Philip & Son Limited

The London Geographical Institute

' I find the governor has names for the villages which differ from those on the chart.   Village No. 1 he calls Dopima, No. 2 Turotere.   The island is Goaribari, a little to the north of Cape Blackwood.   Sir William Macgregor passed it twice, and had trouble both times. So far as is known twenty-four natives were killed and three wounded.'

In a letter written the next day, May 5, Mr. Dauncey states :—

' In one of the dubus at Turotere there were over seven hundred skulls, and at another four hundred. Some of the other dubus were cleared before the party reached them, but I am within the mark in saying that there must have been 10,000 skulls in the twenty dubus burnt.   What a tale that number tells!   The prisoner's village was spared on account of the information he gave.

' Yesterday (Sunday) morning, before we left the anchorage, a memorial service was held in the saloon. Short, but it was hard to get through it.   I never had a harder task than to read the burial service then, and Hunt did not find the address an easy matter.   Try to imagine it!   I can't attempt to describe it.'

Thus runs the account of a brother missionary and an old friend and colleague.   The Lieutenant-Governor of British New Guinea, who was present in person, sent in a full official report of his proceedings, and Mr. Dauncey's narrative may be supplemented with some passages from this :—

' The locality is one which has a very bad reputation ; the population is large and savage.   It was first visited, as far as I know, by Captain Blackwood (after whom the cape to the east of it is named) in 1845.   An interesting account of it, and his search for two of his boats, which parted company with him there, and were subsequently found to have made their way through Torres Straits to Port Essington, beyond the Gulf of Carpentaria, is given by Mr. J. Bete Jukes, naturalist to the expedition, in his book, *Narrative of the Surveying Voyage of H.M.S. Fly*, 1842-1846. Sir William Macgregor visited it twice, in 1892 and 1898, and on one occasion only prevented a collision between his party and the natives of the Omati River, who were stealing from his boat, by with his own hand holding back one of his crew who had struck a thief who had stolen his shirt. I had intended going down there with Mr. Murray during his " north-west " season, but just as I was ready to start from Port Moresby in February last, on my western trip, the news arrived of the death of Mr. Armit, the resident magistrate of the Northern Division, and the murder of the two miners King and Champion on the Upper Kumusi, and I had to alter my plans and go east at once, and it was only an accident due to our not having sufficient coal at Samarai to finish my cruise in that part of the Possession that I came back to Port Moresby, and happened to be there when the news of the massacre arrived.

'I went through the long dubu, which I should say was 300 yards long, divided up on either side into small partitions or cubicles screened off from the centre passage, which was wide and clear from end to end. There were quantities of bows and arrows, many of the latter barbed and of a soft, easily broken wood, probably intentional to make their extraction more difficult. The most curious objects were fantastically carved and painted figures fastened to a sort of seat, with dozens of skulls, some of them carved and painted, in front of them; each skull was attached to the figure or to the frame of the seat by a thick twisted cord with a loop at the end which slipped over a peg; there were hundreds of these skulls before numerous figures, which we take to be idols of some kind, in all the dubus. Some had pieces smashed out by the death-blow, others were uninjured. Some had artificial noses and teeth made of gum and wool. We found bamboo head-knives and the daggers of cassowary bone with which they dispatch their victims. When a man is seized the dagger is plunged downwards into his gullet, and his head is immediately cut off with the bamboo knife.

'I had to decide what punishment I ought to inflict on all those villages which I had reason to believe were implicated or connected in any way with the dreadful tragedy, and I at length, after careful consideration, decided to visit them all with one or other of our parties and burn down the dubus, but not to touch any of the ordinary dwelling-houses of the married men with their women and children. I consulted those of my officers whom I knew were sympathetic and experienced with natives, and we came to the conclusion that it was the right thing to do under the circumstances; but, while I took their opinion, the decision was mine and I was entirely responsible for it. By burning these dubus only, the punishment would fall only on the fighting men. The houses are made of sago-palm, and can be rebuilt, but of course with a considerable amount of time and labour; the blow to the prestige of the village would be greatly felt, and that is of more weight in this case than the material loss of the buildings. It was necessary, in my opinion, to leave a lesson behind me which would not only be felt by those punished, but the report of which would spread amongst their neighbours far and wide. I also decided to destroy several of the large war canoes—dugouts without out-riggers.

'It is in surroundings such as these that the Pioneer Missionary, and one of the mission's latest recruits, and their faithful followers, lost their lives by the hands of those they had come to befriend; the first because he knew of nothing that could stop him, and the others because where their leader went they went too. It was stated by the survivors on the Niue that Mr. Chalmers probably anticipated some danger, as he wished to leave Mr. Tomkins on board; but the latter would not let him go without him, and they were called away together at each other's side. I am not alone in the opinion that Mr. Chalmers has won the death he would have wished for of all others—in New Guinea and for New Guinea—and if I am right in the belief that this sacrifice will prove to be the means of putting an end to such tragedies anywhere on the coast of the Possession—and they could only occur in this last part of it which we had not yet in hand—I know that he, or any others of his brother missionaries here, would unhesitatingly welcome the opportunity for the sake of its end.'

The expedition captured a prisoner at Dopima. One of the native police in the Government expedition was able to speak his language, and through him the prisoner gave the only account of the massacre which has yet been obtained:—

'The name of the village I was captured in is Dopima. I, however, belong to Dubumuba, a village on Baiba Bari Island. I, myself, was not present at the massacre; only the big men at the village went. I have, however, heard all about it. My father, Marawa, sent me to Dopima to get a tomahawk to build a canoe. The name of the village you camped in the first night is Turotere.

'The first suggestion for massacring the London Missionary Society party came from Garopo, off whose village, Dopima, the Niue was anchored. Word was at once sent round that night to villages in the vicinity to come to help. It is the usual custom for people of surrounding villages, when a large boat is sighted, to congregate in one place. The following villages were implicated:—Dopima, Turotere, Bai-ia, Aidio, Eheubi, Goari-ubi, Aimaha, Gewari-Bari, Ubu-Oho, Dubumuba. The next morning all the canoes went off and persuaded Messrs. Chalmers and Tomkins and party to come on shore in the whaleboat. Some of the natives remained to loot the Niue. When they got on shore Messrs. Chalmers and Tomkins and a few boys entered the long house, the rest of the boys remaining to guard the boat. These last, however, were also enticed inside the house on pretence of giving them something to eat. The signal for a general massacre was given by knocking simultaneously from behind both Messrs. Chalmers and Tomkins on the head with stone clubs. This was performed in the case of the former by Iake, of Turotere, in that of the latter by Arau-u, of Turotere. Kaiture, of Dopima, then stabbed Mr. Chalmers in the right side with a cassowary dagger, and then Muroroa cut off his head. Ema cut off Mr. Tomkins' head. They both fell senseless at the first blow of the clubs. Some names of men concerned in the murder of the rest of the party are:—Baibi, Adade, Emai, Utuamu, and Amuke, all of Dopima; also Wahaga and Ema, both of Turotere.

'All the heads were immediately cut off. We, however, lost one man, Gahibai, of Dopima. He was running to knock a big man[1] on the head, when the latter

[1] This was Naragi, chief of Ipisia.

snatched a stone club from a man standing near, and killed Gahibai.  He (Naragi) was, however, immediately overpowered.  The other boys were too small to make any resistance.  In the meantime the people in canoes left at the Niue had come back after looting her.  This party was led by Kautiri, of Dopima.  Finding the party on shore dead, it was determined to go back to the Niue and kill those on board.  However, the Niue got under way, and left, so they could not accomplish their purpose.  I think the crew of the Niue were frightened at the noise on shore.  Then Pakara, of Aimaha, called out to all the people to come and break up the boat, which had been taken right inside the creek, it being high water [1].  This was done, and the pieces were divided amongst people from the various villages.

'Directly the heads had been cut off the bodies some men cut the latter up and handed the pieces over to the women to cook, which they did, mixing the flesh with sago.  They were eaten the same day.  Gebai has got Mr. Chalmers' head at Dopima, and Mahikaha has got Mr. Tomkins' head at Turotere.  The rest of the heads are divided amongst various individuals.  Anybody having a new head would naturally, on seeing strange people coming to the village, hide them away in the bush, and leave only the old skulls in the houses.  The same applies to the loot from the Niue.  As regards the skulls in the houses, those having artificial noses attached to them are of people who have died natural deaths ; those that have no noses attached have been killed.'

A letter from Mr. Hunt at Daru to Dr. Lawes, who

[1] This was the splendid boat which just before her death Mrs. Chalmers had presented to the mission.

was then in England, dated May 11, 1901, contains a
few further particulars :—

'It seems almost as if Tamate must have had a
premonition of what was going to happen; for everything was prepared here. His will was placed uppermost in his desk, and his autobiography was written
almost up to date, and finished. Both men were fully
prepared for death, and all the odd memoranda we
have found breathe a spirit of consecration. How
strange are the workings of Providence! What a mercy
that Tamate Vaine went first, and was thus spared the
shock of this awful news! It is hard for us to think
it for the best that two such men should be suddenly
snatched away. Tamate gave an address at committee that was full of missionary enthusiasm, and few
of us will forget it. Tomkins wrote his diary up to
the night before the massacre, and speaks of the natives
coming off to the Niue.

'Further inquiries have elicited nothing new. It is
evident, I think, that the party were killed in accordance
with the native custom to celebrate the completion of
a dubu by human sacrifice. His Excellency the
governor has been most kind through it all. No one
could have been kinder, and his expedition, although
it involved a certain loss of life, was carried out in
a most fair and humane manner.'

This terrible tragedy produced a profound impression
in all missionary circles, and the tidings of it were
scattered by the press over the whole civilized world.
In Australia, where Chalmers was so well known, the
shock was great and the sorrow deep. One of the last
things the Duke of Cornwall and York did before
leaving Melbourne for Brisbane, was to send an official
expression of his deep sympathy with those who had

been bereaved by the revolting massacre and cannibal outrage at Goaribari.

Lord Hopetoun, the Governor-General of the Commonwealth, also sent a message of kindly sympathy, in which he recognized how much James Chalmers had done for Christianity in New Guinea. These messages from the Heir Apparent and the Governor-General were deeply appreciated by the Christian churches of Australasia, and especially by those who knew best the noble men who had fallen while labouring for the highest well-being of the degraded races which have come under the paternal responsibility of the Commonwealth government.

In Melbourne the confirmation of news came when that community was celebrating the opening of the Commonwealth Parliament, and in that memorable week, when the papers were so full of the one great event, the *Argus* made room for a long leader, in which these words occur:—'The confirmed and detailed account of the Aird River massacre threw a shadow across the Commonwealth in a week of historic rejoicings. It opened up a vista of Commonwealth responsibility. . . . There is no denominational limit to the influence such a splendid character as Chalmers possessed. His record is an inspiration to all who wish to do their duty without regard to consequences. Our heroes transfigure life for us.'

The news reached England when the great anniversaries were being held, and it cast a deep gloom for a time over all the friends and assemblies associated with missionary work. Yet while many a heart was saddened, and multitudes felt that earth had suddenly become poorer by the translation of Tamate, the man whom they loved, yet they did not and could not sorrow as those without hope. Now, as of old, the ways of God are sometimes through the darkness and the storm rather than in the light. To human judgement it seemed as though no men could less easily be spared than the veteran, bravely bearing the last burden of a long and strenuous day, and his eager young colleague, full of hope, full of energy, entirely consecrated to the new and blessed service only just begun. Does not God by visitations such as these teach us that the uplifting of our heathen brothers and sisters ought to be near to the heart and the steady purpose of all His servants?

This closing scene at Dopima is on the one side a cruel and revolting tragedy, on the other it is a glorious close to a noble life. For the man who had faced death a hundred times the King of Terrors had no dread. As confidently as St. Paul Chalmers would have said to any who sought to hinder him in his work, 'I am ready not to be bound only, but also to die at Dopima for the name of the Lord Jesus.' If in the last moment of life he was conscious of what was happening, the prayer on his lips was that of the Master, 'Father, forgive them; for they know not what they do.' The long, courageous, self-denying life, successfully spent by God's grace and sustaining power in leading men out of the darkness of savagery into the light and liberty of the Gospel, received its terrible but glorious coronation when in the horrific dubu of Dopima there descended upon Tamate and his colleague the blood-stained crown of martyrdom.

# CHAPTER XIV

## CHARACTERISTICS

IN the preparation of this book the author has had the hearty and willing co-operation of many of Chalmers' most intimate friends. Some of these have gladly supplied appreciations of their friend and fellow worker, and these are gathered into this final chapter. The first is by his old friend and colleague, Dr. Lawes of Vatorata :—

'It is not easy to delineate any man's character, and reproduce a living personality in cold type. But I find it almost impossible to translate Tamate into black and white. He is not to be measured by ordinary standards, or weighed in the balance of ordinary men. He stood alone, and was hardly amenable to the laws that govern other men. How can I describe him as he was to us in New Guinea, in all his charming personality, and with all his wonderful magnetic influence ?

'He was first and last, always and everywhere, a missionary. He lived for the people among whom he worked, and for the South Sea Islanders who were his helpers and colleagues. His frank and generous nature, his genial, loving disposition soon won the hearts of his fellow workers, and those who knew him best trusted and loved him most.

'He was essentially a pioneer. It was his special gift and mission " to prepare the way." Other men could perhaps more successfully build up and consolidate, but

he was second to none in the initiatory pioneering
work. In physique he was admirably fitted for it.
In long tramps, and in rough boat journeys, he never
seemed to know fatigue or weariness, and could go
without food longer than any man I have ever known.
Tamate had a share in the opening up or establishment
of almost every station in the mission. In many cases
he was the first white man the natives knew, and they
gave him unreservedly their confidence. They named
their little children after him, and it was a common thing
in the early days, when he visited a place after two or
three months' absence, to have three or four little brown
babies brought to him as the most recent editions of
Tamate, in expectation of a godfather's present. His
generous nature was well known. He never went on
a journey but he returned with an impoverished wardrobe, and in almost every native congregation some of
his missing garments might be seen, generally two or
three sizes too large for the wearers. His name became
known far and wide as that of the natives' friend and
the man of peace. Foreigners were looked upon with
suspicion, but Tamate became a talisman and password
with which the natives felt protected and safe. Other
missionaries have come to New Guinea since those early
days, and many names are now honoured, but with the
older people, from east to west, no name can ever be
loved and trusted as that of Tamate. As the true
pioneer of peace, and light, and truth, he is mourned
in New Guinea, and his memory will be revered and
honoured there as nowhere else in the world.

'Every reader of missionary history in New Guinea
knows the splendid service rendered by the South Sea
Island teachers, who, with their lives in their hands,
have gone to that great heathen land as the pioneers of

Christianity. These were in a very especial manner Tamate's delight and joy. Most of them were from the Cook Islands, of which Rarotonga is the principal island, and the one best known. The first ten years of his missionary life were spent in Rarotonga, many of the teachers were trained by him, and he knew their language, habits of thought, and customs, thoroughly well. In New Guinea he looked upon these as his special charge, and was always ready to champion their cause, and defend them against wrong or injustice. And they revered and obeyed him as their own father in Christ. In every South Sea Islander's home in New Guinea Tamate was the beloved and honoured guest. His example was their inspiration, and his approval their stimulus. They lament for him as only loyal brave men can who mourn for a fallen leader and captain.

'Tamate was not distinguished as a teacher. He was interesting and fascinating, but lacked patience and persistency. Steady, plodding, persevering teaching day after day was little to his mind. He would sometimes throw himself into the work of teaching with all his superabundant energy, but he would soon tire and want to be off. The vagabond instinct was strong in him. He used to say it was the gipsy blood in his veins which would not suffer him to be " long tied to a table leg." In later years, when he was not so well able to go on the tramp for long journeys, he did some good educational work at Saguane, but it was contrary to his nature.

'He was restless as a volcano, and as subject to eruptions. He gave way sometimes to violent outbursts, when he would say things which from any other lips would be unkind and unjust, but his brethren knew that there was no grain of bitterness or malice in his great, generous heart. The South Sea Island teachers said of these rash, impetuous speeches, *Tamate ena kara*—" It's Tamate's way." He was very impulsive, and his impulses were mostly generous, but sometimes they led him astray and showed lack of judgement. He was naturally of hasty temper, but of late years especially this was very much under restraint.

' He was a splendid *raconteur*, with plenty of imagination, and a spice of Eastern exaggeration and hyperbole. In his public addresses and sermons he had the same magnetic power over a native audience as that which he wielded over English assemblies. His knowledge of any native language was not very accurate nor complete; but he made himself understood, and any deficiencies in grammar or idiom were more than compensated by voice and eye. A scholar in the ordinary sense of the word he was not, the steady, plodding work of the desk was irksome to him, but he read much and was conversant with most of the literature of the day.

' Tamate was a born optimist, of a sanguine, hopeful temperament. Some of the South Sea Island teachers were not a success. He never liked to see any of them sent home as incompetent, he was always willing to take them over " to give them another chance." He used to say he rather liked the failures, had a tender place for them in his heart, and a hope for the men others had given up.

' He had no children of his own, and this perhaps made him more tender and affectionate for the children of others. His love for children was one of the beautiful traits in his character.

' But that which characterized our beloved Tamate most as a missionary, and as a leader among his brethren, was spiritual power. He was a Christian of the robust, healthy type, with instinctive hatred of all cant and sham. A man of great faith, mighty in prayer, and full of the love of Christ. He realized to a greater degree than most men what it is to live *in* Christ, and to him His presence was very real, and true, and constant. And this spiritual power was the secret of his wonderful influence over men, and of his great success as a missionary: by it " he being dead, yet speaketh." The memory of his Christ life in its consecration and unselfishness, its large-heartedness, its childlike faith, its communion with God, its unwearied service, and in its bright hopefulness is the rich legacy he has left to us in New Guinea, and to all his missionary brethren wherever his name and fame may come.'

The Rev. Joseph King, who was a missionary in Samoa, and who is now the London Missionary Society's representative in Australia, contributes the following recollections :—

'In 1860 I went to London to appear before the Examination Committee of the London Missionary Society. When I entered the waiting-room at the Mission House I found a young Scotchman there present on the same errand as myself. It was James Chalmers; and in that room forty-one years ago commenced a friendship, interrupted now for a brief span, to be renewed again under the brighter conditions of the heavenly service.

' One of the elements of Chalmers' greatness was his extreme modesty; a more modest man I never knew. I never heard him sound his own trumpet. There were trumpets which he could and did sound with marvellous effect, but his own trumpet he never used. His modesty was combined, however, with an intensity of conviction about certain things which often found expression in fearless declamation. He had deep convictions about the Gospel of Jesus Christ, and about the responsibility of churches to make that Gospel known, and when roused by an overpowering conviction that the churches were neglecting their duty, he could declaim and condemn with the force of a Boanerges.

'It was this side of his nature that savages were quick to recognize. They often fell back in his presence when they would certainly have taken advantage of a more timid man. The combinations of his character were striking. Great will-power and dauntless courage were wedded to a most tender heart. He could fight, but he could also weep. He never lost the spirit of schoolboy joviality and fun, but no one could be more sober in earnest talk. The secret of his missionary success was, I think, to be found in this, that he never doubted his possession of a Gospel for savages. All through his missionary career the fire of evangelical fervour was kept alive, and never did he so fully believe that Jesus Christ had a message for the cannibals of New Guinea as when he started on his last expedition.

'I once saw him in his Fly River home, the most oppressively lonely mission station I have ever seen. To have lived at Saguane, in the midst of the mangrove swamps of the Fly Delta, would have been an unbearable exile to most men, but there, on an island mid-stream, which seemed to him to be a strategic position for his work, he planted his home. There was no permanent village near, but he gathered a few friendly natives around him, and formed the nucleus of a Christian community. I was with the Rev. R. Wardlaw Thompson and Mr. William Crosfield, and at daybreak we went into the rudely constructed schoolhouse he had built on the sand, just above high water mark. Twenty-three boys and girls were gathered before him. He knew their language, but he was teaching them English, and with a small bamboo stick for a baton, which I brought away as a memento of the scene, he led them as they sang the first verse of " God save the Queen," and " All hail the power of Jesu's name." I do not think Chalmers ever appeared to me quite so great a man as when I saw him thus teaching that group of Fly River children.

' The night previous to this I saw him amongst friendly savages. Twelve miles up the river we landed at Iasa, a heathen village with which he had succeeded in establishing friendly relationship. It was evening, and the darkness added impressiveness to the scene. Leaving our boat he led the way through a crowd of wild-looking men. The spell his manly figure and strong face threw over them as he went before us toward one of their long houses, and into the weird torch-lighted interior, was a sight not to be forgotten. He walked as a prince amongst those barbarous chiefs. They were disarmed by his manifest human sympathy, and they received us as friends for Chalmers' sake. They knew nothing of Jesus Christ, but there had come to them a sense of brotherhood with one of Christ's faithful followers, and although they were at the time busily engaged preparing a heathen feast they brought us fresh cocoa-nuts to drink, and in the light of the torches we took their proffered cup of hospitality. In that Stone Age interior, surrounded by such sights as can only be seen in savage life, we pledged our friendship and drank to that sense of brotherhood which explained our presence there. Had the wild crowd in the dubu at Goaribari known Chalmers as he was known at Iasa they would have dropped their clubs, and extended to him and his companions the same hospitality.

'The communion service at Port Moresby, at which 450 converted savages gathered around the table of our Lord, is historical. On one side of the chair I occupied sat one of the native deacons, the notorious robber chief of former days, and on the other side James Chalmers. He had never before seen such a large gathering of communicants, and tears of grateful joy filled his eyes as the service proceeded, and as he thought of the previous condition of those people. He was feeling the joy of harvest home after much hardness endured in plowing and sowing. The Christian deacon and the Christian missionary who sat by me at that communion service are both dead, and have they not, think you, met in the presence of Christ? What joy it will be to Chalmers to meet at the marriage supper of the Lamb converts from New Guinea, and what joy it will be to them to see him there wearing his martyr crown.'

While Chalmers could not be called a good correspondent, yet after his visit to England in 1886, and also to certain old and warm friends in Australia, he wrote regularly. Many of these letters are quoted in these pages. Mrs. Arthur Edwards, the English correspondent to whom he probably wrote more frequently than to any other, has noted the following characteristics :—

'One leading characteristic of Tamate was his *enthusiasm*. Friends will remember hearing him when on deputation pray "Give us Christ's enthusiasm," and his love to Christ, which was very intense, must have been the source of his own enthusiasm. His favourite phrase at family prayers was "Spread around us the mantle of Thine own Love."

'Tamate had much humility in his character, and

never seemed to care to be made much of, never pushed himself to the fore. He was upset by applause at public meetings, and would raise his hand to stop it; and would never have himself placed before the work. An instance of this occurs to me. Tamate was eager to see the Lord Mayor's Show the last Saturday before he left England, and Mr. Evan Spicer, hearing of his wish, had kindly arranged for him to see it from the Equitable Office. But that day at eleven o'clock Tamate was fixed to speak at the weekly prayer meeting of the London City Missionaries, and Mr. Spicer meeting us going there, urged me to get it arranged for Tamate to come on first, and so get away in time. When alone, and we were making for Bride-well Place, Tamate turned and said earnestly, "You won't do that, will you? It would vex me. It would be putting Christ second." So nothing was said, but Tamate much enjoyed the enthusiastic meeting, and the private recital he had of the "Coalies' Baby" in Mr. Dawson's room. As usual it was arranged for Tamate to speak last, and so he missed the show at the appointed place, but getting in by a back entrance to the Sunday School Union managed to see it after all.

'Tamate was very shy by nature, and always more so when unsympathetic folk were in the room. In fact, under such circumstances, nothing could be got out of Tamate about his work, and he seemed in a way paralysed. A well-known Congregational minister, who rarely glanced into the London Missionary Society's *Chronicle*, and who considered the "heathen at home" came first—and last—was invited to meet Tamate at dinner, and leaning over the table he remarked to Tamate opposite, "Mr. Chalmers, do you consider the Gospel has made *any* way in New Guinea?" Of this type of home minister he would at times speak in somewhat vehement terms.

'Tamate had great spiritual force, and true Scotch reverence for all that was Divine, rarely speaking of his inmost feelings. But in his letters, as the preceding pages show, he would write often of his longing to be nearer Christ. To him to live was to pray. He wrote to a friend who was in great anxiety about a certain Society in which she was interested, "Don't make plans till you have prayed about it, or you will spoil all." One last memory of him as he left England that dull November morning in 1895 was in prayer. Many friends met at Fenchurch Street Station to bid him God-speed, but only a few went down to the Merkara at Tilbury. And as the first bell sounded for the visitors to leave the boat, Tamate shut the door of his cabin, and asked Dr. Lawson Forster of Queen's Park to engage in prayer. And then we said good-bye. As the tug bore us away, that lonely, God-possessed, earnest Tamate, clad in ulster, with lifted hat, could be seen motionless on the upper deck for a long long way.'

The Rev. James E. Newell, the well-known Samoan missionary, married a daughter of the Rev. W. Wyatt-Gill, of Mangaia. This lady Chalmers had known and loved as a child. He also saw them in their home at Malua in 1890. Mr. Newell has indicated some very striking characteristics in Chalmers' wonderful personality:—

'James Chalmers had a quite remarkable power of remembering and distinguishing faces. Mr. Marriott had twin daughters, so much alike in form and feature that even their parents had to ask, "Are you Elsie or Lily?" On the day of Tamate's arrival at Malua (1890) he saw the two girls, and each told him her name. He never afterwards confounded the two, though we tried several artful little deceptions on him ; but he made no mistake. He visited besides Malua and Apia, the district of Le Faasaleleaga (Savaii), and also the district of Falealili (Upolu). During the subsequent part of his time at Malua several natives whom he had seen at the mission station on Savaii called at Malua. They were astonished and much gratified to find that he remembered their faces, and in cases where he had been told the names saluted the individuals by name. It was a faculty I never saw so acute in any other person I ever met.

'It needs no argument or illustration to show what a marvellous aid this God-given endowment was to Tamate in New Guinea. There can be no question that it was rendered more acute by his alert spiritual nature. Unconsciously perhaps a "passion for souls" (to use a rather abused phrase) was the ruling motive with him. He had scarcely any consciousness of the mere externals of a man—never any incongruity in baptizing a *naked* savage. But he never missed drawing an inference from what a man or a woman *did*, and sometimes these swift judgements were wrong and had to be corrected ; but it was then noticeable that he never remembered the first judgement. He just as swiftly pronounced the revised judgement. It was as though he had come across another person, and not the same one he had seen and written about or spoken about shortly before. In this respect he can be said to have had the chief characteristic endowment of the ideal missionary. It was this which gave zest and interest to his life and work beyond all other endowments and sent him forth to new regions. How often he has remarked that the sturdiest and the most pro-

mising human material in New Guinea were the distinctly
cannibal tribes, and he would rather have to deal with
them than with any other.

'This alertness and zest for the knowledge of those
with whom he came in contact was illustrated by the
vivid and intensely enthusiastic way he spoke of each
of the Malua students, who formed his boat's crew to
Savaii. He did not know Samoan, but he had found
out the names of the men, and gave me his judgement
of the individual men. I was much impressed at the
time with this incident. I think all the men of that
boat's crew offered for service in New Guinea, though
only some eight of them were appointed, there being
obstacles in the way of sending the others.

'His sturdy self-control was also remarkable. The
incidents I recall will appear trivial, but I cannot but
think they are not without value. I noticed at Malua
that Tamate was not smoking. Now he loved the weed.
I asked him why he did not get his pipe. "Oh," he
said, "sometimes I find myself getting too fond of the
pipe, and I have over and over again tested my power
to prevent the thing mastering me by knocking it off
for days." At dinner one day he called for a cocoa-nut,
and pleasantly but decidedly refused any other food,
and sat through the meal eating his cocoa-nut. My wife
quietly acquiesced, and there was no fuss. Will any one
deny that this complete knowledge of his physical needs
and requirements and the common-sense application of
his will to such details was largely the secret of that
physical endurance and strength which enabled him to
cross the bogs in the Fly River territory?

'His will power was remarkable. Discussing at Malua
with him the weaknesses, as well as the other characteristics
of the native South Sea Island missionaries, he spoke of

their lack of will power and their well-known " fatalism," in reference especially to death. He had a deep-rooted conviction that men died in New Guinea from lack of will power as much as anything. And my wife got him to tell of an experience he had had at East Cape in the early days. He had landed there with two Rarotongan teachers, hoping to locate them. He was stricken with fever and became unconscious. As he lay there, his companions expecting every moment that he would breathe his last breath, they began to discuss their own most critical position amongst savages with a dead body. Chalmers overheard the whispers of the men, and the thought occurred to him as he recovered consciousness, " This cannot be God's will," for he knew how true the forecast was. And he said to one of the men, " Bring me my pipe." At first the teacher thought Tamate was delirious, but when the request was repeated it was granted. " Fill it," said the prostrate missionary. And the teacher filled the pipe and inserted it into his leader's mouth. But although Tamate had not strength enough to even draw the pipe, the object that he had had in view was gained. This was to arouse himself, and to inspire hope in the hearts of his dear comrades. And from *that* moment Tamate began to recover.

'I do not think that the published accounts of the Kalo massacre give the real occasion for that tragedy. In his address at Malua (which I interpreted for the students and wives and the boy boarders) Tamate told the story with power and pathos, never surely equalled before any other audience. I shall never forget how I bowed my own head and how my own voice thrilled with the emotion which was almost too great to bear. But the point I want to notice about it is the application he made of the unhappy incident which gave rise to the massacre. The Rarotongan teacher's wife at Kalo had had a visit from the young wife of the chief, who had been rather troublesome begging for tobacco. The Rarotongan woman, going out on the verandah of the house (which was elevated above the ground as such houses are in New Guinea) where the New Guinea woman was standing, pushed her, and the woman fell down from the verandah on to the ground below. She was not injured, but went home, and on the arrival of her husband he found her sulking in the house. Without replying to his questions in words, she pointed to the spears and arrows in the roof of the house, and with a taunt ordered him to avenge the insult. As he gathered his young men together a party of teachers landed, who were calling at Kalo for their colleague to accompany them to a meeting of the mission or district (I think at Port Moresby). The moral of the story for the students and their wives, who might be going to New Guinea, was obvious, and it was trenchantly and very solemnly enforced. I have often quoted the story in my own farewell addresses to outgoing bands of native teachers since that time.

'Tamate ever manifested pride and love for the Rarotongan teachers. This characteristic—the love for his fellow labourers, who, like the first converts to Christianity in the cities of Asia Minor, were a *comfort* to the Apostle Paul—Tamate possessed in common with every missionary who has seen the native Christian come into the realization of the great Divine impulse to evangelize, and has rejoiced in it as the best of all evidence of the power of the Gospel. Still it was a feature in Tamate which made him so irresistible. If you could get Tamate to speak of his Rarotongans you had touched a chord which vibrated with every impulse of his great heart.

'I can see that face lighted up with joy as he told of Piri and of Ruatoka—men much beloved in Samoa. Piri especially had left behind in Samoa, where he laboured for a time, a memory very fragrant of goodness. There are men to-day who call themselves his "sons," and know that heaven will be more of heaven to them when they reach that goal, because of Piri's presence.'

We close this record with two other testimonies, one representing those whose life and work are quite apart from missionary thought and aims; the other representing those whom Tamate most fervently loved, and who were in the closest possible touch with him throughout his missionary life.

Mr. G. Seymour Fort, in a character sketch which appeared in the *Empire Review* shortly after the death of Chalmers, sketched him as he was when helping Sir Peter Scratchley to get to know New Guinea and its people in 1885 :—

'Chalmers' voice in a wonderful way interpreted his rich, many-sided character. My experience of men has been a somewhat varied one, and I can recall no man whose voice had for me the same magnetic quality, ranging from exquisite tenderness to imperial command. For the sick, for the old, for any one who sought his advice in trouble, his tones were deep and sympathetic, but there was no mistaking the note of absolute authority with which I heard him restore order in a panic at sea, and compel fighting natives to lay down their arms.

'Absolutely fearless in action, Chalmers was also wise in counsel, and, when necessary, very prudent and cautious. Natives have often curious codes of signals, whereby they show their attitude and intentions; sometimes even the nature and position of the flowers in their hair signify hostility or friendliness, and for these signals Chalmers was ever watchful. Once we wanted to land on an unknown spot, and amongst natives who had never been visited before. For hours, however, he kept us waiting in the boat until presents had been exchanged, we giving them a coloured pocket-handkerchief, they pushing out to us on a canoe a few cocoanuts. As soon as we landed we were surrounded by wonder-stricken natives, marvelling at our clothes and colour. Suddenly a shout of fear arose, and one and all fled into the bush. We retreated to the boat, but Chalmers went forward and eventually persuaded them to come out. Then we learnt that they had imagined that one of the sailors, who had sat down to take his shoe off, was taking himself to pieces. Hence their alarm and flight.

'New Guinea is an unknown tropical corner of our Empire, and from a commercial point of view of comparatively little value; but the pioneer work done by James Chalmers in opening up communications with the natives, and thus rendering Europeans' exploitation possible, was emphatically imperial in character. As an explorer and pioneer, his name should stand high in the annals of our Imperial history. With regard to the man himself, I can only consider myself as most fortunate to have, in a very small way, shared in his work, and to have been accounted by him amongst his friends. He will ever live in memory as a rich emotional nature allied with finest fighting qualities of our Saxon race, and as one who achieved difficult and disappointing work with noble sympathy and courage.'

The last is a testimony on the principle of our Lord's

saying, 'By their fruits ye shall know them.' The preceding pages of this book contain ample evidence of the nobility of character, of the consistent Christian life, and of the effective working power possessed by Ruatoka, of Port Moresby. We have given[1] Chalmers' own tender and sympathetic sketch of this man, through which there runs an almost paternal pride. Not long after the massacre at Dopima, Ruatoka wrote the following letter to the Rev. H. M. Dauncey:—

'May you have life and happiness. At this time our hearts (insides) are very sad, because Tamate and Mr. Tomkins and the boys are not here, and we shall not see them again. I have wept much. My father Tamate's body I shall not see again, but his spirit we shall certainly see in heaven, if we are strong to do the work of God thoroughly and all the time, till our time (on earth) shall finish. Hear my wish. It is a great wish. The remainder of my strength I would spend in the place where Tamate and Mr. Tomkins were killed. In that village I would live. In that place where they killed men, Jesus Christ's name and His word I would teach to the people, that they may become Jesus' children. My wish is just this. You know it. I have spoken.'

When David said, 'Oh that one would give me drink of the water of the well of Bethlehem, which is by the gate!' three of his mighty men endangered their lives to gratify his wish, and in their action we have one standard of the greatness of David. When James Chalmers falls at Dopima, Ruatoka, his boy, his colleague, his trusted friend, writes, 'It is a great wish. The remainder of my strength I would spend in the place where Tamate and Mr. Tomkins were killed.' Here is the standard by

[1] See pages 132–8.

which to estimate James Chalmers' influence. He was a man who could, and who did, nerve others to become willing and ready to sacrifice even life itself in the effort to help men to become the children of Jesus. Having kept back nothing himself, he was able to inspire in others a burning enthusiasm for the salvation of savage men akin to that with which his own heart was aflame.

P. M<sup>c</sup>Allister
Harbor • Rich I.
Juno • Alexis Haven
P<sup>t</sup> William Haven
mba • Morage
• sorI • C. Rigny
• Astrolabe Bay
• P. Dawai
Mina Boro Boro
M<sup>ts</sup>
or Finisterre
11,000

FRENCH I<sup>s</sup>
Merité I.

Crown I.
Reaumur pk.
Long I.
Lottin I.
C. Herwarth • Iris I<sup>t</sup>
Helmholtz I.
Rook I.
Turpinier I.
Volcano I.
Raoul I.

Gauss Pt.
Reiss Pt.
I Tiliata
Low I<sup>s</sup>

Vitiaz Str.

Dampier Strait

M<sup>t</sup> Hansten

NEW PO

C. King William

Finsch Haven

Rawlinson Range
4000
C. Cretin
Cretin I<sup>s</sup>

HUON GULF
Parsee Pt.
Franziska R.
Solitary I.
Kuper
Range
Longuerue I<sup>s</sup>
Fliegen I<sup>s</sup>
Layard I<sup>s</sup>
Luard I<sup>s</sup>
1500
Hercules B.
Alligator Pt.
Traitor B.
Mitre Rk.
Clyde R. • Douglas I<sup>s</sup>
Caution Pt.
Oro B.
Holnicote B.

GULF

Albert M<sup>ts</sup>

Kerema
Silo
M<sup>t</sup> Chapman
400

Lerbada
Karana
Freshwater I<sup>s</sup>
R. Combe
Tese
Motumotu
Lokea
Maiva
C. Possession
Kabadi
Kawoa
C. Possession
UDU
M<sup>t</sup> Veriveri
Yule I.
Delena
Hall Sound
C. Suckling
Aroa
Redscar B.
Redscar Head
Aplin L.
Boera
Fisherman I.
Round I<sup>d</sup>

C. Chalmers

M<sup>t</sup> Yule
10,046
Alb<sup>t</sup> Edward
12,500

M<sup>t</sup> Gilles
8000
M<sup>t</sup> Parkes
M<sup>t</sup> Scratchley
13,000
Victoria
M<sup>t</sup> Owen Stanley
Range
M<sup>t</sup> Bellamy
Goldie
MOROKA
SOGERI
M<sup>t</sup> Nisbet
M<sup>t</sup> Karadu

C. Killerton
C. Sud Est
Oro
Dyke Ackland B.
Pocklock B.
Port Hennessy
C. Nelson
MacLaren
M<sup>t</sup> Trafalgar
4000
Hardy Pt.
Keppel Pt. (Camp
M<sup>t</sup> Victory
Collingwood
B.

Port Moresby
Astrolabe
Wabedam
M<sup>t</sup> Obree
10,246
Parman

Pasili
Tupusele
Koile
Hula
Hood Pt.
Hood B.
Kerepunu
Contance I.
C. Rodney
Cloudy B.
Baxter I.
Grange I.

AROMA
M<sup>t</sup> Brown
7947
M<sup>t</sup> Clarence
6330
Hornby Rar
M<sup>t</sup> Suckling
11,226
M<sup>t</sup> Simps

C V

Table Bay
P. Glasgow
Millpo
Malo
Orangerie B.
Dufaure I.
Fife
Damono
Deddele

# SOUTH EAST
# NEW GUINEA

Scale 1:5.500.000
Statute Miles

0        50        100        150

# INDEX